CONVERSION IN THE NEW TESTAMENT

DATE DUE

CONVERSION IN THE NEW TESTAMENT

Paul and the Twelve

RICHARD V. PEACE

WILLIAM B. EERDMANS PUBLISHING COMPANY
GRAND RAPIDS, MICHIGAN / CAMBRIDGE, U.K.

© 1999 Wm. B. Eerdmans Publishing Co.

255 Jefferson Ave. S.E., Grand Rapids, Michigan 49503 /

P.O. Box 163, Cambridge CB3 9PU U.K.

Printed in the United States of America

04 03 02 01 00 99   7 6 5 4 3 2 1

Library of Congress Cataloging-in-Publication Data

Peace, Richard.

Conversion in the New Testament: Paul and the Twelve /

Richard V. Peace.

p.   cm.

Includes bibliographical references.

ISBN 0-8028-4235-6 (pbk.: alk. paper)

1. Conversion — Biblical teaching.

2. Christian converts — Palestine Biography.

3. Bible. N.T. Biography.   I. Title.

BV4932.P43   1999

248.2′4′09015 — dc21   99-37660

CIP

For my children
Lisa, Jennifer, Stephen, and Jonathan
with love and gratitude
for who they are

Contents

CONTENTS

PART II: THE EXPERIENCE OF THE TWELVE

Contents

CONTENTS

Foreword

Conversion is a current and critical theme that deserves careful consideration; this book by Richard Peace is a major and responsible contribution to this discussion. Conversion is receiving attention in the scholarly literature of ancient Judaism and early Christianity, in the context of multiple and competing diverse religions in our time, and in the ecumenical discussions about proselytism, and it is even a theme in the best-selling new John Grisham novel, *The Testament*.

In theological circles there is a kind of yearning for the integration and intersection of disciplines. This goal seems elusive, and many are skeptical about achieving it. This book is a genuine attempt, which achieves considerable success, to bring together at least two disciplines: New Testament studies and the practical theological field of evangelism. In fact, the book also brings into the discussion with some clarity debates about religious conversions and mystical experiences from the literature in the field of the psychology of religion. Peace, who has a doctorate in New Testament and a career as an evangelist, as well as being a scholar and professor of evangelism and one who has read widely in the psychological literature of religious experience, is well equipped to undertake this important work.

The results are impressive. Peace's work on the New Testament and its integration with the concerns of present-day work on religious experience, evangelism, conversion, and discipleship is informed, intelligent, independent, and insightful. He has read widely and well; he knows the literature. He reflects both the good insights and the diversity of opinions among scholars. His judgments are fair and intelligent. He often leans heavily on the work of others, but just as often he offers his own critique and judgment. As a former student and frequent devotee of Krister Stendahl, I appreciated and learned, for example, from Peace's substantial critique of Stendahl's famous dictum that what Paul experienced on the Damascus Road was a call, not a conversion. It has been sometimes alleged that Paul's experiences were unique (e.g., an apostolic call from the heavenly Lord Jesus, a mystical trip to Paradise) and should not be used as models for typical Christian experience, but Peace shows that Paul can be understood in both ways and, further, that the presentation of Paul in the Acts of the Apostles does illumine one model of conversion.

Peace's first section is a careful and integrative study of Paul's Damascus Road experience as presented in the Acts of the Apostles, with limited attention to Paul's own discussions of this experience. This approach will make some New Testament Pauline scholars uncomfortable, because such persons (myself included) always stress the priority of Paul's own testimony over that of the Lukan Acts' presentation of Paul with its own agenda. But Peace's book is not about Paul's perception; it is about the New Testament canonical presentations of Paul as a model of conversion. Peace's discussion is a learned dialogue with New Testament scholarship and with the current literature in other disciplines; as such it deserves a careful hearing.

In the second section of the book, Peace argues that the conversion of the Twelve is *the* organizing principle of the Gospel of Mark, the earliest surviving written Gospel of the church. Peace is very careful to show that the major component of their gradual conversion (conversion as a process) was their increasing recognition and understanding of the identity of Jesus. This presents a critical choice: Is the organizing principle of Mark's Gospel conversion or christology? Peace argues well for conversion with a christological focus as the controlling viewpoint. His careful discussion of the structure of Mark, especially his dialogue with Vernon Robbins, shows independent judgment and valuable insight. One could wish that Peace had given more attention to the relationship between the Twelve and the whole group of disciples of Jesus, but minimizing this issue does not undercut the basic values of the model of the gradual process of conversion presented in the Gospel of Mark. As a bibliographic footnote, it is interesting to observe that the once famous work *The Training of the Twelve* (which first appeared in 1871) by Alexander Balmain Bruce (1831-1899), a famous Scottish Free Church theologian, is not in Peace's bibliography; we have passed into a new era.

The third section of the book is Peace's discussion of what he calls encounter evangelism and process evangelism. I recognize that I am not a scholar in this area, but I found this section wholesome, helpful, and compelling. Peace's approach, which respects the values of "traditional evangelism," engages what is for me a more integrative and theologically defensible approach to evangelism that recognizes the place and power of, for example, small groups, spiritual formation, and worship.

Perhaps a personal word could be allowed. The largest section of Peace's book is the second part on the Twelve in the Gospel of Mark, which builds on his doctoral dissertation. It was just over thirty years ago that William B. Eerdmans published Robert P. Meye's *Jesus and the Twelve: Discipleship and Revelation in Mark's Gospel* (1968), his doctoral dissertation. Although not at Fuller Theological Seminary then, Meye later had a distinguished career as Dean and Professor of New Testament at the School of Theology at Fuller (and is now Dean and Professor Emeritus). Now Peace, a professor at Fuller, offers his book. These works are an important "bracket" in the late twentieth-century tradition of evangelical scholarship. It is a joy of my life to count both Bob Meye and Dick Peace as dear friends; my close association with Dick now extends over twenty-five years!

I commend Peace's book to a wide audience — pastors, leaders of virtually any Christian organization, lay leaders and workers in evangelism and discipleship, and scholars in the fields of evangelism, religious experience, and New Testament. I hope that this book helps us think deeply and act wisely with respect to conversion, a concern at the very heart of the gospel to which we owe our lives.

DAVID M. SCHOLER
Professor of New Testament and Associate Dean for the Center
for Advanced Theological Studies, School of Theology,
Fuller Theological Seminary, Pasadena, CA
August 6, 1999

Acknowledgments

This book is based on reading and research begun in the mid-1960s and carried on intermittently over the next twenty-five years. As a result, numerous people have contributed to the outcome. I could not hope to name all these individuals, who include various academic friends and advisers, faculty colleagues, numerous students who have interacted with my presentation of this material, and all the friends who supported me during the seemingly interminable length of time it took me to complete this book. In this context I especially want to thank my wife, Judy, and our children, Lisa, Jennifer, Stephen, and Jonathan, all of whom had to put up with my absence at various points in time when I was engaged in this research. I am more grateful than I can express for their love and patience. Special thanks go to Susan Wood (of the Fuller Seminary Faculty Publications Service) for her preparation of the author and Scripture reference indexes and to John Winson (of the Frontline Group) and Bruce Robinson (of Wm. B. Eerdmans Publishing Company), whose efforts resulted in the publication of this material.

As indicated in the introduction, the core of the argument in this book is taken from my Ph.D. dissertation. It took over twenty years to complete this dissertation, and I am grateful to the School of Theology at the University of Natal in Pietermaritzburg, Natal, South Africa, for its patience and for its willingness to allow me the time I needed to complete this work. I am also grateful to the trustees of Gordon-Conwell Theological Seminary for their very generous sabbatical program, which gave me the opportunity to complete my dissertation, and to the trustees of Fuller Theological Seminary, who provided a sabbatical during which I was able to turn a dissertation into this book. Finally, I owe a debt of appreciation to Tyndale House in Cambridge,

England. It was there, in that special atmosphere dedicated to biblical research, that I completed the crucial work on the Gospel of Mark.

It should be noted that all unattributed quotes from the Bible are taken from the New Revised Standard Version (New York: National Council of Churches, 1989).

INTRODUCTION

What Do We Need to Know about Conversion?

I have been interested in conversion for as long as I can remember. Part of that interest has been professional in orientation. My ministry has focused on evangelism for nearly forty years, and the experience of conversion lies at the very heart of evangelism. In order to be effective in evangelism, it is necessary to have a clear and nuanced understanding of the nature of conversion.

But herein lie the problem and the fascination. The church has not always been clear about conversion. In fact, there is a wide difference of opinion as to what constitutes conversion. Some would understand conversion in quite particular terms: it is like what happened to St. Paul on the Damascus road — a mystical encounter with Christ, a radical reformation of life around Christian principles and ideas, and a reorientation of one's relationships so that they focus on a Christian community. Others would allow more latitude in understanding conversion: it has to do with the decision (rapid or gradual) to align oneself with Christ and with the church. Still others would point to certain liturgical events as the moment of conversion, in particular, baptism or confirmation. Some would even question whether conversion is a useful category, in that the real issue is not some past experience or decision but the ongoing search for spiritual reality and the openness to pursue whatever path promotes such an awareness.

When I began full-time work in evangelism with a group called African Enterprise (which my wife and I and several others helped start when we were students at Fuller Seminary), I brought to that ministry all the typical evangelical assumptions about conversion. Conversion, to me, was that experience which launched one's Christian life. It involved saying yes to Jesus by means of a simple prayer of repentance and faith. Conversion marked the difference between a vital Christian experience and a nominal Christian existence. Mostly conversion looked like what happened to St. Paul, i.e., it was sudden, singular, emotional, and instantaneously transforming.

My understanding of conversion was not so much the product of careful reflection as it was a set of assumptions I had imbibed from my upbringing in the church. However, after two or three years of ministry it became clear to me that while conversion did at times resemble my stereotype, often it did not. This was confusing to me. Sometimes it seemed as if people just slipped silently into the kingdom. They attended a Bible study group and at some point in the process (perhaps even unknown to them) just started thinking, acting, talking, and praying like everybody else in the group. Were they to be questioned about their commitment to Christ, their answers would be as orthodox as anyone's, even though they could not define the moment when they arrived at such a commitment.

Even more confusing was the fact that others had what seemed to me a genuine "conversion experience," but this event appeared to have had little, if any, practical impact on them. Life for such people went on much the same after "conversion" as before. In the South African context this often meant that "being converted" made no appreciable difference in how they treated those of other races.

Others still seemed to be pushed by our evangelistic efforts into more questions than answers. From self-described "happy pagans," they became "discontented seekers" who struggled to know if God existed and if Jesus was God's Son. These "seekers" were often more involved in justice issues than were the "converted" people in the church. Then there were the many folk who assisted us in our evangelistic efforts (in which sudden conversion was our aim) even though they themselves had never had such an experience. They had always loved Jesus and just wanted others to meet him.

So, what was this thing of conversion? My work in an evangelistic ministry had forced me to reconsider whether I actually knew the answer to this fundamental question. That conversion was a real experience which could be described and defined, I never had any doubt. Just what those boundaries might be, however, became the subject of my reading and research. Clearly, my own understanding of conversion was too limited, too circumspect. The Holy Spirit, it seemed, had a broader view of conversion than I did.

Another part of my interest in conversion has been personal. The whole idea of transformation fascinates me, probably because growth and change have never come easily to me. Conversion is a form of transformation that seems, at first glance, to promise complete reformation brought about by the work of God. How wonderful! All a person has to do is to open his or her life to God by trusting in the redeeming power of Jesus' work on the cross, and he or she becomes a new creature. And yet, as I discovered in my own postconversion life, it was not as simple as that. Yes, openness to God by way of commitment to Christ did shift the nature of reality in one's life. Yes, God the Holy Spirit did bring about changes in one's "heart." Yes, conversion to Christ opened up new life. But none of this was easy, automatic, or inevitable. The fruits of conversion unfolded over time — a lot of time in many cases. Again my understanding of the "instantaneousness" of conversion was challenged.

So I started reading and noticing. What had others learned about conversion? How had others experienced (or not experienced) conversion? A few years after I started asking such questions, my individual inquiries became the focus of a doctoral program. As it turned out, this research would not be completed quickly. (While conversion might at times be instantaneous, research never is.) In fact, it took me over twenty years to finish my Ph.D. dissertation. Part of this had to do with my own life circumstances, which never allowed full-time work on this question. But another part had to do with the unwieldy field of inquiry I had picked. As I soon learned, to consider conversion meant that not only did I have to explore various theological byways (church history; systematic, biblical, and practical theology; and biblical studies), I also needed to look into what the social sciences had to say about conversion (psychology, sociology, and communication theory). In the latter case, what began as a curious look at why American psychologists at the turn of the century were fascinated by conversion (psychology was almost equivalent to the psychology of religion during the early years of this discipline in America) turned into a multi-year examination of everyone from William James to Carl Jung as well as the numerous papers in the *Journal of the Scientific Study of Religion* (amongst other journals).

Along the way my interest in conversion converged with my interest in the Gospel of Mark. Mark had become my favorite book of the Bible. I used Mark to teach inductive Bible study — a course I offered in a variety of contexts. Mark was also the first text given to new converts because it was so simple and straightforward (or so I thought at the time). The more I worked with Mark, the more I became fascinated with how Mark told the story of Jesus. In particular, I wondered about how he constructed his Gospel. It was clear that Mark had some sort of agenda in mind when he carefully selected stories from the oral tradition about Jesus and set them side by side so as to convey a meaning beyond the meaning of the individual pericopae. As I wrestled with the question of structure, it gradually became clear to me that Mark had valuable insights into the whole question of conversion.

Mark's aim in writing down the story of Jesus, it seems, was to communicate the gospel (Mark 1:1). The work of evangelism is all about communicating the gospel to those who have not heard it, understood it, or responded to it. And clearly Mark intended for his readers to respond to the Jesus he presented to them. The first unit in his account (1:16–4:34) is all about responding to Jesus. Mark wanted his readers to be amongst those whose lives bore good fruit (4:20). Equally clearly Mark was making use of conversion language in his account. For example, he states in the first chapter: "Now after John was arrested, Jesus came to Galilee, proclaiming the good news of God, and saying, 'The time is fulfilled, and the kingdom of God has come near; repent, and believe in the good news'" (1:14-15). Repentance and faith (belief) are the New Testament definition of conversion.[1] In subsequent chapters of his account, Mark explores in more detail both repentance and faith as well as the nature of discipleship (what it means to continue on in following after Jesus). So Mark was doing the work of evangelism. His aim was to bring about conversion. A careful reflection on his way of doing this would yield valuable insights into the nature of conversion.

It was while I was working on the question of the structure of Mark's Gospel (how he went about "preaching the gospel") that it became clear to me that Mark was offering another paradigm for conversion, different from the Pauline paradigm. *What he was describing in his Gospel was the unfolding conversion of the Twelve.* What Mark sought to communicate in his Gospel was the process by which these twelve men gradually turned, over time, from their culturally derived understanding of Jesus as a great teacher to the amazing discovery that he was actually the Messiah who was the Son of God. In showing how the Twelve turned to Jesus, step-by-step, Mark was inviting his readers to undergo the same journey of conversion.

The implications of this insight became quickly apparent. In its evangelistic work the church has sought to replicate in others what happened to St. Paul: a sudden, point-in-time transformation based on an encounter with Jesus. Thus evangelism has focused on a single issue: accepting Jesus as Lord and Savior now, at this moment in time. It was assumed that all people at every moment in time were able to answer the question: "Will you accept Jesus?" There was little room for those still on the way in understanding who Jesus is. Evangelistic methods were geared around producing instantaneous "decisions for Christ." Mass rallies ended with a call to come forward and

---

1. See the discussion in the appendix, "A Lexical Summary of Conversion," pp. 346-53.

make a decision for Jesus. Visitation evangelism dialogues were designed to confront people with the need to accept Jesus at this moment in time, lest they die and not go to heaven. Tracts were written that always ended with a prayer of commitment. Certainly the impulse behind such efforts was and is positive. Concerned Christian men and women long for others to enter into the kind of life-changing experience of Jesus they themselves have had. But these evangelistic methodologies are derived from an understanding that the model for conversion is what happened to St. Paul. To confront people with the need to decide in a moment for Jesus is derived from a punctiliar understanding of conversion.

But if there is a second paradigm for conversion in the New Testament, this raises the possibility that there are other ways to do evangelism. I began to ask: "What might evangelism look like if we accepted the fact that for a lot of people it is a long-term process by which they come to faith in Jesus?" My reflections on this question are found in the final two chapters of this book.

This research into the nature of conversion eventually became my Ph.D. dissertation. This book presents the core of that work along with further reflections on the work of evangelism derived from my assertion that there is a second paradigm for conversion in the New Testament. It is my sense that to think about conversion as a process and not just an event will be of real value to the church. At this moment in history when so many people are interested in spirituality and open to Christianity, it behooves us to respond to their need in ways that build upon this Spirit-driven desire to know God. We will not be able to help people if we insist that their experience must parallel the experience of St. Paul. Of course, sudden conversions do continue to occur, but this is (and has always been) a minority experience. My hope is that as we explore the process-oriented paradigm for conversion found in Mark's Gospel, we will develop a more holistic way of doing evangelism that yields in our generation the good fruit that Mark desired in his.

Defining Conversion

To define specifically what conversion is would at first glance appear to be a straightforward task.[2] The phenomenon of conversion is, after all, well

2. "A nearly universal assumption in the English-speaking world seems to be that the meaning of 'conversion' is self-evident, and to be thought of along the lines that James proposed," according to Jacob W. Heikkinen, "'Conversion': A Biblical Study," *National Faith and Order Colloquium,* World Council of Churches, June 12-17, 1966, p. 1. The definition to which Heikkinen alludes is that of William James, found in his famous book *The*

known. It ought not be that difficult to point out certain figures in the history of the church and say, "There — what happened to him or her — that is what conversion is." The problem is that even a cursory glance at the conversion stories of individuals down through the ages reveals a plethora of quite different experiences.[3] Even when one is dealing only with Christian conversion, there are so many different types of conversion. Some people, for example, come to faith in a moment, without much discernible preparation. They experience conversion in a flash, and from that point on their lives are of a radically different order. Others, however, struggle for years, coming finally to the end of hope of ever finding salvation, only to discover that out of their despair and without any seeming connection to their past efforts they experience conversion and the despair vanishes. The movement of others toward conversion takes place in fits and starts. In looking back over time they realize that a series of distinct turnings took place before the turning itself was complete. Furthermore, each of the small turnings was marked by a crisis of a different sort. Some come to faith with very little cognitive understanding of what they are doing, much less any theological understanding of what has happened. Still others cannot remember ever being converted, yet by whatever criterion one puts forth to define the genuine Christian, they meet it.[4]

Whatever else one can say about the nature of conversion, it is clear that God created human beings in such a fashion that they are able to experience conversion. This in itself is a remarkable phenomenon that appears not to be duplicated elsewhere in the animal kingdom. Once a bear always a bear, once a porpoise always a porpoise. But human beings have the ability to undergo remarkable transformations of a cognitive, affective, behavioral, social, and religious nature that seem to tip their lives upside down and launch them in whole new and positive directions. This is an important observation since it means that *the essence of conversion is not found in the experience itself but in*

Varieties of Religious Experience. Heikkinen quotes this definition: "To be converted, to be regenerated, to receive grace, to experience religion, to gain an assurance, are so many phrases which denote the process, gradual or sudden, by which a self hitherto divided, and consciously wrong, inferior and unhappy, becomes unified and consciously right, superior and happy, in consequence of its firmer hold upon religious realities."

3. See Hugh T. Kerr and John M. Mulder, eds., *Conversions: The Christian Experience* (Grand Rapids: Wm. B. Eerdmans Publishing Co., 1983).

4. For a discussion of the typology of conversion, see Owen Brandon, *The Battle for the Soul: Aspects of Religious Conversion* (London: Hodder & Stoughton, 1960), pp. 27-33, and Richard Peace, *Pilgrimage: A Workbook on Christian Growth* (Los Angeles: Acton House, 1976), pp. 73-80.

the content of that experience. In the work of ministry, the question then must be: In conversion, from what to whom has a person turned? The question is not: What is the shape of that person's experience, and does it conform to what we consider a normative experience? But even with this qualification, the question still remains: What is genuine conversion?

Approaches to the Issue

There are a variety of ways to tackle the question of the nature of conversion. Perhaps the most straightforward approach would be to immerse oneself in the many and varied *accounts of conversion* that exist in a variety of sources and out of these seek to derive a comprehensive definition. The problem with this approach is the sheer volume of documents testifying to conversion.[5] Furthermore, the nature, quality, and completeness of reports vary enormously, as do the schemas used by respondents (consciously or unconsciously) to report and interpret their experiences. Any definition derived from such materials would be so broad as to be of little practical value.

The implication of this conclusion is that a researcher must therefore limit his or her work to a specific type of conversion. So, for example, it would be possible to consider such experiences as conversion from one Christian denomination to another, as when a member of the Church of England converts to Catholicism.[6] Or conversion from nominal faith to active faith could be explored as, for example, when a person's extrinsic faith becomes intrin-

5. George Jackson, *The Fact of Conversion* (New York: Revell, 1908), pp. 20-21, comments: "How vast and varied the field is perhaps no one realizes who has not made some attempt to survey it and map it out. Most people know something of the great spiritual transformations associated with the names of St. Paul and St. Augustine, of John Bunyan and John Wesley; but how many of us have made any effort seriously to estimate the significance of that great mass of veritable human documents to be found in the New Testament, in the records of great religious awakenings . . . and above all in the biographies and autobiographies, the hymns and prayers and confessions, of religious men and women of all Churches and in all ages?" To this must be added the comment of Edmund S. Conklin, *The Psychology of Religious Adjustment* (New York: Macmillan, 1929), p. viii: "Only ones who have given the subject serious consideration can know how incredibly vast is the literature. . . . If any one claims to have read it all, I shall hereafter think him either pitifully ignorant or suffering from some form of mental aberration." (Both sources are quoted in Barbara E. Jones, "Conversion: An Examination of the Myth of Human Change" [Ph.D. diss., Columbia University, 1970], pp. xxviii-xxxix.) Conklin wrote those words in 1929; Jackson wrote in 1908. Since then the material in which conversions are reported and discussed has grown enormously.

6. As, for example, John Henry Newman in Kerr and Mulder, pp. 121-28.

sic.[7] Conversion from a secular faith to a religious faith (e.g., conversion from communism to Christianity)[8] might be one's topic of consideration. Coercive conversion is another topic of interest, as, for example, when a person is manipulated by a cult or by a government into a new worldview.[9] There are also so-called "secular conversions,"[10] in which, for example, an alcoholic is transformed from dependence on alcohol to a sober lifestyle.[11] Then there is conversion to ideologies quite different from Christianity (e.g., conversion from Shintoism to Judaism).[12] All of these are interesting areas of inquiry, but for the purposes of this study I have chosen to limit my consideration to *conversion to Christianity*, specifically, that which was experienced by certain first-century Jews (such as Paul and the Twelve) who became Christians. My analysis will be even more limited in that I will only look at what I consider to be paradigmatic experiences found in the New Testament literature.

A second way to approach the question of the nature of conversion would be to *examine by means of a questionnaire (or other form of psychological/theological test) the experiences of a representative group of contemporary individuals who report that they have experienced conversion.* Conclusions about conversion could then be derived statistically by analyzing their re-

7. See G. W. Allport, "Religion and Prejudice," *Crane Review* 2 (1959): 1-10; Allport, "The Religious Context of Prejudice," *Journal for the Scientific Study of Religion* 5 (1966): 447-57; and Allport and J. M. Ross, "Personal Religious Orientation and Prejudice," *Journal of Personality and Social Psychology* 5 (1967): 432-43.

8. See, for example, Douglas Hyde, *Dedication and Leadership: Learning from the Communists* (London: Sands & Co., 1966).

9. See Flo Conway and Jim Siegelman, *Snapping: America's Epidemic of Sudden Personality Change* (Philadelphia: Lippincott, 1978); Robert Jay Lifton, *Thought Reform and the Psychology of Totalism: A Study of "Brainwashing" in China* (New York: Norton, 1961); and Duane Arlo Windemiller, "The Psychodynamics of Change in Religious Conversion and Communist Brainwashing: With Particular Reference to the Eighteenth Century Evangelical Revival and the Chinese Thought Control Movement" (Ph.D. diss., Boston University, 1960).

10. Jones, p. xx.

11. B. Jones notes the remarkable similarity of such experiences to religious conversion. She points out "that certain steps which were enunciated in the classic doctrine of conversion are, in fact, the actual occurrences in the transition from hopeless drinking to productive sobriety: despair, admission of defeat, surrender, testifying and good works." She comments that in Alcoholics Anonymous therapy, conversion was not simply one technique used, it was the single essential ingredient. Jones, p. xx.

12. For example, see Abraham Kotsuji, *From Tokyo to Jerusalem* (New York: Geis, 1946). For examples of a variety of conversion-type changes covering all the above categories plus others, see Bernard Dixon, *Journeys in Belief* (London: George Allen & Unwin, 1968).

sponses. This would be less open-ended than the first approach, since the study would be confined to a specific group, and is, in fact, the way psychologists originally went about defining conversion.[13] However, though this has been a popular approach on the part of psychologists, until recently the results have been superficial and not generalizable (due to a lack of adequate test instruments and techniques).[14] Even today, with more sophisticated tests and techniques available, "there has been really little progress beyond James's creative intuitions in his 1901-02 lectures on *Varieties of Religious Experience,* which remains the classic in psychology of religion. Despite an expanded tool kit, the few empirical investigations that have been conducted have tended to rely on questionnaires in forms not much different from that employed by Starbuck in the 1890's."[15] Furthermore, such an empirical approach does not take into account the larger question of the reality of God. How (or if) God is active in conversion cannot be determined by a purely phenomenological study. Yet this is an important consideration given the fact that many in the church would understand Christian conversion to be not merely a species of human turning but the work of God. To attempt to define such an experience only from the point of view of those experiencing the conversion is to disregard the divine dimension.[16] Or, at least, it is to look at this question only in terms of how individuals understand and report what has happened to them. This is one reason why I have chosen to look at Christian conversion *as expressed in the New Testament.* In such a document one not only sees the experience of certain individuals but also finds a theological interpretation of the event.

A third way to probe the nature of conversion might be through an Aristotelian approach. Rather than looking at raw experience itself with all its messiness, with its subjective interpretation on the part of converts and/or

13. William G. T. Douglas and James R. Scroggs, "Issues in the Psychology of Religious Conversion," *Journal of Religion and Health* 6 (1967): 204-5, as well as examples of such research: James Bissett Pratt, *The Religious Consciousness* (New York: Macmillan, 1921), and Edwin Diller Starbuck, *The Psychology of Religion* (New York: Scribner, 1899), both of whom use this method.

14. Douglas and Scroggs, pp. 204-5.

15. Douglas and Scroggs, p. 205. An example of the responsible use of modern testing techniques is John P. Kildahl, "The Personalities of Sudden Religious Converts," *Pastoral Psychology* 16, no. 156 (September 1965): 37-44; Joel Allison, "Recent Empirical Studies of Religious Conversion Experiences," *Pastoral Psychology* 17 (September 1966): 21-23; and Steven M. Silverstein, "A Study of Religious Conversion in North America," *Genetic, Social, and General Psychology Monographs* (1988): 261-305.

16. The New Testament uses the word "conversion" to describe the experience of the individual and the word "regeneration" to describe the work of God in that individual.

their chroniclers, and with the lack of completeness of so many accounts, one could simply *assemble a number of definitions* that have been proposed for conversion.[17] These could then be analyzed on the basis of some predetermined grid, and out of this a general definition could be derived.[18] This methodology shares many of the same problems that occur when one works with accounts of conversion: the sheer number of definitions, the differing perspectives from which these definitions are derived, the faulty basis on which some are developed, and the lack of consistency of analysis. In the end, one is left once again with a highly generalized conclusion that is of little practical value to those in the church who are wrestling with specific questions of ministry.

In contrast to these three approaches, my way of investigating the nature of conversion is *textual in orientation and inductive in methodology and is conducted within the evangelical theological paradigm.* I propose to examine in detail a single, representative experience of conversion (that of St. Paul on the Damascus road), drawn from a particular tradition (Christian) and presented in a specific document (the New Testament, specifically the Acts of the Apostles but with reference also to Paul's own writings on the subject), with the aim of deriving inductively an understanding of what constitutes Christian conversion. Using this as a normative understanding of conversion (with all the limitations already described), I will then seek to show that exactly the same sort of transformation took place in the lives of the twelve disciples, though their experience was quite different from that of Paul. In other words, my aim is to demonstrate that while there is such a phenomenon as Christian conversion and that it has specific characteristics, it occurs in different ways in the lives of different people. What happened to Paul and what happened to the Twelve was identical in terms of theological understanding, though quite different experientially. In this way I hope to articulate an understanding of conversion that will be of use to the church in its inquiry into conversion.

17. There is such a collection in Douglas Clyde MacIntosh, *Personal Religion* (New York: Scribner, 1942).

18. See, for example, the work of Barbara Jones in "Conversion: An Examination of the Myth of Human Change." She uses various accounts of conversion and analyzes them in this fashion. "Moving carefully from discipline to discipline, seeing the material first through one investigative technique and then through another, an effort was made to detail the data multilaterally, to utilize any facts or hypotheses that might shape a coherent theory of conversion" (p. xxx). However, it must also be noted that while she takes advantage of various hypotheses about conversion, she attempts not to "impose a screen of interpretation on it. The method, then, has been a process, an evolution in itself; a living and growing thing which shaped the material and was shaped by it" (p. xxxi).

Hopefully such a definition will also contribute in a small way to the discussion of conversion within the psychological community.[19]

In summary, the way I have approached the subject of conversion in this book is eclectic. It does not fit easily into traditional categories. I examine individual biblical passages, but this is not an exegetical analysis; I combine together various insights taken primarily from Acts and the Gospel of Mark in order to understand one particular theme in these documents, but this is not simply biblical theology; I am touching upon one of the great doctrines of the church, but this is not systematic theology; I discuss various psychological insights, but I am not writing from the vantage point of the social sciences. In fact, *what I am doing can best be described as practical theology, i.e., biblical study as conducted within an evangelical paradigm put in the context of human experience with the hope that this work will assist those who are at work in ministry.*

Overview

My working methodology is as follows. In Part I my aim is to develop a foundational understanding of Christian conversion that will express accurately what lies at the heart of this experience. To this end I will be examining that experience which is considered normative by many: the conversion of St. Paul on the road to Damascus. In Part II I will take the understanding of conversion derived from St. Paul's experience and apply it to quite a different set of experiences, namely, that of the twelve disciples.[20] It is my contention that on

---

19. I need to say a word about my use of psychological materials in this book. This work is sited primarily in the field of biblical theology. However, given a topic such as conversion, one cannot bypass the work that has been done in this area by psychologists of all sorts. From the original work of William James in *The Varieties of Religious Experience* down to the recent articles in the *Journal for the Scientific Study of Religion,* there has been a steady interest on the part of psychologists in the subject of conversion. As the bibliography indicates, I have examined a lot of this material. However, I will not attempt to interact with these psychological materials in any substantial way. To deal adequately with the biblical materials has proved a huge task in itself; to attempt to interact critically with the psychological materials would make this book unwieldy. Still, I will make reference to psychological insights at a number of places in the text when they bear upon the understanding of a particular aspect of the subject. However, this is more by way of enrichment of the argument than critical response to the materials.

20. I am aware that I am taking insights from the writings of one author (Luke, with supporting material from Paul) and applying these to the work of a second, quite different author (Mark). My justification for doing this is that, as Witherup has shown, the concept

the basis of the understanding of conversion derived from Paul's experience, the Twelve were not (nor could have been) converted while they were members of the apostolic band touring Israel with Jesus. But they obviously did have a transforming experience out of which they became the very pillars upon which the Christian church was built. When and how were they converted? How does the understanding of conversion developed in Part I yield useful insights into the nature of the experience of the Twelve?

My argument is that in the Gospel of Mark we see the unfolding conversion experience of the Twelve. Mark is the document that looks most closely at the relationship between Jesus and his twelve disciples. And in fact, as I will argue, the organizing theme in Mark is how the Twelve were brought step-by-step to the experience of repentance and faith. That they did not grasp accurately either who Jesus is or the nature of their own situation (i.e., that they had not repented) is clear right from the beginning of Mark. In fact, up to the time of Jesus' death they persist in crucial misunderstandings. That they did not possess faith in the full sense is also clear right from the beginning. In fact, by virtue of their failure to see and understand who Jesus is, they could not have had proper faith in him. Prior to the death and resurrection of Jesus, their faith was in the Messiah as defined by their culture and not in Jesus as he really was. In the same way that the book of Acts forms the locus for study in Part I, the Gospel of Mark forms the locus of study in Part II.

I argue that a proper biblical understanding of conversion (derived from the seminal experience of St. Paul) will enable us to understand in a new way how the Twelve came to faith. The assumption in biblical studies seems to be (though few address the question)[21] that the act of joining Jesus' apostolic band was equivalent to their conversion. But was this the case? Were they

---

of conversion in the NT remains remarkably consistent across all the documents. "After careful consideration I have come to believe that the NT shows a fairly uniform teaching about conversion with minimal evidence for a dramatic evolution of the concept." Ronald D. Witherup, *Conversion in the New Testament* (Collegeville, Minn.: Liturgical Press, 1994), p. 2. I am not seeking to demonstrate that there was some sort of literary connection between Mark and Luke (though clearly Luke uses Marcan materials in his Gospel). I am attempting to spell out what conversion to Christ looked like in NT times so as to demonstrate that Mark, using this common understanding of conversion, was in fact describing what I call the conversion of the Twelve.

21. Interestingly, a psychologist, André Godin, senses this problem: "What they [the apostles] saw or heard outside was far from matching their indwelling wish in terms of the ego-ideal derived from their Jewish education. So their affirmation of faith could be only gradually transforming, as many episodes in the gospels indicate." André Godin, *The Psychological Dynamics of Religious Experience* (Birmingham, Ala.: Religious Education Press, 1985), p. 202.

converted at the moment they responded to Jesus' invitation to become fishers of men (Mark 1:17-18)? Or did conversion take place when they were
commissioned as apostles (3:13-15)? Perhaps it took place when they affirmed that Jesus was indeed the Messiah (8:29). Or did it occur at the moment of the miracle of the second touch?[22] In fact, on the basis of the understanding derived from Paul's experience, none of these experiences would
qualify as the moment of conversion. Instead, each played a vital part in the
final experience of conversion.

The book unfolds as follows. In Part I the experience of St. Paul on the
Damascus road will be analyzed in order to derive a definition for Christian
conversion. In chapter 1 the core pattern of Paul's conversion will be shown
to have three parts: insight, turning, and transformation. Chapter 2 explores
the new insight Paul has into himself and into God's will, as well as his response to this revelation (repentance). Chapter 3 examines Paul's encounter
with and turning to the resurrected Jesus (faith), while chapter 4 looks at the
transformation that takes place in the life of Paul as he accepts and lives out
the commission he is given to bear the good news of Jesus to the nations (discipleship).

In Part II the experience of the Twelve is examined in the light of the
definition of conversion derived from Paul's conversion. In chapter 5 it is argued that the organizing theme of Mark's Gospel is the conversion of the
Twelve. An outline of the Gospel is developed which reflects the six-part
movement of the Twelve in their unfolding understanding of who Jesus is. In
chapter 6 the stylistic evidence for this outline is examined in detail. In chapters 7–10 the details of Mark's Gospel are examined to demonstrate that each
unit focuses on a different title for Jesus and that each unit has as a subtheme
some aspect of conversion. Specifically, chapter 7 looks at how the Twelve
come to understand that Jesus is the Messiah. Chapter 8 looks at how the
Twelve come to understand that Jesus is the Son of God. Chapter 9 focuses on
the conversion themes in the first half of the Gospel (response to Jesus, faith,
and repentance), while chapter 10 looks at the conversion theme in the second half of the Gospel (discipleship).

Finally, chapters 11–13 discuss the implications for the church in its
ministry of evangelism of the existence of two paradigms for conversion in
the New Testament. The church already understands how to go about the
work of evangelism if it is punctiliar conversion we seek for others. But evangelism will have a different shape if we take seriously that conversion can also
take place over time in an unfolding process. It will be argued that the outline

22. Which Mark portrays in a symbolic way in 10:46-52.

in Mark's Gospel provides a useful outline that might guide how we go about the work of evangelism in a holistic way.

PART I

THE EXPERIENCE OF ST. PAUL

CHAPTER ONE

The Event: The Core Pattern
of Paul's Conversion

I f you were to ask the average person, "What is conversion?" chances are that he or she would reply: "It's what happened to St. Paul on the Damascus road." So it is not a surprise that we begin this study of conversion with a careful examination of the conversion of St. Paul. The story of Paul's conversion is so central to the story of the early church that it is told not once but three times in the Acts of the Apostles. This is all the more striking in the light of the economy of style that characterizes the writing of this New Testament document. In Acts, so much is left out and untold concerning the growth of the church after the resurrection of Jesus that the thrice-repetition of a single event assumes all the more importance. By examining the three accounts of Paul's conversion we will find the core elements that define his conversion and hence those elements that define how conversion was understood in the New Testament.[1]

The Significance of Paul's Conversion

Whatever else one might say about Paul's conversion, it must be conceded that it had a momentous impact on the church. "No single event, apart from the Christ-event itself, has proved so determinant for the course of Christian

1. See the appendix (pp. 346-52) for an examination of the biblical roots of the three key words related to the concept of conversion.

history as the conversion and commissioning of Paul."[2] From that event sprang the ministry of St. Paul. From the ministry of Paul came the Gentile church.[3] From these churches Western Christianity emerged as it is known today. "The importance of Paul's conversion and of the consequences he drew from it can hardly be exaggerated. He made the free development of Gentile Christianity possible. His depreciation of the Law as a Christian may have been as one-sided and extreme as his previous Pharisaic zeal for it, but without his insight into the limitations of a legal religion, Christianity would never have been established in Europe."[4] Furthermore, many consider Paul's conversion to be a central "proof" for the validity of Christianity. As F. F. Bruce writes: "For anyone who accepts Paul's own explanation of his Damascus-road experience, it would be difficult to disagree with the observation of an eighteenth-century writer that 'the conversion and apostleship of St. Paul alone, duly considered, was of itself a demonstration sufficient to prove Christianity to be a divine revelation.'"[5]

Whatever the wider impact, Paul's conversion was for him the most crucial event of his life. His vision of the risen Christ while on the Damascus road literally stopped him in his tracks, turned his whole life around, and launched him in a totally new direction. From a Pharisee of the Pharisees bent on the destruction of the church (Acts 9:1; Phil. 3:4-6), he became a tireless evangelist, planting churches around the Mediterranean, despite great

2. F. F. Bruce, *Paul: Apostle of the Heart Set Free* (Grand Rapids: Wm. B. Eerdmans Publishing Co., 1977), p. 75.

3. There were churches in Gentile areas not founded by Paul, the church at Rome being the prime example. However, it was out of Paul's ministry that the majority of the original Gentile churches emerged.

4. H. G. Wood, "The Conversion of St. Paul: Its Nature, Antecedents and Consequences," *New Testament Studies* 1 (1955): 280.

5. Bruce, *Paul*, p. 75, citing G. Lyttelton, *Observations on the Conversion and Apostleship of St. Paul* (London, 1747), paragraph 1. Joseph Lilly would agree with this assessment in "The Conversion of Saint Paul: The Validity of His Testimony to the Resurrection of Jesus Christ," *Catholic Biblical Quarterly* 6 (1944): 181-82: "As Tricot remarks: 'It can be said without exaggeration that the conversion of Paul ranks after the resurrection of Jesus in the class of miraculous events which determine the fortune of Christianity, since on these two facts depends in large measure the value of the motives of credibility of the traditional faith.' [*Saint Paul, Apôtre des Gentils* (1928), p. 44.] The best witness, historically speaking, to the resurrection of our Lord is St. Paul, the apostle . . . because his testimony is contained in the earliest written documents. . . . [In fact, Paul's] own faith in the resurrection goes back . . . to the time of his conversion which occurred from three to five years after the resurrection. The testimony of Paul, therefore, to the resurrection of Jesus is practically contemporaneous with the event, and is, historically speaking, the most precious we have. . . ."

personal hardship and suffering (2 Cor. 11:16-33). In fact, this very change in Paul himself is a further demonstration of the resurrection of Jesus. It has been asserted that nothing less than an encounter with the living Jesus could have accounted for so radical a change in Paul that he became willing to head up the Gentile mission of the church.

> No motivation residing in Paul nor deriving from his background as a Pharisee can account for his . . . heading up the Gentile mission, for his pride in these [Jewish] distinctives had been so great that he had been as zealous to persecute the Church as the Jews were now zealous to persecute him. The explanation for the Gentile mission must, therefore, derive from something apart from Paul and his background. It must derive from something outside the natural sphere. Paul's explanation is that the risen Jesus appeared to him, and since no explanation from the natural sphere is possible, and since the only proposal for an explanation deriving from the supernatural sphere is the resurrection of Jesus, therefore this is the explanation for the Gentile mission that is to be accepted.[6]

Paul's conversion is significant in yet another way. For countless people in countless generations it has provided the model of what Christian conversion is supposed to be like. Whether individuals have always focused on the key elements in this experience or gotten sidetracked into secondary issues (such as whether a conversion must be sudden to be valid) is beside the point. For many in the church, this is what conversion looks like in its pure form.

For all these reasons, it is important therefore to examine with care the Damascus road event. In these first four chapters the order of analysis is as follows. First, the three accounts of this event in Acts will be presented with some interpretive comment, and then these accounts will be assessed so as to identify the core pattern by which Paul's conversion is defined (chap. 1). Next, each of the three elements of this core pattern will be discussed in some detail in terms of St. Paul and his experience. In chapter 2 the concept of insight as the precursor to conversion will be examined; in chapter 3 the central concept of turning will be the focus of discussion; while in chapter 4 the nature of postconversion transformation will be the topic.

6. Daniel P. Fuller, *Easter Faith and History* (Grand Rapids: Wm. B. Eerdmans Publishing Co., 1965), p. 219. This line of reasoning will be explored more fully in chap. 3.

The Three Accounts of Paul's Conversion

Paul first appears in the Acts of the Apostles at the stoning of Stephen. This incident, as described by Luke, begins with the speech of Stephen to the Sanhedrin. Stephen accuses them of persecuting and murdering God's prophets. The Sanhedrin are, of course, furious. Stephen then has a vision of Jesus "standing at the right hand of God!" (Acts 7:56). This is the final straw for the Sanhedrin. When they heard this, "they covered their ears, and with a loud shout all rushed together against him. Then they dragged him out of the city and began to stone him" (7:57-58). Luke concludes with these words: "and the witnesses laid their coats at the feet of a young man named Saul."[7] Luke then adds that Paul was not just a trustworthy guardian for the garments of those engaged in the act of slaying Stephen, but "Saul approved of their killing him" (8:1a).

This is a transition point in Acts. The stoning of Stephen leads to a general persecution of the church, and as a result it is scattered throughout Judea and Samaria (8:1b). The gospel thus begins to spread from Jerusalem outward into the rest of the region. This general persecution also marks the point at which Paul began his active opposition of the church: "Saul was ravaging the church by entering house after house; dragging off both men and women, he committed them to prison" (8:3). Acts 9 begins with Paul "still breathing threats and murder against the disciples of the Lord" and asking for "letters to the synagogues at Damascus, so that if he found any who belonged to the Way, men or women, he might bring them bound to Jerusalem" (vv. 1-2).

Thus it is that Paul is on the road to Damascus, driven by his "obsession" (26:11),[8] seeking to crush the newly emerging church. His conversion comes in this context, and the story of it enters the account as an unexpected and surprising twist whereby the persecutor becomes one of those he persecuted. The cause of this momentous shift in affiliation is accounted for as the result of an encounter on Paul's part with the resurrected Jesus.

---

7. Acts 7:58. Three names are used in the Greek text, as Krister Stendahl, *Paul among Jews and Gentiles* (Philadelphia: Fortress, 1976), p. 11, points out: "*Saulos* (Saul) through 13:9; and *Paulos* (Paul) from 13:9 on, except for the transliteration of the Hebrew name, *Saoul* in the actual account of the call, used both by the Lord and by Ananias (9:4, 17; 22:7, 13; 26:14)." Stendahl goes on to point out that the event which triggers the shift in name from Saul to Paul is not the conversion/call but Paul's appearance before a Roman proconsul by the name of Sergius Paulus. Acts 13:9 reads: "But Saul, also known as Paul, . . ." and from this point on in the text he is always called Paul because the focus is now on Rome. In this book, for the sake of clarity, only the Greek name will be used, even when referring to those texts in which he is called Saul.

8. NIV. The NRSV says Paul was "furiously enraged at them."

The First Account (Acts 9:1-19)

The first account of Paul's conversion is found in Acts 9:1-19. It is distinguished from the other two accounts in several ways. First, it is given *by Luke* as a description of the next step in the unfolding story of the development of the church. The second and third accounts occur in speeches given *by Paul*. Second, the so-called "double vision" of Paul and Ananias is reported here in 9:10-16.[9] Paul has a vision in which he sees "a man named Ananias come in and lay his hands on him so that he might regain his sight" (9:12), and Ananias has a vision in which he is instructed to "go to the street called Straight, and at the house of Judas look for a man of Tarsus named Saul" (9:11). The two visions are interconnected. They validate each other and demonstrate that a divine hand is at work behind these events.

Ananias is the right person for this task. As the text later reveals, he "was a devout man according to the law and well spoken of by all the Jews living there" (22:12). Ananias himself is not so sure about God's choice of him for this task: "Lord, I have heard from many about this man, how much evil he has done to your saints in Jerusalem; and here he has authority from the chief priests to bind all who invoke your name" (9:13-14). However, he is assured by the Lord: "Go, for he is an instrument whom I have chosen to bring my name before Gentiles and kings and before the people of Israel; I myself will show him how much he must suffer for the sake of my name" (9:15-16). So Ananias goes to Paul, lays hands on his eyes, and Paul recovers his sight. In addition, Ananias recounts the vision that brought him to Paul's room and identifies the one who sent him to Paul. The same Jesus who met Paul on the Damascus road told Ananias to go to Paul (9:17).

9. This is the term used by Gerhard Lohfink. His interest in the double vision is as a Hellenistic literary motif introduced by Luke into the Damascus episode. A similar double vision is found in the next chapter (10) when Cornelius is told in a vision to fetch Peter from Joppa and bring him to Caesarea, and Peter is prepared by a vision to put aside his prejudice against Gentiles. In Peter's vision he is told to go with the men who were sent by Cornelius. Lohfink concludes: "The Cornelius story provides a good indication of what Luke seeks to attain with the motif of the double vision. He intends to show that at the time when the Church turned toward the Gentile mission, God himself was directing the course of events, step by step" (*The Conversion of St. Paul: Narrative and History in Acts*, trans. and ed. Bruce J. Malina [Chicago: Franciscan Herald Press, 1976], p. 76).

The Second Account (Acts 22:3-21)

The second time the story of Paul's conversion is told, Paul himself tells it in a speech to a hostile crowd at the temple in Jerusalem (22:3-21).[10] In an interesting reversal, Paul is now the object of hostility by the sort of crowd of which he had once been a willing part. This illustrates how much had taken place in Paul's life since the Damascus road incident. The reason for Paul's arrest is the mistaken assumption that he had defiled the temple by bringing a Gentile into its confines. A riot ensues, and Paul is about to be led off into confinement when he asks for permission to address the crowd (21:27-40). Thus, in 22:1, Paul begins his defense. He tries to explain to them how he, a true Jew, had become a follower of Jesus. The crowd, however, will have none of this and shouts: "Away with such a fellow from the earth! For he should not be allowed to live" (22:22).

This second account is similar to the first, except that Paul begins by stating his credentials as a Jew (22:3). In addition, he also recounts Ananias's words to him confirming his call to be a witness to all people of what he saw and heard of Jesus (22:14-15). Another difference is Paul's mention of a vision which occurred sometime later in Jerusalem at the temple (where he is now speaking), in which he is told by Jesus that his testimony will not be well received (an appropriate comment given his circumstances at that moment when his testimony is about to be rejected once again). In that second vision, the Lord confirms Paul's mission to the Gentiles (22:21; see also 22:14-15).

The Third Account (Acts 26:1-23)

The third time the story of Paul's conversion is told occurs several years later. Paul now appears before King Agrippa. As he did when he stood before the Jews in the temple, Paul begins by asserting his loyalty to his Jewish upbringing (26:4-8). This time, however, he concludes his list of credentials by pointing out that his Jewishness is not the real issue. The issue is the resurrection of Jesus from the dead. "Why is it thought incredible by any of you that God raises the dead?" Paul asks (26:8).

---

10. Of course, in each case it is Luke as author who is doing the reporting, so not too much weight can be placed on the difference in voice in the various accounts. Still, Luke seeks to "quote" Paul in the second and third accounts, thus placing this testimony directly on the lips of Paul himself and not simply as a report from a third party.

This is not the first time Paul has raised the question of the resurrection. In his various hearings he has increasingly focused on the idea of resurrection. The first time occurred when he stood before the Sanhedrin while the commander of the Roman troops attempted to find out the reason for the temple riot. Paul knew that some of the Sanhedrin were Sadducees while others were Pharisees. He also knew that the one group did not believe in resurrection while the other did (23:6-7). By asserting that he was "on trial concerning the hope of the resurrection of the dead" (23:6), Paul generated a theological argument within the Sanhedrin and actually succeeded in getting the Pharisees on his side, at least for a time (23:9-10)! It did him no ultimate good, however, because the argument got so violent that the commander had to take Paul into protective custody, and so he was not released (23:10).

The second time Paul raised the issue of resurrection was during the follow-up hearing before Felix. The commander of the guard had sent Paul to Caesarea for safety's sake and ordered the Sanhedrin to present its case before the governor (23:30). They did so a few days later (24:1-9). In response, Paul asserts his identity as a Jew (24:14, 16) and his hope in the future resurrection (24:15). Again he does not press the case for Jesus' resurrection. He is only concerned about the reality of resurrection in general because, if he can get Felix to admit that the idea of the resurrection is a valid Jewish belief, then he can move on to the issue of the resurrection of Jesus. If Felix can grasp that Jesus has been raised from the dead, then Paul's whole story becomes clear. Felix would understand that what Paul did by becoming a follower of "the Way" (24:14) made perfect sense, and that, in fact, it was the only thing Paul could have done and still remain faithful to the God of Israel. As Paul asserts: "It is about the resurrection of the dead that I am on trial before you today" (24:21).

The Pharisees had understood what Paul was attempting to do when he first raised the general idea of the resurrection (at the hearing a few days earlier before the Sanhedrin). They quickly related it back to his testimony about his Damascus road experience of the resurrected Jesus. "What if a spirit or an angel has spoken to him?" (23:9) they ask, knowing that it was not just about the final resurrection that Paul was concerned but also about the resurrection of Jesus and his claim that he had met Jesus.

By the time the case is heard before Festus some two years later (24:27), the issue has moved from resurrection in general to the resurrection of Jesus in particular. In explaining Paul's case to King Agrippa, Festus describes what had gone on before by saying: "When the accusers stood up, they did not charge him with any of the crimes that I was expecting. Instead they had certain points of disagreement with him about their own religion and *about a certain Jesus, who had died, but whom Paul asserted to be alive."*[11]

When Paul began his defense before Agrippa, he started with the assertion that he was a faithful Jew who was really on trial because of his belief in the resurrection of Jesus. He then told Agrippa the story of how he persecuted the Christians. With this as background, he then relates the story of his conversion.

In this third account of his conversion, Paul adds a few details not found in the previous versions. For example, he says the voice spoke to him in Aramaic. And he adds that after being asked: "Saul, Saul, why are you persecuting me?" the voice said: "It hurts you to kick against the goads" (26:14). However, the most significant addition is the inclusion of the commissioning statement from the Lord:

> I have appeared to you for this purpose, to appoint you to serve and testify to the things in which you have seen me and to those in which I will appear to you. I will rescue you from your people and from the Gentiles — to whom I am sending you to open their eyes so that they may turn from darkness to light and from the power of Satan to God, so that they may receive forgiveness of sins and a place among those who are sanctified by faith in me. (26:16-18)

Prior to this, the commission has been implied in what was revealed to Ananias (9:15-16), in what Ananias affirmed to Paul (22:14-15), and in Paul's Jerusalem vision (22:17-21). Now it is revealed that Paul heard this directly from the Lord (as he stated in Gal. 1:15-17).[12]

Here, too, for the first time, the nature of Paul's ministry to the Gentiles is defined. In the commissioning statement in Acts 26:18, the reader learns

---

11. Acts 25:18-19, italics mine. Following the story of his conversion, Paul points to the resurrection one final time: "To this day I have had help from God, and so I stand here, testifying to both small and great, saying nothing but what the prophets and Moses said would take place: that the Messiah must suffer, and that, by being the first *to rise from the dead*, he would proclaim light both to our people and to the Gentiles" (26:22-23, italics mine).

12. The question will be asked as to why the reader has not been informed prior to this that the exchange between Paul and Jesus went beyond the terse dialogue previously reported in the first two accounts. However, F. F. Bruce, *Paul*, p. 75, asserts: "Some verbal communication, beyond the heavenly vision in itself, is implied in Paul's statement that 'he who had set me apart before I was born, and had called me by his grace, was pleased to reveal his Son in me, *in order that I might preach him among the Gentiles*' (Galatians 1:15f.)."

that three elements define the process by which Gentiles can come to God. First, their eyes need to be opened ("I am sending you to open their eyes"). They need to *see* their true state in relationship to God. Perception is foundational to change. Second, having seen, they must *turn*. They must turn *from* the way in which they are walking, which is the way of darkness, the way of Satan. They must turn *to* the way of light, which is the way of God. Third, having seen and turned, they will receive forgiveness and sanctification by faith. A new life begins for them.

But this statement concerning how Gentiles are converted to the Way is *also the definition of what happened to Paul on the Damascus road.* These same three elements define the nature of Paul's conversion experience. They provide the outline by which to understand the core elements of Paul's conversion, and thus they give crucial insight into the nature of conversion itself. *This is the paradigm that describes Paul's conversion and thus conversion itself.*

The Core Pattern Defined

At the core of Paul's conversion experience are these same three elements. There are a *seeing* and a *turning* which together result in a *transformation*.

First, there was *insight*. Paul *saw* the truth. He saw two things. Negatively, he saw what his true state really was before God. Positively, he saw who Jesus really was. The two insights are connected. When he saw that Jesus was "the Son of God" (as he himself was preaching a few days later — Acts 9:20), he saw that he had been opposing God in a quite specific way. What he discovered on the Damascus road was not that he had been unfaithful to God because of some sort of laxness or rebellion against the law. In fact, he was the epitome of a committed Jew and was confident he was doing all that God required. No, what Paul saw was quite specific. He saw that in persecuting the Christian church he had been persecuting Jesus, whom he discovered, in that moment, to be of God. In other words, Paul discovered that he was not working for God, as he had assumed, but against God. This is the personal context within which Paul was converted.

Second, there was the *turning*. This also had two parts: a turning *from* and a turning *to*. He turned from persecuting the church to joining the church. He turned from opposing Jesus to following Jesus. He turned from what he discovered to be Satan's way to what he now learned was God's way. Again, this turning is specific, not general. Paul did not simply vow to get it right next time and in the future try to do a better job at doing what God wanted. This was not merely a minor midcourse correction in his theological understanding. No, he turned from being a persecutor of Jesus to being a promoter of Jesus, and this involved a major reordering of his theology. It is not that he rejected one theological system and embraced a totally new system. In fact, he continued to be an orthodox Jew.[13] But now he saw the old facts in a new context. The Messiah had come and been crucified, but then he had risen from the dead by God's power. Paul discovered that God was working in a new way in the world and that he had been blind to this fact. And now that he saw this new reality, he embraced it wholeheartedly. Henceforth Jesus was the focus of his theology, not the law, and his understanding of who God was and what God wanted flowed from this new center. "Acts tells the story of the conversion . . . always with the purpose not merely of explaining how Paul was changed from an unbelieving Jew into a follower of Christ, but of showing how he was changed from a persecutor of the infant church into an apostle, who 'proclaimed Jesus, saying, "He is the Son of God"' (Acts 9:20)."[14]

Third, there was the *transformation* that flowed from Paul's response to Jesus. Paul's life is changed. His first response is to be baptized, to align himself with the church, and to preach the good news about Jesus. He also accepts his commission to be a witness of who Jesus is to all people. He is, in other words, transformed from a zealous Pharisee into a zealous apostle. Henceforth his life takes a radically new direction.

This is not an unfamiliar pattern. The paradigm defined in Acts 26:18 and experienced by Paul during the Damascus road event is connected to the lexical meaning of those words that define conversion in the New Testament.[15] First, there is repentance *(metanoeō)*. Repentance presupposes that a person has seen his or her true state before God. One cannot decide to go in a new direction toward God without the awareness of having hitherto been going in the opposite direction. This is necessary for both Jew and Gentile (26:17), for Paul (26:14), and for the Twelve. Second, the "turning" in 26:18 is *epistrophē*, the very word which can be translated "convert." The two poles of this turning are defined via two vivid metaphors that put God (light) at one end and Satan (darkness) at the other. Third, in 26:20 this connection is further reinforced by Paul's state-

---

13. See Fuller, p. 209, where he points out that even at the end of his ministry Paul continues to maintain his Jewish practices. Thus, on his final trip to Jerusalem, the leaders of the church "recommended that Paul submit to a Jewish vow for seven days in order to demonstrate his loyalty to Judaism. This Paul was willing to do in order to show that for a Jew to acknowledge that salvation was by grace did not mean that he must renounce his distinctively Jewish practices."

14. Charles Buck and Greer Taylor, *Saint Paul: A Study of the Development of His Thought* (New York: Scribner, 1969), p. 220.

15. See the discussion of these NT words in the appendix (pp. 346-52).

ment describing his obedience to this heavenly vision: Paul preached "that they should repent and turn to God and do deeds consistent with repentance." The same three elements are present in this statement — repentance (which is preceded by insight into their true state before God, presumably conveyed via Paul's preaching), turning (to God), and transformation (which is seen in their deeds). In other words, the categories used to understand Paul's conversion are categories derived from Luke's account itself; and furthermore, they are categories that bring one in touch with the New Testament terms describing the phenomenon of conversion.

Call or Conversion?

Having asserted that Acts 26:18 describes the core elements for not only Paul's conversion but for all Christian conversion, we must necessarily take a short excursion into an important question raised by Krister Stendahl in a 1963 lecture series entitled "Paul among Jews and Gentiles."[16] Stendahl contends that the Damascus road experience ought not be considered the story of a conversion at all but the story of a call. "The emphasis in the accounts is always on this assignment, not on the conversion. Rather than being 'converted,' Paul was called to the specific task — made clear to him by his experience of the risen Lord — of apostleship to the Gentiles, one hand-picked through Jesus Christ on behalf of the one God of Jews and Gentiles."[17] If Stendahl is correct, then it is not legitimate to base our understanding of conversion on the experience of Paul on the Damascus road and the various interpretations of that event in Acts and in Paul's own epistles. What we have on the Damascus road is not, in Stendahl's reading, the prime example of conversion but yet another example of God's call to ministry of one already enlisted in his cause.

But Stendahl's argument rests on his understanding of what conversion is. To him, conversion has two elements. First, a person changes religions. "The term 'conversion' easily causes us to bring into play the idea that Paul 'changed his religion': the Jew became a Christian."[18] He rightly contends that

---

16. This was published in 1976 as a book which also includes other essays. Krister Stendahl, *Paul among Jews and Gentiles* (Philadelphia: Fortress, 1976).

17. Stendahl, p. 7.

18. Stendahl, p. 11. See also pp. 7, 9, 11. In describing Paul's Damascus road experience Stendahl states: "Here is not that change of 'religion' that we commonly associate with the word *conversion*" (p. 7, italics in original).

this was not the case for Paul because, in fact, there is a great deal of continuity between Paul's faith before and after the Damascus road experience.[19]

But when conversion is discussed in the biblical literature, it is almost never in the context of "changing religions." In the Old Testament, for example, the word *shubh* ("turn" or "return") is used over one thousand times, and most of the references are to the people of Israel "returning" to their God. As Witherup states in his summary of the concept of conversion in the Old Testament: "It may be surprising to some, but the OT message of conversion is addressed internally to the people of God and not externally to others. That is to say, conversion is not a missionary activity of getting 'converts' to a religion."[20] In the New Testament, even though there are Gentile converts (e.g., the Ethiopian in Acts 8:26-39), the emphasis is never on changing religions. It is on discovering who Jesus is (e.g., Acts 8:32-35; 16:30-31; 17:1-4, 10-12).

Second, Stendahl understands conversion to spring from a guilty conscience, as in the case of Luther. He writes: "In Luther, for example, we have a man who labors under the threatening demands of the law — a man in despair, a man for whom the theological and existential question is 'How am I to find a gracious God?'"[21] He calls the "introspective conscience . . . a Western development and a Western plague,"[22] and finds nothing like this in Paul. "There is no indication that psychologically Paul had some problem of conscience. . . ."[23] What Stendahl contends concerning Paul's state of mind prior to the Damascus road event is accurate, and this will be discussed in chapter 2.

But conversion in the biblical literature is not tied to a "guilty conscience." There are various insights that enable converts to understand that they have not been walking in God's way and need to repent. The Ethiopian is drawn to Jesus out of his interest in prophecy (Acts 8:31-35). It is fear that drives the Philippian jailer to conversion (Acts 16:27-30). Cornelius is a pious Gentile upon whom (along with his whole household) the Holy Spirit descends, leading to their conversion (Acts 10). It is the experience of the power of God that brings about this turning to God. Prior to his conversion Cornelius is described as "a devout man who feared God with all his household; he gave alms generously to the people and prayed constantly to God"

19. Stendahl, p. 7. This same point will be argued in the next chapter.
20. Ronald D. Witherup, *Conversion in the New Testament* (Collegeville, Minn.: Liturgical Press, 1994), p. 18.
21. Stendahl, p. 12.
22. Stendahl, p. 17.
23. Stendahl, p. 13.

(Acts 10:2). The point is that to define conversion as a response to a guilty conscience is to limit the concept far too severely and, in fact, to define conversion in a way that the Bible does not. So it is not legitimate to claim that what happened to Paul was not conversion because it did not arise from a guilty conscience.

Stendahl's assertion that what Paul experienced was call, not conversion, is tied to Stendahl's definition of conversion. And Stendahl gets that definition not from the Bible but from the same Western society he decries in his article. In the Bible conversion means something quite different from "a change of religion in order to find relief from a guilty conscience." Clearly, Paul's commission is an important element within his conversion, but it does not define the whole of the experience. Rather than speaking about conversion *or* call, it is more accurate to speak of conversion *and* call.

Paul's Own Accounts of His Conversion

Having examined the accounts of Paul's conversion in Acts that were written by a third party, we must necessarily look at the references to this event in the letters of Paul himself. As Lohfink points out: "It is of great significance that Paul does in fact attest to the Damascus incident in his letters."[24] However, scholars point out that Paul does not make frequent reference to his conversion. Lohfink states that there are only two texts in which Paul expressly mentions his conversion.[25] Gaventa identifies two major passages and one other that might be read as a description of the turmoil of Paul's preconversion state of mind.[26] Kim points to four major passages.[27] However, as Kim points out: "It cannot be so lightly said that these are only a few places if it is taken into account that these passages represent about half of the churches to which Paul wrote a letter."[28] Kim then points out that there are numerous *allusions* to his conversion in the writings of Paul, and identifies a number of passages in which it has been argued that Paul's conversion is in view. These include Romans 10:2-4; 1 Corinthians 9:16-17; 2 Corinthians 3:4–4:6; 5:16; Ephe-

---

24. Lohfink, p. 21.

25. Lohfink, p. 21. The texts he notes are 1 Cor. 15 and Gal. 1, 2.

26. Beverly Roberts Gaventa, *From Darkness to Light: Aspects of Conversion in the New Testament*, Overtures to Biblical Theology (Philadelphia: Fortress, 1986), p. 22. The texts she notes are Gal. 1:11-17; Phil. 3:2-11; Rom. 7:13-25.

27. Seyoon Kim, *The Origin of Paul's Gospel* (Grand Rapids: Wm. B. Eerdmans Publishing Co., 1981), p. 3. The texts he notes are 1 Cor. 9:1; 15:8-10; Gal. 1:13-17; Phil. 3:4-11.

28. Kim, p. 3.

sians 3:1-13; Colossians 1:23c-29; as well as 1 Timothy 1:11-14 (which many consider to be deutero-Pauline).[29]

These references by Paul to his conversion are illuminating in that they tell us how he understood the meaning of what happened to him on the Damascus road. The four major passages that Kim identifies illustrate this.

For example, Galatians 1:11-17:

> For I want you to know, brothers and sisters, that the gospel that was proclaimed by me is not of human origin; for I did not receive it from a human source, nor was I taught it, but I received it through a revelation of Jesus Christ. You have heard, no doubt, of my earlier life in Judaism. I was violently persecuting the church of God and was trying to destroy it. I advanced in Judaism beyond many among my people of the same age, for I was far more zealous for the traditions of my ancestors. But when God, who had set me apart before I was born and called me through his grace, was pleased to reveal his Son to me, so that I might proclaim him among the Gentiles, I did not confer with any human being, nor did I go up to Jerusalem to those who were already apostles before me, but I went away at once into Arabia, and afterwards I returned to Damascus.

Several aspects of this account require comments. First of all, Paul makes the point that he is not indebted to any human source for his gospel.

> Paul's gospel — Jesus Christ is the Son of God; Jesus Christ is the risen Lord — was revealed to him on the Damascus road. No doubt he had heard such claims made for Jesus in the days of his persecuting zeal, but it was not the witness of the persecuted disciples that convinced him. He rejected their witness as blasphemous until he learned the truth by unmediated disclosure from heaven. On the other hand, facts about the life and teaching of Jesus, about his death, burial and resurrection appearances, were imparted to him after his conversion by those who had prior knowledge of them.[30]

In other words, even though details of Jesus' life and death were given to him by others, the heart of Paul's theology can be traced back to his conversion when he met Christ himself. It was there that he discovered a gospel without law.[31]

---

29. Kim, pp. 3-31.

30. F. F. Bruce, *The Epistle to the Galatians: A Commentary on the Greek Text,* The New International Greek Testament Commentary (Grand Rapids: Wm. B. Eerdmans Publishing Co., 1982), p. 88.

31. See Bruce, *Paul,* pp. 87-88. This same point is argued at length and persuasively by Bruce's doctoral student Seyoon Kim in *The Origin of Paul's Gospel.* This assertion on

Second, the extent of the disruption of Paul's life via this encounter with Jesus is made clear. As Gaventa states, this revelation of Jesus Christ precipitated "a radical disruption of his previous life; his previous cosmos had been crucified (cf. Gal. 6:14)."[32] He went from persecuting the church with excessive zeal because of his deep commitment to Judaism, to preaching Jesus and so bringing men and women into the church. His conversion literally turned his life upside down.

A second passage in which Paul mentions his conversion is Philippians 3:4b-11. Here one gains new understanding of the momentous impact the Damascus road experience had on Paul. He writes:

> If anyone else has reason to be confident in the flesh, I have more: circumcised on the eighth day, a member of the people of Israel, of the tribe of Benjamin, a Hebrew born of Hebrews; as to the law, a Pharisee; as to zeal, a persecutor of the church; as to righteousness under the law, blameless. Yet whatever gains I had, these I have come to regard as loss because of Christ. More than that, I regard everything as loss because of the surpassing value of knowing Christ Jesus my Lord. For his sake I have suffered the loss of all things, and I regard them as rubbish, in order that I may gain Christ and be found in him, not having a righteousness of my own that comes from the law, but one that comes through faith in Christ, the righteousness from God based on faith. I want to know Christ and the power of his resurrection and the sharing of his sufferings by becoming like him in his death, if somehow I may attain the resurrection from the dead.

Paul begins this passage with a recitation of his impressive credentials as a pious Jew. Not only was he blessed by birth with impeccable religious credentials, but as the result of his own accomplishments he had risen to the pinnacle of first-century Jewish spirituality — all of which he describes with ringing phrases in verses 4b-6. However, in verse 8, in one sentence, he dismisses all this as worthless: "I regard everything as loss because of the surpassing value of knowing Christ Jesus my Lord." What happened to undo so dramatically this wall of credentials was his encounter with Jesus on the Damascus road. When he met Jesus he discovered that all he was and all he had

---

the part of Bruce and Kim is questioned by J. Christiaan Beker in his book *Paul the Apostle: The Triumph of God in Life and Thought* (Philadelphia: Fortress, 1980). Beker contends that we know little about Paul and his conversion and that we cannot find the secret of Paul's theology in his conversion experience. See the discussion of the differing views of Bruce and Beker as found in Gaventa, pp. 18-21.

32. Gaventa, p. 28.

done was mere "rubbish" (v. 8).[33] Paul ends this passage by contrasting his old life with his new life. He rejected his former law-based righteousness and gained, in turn, a new, Christ-based righteousness. "It seems clear that the righteous life described in vv. 5-6 *belonged* to Paul; it was his by virtue of both birth and accomplishment. It was also a righteousness that had its origin in the law. Paul has rejected that righteousness in favor of one that comes through faith in Christ."[34]

Note must be made of the contention by Günther Bornkamm that "Paul's own witness about his call in Gal 1 as well as in Phil 3 shows how the understanding of his conversion and sending is completely determined by the content of his preaching and theology and by an arbitrary claim to have received a *revelatio specialissima*." Kim refutes this "strange conclusion," as he calls it, by pointing out, first, that Paul quite clearly claims to have received a special revelation of Jesus Christ and that this is the source of his gospel (Gal. 1:12, 15-16). And second, that

> it is more in line with Paul's own testimony to say that "the content of his preaching and theology" is determined by his "understanding of his conversion and sending" than to say the reverse. For it is inconceivable that "the content of his preaching and theology" which Paul had previously had, led him to interpret his Damascus experience in line with it. In fact, the essential and constitutive character of the Damascus experience for Paul's theology is widely recognized by recent interpreters. . . .[35]

Finally, it is necessary to examine briefly Paul's two statements in 1 Corinthians concerning his encounter with the risen Lord. In 9:1 he states: "Am I not free? Am I not an apostle? Have I not seen Jesus our Lord?" and then in 15:8-10 he writes concerning the risen Lord: "Last of all, as to one untimely born, he appeared also to me. For I am the least of the apostles, unfit to be called an apostle, because I persecuted the church of God. But by the grace of God I am what I am, and his grace toward me has not been in vain. On the contrary, I worked harder than any of them — though it was not I, but the grace of God that is with me." This latter statement comes in the context of Paul's comments on the nature of the gospel which he preached to the Corinthians and which they re-

---

33. The term used here in the Greek is *skubalon*, which can be translated refuse, dirt, or dung, according to Walter Bauer, *A Greek-English Lexicon of the New Testament and Other Early Christian Literature*, translated and adapted by William F. Arndt and F. Wilbur Gingrich from the 4th Ger. ed., 1952 (Chicago: University of Chicago Press, 1957), p. 765.

34. Gaventa, p. 32.

35. See the discussion of this issue in Kim, pp. 101-2.

ceived. In the course of his definition of the gospel he lists various post-resurrection appearances by the risen Jesus. He concludes this listing by noting that the same Christ who had appeared to a variety of other people appeared also to him. He had already asserted this in the 1 Corinthians 9 passage. Though he does not say so explicitly, the best guess is that when he says he has seen Jesus, he is referring to his experience on the Damascus road.

Other texts appear to contain allusions to the Damascus road event. For example, Paul begins the Epistle to the Romans: "Paul, a servant of Jesus Christ, *called to be an apostle*, set apart for the gospel of God . . ." (1:1, italics mine).[36] Romans 1:5 is even more direct, recalling not only Paul's call but the nature of that call: "through whom [Jesus] we have received grace and apostleship to bring about the obedience of faith among all the Gentiles for the sake of his name." A similar statement is found in Romans 15:15-16: "I have written to you rather boldly by way of reminder, because of the grace given me by God to be a minister of Christ Jesus to the Gentiles. . . ." Other related statements are found in 2 Corinthians 5:18-20 and 13:10. Each of these various statements looks back to the commissioning of Paul to be an apostle to the Gentiles. His call stands at the very heart of Paul's understanding of his ministry. Luke records exactly this sort of call in Acts 26:16-18 in his account of Paul's conversion. Although Paul does not place his call in the context of his conversion in the passages from his letters cited above, he would appear to be alluding to it.

Another interesting passage which seems to allude to the language in Acts 26:18 is 2 Corinthians 4:6: "For it is the God who said, 'Let light shine out of darkness,' who has shone in our hearts to give the light of the knowledge of the glory of God in the face of Jesus Christ." Lohfink comments: "We have already indicated the significance ascribed to *light* precisely in the Lukan Damascus accounts. And Acts 22:11 specifically mentions the *doxa*, the brilliance emanating from Christ." Lohfink, however, is not willing to assert a necessary connection between the experience on the Damascus road and the language of this verse: "There is no clear proof to indicate that Paul's vocation vision does in fact stand behind what he says in 2 Cor 4:6."[37] However, other scholars see such a link. For example, S. Kim writes: "The motifs of light and glory in 2 Cor 4.6 point to the Damascus event. . . . He [Paul] is thinking of the radiant face of Christ which he saw on the Damascus road."[38]

36. See also the similar statements at the beginning of other letters of Paul: 1 Cor. 1:1; 2 Cor. 1:1; and Gal. 1:1.

37. Lohfink, pp. 22-23.

38. Kim, p. 8. See Kim's illuminating discussion of this passage on pp. 5-13.

In summary, it would appear that Paul's own mention of the Damascus road event is not at variance with Luke's triple account. "On essential points they agree also with Paul's own accounts in his letters. . . . The similarities between the accounts in Acts themselves, and between them and those in Paul's letters, lead us to think that all three accounts in Acts go back to Paul."[39]

To be sure, Paul does not recount in detail in his epistles the events of his conversion. The trip to Damascus is not mentioned by him (though Damascus is noted in Gal. 1:17), and none of the miraculous events are noted (light, voice, blindness). However, as Lohfink states: "One can argue that this is due to the quite different types of writing involved; in Acts the incident has to be narrated, while in a letter Paul needs only to allude to what he had already told his addressees earlier."[40] Lohfink is not fully satisfied with this explanation, however. He feels that a fuller account was due the Galatians at least, given the fact that Paul's apostolic status was being called into account. No doubt a reiteration of his conversion and call would have helped his case with this difficult church. And yet, as Lohfink points out, "this scarcity of information seems to derive from Paul's personal, deep reserve."[41]

Paul does not provide the details of his conversion experience in his epistles. Still, he "consistently leaves the *impression* that this change was sudden and unexpected, although he never says so explicitly or directly."[42] In both Galatians 1:11-17 and Philippians 3:4-11 there is a sharp contrast between his past and his present life. An event such as the Damascus road experience easily explains such a radical shift. Paul also makes it quite clear in his epistles that at the center of this change was an encounter with Jesus (see Gal. 1:16; Phil. 3:8; 1 Cor. 9:1; 15:8). Again, this fact accords with what the writer of Acts asserts. What Paul does do in these passages is affirm how central the experience was to him personally in his life, ministry, and theology. As a result of the Damascus road experience he was stopped in his tracks and his life was turned in a new direction, a direction in which he continued to walk for the rest of his life. Both the accounts in Acts and in Paul's own writings witness to this fact.

One final question must be addressed. Why does Paul refer to his conversion experience in his letters? What is the purpose of these various autobiographical remarks? The traditional answer to this question is "that Paul writes in the autobiographical mode only reluctantly and almost always apol-

---

39. Kim, pp. 30-31.
40. Lohfink, p. 24. See also Kim, p. 28: "Whereas Luke was writing history, Paul was writing letters to the churches which had already heard of it."
41. Lohfink, p. 24.
42. Gaventa, p. 37.

ogetically."[43] However, George Lyons argues persuasively that there is no evidence to support such a contention. On the one hand, "Paul's apparent reluctance to write autobiographically — despite the frequency with which he does so — probably owes less to an essentially humble disposition than to his attempts to avoid offending the sensibilities of antiquity, which found autobiography patently boastful."[44] On the other hand, the seemingly apologetic stance taken by Paul is due to his use of antithetical constructions, which was a common technique used by ancient writers to avoid the offensiveness of boasting.[45] Lyons goes on to challenge the whole concept of "mirror reading" in which the position of Paul's seeming opponents is deduced from Paul's remarks — when the assumption is made that Paul is writing apologetically. He argues that the conclusions about historical situations drawn from such a method "owe more to the interpreter's conclusions than exegesis."[46]

Lyons gives a different reason for these autobiographical comments as he summarizes his exploration of such remarks in Galatians.

> Various strands of evidence come together to support the conclusion that Paul presents his "autobiography" as a paradigm of the gospel of Christian freedom which he seeks to persuade his reader to reaffirm in the face of the threat presented by the troublemakers.
>
> That Paul offers his autobiographical narrative in [Galatians] 1:13–2:21 as substantiation of his claim in [Galatians] 1:11-12 concerning the nature and origin of his gospel suggests that he considers himself in some sense a prepresentation or even an embodiment of that gospel. . . . He is a paradigm of the gospel he preaches among the Gentiles. The formulation of Paul's autobiographical remarks in terms of "formerly — now" and "Man — God" serves the paradigmatic function of contrasting Paul's conversion from Judaism to Christianity with the Galatians' inverted conversion. . . .[47]

This reading of the autobiographical material adds weight to the evidence. Comments made to prove a point to a critic might not be given as much credence as those offered as an illustration of how Christ impacts one on the level of experience. This, according to Lyons, is Paul's motive: "Succinctly and simply put, Paul's autobiographical remarks function not to dis-

43. George Lyons, *Pauline Autobiography: Toward a New Understanding*, SBL Dissertation Series, no. 73 (Atlanta: Scholars Press, 1985), p. 223. One can see this in the position taken by Lohfink as cited in n. 41 above.

44. Lyons, p. 224.

45. Lyons, p. 224.

46. Lyons, p. 72.

47. Lyons, p. 171.

tinguish him from his converts nor to defend his person or authority but to establish his ethos as an 'incarnation' of the gospel of Jesus Christ. . . . He is concerned that, by imitating him, they too should incarnate the gospel."[48] Paul writes about his experience of Jesus on the Damascus road because he wants his readers to know this same Jesus and to remain faithful to him. His own experience of Jesus is at the heart of his theology and his apostolic ministry.

48. Lyons, p. 226.

CHAPTER TWO

Insight: The Context of Conversion

At the core of the concept of conversion is the idea of turning. On one side of that turning are the conditions that facilitate or enable the turning to take place (insight). On the other side of the turning is the outcome or result of the turning (transformation). This is the pattern defined in Acts 26:18. In the next three chapters this definition will be used as the lens through which Paul's conversion is viewed. The aim of this exploration is twofold. First, the hypothesis that Acts 26:18 describes the essence of Christian conversion will be tested. It will be shown that the three categories of insight, turning, and transformation describe adequately and fully what happened to Paul on the Damascus road. Thus, that event which is paradigmatic for conversion can be described by means of these categories. These same categories will then allow us, in Part II, to assess the significance of the quite different experience of the Twelve. Second, by means of the sheer act of reflecting on the details of Paul's conversion, the concept of conversion will be given form and substance. The result of this, hopefully, will be a much more nuanced understanding of the character of conversion.

In this section the focus is on the first issue: the *insight* that is required before a person can turn. In order for the turning to take place, there must be some sense of what one is turning from and an understanding of what one is turning to. Furthermore, there must be an awareness that what is turned away from is somehow wrong or inadequate and what is being turned to is right and better. It does not matter whether this awareness is internal (a sense of guilt, lostness, pain, etc.) or external (one suddenly confronts truth, hope, Jesus as a compelling person, etc.). A person will not (or for that matter cannot) turn without the motivation to turn, without some

37

reason to change the direction of his or her life in terms of religious commitment.

Paul the Persecutor

In Paul's case, the key insight that launched his conversion had to do with his persecution of the church. Both Paul and Luke insist upon this point over and over again. Paul was a persecutor. In fact, he was obsessed with persecution (Acts 26:11). Not only that, it is repeatedly stressed that Paul carried out this persecution even to the point of death for those he pursued.

By collecting together the references to this fact, the frequency with which this point is made will become clear. There are four categories of text in which Paul's persecution is noted. First are those texts in Acts that describe Paul in this way:

Acts 8:1 — "Saul approved of their killing him." (This comment follows the description of the martyrdom of Stephen, in which Paul played a passive role.)

Acts 8:3 — "Saul was ravaging the church by entering house after house; dragging off both men and women, he committed them to prison."

Acts 9:1-2 — "Meanwhile Saul, still breathing threats and murder against the disciples of the Lord, went to the high priest and asked him for letters to the synagogues at Damascus, so that if he found any who belonged to the Way, men or women, he might bring them bound to Jerusalem."

Acts 9:13-14 — "But Ananias answered, 'Lord, I have heard from many about this man, how much evil he has done to your saints in Jerusalem; and here he has authority from the chief priests to bind all who invoke your name.'"

Acts 22:4-5 — "I persecuted this Way up to the point of death by binding both men and women and putting them in prison, as the high priest and the whole council of elders can testify about me. From them I also received letters to the brothers in Damascus, and I went there in order to bind those who were there and to bring them back to Jerusalem for punishment."

Acts 22:19-20 — "And I said, 'Lord, they themselves know that in every synagogue I imprisoned and beat those who believed in you. And while the blood of your witness Stephen was shed, I myself was standing by, approving and keeping the coats of those who killed him.'"

Acts 26:9-11 — "Indeed, I myself was convinced that I ought to do many things against the name of Jesus of Nazareth. And that is what I did in Jerusalem; with authority received from the chief priests, I not only locked up many of the saints in prison, but I also cast my vote against them when they were being condemned to death. By punishing them often in all the synagogues I tried to force them to blaspheme; and since I was so furiously enraged at them, I pursued them even to foreign cities."

Second, this same emphasis is found in Paul's own description of himself in his epistles:

1 Corinthians 15:9 — "For I am the least of the apostles, unfit to be called an apostle, because I persecuted the church of God."

Galatians 1:13 — "You have heard, no doubt, of my earlier life in Judaism. I was violently persecuting the church of God and was trying to destroy it."

Galatians 1:23 — "They only heard it said, 'The one who formerly was persecuting us is now proclaiming the faith he once tried to destroy.'"

Philippians 3:6 — "As to zeal, a persecutor of the church . . ."

1 Timothy 1:13 — ". . . even though I was formerly a blasphemer, a persecutor, and a man of violence . . . I received mercy because I had acted ignorantly in unbelief. . . ."[1]

Third, in other parts of Acts there is an emphasis on persecution which, while not always directly connected with Paul, nevertheless gives the context for Paul's persecuting activities:

Acts 7:52 — "Which of the prophets did your ancestors not persecute? They killed those who foretold the coming of the Righteous One, and now you have become his betrayers and murderers." (This is the note on which Stephen finished his speech to the Sanhedrin and which made the crowd so angry that it did just what he predicted. Stephen's comment foreshadows Paul's persecuting activities which

---

1. The Pauline authorship of the Pastorals is disputed. However, even if this is not from Paul's hand, it reflects an early understanding of Paul's character.

are about to start. Paul will, in other words, be acting in character. This was the way of Paul's people: they persecuted those whom they felt were blaspheming against the law.)

Acts 8:1 — "That day a severe persecution began against the church in Jerusalem. . . ." (Spearheaded by Paul, persecution spreads from the one individual, Stephen, to all individuals associated with the Way.)

Acts 11:19 — "Now those who were scattered because of the persecution that took place over Stephen traveled as far as Phoenicia, Cyprus, and Antioch, and they spoke the word to no one except Jews." (Luke goes on to describe the fruit of this scattering. Specifically, Greeks began to be converted. The church at Jerusalem sends Barnabas to Antioch to investigate this phenomenon. Finding it of God, Barnabas searches out Paul, and together they minister in Antioch. Interestingly enough, the beginning of Paul's formal ministry is a result of the persecution he helped initiate! See Acts 11:19-26.)

Acts 12:1 — "About that time King Herod laid violent hands upon some who belonged to the church." (Herod's persecution stands as a foil against what Paul did. Its obvious ugliness — he kills James and puts Peter in prison — shows persecution for what it is. Just because the motivation for persecution is zeal for God does not make it acceptable. Although good can come out of persecution, persecution is not seen as legitimate or right in Acts.)

Acts 13:50 — "[They] stirred up persecution against Paul and Barnabas. . . ." (Paul learns firsthand the harshness of persecution.)

Finally, and most important of all, are those texts that describe Paul's encounter with the risen Lord. At the center of that encounter is the issue of persecution. The dialogue in all three accounts is the same, with only minor variations:

Acts 9:4-5 — "'Saul, Saul, why do you persecute me?' He asked, 'Who are you, Lord?' The reply came, 'I am Jesus, whom you are persecuting.'" (See also Acts 22:7-8 and 26:14-15.)

In other words, whatever else one might want to say about Paul's preconversion mind-set or the conditions under which his conversion took place, it is clear that both Luke and Paul consider the fact that he was a persecutor to be central. Luke repeats this idea over and over again, and Paul continues to point to this fact years after his conversion. Furthermore, the risen

Lord makes it the focus of *his* words to Paul! It was Paul's role as persecutor of the church that formed the personal context out of which he was converted.[2]

What did the fact that he was a persecutor mean? In a sentence, it demonstrated that Paul was not, as he had assumed up to that point, walking in God's way and doing God's will. Something was off-kilter at the core of his perception (about himself and about what God wanted) and in how he lived (his moral behavior). An examination of Paul's preconversion assumptions about himself (that he was zealous for the law) and of his preconversion actions toward the Christians (that he was engaged in murder) will reveal the heart of the crisis.

Zeal: The Root of Persecution

Paul persecuted the church because of his zeal for the law. This is the explanation given in the texts for his behavior. His zeal was rooted in his attempt to live as an exemplary first-century Jew. Prior to his conversion Paul assumed that this zeal and the direction it took were good and in accord with God's will. When Jesus, by his pointed question, challenged Paul's assumption about himself, Paul was given a window into his true self. He discovered that in his role as a zealous Pharisee he was not pleasing God but working against God. This was the crucial insight that launched his conversion.

Paul's credentials are mentioned in three types of text. In each case Paul makes the point that his credentials were impeccable from the vantage point of first-century Jewish theological assumptions. First, there are the two recitations by Paul in Acts of his conversion experience. In both cases Paul begins the story of his conversion by describing his background:

> Acts 22:2-3 — "When they heard him addressing them in Hebrew, they became even more quiet. Then he said: 'I am a Jew, born in Tarsus in Cilicia, but brought up in this city at the feet of Gamaliel, educated strictly according to our ancestral law, being zealous for God, just as all of you are today.'" (Then he goes on to point out how he persecuted the followers of the Way.)
>
> Acts 26:4-7 — "All the Jews know my way of life from my youth, a life spent from the beginning among my own people and in Jerusalem.

---

2. "The only concrete sin *qua* sin in his [Paul's] life, *the* sin which he mentions, is that he had persecuted the church (1 Cor. 15:9)." Krister Stendahl, *Paul among Jews and Gentiles* (Philadelphia: Fortress, 1976), p. 14.

They have known for a long time, if they are willing to testify, that I have belonged to the strictest sect of our religion and lived as a Pharisee. And now I stand here on trial on account of my hope in the promise made by God to our ancestors, a promise that our twelve tribes hope to attain, as they earnestly worship day and night. It is for this hope, your Excellency, that I am accused by Jews!"

Second, during his hearing before the Sanhedrin, Paul makes this same point:

Acts 23:6 — "Brothers, I am a Pharisee, a son of Pharisees."

Finally, in his own writings Paul describes the exemplary nature of his background:

Galatians 1:14 — "I advanced in Judaism beyond many among my people of the same age, for I was far more zealous for the traditions of my ancestors."

Philippians 3:4-6 — "If anyone else has reason to be confident in the flesh, I have more: circumcised on the eighth day, a member of the people of Israel, of the tribe of Benjamin, a Hebrew born of Hebrews; as to the law, a Pharisee; as to zeal, a persecutor of the church; as to righteousness under the law, blameless."

The link between who Paul was (a Jew fully committed to Judaism) and what Paul did (persecute the church) is found in the word "zeal." It was because of his deep commitment to all that Judaism stood for that he found the new Christian sect so offensive. And because he was zealous for the law, he had to express this via concrete action which, in this case, meant active persecution. Paul makes this link himself in Philippians 3:6: "as to zeal, a persecutor of the church." Jacques Dupont comments: "Paul associates the violence with which he had persecuted the church with the 'zeal' which motivated him at that time. There is a link between his passion to keep the law in an irreproachable way and the ardor with which he opposed primitive Christianity. . . . One can see in his activity as persecutor the display and proof of his 'zeal.'"[3]

Dupont goes on to give an example from 1 Maccabees 2 of how such

---

3. Jacques Dupont, "The Conversion of Paul, and Its Influence on His Understanding of Salvation by Faith," in *Apostolic History and the Gospel*, ed. W. Ward Gasque and Ralph P. Martin (Grand Rapids: Wm. B. Eerdmans Publishing Co., 1970), p. 183.

"zeal" expressed itself in "devastating wrath."[4] In this account, because of his devotion to the law, Mattathias kills a fellow Jew who is being forced to offer an idolatrous sacrifice by the messengers of Antiochus Epiphanes. Dupont also recalls other examples of zeal, such as that of Phinehas, the priest who killed an Israelite man and a Midianite woman who was a sacred prostitute (Num. 25:1-18), and Jehu, the king who demonstrated his zeal for the Lord by killing Ahab's family (2 Kings 10:16-17).[5] The point is clear. There was a long-standing tradition within Judaism that it was legitimate to express zeal for the Lord by violent acts. Paul was clearly standing in this tradition. His persecuting activities were consonant with his religious commitment. In fact, they demonstrated it. He *assumed* that such persecution was what God wanted.

Conflict: Paul's Inner Struggle?

All of this bears upon an issue that crops up whenever Paul's conversion is discussed: his inner state of mind prior to his conversion. Both those writing from a theological perspective and those who write as psychologists have expressed a range of views, many of them contradictory. Much of the discussion revolves around whether there was an inner struggle within Paul which set the scene for his conversion as he approached Damascus. Some even would assert that this inner conflict created the conversion experience.

For example, G. J. Inglis, theorizing in a 1929 paper, assumes that in each conversion experience there is a "stage of preparation (which) consists of the development of a complex in the unconscious mind." Inglis simply states this hypothesis as if it were accepted fact. He does not discuss it, much less demonstrate it. His viewpoint reflects, of course, the assumptions of psychology in that era (in particular, those of C. G. Jung, who coined the term "complex"). Having asserted that this is how conversion begins, Inglis then sets out to locate the precise nature of Paul's "complex." He proposes that, prior to his conversion, Paul had been gradually inclined toward the Christian viewpoint. However, Paul was not aware of this.

> The fact that Paul was unconscious of any gradual inward inclination towards Christianity is shown, in the first place, by the absence from his writings of any mention of such an inclination. He was conscious, before his conversion, of profound dissatisfaction with the righteousness to which he

4. Dupont, p. 184.
5. See also 1 Kings 19:10; Ps. 106:30-31; Ecclus. 45:23; 1 Macc. 2:26, 54; 4 Macc. 18:12; and Jth. 9:4. Dupont, pp. 184-85.

had attained under the Law (Ph 3:6); but there is no indication that before his conversion he ever contemplated the acceptance of the faith of Christ as a solution of the problem. . . . It has been argued that the liberal tendencies of his teacher Gamaliel, the Scriptural arguments of the Nazarenes, and the impression made by the death of Stephen, forced upon him a better conviction which he resisted, drowning the voice of conscience by a fanatical orgy of persecution. . . . The formation of the Christian complex was due to contingent factors; that is, to the reaction of a personality to its environment and circumstances. Paul's references to his own physical weakness (2 Cr 11 and 12), coupled with the record of his achievements, seem to show him as a man of delicate constitution who was sustained by the nervous energy which belongs to a highly-strung organization. His tendency towards visions, locutions, and trances confirms this view by indicating that he was psychopathic in temperament.[6]

Inglis has been quoted at length because he touches upon so many of the theories one finds elsewhere, both in the biblical and the psychological literature, namely, that (1) Paul was secretly attracted to the faith he saw expressed by the Christians he persecuted;[7] (2) Paul was involved in a moral crisis over his part in the death of Stephen; (3) Paul was dissatisfied over the righteousness one could obtain under the law (here Inglis misuses Philippians 3:6, which certainly does not say this);[8] and (4) Paul was of weak physical and psychological temperament (psychopathic in temperament, in fact).[9]

---

6. G. J. Inglis, "The Problem of St. Paul's Conversion," *Expository Times* 40 (1929): 228.

7. "Goguel suggests that the affirmations of the Christians regarding the resurrection of their Master and the new moral ideal proclaimed by Jesus must have sunk deep into Paul's subconscious, and there in the subconscious was waged the conflict between these Christian elements and his attachment to the religion of his fathers." H. G. Wood, "The Conversion of St. Paul: Its Nature, Antecedents and Consequences," *New Testament Studies* 1 (1955): 279. See Daniel P. Fuller, *Easter Faith and History* (Grand Rapids: Wm. B. Eerdmans Publishing Co., 1965), pp. 247-50, for a critique of Goguel's rather sophisticated argument. A. D. Nock, *St. Paul* (New York: Harper & Brothers, 1938), p. 73, writes: "Analogies suggest that his conversion was not the sudden thing which it seemed to him: the movement had probably fascinated him at the same time that it excited his deepest animosity, and it must have been the question, if the unvoiced question, of his life for some time."

8. "He was dubious, not about his ability to keep the Law, but about the value of such righteousness when he had attained it." Wood, p. 279.

9. Albert Schweitzer writes in *The Mysticism of Paul,* p. 153: "The most natural hypothesis is therefore that Paul suffered from some kind of epileptiform attacks, which does not by any means necessarily mean that he was a real epileptic. It would agree with this

In each case, the problem is that the theorizing has no firm root in the available data. The biblical texts give no evidence that prior to his conversion Paul was attracted to Christianity, that he suffered a moral crisis over his part in Stephen's death (or any other death, for that matter), or that he felt he was off track in terms of what God required of people. In terms of his "temperament," such an assessment depends on the personality theory held by the researcher (as discussed below). Even Inglis's term "temperament" bespeaks an older psychology that is no longer widely held. Given the small amount of evidence that is available, a wide variety of interpretations are possible as to what constituted the core of Paul's personality. One can argue on the basis of analogy to parallel situations in contemporary settings that Paul's mind-set was thus-and-so, but the fact remains that this is mere speculation. *The texts insist that what triggered Paul's turning was the sudden insight into himself which came as a result of his dialogue with Jesus.* Jesus' simple question unlocks for Paul the fact that his zeal to persecute was not of God and was, in fact, against God.

If there is speculation amongst theologians about Paul's preconversion state of mind, there is even more speculation on the part of psychologists. Robert L. Moore, for example, examines several such psychological theories.[10] He begins by outlining the thesis of Richard Rubenstein's 1972 book *My Brother Paul.* Rubenstein contends that first-century Judaism was heavily repressive. It was a superego culture that had no mechanism for "providing satisfactory gratification of the impulses of the id."[11] In this context, Paul's genius

> was to find a means for the recovery of what had been repressed in Judaism. Paul's conflict, we read, was between the infantile yearnings for omnipotence, immortality, and union issuing from his unconscious and the stark world of the reality principle enforced by the faith of his fathers (p. 35). In his conversion on the Damascus road Paul indeed lost his normal ego functions, but the regression proved to be a "creative regression" which was to lead to the resolution of his conflict. Paul's resolution, Rubenstein argues,

---

that on the Damascus road he heard voices during an attack, and suffered afterwards from a temporary affection of the eyesight, if his experience at his conversion really happened during such an attack." Quoted in Joseph L. Lilly, "The Conversion of Saint Paul: The Validity of His Testimony to the Resurrection of Jesus Christ," *Catholic Biblical Quarterly* 6 (1944): 189 n. 41.

10. Robert L. Moore, "Pauline Theology and the Return of the Repressed: Depth Psychology and Early Christian Thought," *Zygon* 13 (June 1978): 158-68.

11. Moore, p. 159.

had liberating psychological consequences not only for himself but for subsequent human history.[12]

Rubenstein's view has not been without its critics. Interestingly, the response to Rubenstein comes not so much from Christian theologians as from Jewish scholars who feel that his reading of both early Christianity and first-century Judaism is in error. For example, there is a book by Ernest A. Rappaport in which, according to Moore, he

> dismisses Rubenstein's treatment of Paul as "absurd." In his view Rubenstein "fails to recognize that the productivity of Paul in the aftermath of his acute schizophrenic episode was a productivity of delusions of persecutions and together with the obsessive pursuit of his missionary goal only proves the relentless persistence of his paranoid psychosis" (p. 34).
>
> Though more scholarly and less vehement, the treatment by Sidney Tarachow offers a more formidable counterpoint to Rubenstein's interpretation of Paul and early Christianity. Compare Tarachow's interpretation of Paul's conversion with Rubenstein's: "The conversion robbed Paul of his compulsive character defense. He gave up both his old aggression and also his religiously displaced obedience to the Law. He was now at the mercy of his aggressions and his homosexuality. Both these tendencies underwent a degree of sublimation in the new religious process taking place in Paul. The son attained equality with the father, but at the same time there was an identification, now, not with the aggressive father, but with the crucified son, an identification carrying many masochistic and homosexual overtones."[13]

After these "heavily Freudian discussions"[14] of the dynamics of Paul's conversion, Moore offers his own, more Jungian assessment. Moore suggests that in some way (by meditation or some other "technology" — he is not clear about this) Paul was able to cultivate receptivity to the Spirit.[15] In this state of psychic openness, contact with archetypal energies became possible. This contact with the depth of the human psyche resulted in the Damascus road experience.

---

12. Moore, p. 159.
13. Moore, p. 164.
14. Moore, p. 166.
15. Moore, pp. 166-67. See the highly speculative paper by J. W. Bowker, "'Merkabah' Visions and the Visions of Paul," *Journal of Semitic Studies* 16 (1971): 157-73, in which he argues that Paul's experience on the Damascus road was triggered by a form of *merkabah* contemplation. According to this theory, Paul was meditating on the chariot chapters of Ezekiel (chaps. 1 and 10), and this induced his vision of Christ.

How can these hypotheses be assessed? The difficulty in analyzing these theories as to the psychological state of Paul that resulted in his conversion is threefold. First, the assertions arise out of particular views of personality. If it is assumed that Freud, for example, has accurately assessed the nature of the human psyche, then the assertions of Rubenstein, Rappaport, and Tarachow become valid options. However — and this is the problem — it is by no means clear that Freud has got it right, as the plethora of non-Freudian views of personality suggest. And without some confidence in the theoretical framework, the suggestions about Paul's preconversion state of mind simply have no basis. Second, even if the Freudian perception is granted, it is necessary to make rather sweeping assertions about the psychosocial state of early Christianity and first-century Judaism in order for the theory to hold. And, as the substantial differences between the three Freudians indicate, such issues are by no means clear. Third, to sustain these interpretations requires that one disregard the New Testament texts, especially when they insist on a real encounter with a historical Jesus who died and rose again. Rubenstein is clearest in his denial of this possibility when he states flatly: "In his vision of the risen Christ Paul encountered the power of the primary processes of his own mind."[16]

Was there inner dissatisfaction on Paul's part? Luke does not point to any. The preconversion state that he emphasizes is Paul's role as persecutor of the church, and even here it is said as a statement of fact, not by way of offering a psychological guess as to why Paul was ripe for conversion. Luke does not even hint that Paul felt any guilt over being a persecutor prior to the Damascus road experience. Nor does Paul offer any psychological explanation when he alludes to his conversion. For him too, the only relevant information is that he persecuted the church because he was a zealous Pharisee. As Lilly comments on Galatians 1:12-17: "There is not the slightest indication that he experienced any interior struggle, was tortured by doubts which gradually led him to a complete change of views relative to Christianity. On the contrary he represents his conversion as coming with complete, lightning rapidity, and attributes it as well as his Christian doctrine to the direct intervention of Jesus Christ."[17]

Romans 7 is often offered as proof of an inner conflict in Paul. Writing in the first person, Paul says: "So I find it to be a law that when I want to do what is good, evil lies close at hand. For I delight in the law of God in my inmost self, but I see in my members another law at war with the law of my

16. Moore, p. 159.
17. Lilly, pp. 198-99.

mind, making me captive to the law of sin that dwells in my members" (vv. 21-23). But, as Dupont comments:

> It does not seem necessary to comment on the fact that one cannot succeed in opposing against this perfectly clear witness [of Paul's view of himself as confident that he was beyond reproach as a zealous Pharisee in the eyes of God] the description which Romans 7 gives of the wretched state of a sinful man under the law's regime. It is admitted, since the dissertation which W. G. Kümmel published in 1929, that we should not look for, in this passage, the reverberation of an experience Paul underwent in Judaism. It is rather the reflection of a Christian theologian who is meditating on the mystery of sin with the experience of redemption as his starting-point.[18]

Menoud adds this further statement: "Against the personal application of Romans 7 to the apostle the following argument, taken from among others which could be put forward, must be mentioned. We have no other example of the fact that the law had ever been considered by any Jew as a burden. This is the Christian interpretation of Jewish law. On the contrary, for the Jews, the law is the privilege and the pride of the nation. . . ."[19]

What, then, was Paul's preconversion assessment of himself? In the texts collected above, one finds the portrait of a man who is confident in his relationship to God. After all, he was living in accord with the law, which was God's revelation of what God required of humankind. In fact, Paul took the law more seriously than most. He was a strict Pharisee, and his deep devotion was shown by his zeal. Dupont says: "A number of features of Pharisaic theology provide Paul with reason for being satisfied with himself." Dupont goes on to point to "his pride which membership of the elect race gave him," to his awareness "of belonging to a spiritual elite," to the fact that Paul was "a fanatic among fanatics," and to "the exertion with which he observed scrupulously the law's prescriptions, interpreted in their most rigid sense, [which] led him to attain a perfection which was without lapse or defect."[20] Dupont's conclusion is:

> In all the evidence none is found which expresses a recollection of his being restless, tortured by an unattainable ideal. As he saw himself, Paul was, at the eve of his conversion, a man well satisfied, contented with his member-

18. Dupont, p. 183.
19. Philippe H. Menoud, "Revelation and Tradition: The Influence of Paul's Conversion on His Theology," *Catholic Biblical Quarterly* 6 (1953): 133. See also Wood, p. 278, for the same conclusion.
20. Dupont, pp. 182-83.

ship of the elect race and of an elite group of his people, and confident of attaining by his religious observance an ideal of righteousness which would make him beyond reproach in the eyes of God, men and his own conscience.[21]

Stendahl perhaps captures best the reality of Paul's preconversion state of mind by calling him "a very happy and successful Jew. . . . He experiences no troubles, no problems, no qualms of conscience, no feelings of shortcomings. He is a star pupil, the student to get the thousand dollar graduate scholarship in Gamaliel's Seminary, if we can trust Acts (22:3) — both for character and for achievements of scholarship — a very happy Jew."[22]

In conclusion, then, it must be stated that whether explanations of Paul's preconversion state are offered because one assumes (on the basis of psychology) that, of necessity, conflict must precede conversion, because one feels the evidence points to such a conflict, or because it is asserted that the inner crisis actually causes the conversion experience,[23] all this goes beyond what the New Testament documents assert. In the New Testament the matter is quite plain. Paul was a model Jew. Because of his deep attachment to the law, he was outraged that Christians claimed that Jesus and not the law was the way to salvation. His zeal for the law led him to persecute these heretics — as his forefathers in the faith had persecuted those who abused the law. He felt no inner frustration. There was no turmoil over the question of his righteousness. But on the way to Damascus, the Lord stopped him in his tracks and asked him about his persecution. In the context of his discovery that Jesus was of God, Paul suddenly saw that in persecuting the church, he was persecuting God. He was *not* walking in God's way as he had supposed.

Thus it is clear: *conversion begins with insight*. When people are confronted with the reality of their situation before God, the option is presented

---

21. Dupont, p. 183. Menoud, p. 132, agrees: "According to his own testimony Paul, when still a Jew, does not seem to have been morally troubled — he was a sincere Pharisee — nor to have been spiritually restless when he was trying to destroy the church of God — he was a sincere persecutor."

22. Stendahl, pp. 12-13.

23. "Next comes the psychological explanation. This theory tells us that St. Paul's conversion was not altogether sudden: that there was a long period of doubt and perplexity, a gradually strengthening attraction to Jesus Christ and His followers, a dissatisfaction with the Mosaic religion, and that the quest for religious truth and peace amidst anguish of mind and torturing doubts about the justice of his savage persecution of the Christians finally reached a crisis near Damascus, and with complete suddenness the conviction that Christianity was true burst upon Saul with such clearness and force that he *imagined* he saw the risen Lord and heard Him speaking." Lilly, p. 196.

to them to correct their errant ways. They now *see,* and in seeing it becomes possible for them to say no to the old way while embracing a new way. Without such insight into their true states before God, there would be no reason to embrace a new way. Without insight there cannot be conversion.

Murder: The Underlying Issue

One more point remains to be made about Paul's assessment of himself and how it came to be called into question by the encounter with Jesus. There is a subtheme within the description of Paul as a persecutor that requires notice. On four occasions Paul is connected in one way or another with the death of Christians.

First, there is the stoning of Stephen (Acts 7:54–8:1). While Paul is not directly involved with the actual killing, Luke makes a point of saying that he "approved of their killing him." Second, the adjective Luke uses to describe Paul's threats against the Lord's disciples is "murderous," as the NIV translates this passage, or "breathing threats and murder against the disciples of the Lord," in the case of the NRSV (9:1). Third, Paul himself, in his recitation of his conversion experience before the crowd at the temple, says: "I persecuted the followers of this Way *to their death*" (22:4 NIV, italics mine). Finally, during his address to King Agrippa, Paul says: "I not only locked up many of the saints in prison, but I also cast my vote against them when they were being condemned to death" (26:10).

In other words, Paul's persecution was not simply a matter of threatening people or harassing them. It was not even a matter of jailing them (though this was involved and was bad enough). It was a matter of killing people. This was zeal gone amok. There may have been a tradition within Judaism that offenses against the law deserved death, but there was also the sixth command: "You shall not murder" (Exod. 20:13).

When the risen Lord raised the issue of persecution, it can be argued that not only did Paul become aware that he was persecuting the wrong people (because they were of God), but he also became aware that by his behavior he was responsible for the death of innocent people. In this case, his assumed morality (he kept the law) would have been called into question along with his mistaken theology (he was wrong about Jesus).

There is a curious nuance in the above texts. Nowhere is Paul charged directly with the *murder* of Christians. He is always the one behind the scene. He approves of the crowd's desire to kill Stephen. He hints at murder in his threats. He hounds Christians and brings them before the synagogue courts where they are tried. He casts his vote for them to die. This is another level of moral corruption. Paul, in essence, hid behind his authority. He did not actually have to kill Christians. He saw to it that others did the killing. The pretense (and this is speculation) that it was not actually he who killed people — the law and the courts did that as a result of due process — would also have evaporated in the face of Jesus' question on the Damascus road. After all, it was Jesus who not only upheld the prohibition against murder but went on to point out that anger was a form of murder (Matt. 5:21-22; 19:18). And it was Jesus who accused the Pharisees (of whom Paul was one) of this very thing:

> Woe to you, scribes and Pharisees, hypocrites! For you build the tombs of the prophets and decorate the graves of the righteous, and you say, "If we had lived in the days of our ancestors, we would not have taken part with them in shedding the blood of the prophets." Thus you testify against yourselves that you are descendants of those who murdered the prophets. . . . Therefore I send you prophets, sages, and scribes, some of whom you will kill and crucify, and some you will flog in your synagogues and pursue from town to town. (Matt. 23:29-31, 34)

And in fact, the Pharisees did just this to Jesus. They were in on the plot to kill Jesus (Matt. 26:4). The Jesus that Paul met on the Damascus road had been killed by Paul's colleagues! And Paul himself had continued this tradition of persecution about which Jesus spoke. Stephen predicted the same thing that Jesus had, presumably within the hearing of Paul: "You stiff-necked people, uncircumcised in heart and ears, you are forever opposing the Holy Spirit, just as your ancestors used to do. Which of the prophets did your ancestors not persecute? They killed those who foretold the coming of the Righteous One, and now you have become his betrayers and murderers" (Acts 7:51-52). Later in his own writings, Paul would affirm the validity of the commandment not to murder. He knew it well, and in Romans 13 he connects the commandment not to murder to the law of love (vv. 9-10).

Jesus makes an interesting comment in John 8:44 while speaking to the Pharisees. He connects Satan with the desire to murder: "You are from your father the devil, and you choose to do your father's desires. He was a murderer from the beginning. . . ." In Paul's commissioning statement, mention is made of rescuing people "from the power of Satan" (Acts 26:18). Perhaps Paul was chosen to call people away from Satan because he, as a Pharisee, had personally experienced a desire to kill induced by the power of Satan, and had been rescued by Jesus from it.

51

A Shift in Assumptions

So for Paul, as a result of his encounter with Jesus, there was a significant shift in his understanding of who he was as a Jew trying to follow God. The assumption prior to that encounter was that he, Paul, was righteous. He had followed the law with sincerity and severity, therefore he was right with God. If anyone was on God's side, then certainly he was. He had been blessed with all the advantages of birth and background.

Paul had every right to be satisfied with himself. But then he had his encounter with Jesus, and this assumption about himself is called into question. Paul's view of himself is shattered by a single question: "Saul, Saul, why do you persecute me?" By this question his true state is revealed. His assumptions about what God wanted, about what he was doing, and about whether he was really walking in the way of God are all shown to be faulty. It was not that the facts had changed. Rather, now he saw them in a completely new light. Paul had a new organizing framework so that what he once valued he now saw as worthless. Commenting on what he said in Philippians 3:5-6 about the advantages of his birth and conduct, Paul says: "Yet whatever gains I had, these I have come to regard as loss because of Christ. . . . I regard them as rubbish, in order that I may gain Christ and be found in him, not having a righteousness of my own that comes from the law, but one that comes through faith in Christ, the righteousness from God based on faith" (Phil. 3:7-9).

It was not that Paul had been unfamiliar with the tenets of the movement he was persecuting prior to this experience.[24] But before his conversion he was blind to the significance and truth of the Christian way. He saw these ideas as heretical, a threat. They needed to be crushed. But in his conversion, his defenses were shattered and he saw Christianity in a whole new way. Exiting from the Damascus road experience, Paul had a new view of reality. As Bultmann comments:

> For just this is what his conversion meant: in it he surrendered his previous understanding of himself, i.e. he surrendered what had up to then been the norm and meaning of his life, he sacrificed what had hitherto been his pride and joy (Phil. iii.4-7). His conversion was not the result of an inner moral collapse (which it is frequently assumed to have been on the basis of a mis-interpretation of Rom. vii.7ff. as autobiographical confession). It was not deliverance from the despair into which the cleavage between willing

24. Nock, p. 67.

and doing had allegedly driven him. His was not a conversion of repentance, neither of course was it one of emancipating enlightenment. Rather it was submission to the judgments of God, made known in the cross of Christ, upon all human accomplishments and boasting. It is as such that his conversion is reflected in his theology.[25]

This new perspective is not forced on Paul. It is not the result of long hours of study or indoctrination. It is not the product of intense peer pressure. Rather, it comes out of a single question asked in the sorts of circumstances that shed a whole new light on the situation. There is no accusation or judgment on the part of Jesus. If anything, a certain sadness is in his question. There is no force behind it which compels Paul to answer in one way only, and yet an irresistible force is present.[26] It is the force of truth and reality. The question reveals the way things really are over against the errant religious and cultural assumptions that led Paul to the Damascus road in the first place, seeking out Christians to arrest, try, and perhaps kill.

The pattern by which insight comes, then, is this. There is an entering set of assumptions — about God and about oneself. The encounter with Christ reveals these to be faulty, wrong, and inadequate — out of touch with reality. As a result of that confrontation with reality, the old assumptions are

25. Rudolph Bultmann, *Theology of the New Testament,* trans. Kendrick Brobel (New York: Scribner, 1965), p. 188. The general outlines of what Bultmann says are accurate. However, it is not true to say that repentance does not characterize Paul's conversion. Repentance describes accurately the shift in perspective whereby Paul gave up his assumptions about himself and about the law as a way to please God and, in turn, accepted the way of the cross as the path to God. He literally "changed his mind," which is what repentance means. Wood, p. 281, takes exception to Bultmann's assertion that this was not a conversion of emancipating enlightenment, feeling that Bultmann seems "to merge the actual conversion-experience too simply with its immediate and most important consequences for Paul's faith and theology." See also the comments of Menoud, pp. 131-32, who agrees with Bultmann that this was not a conversion born out of a moral revolution: Paul had what may be called an ethical nature, and as a Pharisee had moral conduct high above the common average. Again, Saul the Pharisee sincerely believed in righteousness by observing the law of Moses; he was at peace with the God of his fathers, and was assured of being saved in the last judgment. To him, his conversion means a new revelation of the God of Israel, a new act of God in Christ, and consequently, a reorganization of his Jewish messianic faith and hope. In one word, his conversion is the model of a theological conversion. The effects of that conversion are not so much a new spiritual or ethical life as a new theological position, at least in the sense that the new spiritual life of Paul the apostle has its source in a new theological truth.

26. See the comments in the next chapter (pp. 86-87) on the phrase "It is hard for you to kick against the goads" (Acts 26:14 NIV).

shattered — they no longer can contain reality. One exits with a new set of assumptions — a new framework that better contains reality.[27]

The new insight that overwhelmed Paul on the Damascus road came to pass in a moment. Perhaps this is what ought to distinguish sudden conversion from other forms of conversion, not the rapid turning as much as the suddenness of insight. The turning follows almost by reflex when the insight is there: insight into truth, God, oneself, Jesus, the way the world works. The pieces, hitherto discrete and unconnected, suddenly fall into place and make a whole where once there was confusion. All one can do is gasp "Aha . . . so that is what it is all about." Paul's "aha" was in two directions: "So that is who Jesus really is" and "so that is who I really am." On both counts Paul had got it wrong. Up to that point in time he had seen Jesus as a fake Messiah and himself as one faithfully doing God's work in accord with God's will. But in that instance on the Damascus road, all this changed.

Insight drives conversion. Without insight there literally cannot be conversion. It does not matter if that insight is slow or sudden, or if the insight comes by means of careful sifting of the facts so as to reveal truth or by means of a flash of creative intuition. It does not matter if the precipitating cause is internal or external: guilt that drives one to a new way or encounter that opens up that new way. But there must be some trigger, otherwise the turning cannot even begin.

Conversion begins with insight into one's own condition as it concerns God. Without such insight there is no motive for change. Still, insight is but the first step. Theoretically, Paul could have seen all this about himself and still turned his back on it, refused the power of the insight, and continued on his way to Damascus as an agent of the Pharisees, seeking out Christians to arrest them. This is "theoretical" since such a refusal to see would be difficult indeed given the power of the numinous encounter that has taken place. Yet, in less powerful moments of insight, clearly it is possible to dismiss the insight. Every therapist has seen patients confront a new insight into themselves, only to deny it or repress it the next week. The point is that a second step is necessary in order for conversion to take place. A decision has to be made about the insight. Will the person turn from the old way to a new way? The term for this second step is "repentance."[28] Insight is the precursor to repentance; without insight no decision can be made about following a new way instead of the old way.

27. This is not to suggest that there is no continuity between the old and new, as will be discussed in the next chapter. The point is that the old facts are given a new context and take on new meaning as a result of this confrontation with reality.

28. See the discussion of *metanoeō* in the appendix (pp. 349-51).

Thus the first question that must be asked of the Twelve (when their conversion is considered) is this: Have they confronted themselves in this way? Have their assumptions about God (and what God is doing) and about their relationship to God been called into question? If so, how, when, and why? Unless there is new insight akin to what happened to St. Paul, they cannot be said to have undergone conversion.

CHAPTER THREE

Turning: Encounter with Jesus

From the three conversion accounts in Acts, it is evident that at the core of Paul's experience is a three-part movement. First, there is insight: Paul came to understand his true state before God, just as he came to understand who Jesus is. Second, there is a turning: Paul embraced Jesus. Third, there is transformation: Paul accepted the new life he was offered. In chapter 2 the first of these three movements was discussed: the nature of the insight which provided the context for Paul's conversion. In this chapter the second movement will be analyzed: Paul's encounter with Jesus whereby he turned around and started walking in a new direction and a new way.

A Vision of Jesus

What changed everything for Paul was his encounter with Jesus of Nazareth, a man Paul knew to have been crucified. But what exactly happened during this encounter in the noonday heat there on that road to Damascus? Apart from anything else, the three accounts in Acts record extraordinary phenomena.

For one thing, there was *light:*

Acts 9:3 — "a light from heaven flashed around him."

Acts 22:6 — "about noon a great light from heaven suddenly shone about me."

Acts 26:13 — "when at midday along the road, your Excellency, I saw a light from heaven, brighter than the sun, shining around me and my companions."

There was a *voice:*

> Acts 9:4 — "a voice saying to him, 'Saul, Saul. . . .'"
> Acts 22:7 — "I fell to the ground and heard a voice saying to me, 'Saul, Saul. . . .'"
> Acts 26:14 — "When we had all fallen to the ground, I heard a voice saying to me in the Hebrew language, 'Saul, Saul. . . .'"

In the midst of the light and the voice speaking to Paul was the *vision of a man:*

> Acts 9:5; 22:8; 26:15 — "Who are you, Lord?"

These *effects spilled over* to Paul's companions:

> Acts 9:7 — "The men who were traveling with him stood speechless because they heard the voice but saw no one."
> Acts 22:9 — "Now those who were with me saw the light but did not hear the voice of the one who was speaking to me."
> Acts 26:14 — "we had all fallen to the ground. . . ."

And there was a *physical impact* on Paul:

> Acts 9:8 — "Saul got up from the ground, and though his eyes were open, he could see nothing; so they led him by the hand and brought him into Damascus."
> Acts 22:11 — "Since I could not see because of the brightness of that light, those who were with me took my hand and led me to Damascus."

What does one make of this description? Several questions must be considered. First, are the documents telling the truth? Did this really happen, or was all this just pious fiction which was given these dramatic touches in an attempt to convince the gullible that Jesus was actually there? Second, if it is granted that something happened, what exactly was it? What is a vision, and how does one talk about such events? Are there other examples in history of this sort of thing happening? Then third, what was it about the dialogue with Jesus that made such an impact on Paul?

The Reliability of the Reports

Are the documents reporting historical truth? This is, of course, an enormous question, asked not just of these accounts but of the whole New Testament. It is a subject that is complex, the object of much debate, and around which a great deal of literature has been generated. It is a question that goes well beyond the scope of this particular book. Suffice it to say that it is not an uncommon conclusion on the part of scholars that what is reported in Acts is the substance of real events, shaped by Luke in accord with his purposes in writing Acts. Lohfink expresses this well in the final chapter of his book on the conversion of Paul:

> In conclusion, I would like to offer a brief statement on the relationship between the Lukan Damascus story and historical reality: *The report in Acts is not an exact verbal transcript of what really happened, yet it certainly is not pure fiction either. Rather it is both a report of a well attested historical tradition (cf. the Pauline letters) as well as Luke's interpretation and explanation of this historical tradition presented in conventionally accepted literary forms and literary techniques.*[1]

It is useful to examine representative examples of the debate over the reliability of the documents as it relates to the question of Paul's conversion since such an examination will add useful background information that assists in understanding Paul's conversion.

On one side of the debate is the perspective of G. J. Inglis, who understands Paul's experience of Jesus to be purely subjective, the product of internal mental processes with no cause beyond his own psychic state. Inglis examines the texts with this assumption, and thus has no problem accepting Paul's report of the various phenomena at the time of his conversion. This is what a man in that mental state might imagine to have happened. The problem for Inglis comes with the companions who are said to have witnessed the light and heard, if not a voice, then a sound. It is one thing for Paul to have a vision. It is quite another for that vision to spill over to those around him. He explains away the testimony of Paul's companions by asserting that Luke could not have interviewed them himself and so had to rely on Paul's report as to the external effects of the vision.

> Hence the Apostle's words provide the only evidence as to the effect of the vision upon the escort; and it may well be doubted whether this evidence is reli-

---

1. Gerhard Lohfink, *The Conversion of St. Paul: Narrative and History in Acts,* trans. and ed. Bruce J. Malina (Chicago: Franciscan Herald Press, 1976), p. 101.

able. Paul speaks with unquestioned authority concerning what he himself saw and heard, but his words carry much less weight when he describes the effect of his own spiritual experiences upon other people. It is most improbable that such description is based on the Apostle's own observation. There is no indication that, when the light flashed out suddenly, Paul had either the inclination or the opportunity to note the behaviour of those with him: he was so dazzled that he fell to the ground at once, and when the vision was over he rose up unable to see. Hence the information must have been drawn by Paul from the escort themselves, and such testimony is precarious. The sight of their master suddenly prostrated in the dust would probably be enough to fill them with astonishment and alarm; and it is unlikely that he would be in a fit condition to discuss his experience with them. On these grounds it is contended that the evidence for the behaviour of the escort must be viewed with suspicion; and this view is confirmed by the contradictory or at least inconsistent nature of the three narratives in this respect.[2]

In other words, Inglis's assumptions about the nature of Paul's experience (based on the authority of psychology) force him to read the texts in a certain way. This, of course, says nothing about the validity of the texts. It simply raises the question of what lens one uses to view the texts if they are not treated as reliable reports.

The so-called contradictions in the three reports, to which Inglis refers, are a common concern. In his article, Lilly examines with some care those statements that are said to conflict and concludes "that there is no reason to discount the historical credibility of the various records of St. Paul's conversion given in Acts because of the supposed intrinsic 'formal contradictions,' because there are none. . . ."[3] What Lilly demonstrates is that if one approaches the texts with the sense that they are reliable, it is a fairly straightforward process to read them in such a way that they do not contradict. In other words, the reliability of the texts is an issue to be decided on other grounds (beyond the scope of this book).

Lohfink approaches this question of establishing the reliability of the documents from a different angle. He rejects both what he calls "the conservative way" (in which an attempt is made to reconcile differences, such as Lilly does)[4] and "the attempted solutions of literary criticism"[5] in favor of

2. G. J. Inglis, "The Problem of St. Paul's Conversion," *Expository Times* (1929): 230.
3. Joseph L. Lilly, "The Conversion of Saint Paul: The Validity of His Testimony to the Resurrection of Jesus Christ," *Catholic Biblical Quarterly* 6 (1944): 189.
4. Lohfink, pp. 33-40.
5. Lohfink, pp. 40-46.

"the methods of contemporary exegesis" or "form-critical thinking" which takes into account the *"literary forms of expression* and *styles of literary composition."*[6] His conclusion about the documents, drawn from this perspective, is given at the beginning of this chapter.[7] To this statement he adds the following comments: "Luke's interpretation of events is not just his personal opinion, it is not just one of many possible interpretations of history, burdened as they are with the many possibilities for error which accompany any human endeavor; rather it is an interpretation wrought by the Holy Spirit. And this interpretation, which takes shape in what the author says and intends to say, cannot be erroneous."[8]

Perhaps the most telling argument as to the reliability of the reports of Paul's conversion comes from Daniel Fuller in his book *Easter Faith and History.* Fuller seeks to show that on the grounds of logic and history, *something like the encounter with the risen Lord had to take place, otherwise there is no adequate explanation of events about which there is historical certainty.* If Fuller can demonstrate that Paul's encounter with the resurrected Jesus has a high historical probability, then Luke's record of that event will also be seen to have high reliability. What follows is a summary and extension of Fuller's basic argument as developed in chapters 7 and 8 of his book. In these chapters he seeks to show that without a conversion of the sort St. Paul claims to have experienced and which Luke reports, it is impossible to explain the Gentile mission of the early church. In other words, this well-accepted historical reality (the Gentile mission) would have no adequate explanation were it not for Paul's conversion encounter with Jesus.

Fuller begins his argument by asking how it is possible that an orthodox Pharisee like Paul came to head up the Christian mission to the Gentiles. He asserts that this question lies at the heart of the various examinations which Paul underwent after his arrest at the temple. Fuller points to the riot that broke out when it was rumored that "Paul had committed the supreme sacrilege of bringing a Gentile into the temple precincts."[9] Paul is arrested and then given a chance to present his case to the mob. He tries to explain how he, an orthodox Jew, could be leading a mission to *Gentiles.* (The riot is about Gentiles.) Paul begins by recounting his credentials, which show that he was a true Jew committed to the faith of the fathers. In fact, he was so zealous that he even became a persecutor of the Christians (Acts 22:1-5). Next, he tells the

6. Lohfink, p. xii.
7. See p. 58 above.
8. Lohfink, p. 101.
9. Daniel P. Fuller, *Easter Faith and History* (Grand Rapids: Wm. B. Eerdmans Publishing Co., 1965), pp. 209-10.

story of his encounter with the risen Jesus on the Damascus road (22:6-16). He follows this up by recounting a second vision which took place later in Jerusalem (22:17-21). So far, so good. The crowd listened to what he was saying. But when Paul concludes with the comment: "Then the Lord said to me, 'Go; I will send you far away to the Gentiles'" (22:21 NIV), this gets a strong reaction from the crowd. Luke says:[10] "The crowd listened to Paul until he said this. Then they raised their voices and shouted, 'Rid the earth of him! He's not fit to live!'" (22:22 NIV).

Why this strong reaction to the idea that God might send Paul to the Gentiles? Why the riot over the idea that a Gentile might have been inside the temple? The answer to these questions is connected to the way the Jews viewed the Gentiles, particularly "the Jewish sense of superiority over the Gentiles."[11] The Jews were God's chosen people to whom the law had been revealed. But "the message of grace that Paul preached to the Gentiles . . . made the Jewish distinctive of no ultimate value."[12] "Apart from this grace of God that was evident in the resurrection appearances of Jesus, there was no force on earth that could have led a Jew to admit that an uncircumcised Gentile who ate unclean food was equally the partaker of the blessings promised in the Old Testament."[13] That somehow God could be seeking out Gentiles was beyond their imagination and an affront to their whole view of God. The point Fuller is trying to make is that, within first-century orthodox Judaism, nothing could have motivated a mission to the Gentiles and certainly not a mission of the sort Paul had undertaken, in which the law seemed to count for nothing and Jew and Gentile were considered equal before God, both receiving salvation by grace through faith in Jesus Christ.[14]

How, then, did an orthodox Jew like Paul come to head up the Gentile mission if nothing within Judaism could have motivated such an undertaking? Was he simply "a renegade Jew"? Fuller asks.[15] But this possibility was discounted during Paul's various hearings before the Romans. The three

---

10. There is a good chance that Luke did not just hear about all this from other people but actually witnessed it for himself, since in Acts 21:17 he indicates that he had come to Jerusalem with Paul.

11. Fuller, p. 210.

12. Fuller, p. 212.

13. Fuller, pp. 222-23.

14. Fuller, p. 217. Fuller does point out: "The Jews did seek to make converts among the Gentiles. Jesus spoke of the Pharisees compassing land and sea to make one proselyte (Matt. 23:15). But a Gentile could only become a full-fledged Jew to the extent that he was willing to submit to all the Jewish distinctives" (p. 218 n. 34).

15. Fuller, p. 218.

charges brought to Felix were that Paul was an agitator, stirring up riots among the Jews; that he was the ringleader of a sect; and that he tried to desecrate the temple (Acts 24:5-6). Any of these charges would have been sufficient to convict Paul. As to agitation, "such a charge could well have reminded Felix of the Egyptian whom some had confused with Paul at the time of his arrest (21:38). This Egyptian was stopped only after Felix had sent troops against him and his 4,000 followers, who had encamped on the Mount of Olives waiting to invade Jerusalem after its walls had fallen down (Josephus, *Antiquities*, XX.8.6)." Felix had dealt with agitators before, and would do so again were it proved that Paul was such. As to the other two charges:

> If they could prove that Paul headed up a sect which was contrary to Judaism, then he would be guilty of transgressing the law, in effect since the reign of Julius Caesar, which banned all *collegia* or "special societies" (Suetonius, *The Deified Julius*, XLII.3). The third charge the Jews brought against Paul was that he had profaned the temple. The Romans had given the Jews the right to execute even a Roman citizen if he defiled the temple by bringing a Gentile beyond the Court of the Gentiles (Josephus, *Jewish Wars*, VI.126). If the Jews could prove any of these charges, then they would be rid of Paul.[16]

Paul denied each charge, and apparently his defense convinced Felix: "Because the procurator Felix understood about Christianity, he was convinced of Paul's innocence, but because he did not want to displease the Jews by releasing Paul, he made it appear that he wished to investigate further (Acts 24:22). However, nothing more was done during the remainder of Felix' procuratorship, and Paul remained in prison in Caesarea."[17]

Two years later Festus heard the charges against Paul and likewise was not convinced of Paul's guilt. He shrewdly deduced that the Jews "had certain points of disagreement with him about their own religion and about a certain Jesus, who had died, but whom Paul asserted to be alive" (Acts 25:19). However, it was required that Festus write a letter, which would accompany Paul to Rome, specifying the charges.[18] So Festus asked King Agrippa to help

> ascertain whether Paul was a bona fide Jew or whether he was to be condemned for propagating a *religio illicita*. Rome had to investigate, and in the person of Agrippa it was capable of discerning how far Paul might have

16. Fuller, p. 213.
17. Fuller, pp. 213-14.
18. Fuller, p. 214.

deviated from Judaism so that something definite could be written to Rome.

In his defense before Agrippa (Acts 26:1-32), Paul's point was that there was nothing about his leadership of the Gentile mission that made him any less than the most orthodox Pharisee. Orthodox Judaism believed in the resurrection of the dead, and Paul spearheaded the Gentile mission because the risen Jesus had commissioned him to carry it out. So long as Paul could show that his work was the result of his belief in the resurrection, he could not be charged with a departure from Judaism, for the hope of the resurrection was of the very essence of Judaism.[19]

Thus Paul was given the opportunity to defend himself before King Agrippa, in the course of which he repeated once again the familiar litany: he was a fully orthodox Jew and engaged in the mission to the Gentiles only because the resurrected Jesus told him to do so.

Fuller then makes the point to which all this is leading:

During Paul's trial before the Romans, the two possible explanations of why Paul had led the Gentile mission had been advanced. Since Judaism itself would never produce such a mission, the only possible explanations for it were that (1) Paul led it as a renegade Jew, or that (2) somehow Paul's understanding of Judaism became modified to the extent that he felt compelled to carry out this mission while remaining loyal in every other way to the tenets of Judaism. The Romans became convinced of the falsity of the first possibility, for the letter that Agrippa II sent to Rome must have declared that Paul was a bona fide Jew who, even while he remained a prisoner, had every right to practice and propagate his religion. This fact having been established, the only other possibility was that Paul's orthodox Judaism had become modified so that he felt impelled to head up the Gentile mission. In rejecting the first possibility, the Romans, without realizing it, provided support for Paul's claim that he had led the mission because of a command received from the risen Christ. Somehow it must be understood how Paul, who remained completely loyal to the basic tenets of orthodox Judaism, could nevertheless cease to glory in the Jewish distinctives. No motivation residing in Paul nor deriving from his background as a Pharisee can account for his doing this in heading up the Gentile mission, for his pride in these distinctives had been so great that he had been as zealous to persecute the Church as the Jews were now zealous to persecute him. The explanation for the Gentile mission must, therefore, derive from something apart from Paul and his background. It must derive from something out-

19. Fuller, p. 215.

side the natural sphere. Paul's explanation is that the risen Jesus appeared to him, and since no explanation from the natural sphere is possible, and since the only proposal for an explanation deriving from the supernatural sphere is the resurrection of Jesus, therefore this is the explanation for the Gentile mission that is to be accepted.[20]

The single point at which Paul deviated from orthodox Judaism was in asserting that the resurrection — which Jews believed to be in the future — had already occurred for one man: Jesus of Nazareth. Paul knew this because he had encountered the risen Jesus on the road to Damascus. "The Gentile mission could only have resulted from the resurrection. . . . The risen Jesus appeared to him and commissioned him to preach."[21] "Paul's leadership of it really could not be explained either by his loyalty to Judaism or by his revolt against Judaism, but only by recourse to the fact that Jesus appeared to him."[22]

Having established this point by examining the material in Acts, Fuller goes on to show that exactly the same case can be made on the basis of Paul's own epistles.

> Thus Luke's argument can be formed from the data of the Pauline epistles: since the Gentile mission stemmed from a man who was and who remained a loyal Jew, and since this mission was opposed by the Jews who thought and felt as Paul did before his conversion, therefore Paul's testimony that it was the gracious appearance of the risen Christ to him that changed him and led to the Gentile mission must be true.
>
> The fact that there are two sources for the data essential to this argument would have little weight if it were evident that the material in Acts was derived simply from the Pauline epistles. However, there is almost unanimous agreement that Acts does not have a literary dependence on the Pauline epistles. . . . Hence, there is a real sense in which Acts and the Pauline epistles are independent sources for our knowledge of Paul, and consequently we have an historical control which validates the three essentials for the argument.[23]

Since "the Gentile mission is an unquestioned fact of history"[24] and cannot be explained apart from Paul's conversion, this is a strong case indeed for the fact of that conversion. As to Luke's account, it must therefore be given

20. Fuller, pp. 218-19.
21. Fuller, p. 220.
22. Fuller, p. 245.
23. Fuller, pp. 246-47.
24. Fuller, p. 226.

weight as being true. Something happened to Paul. If not exactly what Luke reports, then something very much like it. As Wood points out: "In short, if we do not accept the stories in Acts of the event on the road to Damascus, and of the martyrdom of Stephen, as history, we shall have to invent for ourselves stories of the same character, which seems to me a work of supererogation."[25] *Why would Luke bother to report a make-believe incident if there were a real event of the same unexpected quality and the same magnitude?*

The only other possibility in all this is that Paul was lying. Back to Fuller:

> But it might be suggested that Paul was simply an impostor, who fabricated these statements in his epistles and misled the author of Acts. It would be difficult to support such an hypothesis, however, because the same objection would rise against such a reconstruction as arose against Reimarus' hypothesis that the disciples stole the body of Jesus so that the empty tomb could argue for their claim that Jesus had risen. How could Paul be willing to suffer deprivation and the threat of death for an idea he knew was only a fabrication?[26]

The Nature of the Vision

Something happened to Paul on the Damascus road. It is reported that there was a great light, so intense that it caused Paul and his companions to fall to the ground even though it was noon and the hot Middle Eastern sun shown brightly in the sky. A voice spoke. There was coherent dialogue out of which life-changing insight flowed. There was a person — someone was there who had not been there before. And there was physical impact. Paul was blinded. His companions were even caught up in the effects of the vision. What was this thing that happened to Paul? Does this sort of thing still happen? Are there records of this kind of experience occurring to other people?

The Insights of Marghanita Laski

In fact, there are abundant records indicating that these sorts of numinous encounters continue to take place even today. Several survey studies demonstrate this. One such study was undertaken by Marghanita Laski in the 1950s.

---

25. H. G. Wood, "The Conversion of St. Paul: Its Nature, Antecedents and Consequences," *New Testament Studies* 1 (1955): 278.
26. Fuller, p. 247.

She published her results in a book entitled *Ecstasy: A Study of Some Secular and Religious Experiences* (1961). Laski got interested in ecstatic experiences in the course of writing a novel in which her heroine had a mystical experience. She wondered if this sort of thing was common, and if so, what such experiences looked like. Finding no studies that answered her questions, she endeavored to undertake an "empirical investigation of ecstatic experiences," even though she counted herself an "amateur." Because "no professional has undertaken it, or, so far as I know, considered doing so," she took this on as her project.[27] She sought examples of ecstatic experiences from three sources: individuals she happened to know (or met in the course of her study), accounts from literary sources, and accounts from religious sources. She began her research by interviewing friends and acquaintances, using a nine-part questionnaire she had developed. Then she undertook a literature survey, "looking for experiences superficially similar to those of the questionnaire group which their authors had thought worth communicating to the public."[28] Her content analysis of these materials was "divided into two main parts, the first (Section I) classifying the circumstances in which the experiences took place (the triggers), the second (Sections II to V) what people said about their experiences."[29] In the second section Laski was mainly interested in what people *felt* during ecstatic episodes — hence her four categories: feelings of loss (such as the loss of a sense of time or place, or the loss of human desire);[30] feelings of gain (such as achievement of complete satisfaction or joy, a sense of contact with the divine, or the discovery of new insight);[31] quasi-physical feelings (such as floating, pain, or peace);[32] and the sense of intensity or withdrawal (by which one experiences a great bursting out or a merging into).[33]

Laski's work is not as useful as it might be in understanding Paul's experience because of her focus on inward experience (what it felt like) and not on outward experience (the nature of the event itself). She herself recognizes this limitation when she suggests that further research needs to be done in order to answer the question, "what physical events accompany ecstatic experi-

27. Marghanita Laski, *Ecstasy: A Study of Some Secular and Religious Experiences* (New York: Greenwood, 1968), p. 2.
28. Laski, p. 12.
29. Laski, p. 16.
30. Laski, p. 24.
31. Laski, p. 30.
32. Laski, p. 32.
33. Laski, p. 32.

ences? Do these have any kind of reference to the physical events that ecstatics describe?"[34]

A second limitation is the small size and random nature of her sample. She and a colleague did sixty-three brief interviews using Laski's questionnaire. In addition, Laski uncovered accounts from twenty-seven literary sources and twenty-two religious sources. Of these twenty-two religious accounts, ten are taken from *The Mystic Way* by Evelyn Underhill and six from *The Varieties of Religious Experience* by William James. Not only are her sources limited, but the data were not gathered in any systematic or representative way. She got her data from friends and a few books. Still, since this was the first such study, it was perhaps the only way by which categories could be established that can (and did) serve as the basis for more systematic research.

Despite these limitations, two pieces of data intersect with Paul's experience. First, Laski found individuals who had experienced "light" during their ecstatic encounters, and second, she came across individuals who encountered some sort of "being" during their experiences. The following are examples of the kinds of data she included in these two categories. The material below consists of the actual phrases used by respondents to describe their experiences.

Light and/or Heat words and phrases:

Group L:[35] whitening, flashing, ebbing light — his face . . . with its exceeding brightness, and the light of the great Angel Mind which look'd from out the starry glowing of his restless eyes — each failing sense, as with a momentary flash of light, grew . . . distinct and keen — thought . . . rapid as fire (L2); [. . .] flashed up lightning-wise — Illumination . . . like a sunbeam striking with iridescence — Enlightenment (L 11); [. . .] he and they struck with the same pulse of fire — in an immense tongue of flame (L17b); [. . .] ground shone with purple light (L22). [. . .]

Group R: Shining Brightness — heavenly lightnings passed and repassed in the deeps of his being (R 1); [. . .] there is seen the brightness of the Lord (R 19).[36]

34. Laski, p. 372.
35. Group L designates those sources drawn from literature, Group R those drawn from religious sources, and Group Q are reports from the questionnaires. Each source is then given a number to identify it.
36. Laski, pp. 464-65. These are samples of responses Laski got, chosen from a larger group because they most closely paralleled Paul's experience.

Feelings of contact:

Group Q: [. . .] communion — direct communication (Q 5); in touch with the Creator (Q 15); [. . .] communion with something else (Q 27); [. . .]

Group L: felt a presence — a sense . . . of something far more deeply interfused . . . a motion and a spirit (L 1a); visitation from the living God — rapt into still communion (L 1b); [. . .] in the presence of a being (L 5); [. . .] Union with God (L 11); [. . .] the very obvious, tangible presence of the Creator (L 23b). [. . .]

Group R: [. . .] my soul opened out . . . into the Infinite — I stood alone with Him — perfect unison of my spirit with His — a presence that was all the more felt because it was not seen — I stood face to face with God (R 3); [. . .] intimate communion with the divine (R 6).[37]

This is not as illustrative as might be wished because Laski was more concerned with the particular words used to describe the feelings during such an experience than with the description of the actual event itself. Still, as has been seen, her material correlates with two of the five components of Paul's experience.

Laski makes an interesting comment that connects with a third element in Paul's experience. She notes that certain anti-triggers tend to inhibit ecstasy, the chief of which is the presence of other people.[38] Laski is pointing out that most ecstatic experiences are solitary in nature. This means that it may well be difficult to find examples of numinous experiences that spill over to other people (as it did to Paul's companions), because generally no one else would be present.

The Insights of the Religious Experience Research Unit

A more recent, more systematic, and more illuminating study of these sorts of experiences was undertaken by Sir Alister Hardy and the Religious Experience Research Unit (RERU) at Oxford. Their initial findings were published in 1979 in a volume entitled *The Spiritual Nature of Man*. Hardy, an eminent zoologist who was Linacre Professor of Zoology in the University of Oxford

37. Laski, pp. 456-57.
38. Laski, p. 177.

from 1946 to 1961, studied contemporary religious experience by analyzing reports of people who responded to a request (published in newspapers and elsewhere) to communicate in writing their experiences of being influenced "by some Power, whether they call it God or not, which may either appear to be beyond their individual selves or partly, or even entirely, within their being. . . ."[39] In his book, the first 3,000 responses are analyzed.

As with Laski, Hardy's aims (and his resultant classification system) are somewhat different from that required by this present study. Still, two of the twelve main divisions by which he classifies the reports relate to the Damascus road experience. In his first category he identifies experiences that have *visual* sensory or quasi-sensory components, and in his second category he places those experiences with *auditory* sensory or quasi-sensory qualities.

In the first category (visual experiences), of the 3,000 accounts, some 544 reported "visions," 135 reported "illuminations" in which the respondents felt "bathed in a general glowing light,"[40] while an additional 264 saw a particular pattern of light (as, for example, a patch of light in the shape of a cross when there was no external source of light to account for the pattern).[41] In the second category (auditory experiences), there were 431 reports of voices which were part of a religious experience.[42]

The problem with Hardy's report in terms of the questions asked in this study is that he summarizes a wide range of experiences and reports only his generalized conclusions according to his own categories. Few specific incidents are reported, so it is difficult to ascertain the precise nature of the experience of light, the kind of vision that takes place, or the nature of the voices. Did people ever experience light as bright and intense as that which blinded Paul? Was the figure ever recognizable in these experiences? Was there dialogue? No data are presented that enable such questions to be answered since specific incidents are hidden behind the classification system. In order to ascertain whether contemporary experiences parallel that of Paul, a researcher would have to examine the RERU database via a different classification system. At this point, in terms of the published findings, all that can be said is that, like Paul, people do have visions in which they see light and hear voices.

A more promising approach is that of Timothy Beardsworth, one of Hardy's colleagues who, several years before Hardy's summary, approached this same database looking for a very specific kind of experience. What inter-

39. Alister Hardy, *The Spiritual Nature of Man: A Study of Contemporary Religious Experience* (Oxford: Clarendon Press, 1979), p. 20.
40. Hardy, p. 34.
41. Hardy, p. 35.
42. Hardy, p. 39.

ested Beardsworth were those experiences in which people reported that they had encountered a "presence." From the first 1,000 responses sent into the RERU, Beardsworth extracted those reports that told of this type of encounter. Then he divided these reports into five categories. He looked for physical or quasi-physical experiences of four types: Did the incident involve a visual experience of any sort? Was there an auditory component? Was there a tactile experience? Was there any sort of "inward sensation"? In his fifth category he placed those reports in which there was a feeling of presence not based on any evident sensory experience.

This is more nearly the grid that should uncover parallels to Paul's experience than those used in the previous two classification systems. And certainly Beardsworth did come across incidents that are strongly reminiscent of what happened on the Damascus road. For example, he did find a number of "speaking apparitions." This is Beardsworth's terminology for what Paul experienced. He notes that the sorts of experiences in which there are both voice and vision are "nearly as common as 'silent' visions." He goes on to say that these "apparitions were sometimes bathed in a 'warm glow' or 'dazzling light.'"[43] Here is one example that he gives: "Awaking at about 4.00 p.m., I became aware of a fragrant perfume and a tremendous feeling of power, and looking through the bottom of the net at the end of my bed I was amazed to see a beautiful figure shrouded in a tremendous light. I could not believe in the reality of this phenomenon at first and rubbed my eyes to ensure that this was an experience in the realm of reality."[44]

After examining a variety of visual experiences in which there is a vision of some sort, Beardsworth next examines visual experiences in which there was illumination of the surroundings in general or the experience of a very specific light or lights. Again there are numerous examples, and again, some of these parallel what happened to Paul. For example:

> One lunch time I had been helping to dry dishes after the meal, and was standing before the open drawer of the sideboard putting knives and forks away. I was not thinking of anything, apart from vague attention to the job I was doing. Suddenly, without warning, I was flooded with the most intense blue-white light I have ever seen. Words can never adequately nor remotely touch the depth of this experience. It was like looking into the face of the sun, magnified several times in its light-intensity. But more "real" than the Light itself was the unbearable ecstasy that accompanied it. All

43. Timothy Beardsworth, *A Sense of Presence* (Oxford: Religious Experience Research Unit, Manchester College, 1977), p. 9.
44. Beardsworth, p. 9, account #28.

sense of time or self disappeared, yet it could only have been a fraction of a second. I knew only a sense of infinite dimension, and a knowledge that this was the Spirit of God Almighty, which was the hidden Life-Light-Love in all me, all life and all creation. . . . Then after the fraction of a second — I became myself again, still standing beside the open drawer putting knives and forks away. That one moment was and remains the most vital moment of my life, for there has never been a repetition. But out of it was born the Mission to which I have for many years dedicated my life. . . .[45]

It is worth noting that the duration of such experiences varies from "a fraction of a second," as above, to "over an hour" in other instances. The after-effects for many are "lasting." As in the above incident, this sort of experience can change a person's whole life. For others, however, such experiences have no discernible impact apart from being remembered as a happy experience. During the experience of light itself, on an affective level there was a strong, positive impact (e.g., "a feeling of absolute bliss . . .")[46] for all of Beardsworth's subjects. On a cognitive level, many report that the experience was revelatory for them.[47]

Auditory experiences, in which people hear cogent voices, provide additional parallels to Paul's experience. Beardsworth divides this experience into two categories: voices that are comforting and voices that provide guidance. It is interesting to note that while some of the voices are unidentifiable, others are assumed to be the voice of God (or at least the voice of some supernatural being). Many of the voices are of friends or relatives who had died recently. In these cases the identity of the speaker is quite evident to the recipient.

As to experiences in which more than one person was involved, Beardsworth reports only one (though it must be remembered that he was not looking for this sort of thing and the shared nature of this one incident was mentioned only incidentally). In this case a man reports being wakened one night while in Africa by the cries of birds and the barking of dogs. Going outside, he saw "a large bright light ascend from the sea and sway in the sky within my vision, and after some time it moved straight over the Rest House." He then reports a similar incident one month later in a place some 180 miles from the first scene, in which, as he says, "*I was awakened by a shout from my servant that there was a 'big moon' over the house.* Putting on a gown I stood outside and saw this huge bright light over the house."[48] This experience, however, has quite a different quality to it from most of the other reports ana-

45. Beardsworth, p. 20, account #15.
46. Beardsworth, p. 24, account #17.
47. Beardsworth, pp. 23-25.
48. Beardsworth, pp. 40-41, account #17 (italics mine).

lyzed by Beardsworth. In this case the correspondent is merely an impassive "observer" of an unusual event that has no impact on him personally, apart from leaving him "mystified." This account is more akin to reports of UFOs than to accounts of ecstatic experiences and therefore does not yield a proper parallel to the shared experience between Paul and his companions. Beardsworth also mentions some experiences in which other people are present but seem oblivious to what is perceived by the correspondent.[49]

The Insights of Phillip Wiebe

The most interesting study of mystical experiences is found in the recent book by Phillip H. Wiebe entitled *Visions of Jesus: Direct Encounters from the New Testament to Today.* Wiebe, who is professor of philosophy and dean of Arts and Religious Studies at Trinity Western University in Canada, undertakes a rigorous examination of "[v]ision and apparition experiences in which people believe they encounter Jesus Christ. . . ."[50] Here are the kinds of parallels for which we are looking. And indeed, Wiebe recounts various experiences that contain the elements found in Paul's encounter with Jesus.

Wiebe describes in some detail twenty-eight contemporary Christic encounters. He groups these experiences into five categories. The first group (of four cases) consists of experiences in which people seem to have fallen into trances or where the experience had a dreamlike quality to it. The second group consists of five examples in which percipients experienced a change in their physical environment. For example, one man was watching television when the screen became invisible and the walls of the room disappeared. It was into this setting that Jesus came.[51] In the third group (of fifteen experiences) the encounter took place in familiar and unaltered physical surroundings. In each case this was a private experience, since only the percipient had the experience, even though some of these events took place in public settings. The fourth, and most interesting, group (of four cases) consists of experiences in which several people were simultaneously affected. The fifth category is identified but not described via case studies. Here the percipients see events in the life of Jesus reenacted, such as Jesus suffering on the cross.[52]

---

49. Beardsworth, pp. 40-41. See p. 19, account #14; p. 28, the account in footnote 5; and p. 31, account #4.

50. Phillip H. Wiebe, *Visions of Jesus: Direct Encounters from the New Testament to Today* (New York and Oxford: Oxford University Press, 1997), p. vii.

51. Wiebe, p. 3.

52. Wiebe, p. 3. These categories are defined on pp. 41-42, and the cases themselves are described on pp. 3-4, 42-86.

In the contemporary examples that Wiebe amasses, each of the components of Paul's experience is present in one case or another. For example, in several cases there is intense light. In Marian Gallife's experience (group II), "a light brighter than anything she had ever seen exploded upon her and filled the room."[53] And Deby Stamm-Loya (group III) saw a figure whom she identified as Jesus standing at the end of her bed. "A radiance enveloped him in a pure white light that gradually increased in intensity. As this radiance intensified, it extended farther and farther beyond him, so that it finally consisted of a pure white light. . . ."[54]

In several cases a dialogue took place between the person and Jesus. For example, in his second Christic experience Jim Link (group II) was "flattened by a force that pinned him to the floor. For about three hours he was interrogated by this being [whom he later identified as Jesus] about what he valued most — his job, his family, his wife, his possessions, and so on. The others in the group watched in awe but said nothing. They heard Jim's responses, but not the questions that were put to him."[55] Ron Lindsay (group III) was in church one Sunday morning when he was startled to see Jesus at the front of the church. Ron entered into a dialogue with Jesus in which Jesus promised to heal him from his epileptic seizures. Ron reported that Jesus' lips moved as he spoke. The congregation heard Ron but not the other voice. Ron reports that nine months after this vision he was healed.[56]

In several cases there was a physical impact. Henry Hinn (group IV) was walking in snow a foot and a half deep when Jesus suddenly appeared eight feet away. "Henry reported that the snow had mysteriously disappeared at the spot where Jesus stood, and that dead grass was visible in an area about three feet in diameter. No tracks to or from this spot could be seen, however." Henry also reported a brief dialogue with Jesus.[57] After a ski accident Barry Dyck (group IV) was hospitalized and in serious condition. He broke three vertebrae and herniated one disc; swelling in his head created pressure on his brain. He could not see clearly and was in great pain. Eight days after the accident Jesus appeared to him and indicated that everything would be fine. The next morning Barry awoke to find that the swelling and pain were gone and he could see clearly. He convinced the reluctant doctor to release him. Within three or four days he was running again without any ill effect. "X-rays taken by his family doctor in Seattle several weeks later showed no evidence of frac-

53. Wiebe, p. 50.
54. Wiebe, p. 65.
55. Wiebe, p. 4.
56. Wiebe, pp. 58-60.
57. Wiebe, p. 74.

ture in his neck vertebrae [even though] the many x-rays taken during the week in the hospital had shown obvious signs of fracture."[58] In Wiebe's Case 27, John Occhipinti (group IV) saw someone whom he identified as Jesus standing over his ill roommate, Nathan. As John was about to tell Nathan what he was seeing, Jesus reached over and placed his hand on Nathan's forehead and then disappeared. "At that instant Nathan leaped out of bed and ran down the halls of the dormitory shouting 'I've been healed, I've been healed.' Nathan later said that although he did not see anyone, he felt something touch his head."[59]

The parallels to Paul's experience are striking. While each Christic experience is unique, within the variety of experiences are a host of phenomena. Wiebe comments that Christic visions are more common than realized. These visions happen mostly to "ordinary people" and not just to those who might be considered "saints." And these experiences have great religious import for those having them. About these reports Wiebe asserts: "I believe that enough reports of Christic apparitions come from people with strong education backgrounds to warrant giving serious attention to the whole body of evidence, including that from percipients with weak educational backgrounds."[60]

In his book Wiebe explores ways to understand Christic experiences. He evaluates the evidence from various vantage points, including mentalistic, psychological, neurophysiological, and supernaturalist explanations. The nature of his reflection moves beyond the intentions of this book. However, one track is worth noting. Wiebe believes that

> contemporary Christic visions seem to confirm some of the claim of NT accounts. That people now attest to experiences in which Jesus is perceived by both sight and touch, or is seen by groups, or leaves some intersubjectively observed effects, lends credence to claims that similar experiences occurred in NT times and are not merely legendary accretions. This is not a "knock-down" argument, to be sure, but it warrants careful (and further) consideration.[61]

The Significance of the Research into Mystical Experiences

What is the meaning of these accounts compiled by Laski, Hardy, Beardsworth, and Wiebe? First, it is obvious that such ecstatic or mystical ex-

58. Wiebe, pp. 74-75.
59. Wiebe, pp. 76-77.
60. Wiebe, p. 107.
61. Wiebe, p. 142.

periences are by no means uncommon. This sort of thing happens to a lot of people in a variety of circumstances. Second, there is great variation in the types of experiences people have. There does not seem to be a single pattern that can be identified apart from the fact that these events are not normal occurrences for most people and that they have about them the "feel" of otherness. Third, all this points to the fact that human beings do have some sort of innate capability to experience nonnatural phenomena, however one defines such phenomena. In other words, Paul was not unique in his Damascus road encounter. Potentially, all human beings are capable of having religious experiences like this. Finally, the question as to the source of the experience cannot be decided on the basis of the experience itself, as demonstrated by the variety of "explanations" given by respondents as to what happened, who was experienced, and what it meant.

Thus, by its very nature as a subjective experience, it is not possible from the experience alone to say who Paul met on the Damascus road. It is clear that in Paul's mind there was no question that he encountered Jesus of Nazareth, who had been resurrected. But whether this was so must be decided on other grounds. First, the whole question of the resurrection of Jesus must be examined. Did this happen in history? Was a man by the name of Jesus of Nazareth killed, and did he then rise from the dead a few days later? It is, of course, well beyond the scope of this book to evaluate the evidence bearing on this question. However, as is already apparent, the assumption is made here that the resurrection of Jesus is a fact of history.

If, on the other hand, the resurrection did not happen, then what Paul experienced was one of the following: a product of his own inner processes (a hallucination-type experience), an intrusion from whatever lies beyond human consciousness, or an experience similar to encountering a dead person speaking from beyond the grave. In fact, there are elements of each of these in Paul's experience. What happened to him did involve psychological processes; it was contact of some sort with transpersonal reality; and Jesus had, in fact, already ascended to heaven (Acts 1:9-11). But it was *not just* any or all of these taken together. Paul insists there was something else. He was met by Jesus who had died, was buried, and was raised from the dead on the third day, and who had appeared to the disciples and others. Paul puts his experience in the same category as that of the disciples (1 Cor. 15:3-8). And the resurrected Jesus they met was no apparition. He was flesh that could be touched, and he had a body that could consume food (Luke 24:37-43). In other words, he had been resurrected to new life.

If one makes the assumption that Jesus was raised from the dead, then what other evidence is there that this is whom Paul met on the Damascus road? For one thing, there is Paul's conviction that he met Jesus. While not sufficient in and of itself, it is striking that he was convinced on the deepest level of his being that he met Jesus. There is never any hint of doubt in his epistles that this is whom he met. This conviction is consonant with what one would expect if he did really meet Jesus. Furthermore, there is the unexpectedness of all this for Paul. Jesus was the last person he could have anticipated meeting. An angel maybe, but not Jesus. And certainly not when he was traveling to Damascus to persecute the disciples of Jesus. Paul would not have been doing this had he not felt Jesus to be merely a deluded teacher who got himself killed. Then there is the dialogue itself. Just the right question is asked of Paul to puncture his strongly defended self-understanding and so cause him to see reality in a whole new way. It is the sort of question that would arise from the penetrating wisdom of the risen Lord. Third, there are the parallel vision of Ananias and the verification that he brings that it is indeed Jesus who had been encountered. Finally, Paul continues to experience the presence of this same Jesus, as is evinced in the dialogue that took place between Paul and Jesus in the temple in Jerusalem (Acts 22:17-21). All of these facts corroborate Paul's conclusion that he met the resurrected Lord.

In summary then, what can one say about the line of inquiry pursued by these four researchers? For one thing, it is important to note that their work is phenomenological in nature; that is, it is "concerned with each individual's exact description of his experience (assuming that he is telling the truth), regardless of whether what seemed to him to happen 'really' happened or not. Indeed, the question of establishing whether something 'really' happened can hardly arise in this field. It makes no sense to talk of overhearing the voice of God talking to somebody else (it is not that kind of 'voice'). . . ."[62] In other words, all that such studies can do is establish that people do report having mystical or numinous experiences. Furthermore, such studies can analyze how many people report having what kind of experiences, but they can never, by definition, get at the truth of the situation, much less the reality (if any) behind the experience. As James Loder points out, these studies almost without exception concentrate "on description, classification, and the general question of *how* people believe or come to belief. The human sciences have given considerably less attention to *what* people believe and the power that content may have in determining the truth of a crisis situation in which some degree of conviction occurs." Loder goes on to show that the human sciences cannot understand those experiences where there is the conviction, arising out of an encounter with a Spiritual Presence known to be greater than oneself, that one has encountered truth. Human

62. Beardsworth, p. viii.

sciences cannot become "normative for those experiences that to the experiencer are disclosing a reality of a related but distinctly different order."[63] To allow the conclusions of these empirical studies to reinterpret such experiences is to mute their power and meaning, as well as their truth.

The Insights of Rudolf Otto

One further line of investigation needs to be noted. Rudolf Otto, who wrote about these phenomena in his classic study *The Idea of the Holy,* attempts to define the nature of a numinous encounter. In so doing he gives us a vocabulary by which to discuss the mystical. According to Otto, in broad terms a numinous encounter is the kind of experience that takes place when a person is confronted with reality as it really is. It is a moment when the veil across a person's eyes (which he or she had not hitherto been aware of) is drawn aside and that person says, "Yes, here is what life is all about." This is what James Loder would call a "convictional experience" — an event which discloses reality as it really is.[64] In that moment, caught up in this experience, suddenly a person "knows." No argument or proofs are necessary to understand that one has encountered God. The experience is self-validating. It is its own proof.

In developing a vocabulary by which to talk about these experiences, Otto casts light on the experiences themselves. He begins by calling attention to what he calls the *numinous.* Derived from the Latin *numen,* this word refers to the mental state of the person who has confronted the supernatural. This is "the reaction in a man to some apprehension of a reality beyond himself, which affects him. . . ."[65] Otto argues that the word "holy," which originally referred to this quality, has become too laden with ethical content and has come to mean the state of being "morally good." No longer does "holy" describe a unique feeling-response. It is this feeling-response which Otto seeks to define by his word "numinous."[66] The numinous state of mind, then, is at its heart a "'creature-consciousness' or creature-feeling. It is the emotion of a creature, submerged and overwhelmed by its own nothingness in contrast to that which is supreme above all creatures."[67]

---

63. James E. Loder, *The Transforming Moment: Understanding Convictional Experiences* (San Francisco: Harper & Row, 1981), p. 9.

64. Loder, p. 6.

65. Rudolf Otto, *The Idea of the Holy,* trans. John W. Harvey (Harmondsworth, Middlesex, England: Penguin Books, 1959), p. 10. This comment comes in the anonymous introduction to the book.

66. Otto, p. 10; see pp. 15-21.

67. Otto, p. 24.

Otto goes on to say that this numinous feeling is understood to be gen-erated by "an object outside the self."[68] This object is thus spoken of as "'the numinous.' For the 'creature-feeling' and the sense of dependence to arise in the mind the 'numen' must be experienced as present, a *numen praesens*. . . . The numinous is thus felt as objective and outside the self."[69]

In his book, Otto next defines more precisely the nature of this numin-ous presence which he calls the *mysterium tremendum*, the "aweful mys-tery."[70] First he describes the three elements within the concept of *tremendum*. An entity that is encountered in such an experience possesses *awefulness, majesty, and energy*. The numinous object, by virtue of being filled with awe, creates a sense of *fear*, though this is not so much "being afraid" as it is a sense of dread or shuddering — a kind of "holy terror." The numinous object is also seen to be filled with might and power, or "absolute overpoweringness," which is the root idea behind the concept of "majesty." Finally, there is an energy or urgency connected to the numinous object.[71]

Second, Otto gives content to the idea of *mysterium*. The *numen* is seen as "'wholly other' . . . that which is quite beyond the sphere of the usual, the intelligible, and the familiar, which therefore falls quite outside the limits of the 'canny,' and is contrasted with it, filling the mind with blank wonder and astonishment."[72] This "wholly other" evokes a sense of fascination which is not unrelated to the daunting sense evoked by the "awefulness" and "majesty" already noted.

> These two qualities, the daunting and the fascinating, now combine in a strange harmony of contrast, and the resultant dual character of the nu-minous consciousness, to which the entire religious development bears witness, at any rate from the level of the "daemonic dread" onwards, is at once the strangest and most noteworthy phenomenon in the whole history of religion. The daemonic-divine object may appear to the mind an object of horror and dread, but at the same time it is no less something that allures with a potent charm, and the creature, who trembles before it, utterly cowed and cast down, has always at the same time the impulse to turn to it, nay even to make it somehow his own. The "mystery" is for him not merely

68. Otto, p. 24.

69. Otto, p. 25.

70. Otto's translator calls attention to the fact that "awe" lies at the heart of this mys-tery by spelling "awful" as "aweful." This spelling will be used at those points in the discus-sion where Otto's meaning is found.

71. Otto, pp. 26-39.

72. Otto, p. 40.

something to be wondered at but something that entrances him; and beside that in it which bewilders and confounds, he feels a something that captivates and transports him with a strange ravishment, rising often enough to the pitch of dizzy intoxication; it is the Dionysiac-element in the numen.[73]

As Otto points out, one's feelings in the presence of the Holy Other are twofold. There is a strong urge to flee, to leave this dangerous place and this frightening being. On the other hand, one wants nothing more than to be one with the Other, to draw near and remain in the aura of that love, power, and presence. There is terror (you want to run away) and there is joy (you want to remain at that place forever).

Thus Otto's description of a numinous encounter fills in the background to Paul's experience. Something of this sort must have happened to Paul. One catches a glimpse of this in the terse description of the event given by Luke. This is why Paul broaches no argument when given his new calling, despite all the danger and persecution that it will bring him. This is why the experience has a self-validating quality to it for Paul. This is why there is the sense that it would be useless to fight against what the Other is saying. Paul stood within the presence of the "wholly other" Lord, who was filled with awefulness, majesty, and energy. He experienced the daunting nature of these characteristics while simultaneously being fascinated with and drawn to this Other who knew his name. It is within this context that one must hear the dialogue between the resurrected Jesus and Paul.

The Dialogue

Jesus initiates the dialogue: "Saul, Saul, why are you persecuting me?" There are four things to note in this opening statement. First, this is not a generalized encounter with a numinous force that is impersonal and detached. This is an encounter with someone who knows Paul's name ("Saul, Saul"). The experience is individual and particular. This is a presence who knows Paul (the sense is) as deeply as he can be known and who cares for Paul so much that he stops him in his murderous way and confronts him with reality.

Second, once Paul is named it might be expected that the next statement would be accusatory. After all, Paul had been persecuting the followers of Jesus. But only a question is asked: "Why?" This is, of course, the right question (by it Paul's whole purpose in life, his motivation and his assump-

73. Otto, p. 45.

tions are called into question) in the right context (Paul's defenses are down). In any other circumstance Paul would probably have given an eloquent rationalization of why he persecuted Christians, based on the law and illustrated from the traditions of Judaism. But here, in this numinous context, defense and justification are not even considered. This is reality speaking. This is the truth confronting Paul.

Third, the heart of the first question revolves around the issue of persecution. "Why are you *persecuting* me?" As has been shown in chapter 2, it is by confronting this particular issue that Paul discovers both his theological error (he was persecuting God's own people, all the while thinking he was doing God's will) and his behavioral aberration (he was having innocent people killed and thinking this was pleasing to God). The question reveals to Paul his life as it really is in such a way that he cannot deny that his path was leading him away from God and not to God as he had supposed.

Fourth, the final part of this initial question in the dialogue raises the central issue. The voice says, "Why are you persecuting *me?*" Who is speaking to Paul? Who is this mysterious "me"? Paul knows well enough whom he wants to find and imprison in Damascus, but who is speaking on behalf of the followers of the Way? Who is claiming that in persecuting them, he is being persecuted? Is it an angel? Is it a martyred leader of the church like Stephen? Is it God? Is it Jesus? It is one thing to discover that you are going in the wrong direction. It is another to discover the right direction you ought to take. The correct direction will become clear only when the identity of the person in the vision is revealed.

So Paul asks, "Who are you, Lord?" This is the second statement in the dialogue. By calling the figure "Lord," Paul indicates his posture toward him. It is one of submission. (This is the same response Ananias makes when his name is called. "Yes, Lord," he answers [Acts 9:10]. This is the title by which the resurrected Jesus is known to his disciples.)[74]

The response by which the figure reveals himself — the third statement in the dialogue — is clear-cut and unambiguous. "I am Jesus of Nazareth whom you are persecuting." By means of the first question ("Saul, Saul, why are you persecuting me?"), Paul knows *from what* he must turn. Now, by means of this response to his question ("Who are you, Lord?"), he knows *to whom* he must turn. It is Jesus of Nazareth who will chart the way ahead for Paul. Interestingly, it is not by means of one of his messianic titles that Jesus identifies himself; it is with his human name. There is continuity between the resurrected Lord whom Paul encounters and Jesus who lived in Nazareth.

74. See also Acts 9:11, 13, 15, and 17.

Once his question was answered, there was never any doubt in Paul's mind about the identity of the figure in the vision. From that point on he will insist that it is Jesus he met. This comes out in his two recitations of his conversion experience (Acts 22:8; 26:15). This same clear identity is found in his own writings. When asserting his legitimacy as an apostle, he insists that he met *Jesus* on that road. "Am I not an apostle? Have I not seen Jesus our Lord?" (1 Cor. 9:1). Elsewhere he says: "Christ died for our sins . . . he was raised on the third day . . . he appeared to Cephas, then to the twelve. . . . Last of all, as to one untimely born, he appeared also to me" (1 Cor. 15:3-8). And:

> For I want you to know, brothers and sisters, that the gospel that was proclaimed by me is not of human origin; for I did not receive it from a human source, nor was I taught it, but I received it through a revelation of Jesus Christ. . . . God, who had set me apart before I was born and called me through his grace, was pleased to reveal his Son to me, so that I might proclaim him among the Gentiles. . . . (Gal. 1:11-12, 15-16)

Discovering Who Jesus Is

Thus Paul discovers who Jesus really is. Prior to this encounter his assessment of Jesus was undoubtedly similar to that of his colleagues in the Sanhedrin; otherwise his persecution of those who followed Jesus cannot be explained. Paul does not tell us directly what his preconversion view of Jesus was. But the Pharisees and other Jewish religious leaders variously described Jesus, and these descriptions probably reflect Paul's own view. They said Jesus was motivated by an evil spirit (Mark 3:30). They thought him to be a troublemaker who was in opposition to the legitimate religious authority in the land and therefore deserving of death (Mark 11:18, 27-28). They saw him as a false Messiah (Mark 14:61-64).

> But that Jesus of Nazareth could be the expected Messiah, as his disciples maintained, was out of the question. It is unlikely that the status, career and teaching of Jesus conformed in any way with Paul's conception of the status, career and teaching of the Messiah — but that was not the conclusive argument in Paul's mind. The conclusive argument was simply this: Jesus had been crucified. A crucified Messiah was a contradiction in terms. Whether his death by crucifixion was deserved or resulted from a miscarriage of justice was beside the point: the point was that he was crucified, and therefore came within the meaning of the pronouncement in Deuteronomy 21:23, "a hanged man is accursed by God." True, the pronouncement envisaged the hanging until sundown, on a tree or wooden gibbet, of

the dead body of an executed criminal, but as formulated it covered the situation in which someone was hanged up alive. It stood to reason, therefore, that Jesus could not be the Messiah.[75]

However his views were formulated, Paul discovered in that moment on the road that they were wrong. What is immediately obvious to Paul about Jesus is that he was somehow imbued with the aura of God. The numinous context of the experience made this much clear. Whoever he was, Jesus was not simply a deluded Galilean peasant who dared to challenge the religious structure of Israel. He had God's approval. He was of God. The second thing that is clear to Paul is that Jesus was most definitely alive, as the Christians claimed. He was there, present with Paul, in conversation with him. The third thing that is clear to Paul is that Jesus was worthy of the title "Lord."

How much of Jesus' nature Paul grasped intuitively in that moment and how much he was told by Jesus (Gal. 1:12) is not made clear in the texts. That there was self-revelation on Jesus' part is evident from the commissioning statement in Acts 26:17-18. Paul is told that Jesus is powerful, of the light, of God and not of Satan, able to offer forgiveness, and the one who brings sanctification through faith in him. Whatever Paul learned, soon afterward it is confirmed by Ananias and, presumably, by the other Christians he then met. For example, Ananias calls Jesus the "Lord" during his visit to Paul, confirming Paul's first response to the figure before him on the road. In addition, Ananias asserts that Jesus is of God. In confirming Paul's commission, Ananias calls Jesus by one of his messianic titles: "The God of our ancestors has chosen you to know his will, to see *the Righteous One* and to hear his own voice" (Acts 22:14, italics mine). Whatever Paul had learned about Jesus' essential nature, it was enough so that soon after his conversion he is out in the synagogues of Damascus preaching that Jesus "is the Son of God" (Acts 9:20) and "proving that Jesus was the Messiah" (Acts 9:22).

Menoud argues that three things were revealed to Paul in his encounter with Jesus: "the unity of the divine work in the Old and New Covenant, the redemptive value of the Cross, and the two stages in salvation."[76] First, Paul discovers that the God who revealed his Son to him is the same God that he had served as a Pharisee. The coming of Jesus fulfills the old covenant and creates a new covenant. But it is still the same God at work. Paul has not joined a new religious movement or altered all his ideas about God. His con-

---

75. F. F. Bruce, *Paul: Apostle of the Heart Set Free* (Grand Rapids: Wm. B. Eerdmans Publishing Co., 1977), pp. 70-71.

76. Philippe Menoud, "Revelation and Tradition: The Influence of Paul's Conversion on His Theology," *Catholic Biblical Quarterly* 6 (1953): 134.

version does not "conduct Paul to an entirely new theology." There is one new element, however:

> Paul now no longer expects in the future a still unknown Messiah. On the contrary he knows from the revelation given to him by God that the Messiah did come indeed in "Jesus our Lord, who was put to death for our trespasses and raised for our justification" (Rom. 4:25). The central quest of religion is still the same: How can men be saved and be admitted finally into the kingdom of God? But the answer is now different, because a new fact has been revealed. The new fact is the christological faith of the apostle, and its main consequence: salvation is not to be gained by observing the law; it has been brought about by Christ on the cross and it is granted by grace to the believers.[77]

Second, in discovering that Jesus was the long-promised Messiah who brought salvation, Paul also discovered that the cross was not the curse spoken of in Deuteronomy. Instead, he came to see that the cross had redemptive value. "The Cross was the means chosen by God to save men."[78] Third, Paul came to see that salvation was a two-part process. "He speaks of redemption as at the same time an actual and a future experience."[79]

The result of Paul's encounter with Jesus was the restructuring of his theological understanding. "Paul's conversion meant for him the recognition that the condemned criminal was in fact the Anointed One of God, living now in the glory of the Spirit world, and that through this Anointed One an imperious call to tell the good tidings had come to him, Paul. This was a sudden intuition; thereafter Paul had to readjust his whole thinking."[80]

By the addition of one new fact only — Jesus crucified and resurrected — Paul experienced a shift in context that put him at odds with orthodox Judaism. He kept claiming, rightly, that he was still faithful to his Jewish roots and that the only thing which had happened to him on the Damascus road was the revelation that Jesus was who he claimed to be — the Son of God who came to save all peoples. To his Jewish colleagues, however, this was seen as a fatal shift that put him outside the camp and thus made him a legitimate target for the persecution that was directed at those who corrupted the law.

77. Menoud, p. 135.
78. Menoud, p. 136.
79. Menoud, p. 137.
80. A. D. Nock, *St. Paul* (New York: Harper & Brothers, 1938), p. 74.

Encountering the Exalted Lord

There is yet another aspect to Paul's encounter with Jesus. As Stanley notes:

> Christ's appearance to Paul, Luke knows, differs in one very notable respect from His visits with His own in Jerusalem or Galilee: it is *the Christ exalted in divine glory,* Who appears to Saul. We possess no record of any such revelation of His glorified Humanity to the Twelve during the forty days before the Ascension. In fact, as Père Benoit has rightly observed, Luke's description of the Ascension is rendered remarkable by the absence of any light of glory; and thus differs from the *coelestis exaltatio* described elsewhere in the New Testament.[81]

Dupont makes the same point:

> Paul saw *Christ in his glory.* In this respect the Damascus appearance is plainly different from the Easter appearances which are recorded in the gospels.
>
> In Galatians 1:12, 16 Paul speaks of this appearance as an "apocalypse," a glorious manifestation in which Christ revealed himself to Paul in his state as Son of God, such as will be his appearance at the end-time.[82]

Both Stanley and Dupont make reference to 2 Corinthians 4:4-6, which Dupont describes as an allusion to Paul's conversion. This text says:

> In their case the god of this world has blinded the minds of the unbelievers, to keep them from seeing the light of the gospel of the glory of Christ, who is the image of God. For we do not proclaim ourselves; we proclaim Jesus Christ as Lord and ourselves as your slaves for Jesus' sake. For it is the God who said, "Let light shine out of darkness," who has shone in our hearts to give the light of the knowledge of the glory of God in the face of Jesus Christ.

This is, in fact, what Paul encountered when he met Jesus on the Damascus road, and this is what swept away the old and ushered in the new. He saw the "glory of God in the face of Jesus." He might eventually come to know all the titles for Jesus whereby his character and office are defined, but in that

---

81. David M. Stanley, "Paul's Conversion in Acts: Why the Three Accounts?" *Catholic Biblical Quarterly* 15 (1953): 330-31.

82. Jacques Dupont, "The Conversion of Paul, and Its Influence on His Understanding of Salvation by Faith," in *Apostolic History and the Gospel,* ed. W. Ward Gasque and Ralph P. Martin (Grand Rapids: Wm. B. Eerdmans Publishing Co., 1970), p. 192.

first moment what he saw was Christ exalted in glory. This made all the difference.

The Inner Experience of Jesus

There was an inner dimension to what happened. Paul hints at this in Galatians 1:15-16: "But when God, who set me apart from birth and called me by his grace, was pleased to reveal his Son in me . . ." (NIV). By the phrase "in me" or "within me" Paul calls attention to the interior quality of his experience. It was not merely a dialogue with spoken words. There was an inner knowing and an inner conviction. It was not just Paul's mind that was touched but his whole being at its depth.

This must not be interpreted to mean that this was merely an internal vision, i.e., that it was generated solely by psychological forces at work in Paul. Lilly responds to this charge:

> St. John Chrysostom gave a very satisfying interpretation of this expression centuries ago when he wrote: "Why did he not say 'reveal his son to me' but 'in me'? To show that not through words alone did he hear the truths of faith, but that he was filled with an abundance of the Spirit, that since revelation was illumining his soul, he had Christ speaking within him" (*Com. in cap. 1 Ep. ad Gal.* MPG 61, 628). And that equivalently has been the interpretation ever since, and it is only in relatively recent times, when rationalist presuppositions require the elimination of the supernatural, that recourse is had to the explanation that the phrase means a purely internal vision excluding any appearance to the senses on the road to Damascus. How, it may reasonably be asked, can these critics insist that the phrase "in me" implies merely an internal vision when St. Paul himself, our best witness, insists that he saw the risen Lord (1 Cor. 9:1; 15:8)?[83]

The Turning

So there was a turning on Paul's part — from the law to Christ, from persecution to apostleship, from killing Jews who had become Christians to calling Gentiles to become Christians. This is what lies at the heart of the word "conversion" — the image of turning. There are a *from* and a *to*. The old is renounced (turned from) and the new is embraced (turned to). Paul left behind one image of how to serve God (by persecuting those who deny the law) and

83. Lilly, p. 201.

took up a new image of how to serve God (he was appointed to "serve and testify" [Acts 26:16]). He left behind one view of Christ (a rebel and a pretender) and took up a new view (the Messiah and the Son of God).

Looked at another way, this turning takes place around Jesus. Jesus stands at the pivot point. On the one side is the old life, flawed, marred, out of step with what God wants. On the other side of the turning is the new life, grounded in forgiveness, expressed in service, encompassed about by a new community of God's people, and opening out into new horizons of growth (sanctification). At the center stands Jesus, who reveals the old life for what it really is and who gives the focus, direction, and commission for the new life. It is Jesus, by lifting Paul's eyes to himself, who puts Paul's old life into a new perspective and gives him vision for the new life. It is Jesus to whom Paul turns and from whom he proceeds. Jesus is the axis around which Paul's conversion rotates.

There is an inevitability to all this which is perhaps best captured in the phrase by which Paul amplifies the Lord's opening question to him. Paul cites this when he relates his conversion experience to King Agrippa. The Lord says to him: "Saul, Saul, why are you persecuting me? *It hurts you to kick against the goads*" (italics mine).[84] This was a common proverb in the first century

---

84. Acts 26:14. This phrase has caused concern amongst critics because it is, apparently, a Greek proverb and they find it hard to imagine it on the lips of Jesus. So the assumption is made that this was a later insertion by Luke, or perhaps even by Paul, who in this case would be putting his experience into images that will communicate the proper meaning to this particular audience. This conclusion is reached for two reasons, according to Lohfink: "First, the form critical analysis of the context (the proverb stands within an apparition dialogue!) and second, the fact that Luke's report of Paul's speech in chapter 26 sparkles with many other high-class Greek expressions. And we need not go far to find the reason for this high-class literary style here — in Acts 26 Paul addresses a royal audience and not the Jewish masses as in Acts 22." Still, Lohfink admits, based on the work of Rahner in *Visions and Prophecies*, that "The question is more complicated than it might first appear. For what a person sees and hears in a vision is invariably perceived and understood in terms of the experiences provided by his own culture." Lohfink, p. 78.

Carsten Peter Thiede and Matthew D'Ancona, *Eyewitness to Jesus* (New York: Doubleday, 1996), p. 133, point out that this reference would have been a familiar allusion to Agrippa and Festus, who would have recognized that it was used not only in the popular Oresteian trilogy by Aeschylus but in other plays as well. Their point is that Agrippa and Festus "could not have escaped the notion that Jesus of Nazareth, the crucified Galilean, was familiar with such idioms, and that his apostle Paul could quote him in Greek with ease." Previously Thiede and D'Ancona made the point that Jesus lived only six kilometers (or one and a half hours' walking distance) from Sepphoris; that Sepphoris was being rebuilt when Jesus was a young man; that Joseph his father was a builder who might well have participated in the construction of Sepphoris; and therefore that Jesus might well have attended Greek plays in the theater of Sepphoris, thus making it possible for him to have known this phrase from Greek theater (pp. 129-130).

and referred to the practice by animal drivers of prodding an ox with a sharply pointed stick (a goad) in order to get it to go faster. It made no sense for the beast to kick at the goad. It only cut him more deeply and increased his pain. So the idea conveyed by this proverb is that for Paul to work any longer against Christ (by persecuting the church) was as futile as an ox kicking against a goad.[85]

Certainly there was an irresistibility to this encounter and call. After all, it was initiated by God, not by Paul (Gal. 1:16). And the vision came with all the power and conviction of the numinous. It rings of truth and reality and certainly caused a deep resonance within Paul. "Christ Jesus has made me his own," Paul says in Philippians 3:12, in a reference to his conversion.[86] First Corinthians 9:16-17 strikes the same note of irresistibility: "If I proclaim the gospel, this gives me no ground for boasting, for an obligation is laid on me, and woe to me if I do not proclaim the gospel! For if I do this of my own will, I have a reward; but if not of my own will, I am entrusted with a commission." Who could resist the resurrected Christ? Certainly not Paul, who, burning with zeal to be God's person, discovers to his horror that he has been doing exactly the opposite but that now, through God's grace, he is being given another chance. In fact, he is asked to accept a special commission, to become a witness of the Lord he persecuted. Who can resist such forgiveness and love?

In conclusion, then, it is clear that the second stage in Christian conversion involves *turning,* based on insight that has been gained into one's relationship to God. Conversion is not, however, simply turning away from the old. It is turning to Jesus. A person cannot experience Christian conversion without an encounter (in one way or another) with Jesus and a turning to him. This, then, is the second factor which must be assessed when analyzing the experience of the Twelve. What happens to their view of Jesus? Is there an awareness of who he really is (over against a cultural assessment of him)? Is there a turning to Jesus? Does Jesus become the center of their faith?

85. Fuller, p. 216.
86. The NIV translates the phrase "I press on to take hold of that for which Christ Jesus *took hold of me*" (italics mine).

CHAPTER FOUR

Transformation:
The Emergence of New Life

To have a numinous experience is one thing; to be converted is another. A numinous experience can lead to conversion if it is acted upon, but if not, it may simply remain "an experience" — valued but not life changing.

Numinous experiences are, it appears, quite numerous. According to a study done by Andrew M. Greeley and William C. McCready for the National Opinion Research Center at the University of Chicago, fully 35 percent of adult Americans have had, at one time or another, an experience that has all the characteristics of a classic mystical experience.[1] Such experiences are overpowering and highly valued. Recipients count them as the most valuable or amongst the most significant experiences they have ever had.[2] And yet, as far as can be known, few numinous encounters seem to result in conversion.[3]

1. Andrew M. Greeley and William C. McCready, *The Ultimate Values of the American Population*, Sage Library of Social Research, vol. 23 (Beverly Hills, Calif.: Sage, 1976), p. 133. This was a carefully selected, statistically representative sample population, according to Andrew M. Greeley, *The Sociology of the Paranormal: A Reconnaissance* (Beverly Hills, Calif.: Sage, 1975), pp. 8-9. These two volumes report on the same study.

2. Andrew M. Greeley and William C. McCready, "Are We a Nation of Mystics?" *New York Times Magazine,* January 25, 1975, pp. 12-25.

3. It should be noted that such experiences increase the psychological well-being of most recipients. "Professor Norman Bradburn, whose psychological well-being scale is one of the principal dependent variables used in this monograph, commented at a National Opinion Research Center (NORC) staff seminar that there are no other variables he knows of that correlate as strongly with psychological well-being as does frequent mystical experience." Greeley, p. 7. See also pp. 61-62 and 75.

In other words, it is one thing to have a mystical experience. It is another to have a conversion experience.

There are at least two differences between a numinous experience and a conversion experience. First, as was argued in chapter 2, conversion begins with insight. It occurs within a context that reveals that one's relationship with God is somehow askew and in need of correction. There is the awareness that one needs to turn around from the old way and adopt a new way in regard to God. A mystical experience, on the other hand, is simply an experience. It may not reveal anything about one's relationship to God. The second difference involves the adopting of this new way. Again, a mystical experience simply happens. No response is required. Conversion, however, involves choice, turning, and a new way of living. Insight gives the direction and provides the mental picture of what should be. The turning launches a person in the right direction. But the turning is not complete until the new way is actively pursued. This is the subject of this chapter: the new life that Paul, to complete his conversion experience, embraced as a result of his encounter with Jesus.

The Response

In Acts 22:10 Paul asks: "What am I to do, Lord?" Paul immediately recognizes that what happened to him requires a response. This is not an event that could be experienced and then let go. Something new is in the process of being born here. There is a new path to be followed, a new obligation to be fulfilled.

The answer to Paul's question comes on two levels. First, immediate action is to be taken. He is to get up and go into Damascus and wait for events to unfold there. And second, a long-term call is to be followed. He is to go to all people, but especially the Gentiles, as a witness and a servant. The relevant texts are as follows:

> Acts 9:6, 8-9 — "'But get up and enter the city, and you will be told what you are to do.' . . . Saul got up from the ground, and though his eyes were open, he could see nothing; so they led him by the hand and brought him into Damascus. For three days he was without sight, and neither ate nor drank."
>
> Acts 9:17-19a — "So Ananias went and entered the house. He laid his hands on Saul and said, 'Brother Saul, the Lord Jesus, who appeared to you on your way here, has sent me so that you may regain your sight and be filled with the Holy Spirit.' And immediately something like scales fell from his eyes, and his sight was restored. Then he got

up and was baptized, and after taking some food, he regained his strength."

Acts 9:19b-20, 22 — "For several days he was with the disciples in Damascus, and immediately he began to proclaim Jesus in the synagogues, saying, 'He is the Son of God.' . . . Saul became increasingly more powerful and confounded the Jews who lived in Damascus by proving that Jesus was the Messiah."

Acts 22:10-11 — "I asked, 'What am I to do, Lord?' The Lord said to me, 'Get up and go to Damascus; there you will be told everything that has been assigned to you to do.' Since I could not see because of the brightness of that light, those who were with me took my hand and led me to Damascus."

Acts 22:12-16 — "A certain Ananias, who was a devout man according to the law and well spoken of by all the Jews living there, came to me; and standing beside me, he said, 'Brother Saul, regain your sight!' In that very hour I regained my sight and saw him. Then he said, 'The God of our ancestors has chosen you to know his will, to see the Righteous One and to hear his own voice; for you will be his witness to all the world of what you have seen and heard. And now why do you delay? Get up, be baptized, and have your sins washed away, calling on his name.'"

Acts 26:16-18 — "But get up and stand on your feet; for I have appeared to you for this purpose, to appoint you to serve and testify to the things in which you have seen me and to those in which I will appear to you. I will rescue you from your people and from the Gentiles — to whom I am sending you to open their eyes so that they may turn from darkness to light and from the power of Satan to God, so that they may receive forgiveness of sins and a place among those who are sanctified by faith in me.'"

Paul Joins the Christian Community

As to the immediate actions required of Paul, some are related to Paul's personal needs following his blinding, others involve linking up with the Christian community, while still others move Paul out into the wider community as a witness to Jesus. First, there are Paul's needs. The disorientation of such an experience must have been enormous. There he is, lying in the road, blind and overwhelmed by a vision that has changed his whole perspective on life. Paul's initial instructions are designed to overcome the paralysis of such an experience and move him into a place where he can be helped. "Get up. Go into Damascus. Wait." This is all he needs to know for the moment.

Once in Damascus, the second step for Paul is to make contact with the Christian community there. This involves Ananias. Just as it took a vision for Peter to accept Cornelius, who was a Gentile, it took a vision for Ananias to accept Paul, who was a persecutor (Acts 9:10-16). Ananias seeks out Paul (his location having been revealed in the vision) and immediately welcomes him into the Christian community. "Brother Saul" is how he addresses this man who a few days before was known to be a deadly enemy of the church. The term "brother" is, of course, how Christians referred to one another. Ananias welcomes Paul as one who is a follower of Jesus.

In this first meeting between the two, not only does Ananias accept Paul as a part of the Christian community, he also indirectly demonstrates to Paul that this new community is in touch with the very power of God. Ananias reveals the power of God in three ways. First, he lays his hands on Paul and his blindness is healed. Second, in the same instance Paul is filled with the Holy Spirit (Acts 9:17-18). Then, third, Ananias speaks in a prophetic way by repeating the word of God that has come to Paul (22:14-15). Paul knows this is God's word because he too heard the same thing from Jesus (26:16-18). All of this speaks of God's power and presence.

After meeting Ananias, Paul breaks his fast and is strengthened by the food. He meets other Christians in Damascus. He is baptized and in this way publicly takes upon himself the name of Jesus. And so Paul becomes a part of this new community (9:18-19).

Ananias does one other thing for Paul. Because of who Ananias is, namely, "a devout man according to the law and well spoken of by all the Jews living there" (22:12), he confirms for Paul that continuity exists between Judaism and Christianity. This is no new religion with which Paul has come into contact. This is the extension and fulfillment of Old Testament hopes and promises.

If step one was to get Paul up from the dust of the road and into the city and step two was for Ananias to introduce Paul to the Christian community, then step three was for Paul to begin to move out into the world with his new faith. After a few days Paul goes back to his original Jewish community and preaches in the synagogues that Jesus is the Son of God (9:20). He now declares publicly what he had affirmed privately.[4] All the while Paul is obviously

---

4. He later confirms that such public admission of faith is indeed vital. In Rom. 10:9 he says: "if you confess with your lips that Jesus is Lord and believe in your heart that God raised him from the dead, you will be saved."

integrating his new discovery (that Jesus is alive and is God's Son) into his old understanding of the law and the prophets. He apparently grows rapidly in his understanding, since he is able to demonstrate to the Jews in Damascus that Jesus is indeed the Messiah (9:22).

Paul Accepts His New Commission

Once Paul is back on his feet, so to speak, and in touch with the Christian community, it is time for him to consider the commission given him to be a witness of the resurrection. At the time of his conversion, Paul is told that he has an assignment and that the details of it will be made clear in Damascus (Acts 9:6; 22:10). He knows in general what this is because during his conversion experience Jesus tells him that he is to be a servant and witness (26:16). This is later confirmed by Ananias, who has also heard it from the Lord.[5]

The elements of that commission are as follows. First, there is the sense of selection. Paul did not simply decide to become a witness to the resurrection. It was God who chose him. "He is an instrument whom I have chosen . . ." (9:15). Ananias repeats this to him: "The God of our ancestors has chosen you . . ." (22:14). Jesus told Paul that he has been "appointed" to this function and that he was being "sent" (26:16-17).

Second, the nature of his task is defined. He is to be a witness and a servant (22:15; 26:16). He is to "bring [the Lord's] name" (9:15) to the world. The content of this witness is also defined. He is to witness to what he sees and hears from God (22:15) and from Jesus (26:16). Specifically, this involves three things according to 22:14. Paul will know the will of God, he will see the resurrected Jesus ("the Righteous One"), and he will hear from Jesus the words he is to communicate. In other words, it is not up to Paul to devise the content of his witness. This is given to him by revelation.

Third, Paul's audience is defined. He is to witness to "all the world" (22:15). He is being sent to both Jews and Gentiles. In all three accounts of his conversion, the universality of his call is noted. In Acts 9 the text reads: "he is an instrument whom I have chosen to bring my name before Gentiles and kings and before the people of Israel" (v. 15). The text from Acts 22 has already been noted: "you will be his witness to all the world . . ." (v. 15). And in

---

5. See Acts 22:14-15 and 9:15-16. Many critics do not understand the Acts 26:16-18 commission to have come at the time of the conversion but see it, rather, as a later summation by Paul (or Luke) of what Paul came to understand his commission to be. However, nothing in any of the accounts requires it to be read this way.

Acts 26 he is told: "I will rescue you from your people and from the Gentiles — to whom I am sending you to open their eyes so that they may turn . . ." (vv. 17-18).

Finally, the goal (or outcome) of Paul's witness is defined. It is threefold. He is (1) to open their eyes and (2) to turn them from Satan (darkness) to God (light) so that (3) they receive forgiveness of their sins and become part of the community of the saints (26:18). This statement not only defines what will happen in the lives of those to whom he witnesses. It also defines what has just happened to Paul. He has had his eyes opened (insight), and he has turned from the darkness of his persecution to the light of God (turning). He has been forgiven for his persecution and has been given a place in the community of faith (transformation).

In order for his conversion to be complete, it was necessary that Paul accept that what happened to him was true, confess it publicly, and live it out as an apostle of the church. Otherwise the experience would remain on the periphery of his life — dramatic but not life changing. God acted. Paul needs to react (respond). In quite another context, this same point is made by the Epistle of James. James 2:14-26 says it is not good enough to talk about having faith. Faith is an intangible substance. One cannot see it or feel it until it shows itself in actions that are consonant with what is professed to be believed. Unless faith spills over into life, it is merely an intellectual game. So too conversion. It is merely an idea or experience until it reveals itself by the new way one lives. *Unless there is transformation, there is no conversion.*

For Paul this meant that he had to relinquish one commission and take up quite another. At the start of his journey to Damascus he is commissioned to take prisoners on behalf of the high priest, who had given him letters of authorization (Acts 9:1-2). At the conclusion of his journey to Damascus he is commissioned to make disciples on behalf of Jesus, who changed his heart and then appointed him to tell others what happened. Paul's original intent was to go to the synagogues of Damascus to search out followers of the Way. Once in Damascus he does go to the synagogues, but now it is to convince people to become followers of the Way (9:20-22). It was by this switch of commissions that Paul demonstrated the authenticity of his conversion experience.

In Paul's case, as has been noted, the response to his conversion has two parts. There was an immediate living out of his new commitment by linking up with the Christian community, by being baptized, and by proclaiming his faith. The long-term response was to accept the commission and become an apostle. Not all people receive a commission in the context of conversion, of course. The commission is a separate issue. But all people do need to make some kind of public declaration of their act of repentance and faith in order for conversion to be complete.

The Commission

A Real or Invented Commission?

It has been widely recognized that the commission by which Paul is called to his apostolic ministry is remarkably parallel to the commissions given to three Old Testament prophets.[6] Specifically, Paul's commission as recorded in Acts 26:16-18 is reminiscent of the calls given Isaiah (Isa. 6:1-9a), Ezekiel (Ezek. 1:3–3:11), and Jeremiah (Jer. 1:4-9). In each instance the events are parallel. Each call came in the context of a vision. When Isaiah was called, he, like Paul, had a sense of personal sinfulness and unworthiness. The call of Jeremiah is significant since, unlike the other two prophets who were sent to the nation of Israel, he, like Paul, was called to be "a prophet to the nations" (Jer. 1:5).[7]

Not only are there parallel events, but the words of the Acts 26 commission are reminiscent of the words spoken to the three prophets. Lohfink contends that "the first part of the passage [in Acts 26] is a veritable mosaic of citations from the prophets."[8] He identifies a whole series of phrases drawn from Isaiah, Jeremiah, and Ezekiel and goes on to conclude: "In other words, the mission speech of Acts 26:16-18 has been constructed of references to the famous mission and vocation texts of the Old Testament — and this by Luke himself."[9] In addition, it needs to be noted that when Paul himself wrote about his call in Galatians 1:13-16, he too expressed it in phrases drawn from Isaiah and Jeremiah.[10]

But it is not necessary to conclude that the text of the commission was therefore invented by Luke just because the phrases are reminiscent of the Old

6. See, for example, F. F. Bruce, *Paul: Apostle of the Heart Set Free* (Grand Rapids: Wm. B. Eerdmans Publishing Co., 1977), p. 75; Günther Bornkamm, *Paul,* trans. D. M. G. Stalker (New York: Harper & Row, 1969), pp. 13-25; and A. D. Nock, *St. Paul* (New York: Harper & Brothers, 1938), p. 65.

7. The Greek word used in the Septuagint is *ethnē,* which can be translated either "nations" or "Gentiles."

8. Gerhard Lohfink, *The Conversion of St. Paul: Narrative and History in Acts,* trans. and ed. Bruce J. Malina (Chicago: Franciscan Herald Press, 1976), p. 70.

9. Lohfink, p. 71. Lohfink uses the work of Clarke, "The Use of the Septuagint in Acts," in *The Beginnings of Christianity,* ed. F. J. Foakes Jackson and K. Lake, vol. 2 (London: Macmillan, 1920), pp. 99-100. See also Krister Stendahl, *Paul among Jews and Gentiles* (Philadelphia: Fortress, 1976), pp. 9-10.

10. Isa. 49:1, 6; Jer. 1:5. Stendahl, p. 8.

Testament.[11] There is another option. This may simply be the way God addresses people at crucial points in the history of Israel. This is the way he spoke to Jacob and Moses (not to mention Isaiah, Jeremiah, and Ezekiel) when they were needed to lead the people of God to a new place. Thus, when Paul finds himself in this same sort of situation — confronted with a heavenly being — his (perhaps unconscious) anticipation, drawn from his rabbinical training, would be of dialogue of exactly this sort. As Lohfink said in another context: "What a person sees and hears in a vision is invariably perceived and understood in terms of the experiences provided by his own culture."[12] Furthermore, when Paul later recalled this dialogue, he would realize that it was similar to dialogue in the Old Testament that occurred at turning points in the history of Israel. Thus he would realize the significance of what had happened to him. "Was this another such turning point for my people?" he would ask.

It must also be remembered that the sole source of information about what took place in the dialogue on the Damascus road is Paul. His companions did not grasp the content of the words, so Paul, by definition, could be the only reporter. Furthermore, by the time he told his story to Luke, Paul would have recounted the event numerous times. It was, after all, the only explanation of his new role as apostle to the Gentiles. In the process of repeating his story, he would have evolved a way of talking about it. He would have reduced it to its essence — which is the sense one gets in hearing the conversion dialogue. What has been reported is the heart of whatever conversation went on between Paul and Jesus.[13]

That there was additional dialogue between Paul and Jesus becomes clear when the three accounts are compared. For example, in Acts 9:5, in response to Paul's question, the Lord identifies himself by saying: "I am Jesus . . . ," whereas in Acts 22:8 the reply is: "I am Jesus *of Nazareth. . . .*" In the Acts 9 account, Paul's second question is left out of the report and Paul is told straightaway by the Lord to go into the city, whereas in Acts 22:10 he asks:

---

11. As Lohfink seems to do when speaking about the dialogues between Jesus and Paul on the Damascus road: "The apparition dialogues are certainly not historical reports of what really happened between Christ and Paul" (p. 68).

12. Lohfink, p. 78.

13. It must be noted that this is a conservative reading of the text and that many scholars would feel, as does Lohfink, that Luke shaped the text here as elsewhere to serve his own purposes in writing. This will always be an issue when it comes to NT narrative. Clearly the Gospel writers shape the text in accord with their own intentions, if in no other way than by the simple act of selecting certain stories and leaving out others and by the decision to set these stories side by side with other stories so as to make a point that goes beyond any of the individual stories. The nature and character of authorial intervention, under the guidance of the Holy Spirit, is a subject beyond the scope of this book.

"What am I to do, Lord?" and then the reply comes. In terms of what Paul should do, in the Acts 9 account he is told: "But get up and enter the city, and you will be told what you are to do" (v. 6). In the Acts 22 account the response is fuller: "Get up and go to Damascus; there you will be told everything that has been assigned to you to do" (v. 10). Only in Acts 26:16-18 is it discovered that the Lord actually commissioned Paul then and there.

In other words, a principle of selectivity is operating both in Paul's telling of the story and in Luke's reporting of it. But in either case, the core event is presented with historical accuracy.[14] What is found in the speeches in Acts is not a *summary* as Wikenhauser contends when he says that Luke gives "as a rule only short summaries of the main thought."[15] Lohfink rightly asserts that it is not possible simply to blow up these speeches like balloons and discover the size and shape of the original.[16] Instead of summaries, what Luke gives is selected passages that convey the essence of the speech, in accord with his editorial purposes.

Of course, the same problem confronts anyone working with the synoptic Gospels, which consist of compilations of short stories called pericopae. A pericope is a literary form (derived from an oral form) in which the same sort of compression and selection is found. Form is one thing. Content is another. Simply because a particular form has been chosen by which to report an event or dialogue, it does not necessarily follow that the content is invented. In fact, the form may aid in the focus and selection process so as to get at the essence of the material.

An Immediate or Gradual Call to the Gentiles?

There is yet another question concerning Paul's commissioning. *When* did Paul become conscious of his particular call to the Gentiles? Inglis states the problem as follows:

14. "Granted that the speeches in Acts are compositions of the author, there is good reason to hold that he knew what was fitting to each occasion, and that the speeches are not exercises in pure imagination. There is certainly primitive tradition in the speeches of Peter in Acts, and as Paul must often have told the story of his conversion, it is not likely that the writer has substituted a romantic story of his own invention for Paul's own account of his change-over from persecutor to a disciple and an apostle." H. G. Wood, "The Conversion of St. Paul: Its Nature, Antecedents and Consequences," *New Testament Studies* 1 (1955): 276-77.

15. *Die Apostelgeschichte und ihr Geschichtswert*, Neutestamentliche Abhandlungen 8, p. 17, quoted in Lohfink, p. 54.

16. Lohfink, p. 54.

Connected with the content of the Divine message is the problem concerning the time at which the Apostle became conscious of his vocation to the Gentile mission. In Ac 9:15 Saul's vocation is revealed to Ananias in his vision, but Ananias does not mention this revelation to Saul. In chap. 22 there is no account of Ananias' vision, but, in his interview with Saul, Ananias declares that "thou shalt be a witness for him unto all men of what thou hast seen and heard" (22:15); while, in the verses which follow, the call is represented definitely as coming during a subsequent vision in the Temple at Jerusalem (22:17-21). The third account (chap. 26) ascribes the call to the words of the risen Lord. But, in the elaborate apologia before Agrippa and Festus, Paul is anxious to prove to an audience of Jews and Gentiles that it was the very God of the former who sent him to work among the latter. Hence he makes his call to the Gentile mission part and parcel of his supreme experience. In his eagerness to show that it was in obedience to the heavenly vision that he had spent his life urging both Jew and Gentile to "repent and turn to God" (Ac 26:20), he identifies his call with his conversion, and passes straight from his spiritual crisis to the evangelistic work which resulted from it. In view of these inconsistencies and in view of "the tendency in the light of after events to regard a decision as definitely formed and realized at a period when it was in fact only implicit and tentative," it is impossible to say with certainty when the Apostle became conscious of his vocation to the Gentiles.[17]

This comment has been quoted at length because it reflects well the views of certain scholars.[18] But as shown above, this is not the only way to handle the texts. If Luke is understood to be selective and to use material as it suits his narrative needs, it is not necessary to require that the call to the Gentiles be stated in Acts 9 when it better fits the context of Acts 26. In any case, it is clear that Paul's original call was universal. He was to go to all peoples. This is why, when he came to a new city while on his missionary journeys, Paul typically first went to the synagogue. He moved on to the Gentiles only when he was rejected by the Jews.[19] It must also be remembered that

17. G. J. Inglis, "The Problem of St. Paul's Conversion," *Expository Times* 40 (1929): 229-30. The quoted material is from C. W. Emmet's essay "The Apostolic Age and the Life of Paul," in *Peake's Commentary on the Bible* (London, 1920), p. 768.

18. See, for example, Jacques Dupont, "The Conversion of Paul, and Its Influence on His Understanding of Salvation by Faith," in *Apostolic History and the Gospel*, ed. W. Ward Gasque and Ralph P. Martin (Grand Rapids: Wm. B. Eerdmans Publishing Co., 1970), pp. 192-93.

19. For example, note his experience in Pisidian Antioch. Compare Acts 13:14-15 with 13:44-48.

Paul's initial ministry following his conversion was to the Jewish community. In Acts 9:19b-30 the story is told of how Paul's ministry to the Jews in Damascus and Jerusalem provoked them in both places to seek to kill him, so that eventually he was sent back to his hometown of Tarsus. Paul returns to ministry only after Barnabas journeys to Tarsus to enlist him in the emerging ministry in Antioch (11:19-26). This time his work is primarily amongst Gentiles who have started to respond to the gospel. In other words, Paul's special ministry to the Gentiles is something that emerged over time and was eventually confirmed by the leaders in Jerusalem (Gal. 2:7-10). However, Paul never forgot that his original call was to *all* peoples, and even while he was the apostle to the Gentiles, he also sought out Jews in order to tell them about Jesus.

The Continuity

Stendahl has pointed out convincingly the continuity that existed between the religious views of Paul the Pharisee and those of Paul the apostle.[20] After his conversion Paul continued to serve the same God. Paul insists that he has continued to obey God. In his response to the Sanhedrin he says: "Brothers, up to this day I have lived my life with a clear conscience before God" (Acts 23:1). It is striking that he continues to call these men "brothers." On another occasion he says, "I worship the God of our ancestors, believing everything laid down according to the law or written in the prophets. I have a hope in God — a hope that they themselves also accept — that there will be a resurrection of both the righteous and the unrighteous" (24:14-15). In fact, Paul got into the trouble in Jerusalem because he undertook a vow of purification to demonstrate that he "observe[d] and guard[ed] the law" (21:24). In two accounts of his conversion, he begins by reciting his impeccable credentials as a Jew, which he affirms and does not deny (22:2-5; 26:4-8). Paul insists that he has done what he has done because he is an orthodox Jew.

The Jews did not agree with Paul's assessment. When he contended in 23:1 that he had fulfilled his duty to God, the high priest was so outraged that he ordered Paul struck. And then, once Paul was in custody as a result of the temple riot, the Jewish leaders conspired together how they might kill him[21] — which was the only fit end for one who abused the law. The problem for the religious leaders was that Paul did deviate from his former beliefs at one major point. He knew Jesus to be the Messiah because he had met him on the

---

20. Stendahl, pp. 7-23. See also Inglis, p. 231.
21. For example, see Acts 23:12ff.

Damascus road, alive and surrounded by a light from heaven. This made all the difference. If Jesus was the Messiah, then Jesus and not the law was the way of salvation. If Jesus was the Messiah and had called Paul to go to the Gentiles, then this was God's will. To Paul this was not deviation from the faith of his fathers. It was the extension and fulfillment of that faith. He would have considered himself a "completed" or "fulfilled" Jew, not a heretical Jew.[22]

So, for Paul, his conversion marked not only the moment when he started to follow Jesus. It also included his call to be an apostle. For Paul, then, part of the response whereby he completes his turning from sin to Jesus involves accepting the commission to be a witness of the resurrection to all peoples, but primarily the Gentiles. He accepts this call despite the warning within the commissioning itself that this role would not be without cost. And he was faithful to this call. In the concluding remarks of his defense before King Agrippa, he describes what this new life was like that flowed from his conversion:

> After that, King Agrippa, I was not disobedient to the heavenly vision, but declared first to those in Damascus, then in Jerusalem and throughout the countryside of Judea, and also to the Gentiles, that they should repent and turn to God and do deeds consistent with repentance. For this reason the Jews seized me in the temple and tried to kill me. To this day I have had help from God, and so I stand here, testifying to both small and great, saying nothing but what the prophets and Moses said would take place: that the Messiah must suffer, and that, by being the first to rise from the dead, he would proclaim light both to our people and to the Gentiles. (Acts 26:19-23)

Conclusion

What, then, lies at the heart of Paul's conversion? What is the foundational pattern that characterizes this experience? What are the core elements without which this would not be Christian conversion? In other words, what are the elements that must characterize the experience of the Twelve if it is to be called conversion?

On one level, Paul's conversion can be viewed as having three movements or phases. Phase 1 is insight: he sees himself for who he really is in terms of his understanding of and relationship to God. Phase 2 is turning: he encounters Jesus Christ and submits to him as the Lord, the Son of God.

22. To use the slogans of the contemporary group Jews for Jesus.

Phase 3 is transformation: his commitment is translated into a new life experience in which there is a different inner dynamic as well as a different outer lifestyle and calling.

On another level, each of these elements — insight, turning, and transformation — is found in *each* of the phases. The central motif in Phase 1 is insight into himself and into who Jesus is. But there is also turning. Seeing this about his old way of life, Paul turns away from it to a new pattern of life. Seeing who Jesus is, he turns to him. And there is transformation. By his discovery of who he is and who Jesus is, Paul discovers a whole new way of living which he comes to accept as the new pattern for his life. His thinking about how to live has been transformed.

The central motif in Phase 2 is turning to Jesus. But there is also insight. In encountering the risen Jesus, Paul grasps for the first time who Jesus really is. And there is transformation. He begins a new life with Jesus as the central figure in it.

The central motif in Phase 3 is transformation of his life. The insight at this point involves the nature of this new life. Paul had met Christians in the course of his persecution. He saw how they lived and heard what they believed. At his conversion he would have realized that this now will be the pattern for his life. There is also turning. In embracing this new life, he turns from his old commission to persecute Christians to his new commission to make Christians.

There is still another way of looking at all this. Paul's conversion involves three spheres. It was an encounter with himself. It was an encounter with Jesus. And it was an encounter with his culture. In each encounter, all three movements are visible. There is insight in his encounter with himself: he sees himself for who he really is. There is turning: he leaves the old way of life and embraces the new. There is transformation: he links up with a new community and begins to function in a new role with a new vocation.

In his encounter with Jesus these same three phases come into play. There is insight: he see Jesus for who he really is. There is turning: he turns to Jesus and embraces him as Lord and Savior. There is transformation: his worship and obedience are now given to Jesus, not to the law. This same pattern applies to his encounter with his culture (both Jewish and Greek). He has insight into the deficiencies of Judaism and into the fact that God is also calling Gentiles to be his people. He turns from the exclusivism of Judaism to the inclusiveness of the Christian way. He stops persecuting Christians as heretical Jews and starts pursuing Jews as potential Christians. He seeks out Gentiles to enlist them in God's kingdom. As for transformation, he now ceases to be a persecutor (a negative role) and starts acting as an apostle by being a witness to the resurrection both among his own people and, especially, among the Gentiles (a positive role).

In other words, Paul's conversion is marked by three movements within three spheres. *There are insight, turning, and transformation that affect who he is, how he relates to Jesus, and what he does within his culture.* Furthermore, these movements within these spheres are all in the context of God. Christian conversion is not a generalized movement of transformation within the context of one's relationships to other people and to the world around one. It involves new insight into God, new turning toward God, and a new life lived in response to God. It involves seeing oneself in the light of God's truth, embracing a new relationship to God, and living this out within the community of God's people as a servant and witness to all people.

Thus, in evaluating the experience of the Twelve, these same three movements within these three spheres, all within the context of their relationship to God, will be the subject of the investigation. Had they been living somehow askew from God's way? Do they encounter Jesus and discover who he really is? Does this translate over into a new lifestyle?

PART II

THE EXPERIENCE
OF THE TWELVE

CHAPTER FIVE

The Theme of Conversion in the Gospel of Mark: An Outline of the Gospel

aul's conversion is presented in stark black-and-white terms: he goes from killing Christians to converting people to Christ; he is changed from a zealous Pharisee into a zealous Christian. And all this happened in a flash: there is a vision, a single question, and his life is transformed.

But what about the Twelve?[1] They never hated Jesus and what he stood for (as did Paul). When Jesus calls them to become a part of his rabbinical band, they do so willingly, though this was an act undertaken at no small cost to them, since it necessitated turning their backs on occupation and family. When these twelve men joined Jesus' band, they were not notorious sinners in need of radical moral transformation. As far as one can tell, they were for the most part quite conventional both in terms of religious belief and lifestyle.[2]

---

1. The terms "the Twelve" and "the disciples" will be used interchangeably, both referring to the small band of men who had been called by Jesus to be "apostles." Of course, Jesus had other "disciples," but the context will make clear when this term is used to refer to those other than the Twelve. The issues relating to the identity of the Twelve and to the question of whether "disciples," "the Twelve," and "apostles" refer to the same group or different groups will be discussed in chap. 8.

2. Of course, what we know about the Twelve is what has been recorded in the narratives. And what we know is not great. Who knows what has been left out of the record? Perhaps there were "notorious sinners" within this group. Certainly it was an interesting group. The mix of Matthew the tax collector and Simon the Zealot alone would have created a fascinating dynamic. In any case, the Twelve are not presented in the text as anything other than "ordinary" people, and this sets them apart from Paul, who was by anyone's reckoning an extraordinary person.

They were not out hunting down people in the name of God, as Paul had done. And furthermore, whatever change took place in their lives happened over time. It was not instantaneous, and it was not complete during the period of time they spent with Jesus. In fact, although Jesus spent an extended length of time with the disciples,[3] patiently teaching them by word and deed, they repeatedly failed to grasp what he was trying to communicate. However, in the end they are transformed — as radically as Paul had been. One need only look at the disciples as portrayed in the Gospels and the disciples as portrayed in Acts to see the difference. They have been changed from frightened men, in hiding from the abductors of Jesus, to bold, public witnesses of his resurrection.[4] How did this happen? What went into their "conversion"? Can their experience even be called "conversion," or was some other process at work? What were the elements that combined together to produce this change? What is the nature of their transformation? And where does one find information about how this "conversion" took place in the lives of the Twelve?

The thesis of Part II of this book is that what happened to the Twelve can indeed be called "conversion" in the full New Testament sense. It is certainly conversion in the strict lexical sense of the word, and even more importantly, it is conversion in that it bears the same three core characteristics found in Paul's conversion. However, the *dynamics of their conversion* were quite different in comparison to the experience of Paul. The main difference is that what was an *event* for St. Paul is described by Mark as a *process* for the Twelve. It took the Twelve a long time to "see" their true states before God and to understand who Jesus really was, whereas it took only one question to reveal to Paul his state before God and one response for him to understand who Jesus was. It took the Twelve a long time to turn fully to Jesus. If Paul's turning took place in a flash, theirs took place in fits and starts over the course of their years with Jesus. It took a long time for the Twelve to understand what Jesus was saying about true discipleship, whereas Paul's transformation was immediate. But what happened to the Twelve bears the same fundamental marks of New Testament conversion as found in the prototype of St. Paul. It just happened in a different way. As such, the conversion of the Twelve offers another model for how conversion can come about, one that has the potential to alter the way in which the church goes about its ministry of evangelism.

It is also the thesis of Part II that the Gospel of Mark recounts the

---

3. Taking all the Gospels into account, this was probably three years.

4. For example, compare the Peter who refuses to own up to his allegiance to Jesus before a servant girl (Mark 14:66-72) and the Peter who boldly preaches the resurrected Christ right in the heart of Jerusalem (Acts 2:14ff.; 3) and openly confronts the religious leaders (Acts 4:1-22).

story of the conversion of the Twelve. *It will be argued that the conversion of the Twelve is a major theme in the Gospel of Mark and, in fact, the organizing principle by which Mark structures his Gospel.* What a reader finds in the Gospel of Mark is the story of how the Twelve moved step-by-step from their limited, culturally based assumptions about Jesus to a full theological understanding of who Jesus actually was. In the course of this six-step process of turning, they learn about repentance, faith, and transformation, i.e., conversion. It is thus necessary to examine the Gospel of Mark with some care in order to determine whether it is, as claimed, the intention of the author to relate the conversion of the Twelve. In this chapter a comprehensive outline will be developed which describes the structure of the Gospel of Mark from this perspective. In subsequent chapters this outline will be defended.

A word is necessary as to how the Gospel of Mark will be treated in this analysis. Form criticism and (especially) redaction criticism have undoubtedly produced valuable insights into Mark. They have, however, tended to so dissect the Gospel that in the end one is left with a rather "clumsy compilation" (to use W. Harrington's phrase) of certain first-century stories about Jesus rather than a complete manuscript with its own integrity. "Preoccupation with the pre-Gospel units of tradition and with the editorial modification of those units obscured the fact that Mark is a continuous narrative presenting a meaningful development to a climax and that each episode should be understood in light of its relations to the story as a whole."[5] However, when the text is discussed using biblical literary criticism as the approach, the focus shifts from a preoccupation with the pieces of Mark to a consideration of the whole of the composition. This approach has the effect of putting Mark back together, with the result that it is now being recognized for the fine piece of work that it is.[6]

> Once we have accepted that a gospel is a book and an evangelist is an author, remarkable things begin to happen — remarkable only because we have faced the obvious. We had tended to regard a gospel as a string of passages. We had been mesmerized by the analysis of the form-critics and had grown accustomed to a synoptic study: constantly comparing two or more

---

5. Robert C. Tannehill, "Tension in Synoptic Sayings and Stories," *Interpretation* 34 (1980): 148, quoted in Augustine Stock, *Call to Discipleship: A Literary Study of Mark's Gospel* (Dublin: Veritas Publications, 1982), p. 12.

6. For example, David Rhoads and Donald Michie, *Mark as Story: An Introduction to the Narrative of a Gospel* (Philadelphia: Fortress, 1982).

parallel passages. Once the gospel is taken as a literary whole it appears in a refreshingly new light.

Viewed this way, the second gospel takes on further depth and meaning. Mark is recognized as a writer who had written purposefully and planned his writing with care. He had, of course, made extensive use of traditional material because he wrote for a community with a firm Christian tradition. But he knew what he was about and he exploited his sources with notable freedom and with skill. He has written our gospel: a literary work and a document of sterling theological worth.[7]

Harrington captures precisely the attitude taken in this book toward the Gospel of Mark. Mark is considered to be a writer of great skill who put together traditional materials in a unique way so as not only to tell the story of Jesus but to communicate to his readers the meaning of this story.[8] Mark did all this in a thoughtful, structured way. He carefully lays one pericope alongside another so that, taken together, they say more than either pericope says alone. Mark has particular themes that he wants to communicate and an outline that guides his construction of the Gospel.

In this chapter the Gospel of Mark will be examined as a whole. Broad patterns are considered rather than details of the text, except where these reveal or demonstrate the larger patterns. The Gospel is analyzed on its own terms, without comparison to the other synoptic Gospels or other parts of the Bible, except where such comparison elucidates what Mark is saying.[9] The aim is to understand how Mark tells the story of Jesus.

So, when the experience of the Twelve is discussed, it will be from the vantage point of the original readers of the Gospel of Mark. Thus such themes as "the unfolding conversion of the Twelve" will be written about as if this were a single experience for all Twelve because this is how Mark presents the material. Of course, in reality each of the Twelve would have had a different (though

---

7. Wilfrid Harrington, foreword to *Call to Discipleship*, by Augustine Stock, pp. 7-8.

8. There is strong evidence that John Mark, the son of Mary (Acts 12:12), is the author of the Second Gospel. See William L. Lane, *The Gospel according to Mark* (Grand Rapids: Wm. B. Eerdmans Publishing Co., 1974), pp. 7-12. However, for the sake of this discussion it is not important that the author be fully identified. The issue in question is how this particular author (be he John Mark, some other Mark, or an unknown person) presents the story of Jesus. It is useful, however, to be able to name a person rather than referring constantly to "the author of this Gospel," and so for compositional purposes I have chosen to refer to "Mark" as author.

9. "In reading Mark one must refrain from injecting Matthean, Lukan, or Johannine elements into his Gospel. Mark deserves to be read on his own terms." Werner H. Kelber, *Mark's Story of Jesus* (Philadelphia: Fortress, 1979), p. 11.

common) experience of Jesus. They would not have walked lockstep together, even though Mark might write as if this were the case.[10] For example, at the end of Mark's account Judas is not convinced by, or at least he is not satisfied with, the path Jesus is taking. He takes events into his own hands. Up to this point in Mark Judas has been invisible, one of the Twelve whose individual experience is written of as if it were the same for all. Clearly this was not the case.

Likewise, the Twelve will be spoken of as walking on a path of discovery so that first they find out that Jesus is not just a teacher but also a prophet. Next they discover that Jesus is the Messiah, and so on, until they confront each of the six titles used by Mark for Jesus. This language will be used because it is the language of Mark and the experience of his readers as they follow his account. But other Gospels, written from different vantage points and for different purposes, do not make such careful distinctions. For example, in the first chapter of the Gospel of John, certain of the Twelve seem fully aware of who Jesus is right from the beginning. In that account John the Baptist declares quite openly that Jesus is the Lamb of God who will take away the sin of the world (John 1:29). He then calls Jesus the Son of God (1:34). No mystery here; no confusion of identity. The next day John the Baptist is standing with two of his disciples, one of whom turns out to be Andrew, who later became one of the Twelve (1:35, 40). Andrew hears the Baptist call Jesus "the Lamb of God" (1:36). He then fetches Peter (another of the Twelve), telling him that "We have found the Messiah" (1:41). No attempt will be made to assess these differing accounts, since the focus of the book is on Mark and his story.[11]

But it must also be pointed out that Mark's Gospel, according to most scholars, is the earliest of the four Gospels. As such it must be accorded great respect when it comes to understanding what went on in the lives of the Twelve. Furthermore, it is the Gospel most concerned about the experience of the Twelve. And certainly, when one reflects on the profound changes that went on in their lives, Mark's account rings true. Certainly they needed time

---

10. Clearly Mark was involved in making editorial decisions all along the way. The sheer limitation of space meant that he could not include all that took place in the lives of each of the Twelve. In the same way that a pericope is a condensation of an event that captures the central truth of that event, so too the whole book of Mark is a condensation of the experience of each of the Twelve in a way that expresses the truth of their experience. However, in all this the experience of the reader must be kept central. Mark is writing for his readers, and we need to hear the story through their ears. Likewise, that story will be expressed in terms of what they would have heard.

11. There is a whole genre of literature which examines and compares the material in the four Gospels. To explore this voluminous material is well beyond the scope of this book.

to grasp the significance of each title that described who Jesus was. After all, Jesus was unique. He broke all the old categories. So it stands to reason that it took time to grasp who he was. The Twelve underwent a profound paradigm shift. In the end, the only point that needs to be made is that Mark has chosen to write an account of Jesus for evangelistic purposes from the vantage point of the Twelve, with the hope that his readers will follow this same path of discovery as the Twelve and so become, like them, disciples of Jesus.

It should also be noted that although at first glance Mark appears to be a simple, straightforward account of the life of Jesus, it is in fact a highly complex piece of writing.[12] Part of its genius is that it reads so easily while at the same time developing several major themes. In addition, subthemes weave in and out — punctuating certain points, amplifying others, providing a foil to still others, and always enriching the whole. An in-depth look at the Gospel of Mark leaves the reader with the sense that it is like a symphony with theme and subtheme interacting to create complex resonances that make the whole so much greater than any of the parts. There is a richness to Mark that defies full analysis.[13]

The Structure of Mark's Gospel

Themes in Mark

It is clear that Mark wrote his Gospel with a purpose in mind.[14] Just what that purpose might be has been the subject of much research. In fact, as H. C. Kee

12. Ralph Martin, *Mark: Evangelist and Theologian* (Grand Rapids: Zondervan, 1973), states this view well: "[The Gospel of Mark's] language is clear, its narrative of Jesus' life swift-flowing and entertaining, and its appeal to the non-theological mind is direct. The inference is that all readers appreciate a biography simply told. Mark's Gospel is a good story, told with an economy of words and a forthrightness of style." Martin then points out that to this popular picture of Mark as a simple story must be added the fact that interwoven with the story of this "simple Galilean peasant-teacher" is also the story of the enigmatic Son of God, who is, at times, quite mysterious and who acts as if he is the king of Israel (pp. 11-12).

13. As a result, there is not yet consensus as to the structure of Mark's Gospel. The explosion of Marcan studies since the 1980s has uncovered the variety of themes found in the Gospel, but scholarship has yet to identify adequately the structure that unifies these various themes. William L. Lane, "The Present State of Markan Studies" (unpublished article, 1988), p. 1.

14. The work of form criticism made this evident. The question is: "According to what kind of plan did Mark assemble his pre-canonical material and fit it together into what we know as his gospel?" Martin, p. 85.

comments: "The history of recent research on the Gospel of Mark can be seen as the record of an attempt to discern the aim of the Evangelist and so to discover the perspective which gives coherence to all the features of the Second Gospel."[15] However, as R. T. France rightly cautions, the search for a single purpose might be misguided. Few authors (ancient or modern) have one controlling aim.[16] It is more realistic to note the various themes that are interwoven into a single work. And indeed, it is clear that Mark had a variety of aims in writing his Gospel. For example, the centrality of the passion to the Gospel of Mark has been noted by a number of scholars. P. Achtemeier states: "The hermeneutical key Mark chose was the passion of Jesus, his death and resurrection."[17] As M. Kähler declared in his now famous footnote: the Gospels should be called "passion narratives with extended introductions."[18] In his seminal study, W. Wrede identified the so-called messianic secret and the importance it plays in the revelation of Jesus' identity in Mark.[19] Both R. Meye and V. Robbins have pointed out the importance in Mark of the theme of Jesus as teacher.[20] Quentin Quesnell finds the Eucharist to be the interpretive key to Mark.[21] Don Juel thinks the declaration that Jesus is king is central to understanding the Gospel.[22] W. G. Kümmel concludes: "A clear explanation of the aim of the evangelist has not yet been elicited from the text."[23]

15. Howard Clark Kee, "Mark's Gospel in Recent Research," *Interpretation* 32 (October 1978): 353. In this article Kee identifies many of the attempts to identify the central purpose of Mark from Johannes Weiss in 1892 onwards.

16. R. T. France, "Mark and the Teaching of Jesus," in *Gospel Perspectives: Studies of History and Tradition in the Four Gospels*, ed. R. T. France and David Wenham, vol. 1 (Sheffield: University of Sheffield, 1980), p. 101.

17. Paul Achtemeier, "Mark as Interpreter of the Jesus Traditions," *Interpretation* 32 (October 1978): 340.

18. Martin Kähler, *The So-Called Historical Jesus and the Historic, Biblical Christ*, trans. Carl E. Braaten (Philadelphia: Fortress, 1964), p. 80 n. 11.

19. W. Wrede, *The Messianic Secret*, trans. J. C. G. Greig (Greenwood, S.C.: Attic Press, 1971).

20. Robert P. Meye, *Jesus and the Twelve: Discipleship and Revelation in Mark's Gospel* (Grand Rapids: Wm. B. Eerdmans Publishing Co., 1968), and V. K. Robbins, *Jesus the Teacher: A Socio-Rhetorical Interpretation of Mark* (Philadelphia: Fortress, 1984).

21. Quentin Quesnell, *The Mind of Mark: Interpretation and Method through the Exegesis of Mark 6:52*, Analecta Biblica 38 (Rome: Pontifical Biblical Institute, 1969).

22. Donald Juel, *Messiah and Temple: The Trial of Jesus in the Gospel of Mark*, SBL Dissertation Series 31 (Missoula, Mont.: Scholars Press, 1977).

23. W. G. Kümmel, *Introduction to the New Testament*, trans. Howard C. Kee (Nashville: Abingdon, 1975), p. 92, quoted in Kee, p. 355. The above material on Quesnell and Juel is found in Kee, pp. 356-58. The question of the theme of the Gospel is connected to the question of the organizing principle by which the Gospel is structured.

This book proposes that the theme which plays the controlling part in the unfolding of the Gospel of Mark is the conversion of the Twelve. As has been shown, Christian conversion involves, at its center, an encounter with Jesus. But to encounter Jesus, one must know Jesus for who he truly is. Mark tells the step-by-step story of how the disciples come to understand who Jesus actually is. This is the primary organizing theme for the Gospel. So the central focus of the Second Gospel is on the *turning* aspect of conversion. It describes the slow, step-by-step turning of the Twelve *from* a misunderstanding of Jesus *to* a full and radical new understanding of who he is.

Yet, it is not enough simply to know who Jesus is. Conversion involves responding to Jesus. Thus Mark traces, on a secondary level, the themes of repentance, faith, and discipleship. Taken together, Mark's emphasis on responding properly to Jesus (the process of repentance and faith), on Christology (who Jesus is), and on discipleship (how to follow him) adds up to a discussion of conversion. Although what is proposed here is a new way of looking at the Gospel of Mark, this view builds upon two theological themes that have long been recognized as central to the Gospel: Christology and discipleship.[24] These two themes are essential aspects of conversion, which is the larger, controlling aim.

In other words, Mark portrays the disciples coming, over time, to understand the unique nature of Jesus. "Jesus himself is the parable whose meaning the disciples have been brought to understand through his [Jesus'] own patient, didactic ministry to them."[25] Specifically, Mark shows them moving from a cultural view of Jesus (he is a teacher) to a complete view of Jesus (he is the Messiah, the Son of God). This is repentance in the broad sense of the word (changing one's mind about religious truth). The reader sees the disciples moving from little insight into Jesus to full insight into him. Their minds are changed. Their views have turned around.

It is important to note that Mark does not treat conversion as a theoretical subject in his Gospel. Instead, he shows it happening. His readers watch the disciples turning around in their views of Jesus and in their understanding of themselves. They watch them grow in faith. They watch them wrestle with the question of discipleship. The readers come to understand the character of conversion as a result of the case study that Mark has presented focusing on the Twelve.

24. "The central theological concerns in Mark are the identity of Jesus (Christology) and the appropriate response to Jesus (discipleship)." Daniel J. Harrington, "A Map of Books on Mark (1975-1984)," *Biblical Theology Bulletin* 15 (January 1985): 14. See also Jack Dean Kingsbury, *The Christology of Mark's Gospel* (Philadelphia: Fortress, 1983), p. ix.

25. Meye, p. 103.

A Thematic Outline of the Gospel of Mark

Various Outlines of Mark

Recent New Testament scholarship has concerned itself with the question of how Mark arranged the various materials available to him (the oral tradition about Jesus as preserved by his followers) into a coherent account.[26] That Mark did indeed play the role of editor (as against creator) of the materials is clear.[27] What is not clear is just what selection process he used in his role as redactor. Why did he include one pericope and exclude others? What guided the way in which he set one pericope alongside another? "Virtually every literary document has a formal structure that is a planned framework, and the framework is likely to provide a clue to the interrelation of forms in the document."[28] The aim, therefore, is to uncover the outline Mark has for his Gospel.

Various proposals have been made as to how Mark organized the Gospel. P. Carrington argues that Mark followed a calendar known in the early church. A. M. Farrer says he was "artistically governed by Old Testament examples of typology and prefigurations." J. Bowman suggests that Mark "wished to compose his gospel as a Christianized version of the Passover *haggadah* in the Jewish festival." And G. Schille thinks Mark "sought to convey through a dramatized 'life of Jesus' the steps of catechetical instruction and training for new converts on the road to church membership."[29]

A. Stock feels that Mark was consciously following the forms of Greek drama.[30] V. K. Robbins asserts that "the three-step progressions that cover two or three pericopes form interludes in the narrative that establish the basic outline for the Marcan narrative."[31] J. Donahue argues that the Gospel of Mark is actually a narrative parable of the meaning of the life and death of Jesus.[32] C. Faw uses four stylistic characteristics to derive his out-

---

26. Laurence F. X. Brett, "Suggestions for an Analysis of Mark's Arrangement," in *Mark: A New Translation with Introduction and Commentary,* by C. S. Mann (Garden City, N.Y.: Doubleday, 1986), p. 174.

27. France, pp. 124-26.

28. Robbins, *Jesus the Teacher,* p. 19.

29. Martin, p. 85.

30. Augustine Stock, *Call to Discipleship: A Literary Study of Mark's Gospel* (Dublin: Veritas Publications, 1982). See chap. 3 especially, pp. 24ff.

31. Vernon K. Robbins, "Summons and Outline in Mark: The Three-Step Progression," *Novum Testamentum* 23 (April 1981): 98. See also Robbins's book *Jesus the Teacher,* in which he expands upon the argument in his earlier paper.

32. John R. Donahue, "Jesus as the Parable of God in the Gospel of Mark," *Interpretation* 32 (October 1978): 369-85.

line.[33] D. Hawkins argues that the recognition of the symbolism in Mark is the key to understanding the outline of the Gospel. He produces a useful outline around the idea of the revelation of "the mysterious person of Jesus."[34] Laurence Brett uses ten compositional categories by which he derives an outline of Mark.[35] Dame Helen Gardner understands Mark as a poem: "By the time we have read through the Gospel of St. Mark nothing has been proved, and we have not acquired a stock of verifiable information of which we can make practical use. In that sense reading the Gospel is like reading a poem. It is an imaginative experience. It presents us with a sequence of events and sayings which combine to create in our minds a single complex and powerful symbol, a pattern of meaning."[36]

Despite this plethora of proposals and their different viewpoints, some of Mark's organizing principles are readily evident. It is clear, for example, that geography plays an outlining role. Following his preparation for ministry in Judea (Mark 1:1-13), Jesus then ministers in and around Galilee (1:14–9:50). Mark 10 traces his movement from Galilee through the region of Perea toward Jerusalem. The rest of the story is set in Jerusalem (chaps. 11–16).[37] It is also clear that chronology is *not* a key organizing principle (as might be expected from a Western, sequential point of view). The sequence of events in time is of only secondary interest to Mark. While Mark organizes certain sec-

33. Chalmer E. Faw, "The Outline of Mark," *Journal of Bible and Religion* 25 (1957): 19-23.

34. David J. Hawkins, "The Symbolism and Structure of the Marcan Redaction," *Evangelical Quarterly* 49 (1977): 109-110.

35. Brett, pp. 174-90.

36. Helen Gardner, "The Poetry of St. Mark," in *The Business of Criticism* (Oxford: Clarendon Press, 1959), p. 102.

37. "Geographically, the remainder of the book [following the prologue] falls into two clearly marked divisions, of almost equal length; first, the Lord's work in northern Palestine: this is described in chapters 1 to 9; and secondly, His work in and near Jerusalem; this is described in chapters 11 to 16. These two chief divisions of the book are joined together by chapter 10, which contains incidents and conversations placed between the departure from Galilee and the arrival at the capital, Jerusalem. . . ." R. H. Lightfoot, *The Gospel Message of St. Mark* (London: Oxford University Press, 1950), p. 9.

W. Kelber goes beyond this broad outline of the movements of Jesus and suggests that Mark's Gospel can be viewed as a dramatically plotted journey of Jesus. He says: "Throughout the Gospel Jesus is depicted as being in movement from one place to another. He journeys through Galilee, undertakes six boat trips on and across the Lake of Galilee, travels from Galilee to Jerusalem, makes three trips into the temple, and toward the end signals the return to Galilee" (p. 9). In other words, he is suggesting that geography provides the structure for Mark not only in broad terms but in the organization of smaller units.

tions of the Gospel around the unfolding chronology of the events (e.g., 14:1–16:8), in other places this is clearly not the case (e.g., 2:1–3:6).

However, despite all the work that has been done on this issue, there is still no clear answer to the question of structure. "The studies to date . . . have yet to reveal an overall schema to the entire gospel, while each attempt to uncover a unifying pattern has added to our insights."[38] The outline in this chapter is one more attempt at discerning how Mark has structured his Gospel.[39]

The argument for this particular outline will be presented as follows. First, in this chapter a series of comments will be made on each of the proposed six units (plus the prologue and epilogue)[40] that make up the Gospel of Mark.[41] The aim of these comments is to identify (1) the title by which the Twelve come to understand Jesus in each unit and (2) the aspect of conversion which is singled out for discussion in each unit. This chapter will conclude with a detailed outline for Mark that is derived from this line of reasoning.

The validity of this outline will be defended on structural grounds in chapter 6. This will be done in four ways: (1) by showing that each unit has an independent literary structure that consciously sets it apart from the other units; (2) by showing that each of the proposed transition points between units bears similar stylistic characteristics indicating that it was Mark's intention to shift at that point to a new topic; (3) by showing that Mark has bracketed each unit so as to identify it as a unit of material that is to be interpreted together; and (4) by showing that Mark carefully uses the titles for Jesus so

---

38. Brett, p. 174.

39. A variety of outlines have been suggested for the Gospel of Mark. See, for example, the outline of E. Schweizer in "The Portrayal of the Life of Faith in the Gospel of Mark," *Interpretation* 32 (October 1978): 388-89; Norman Perrin, "Towards an Interpretation of the Gospel of Mark," in *Christology and a Modern Pilgrimage: A Discussion with Norman Perrin,* ed. Hans Dieter Betz (n.p.: Society of Biblical Literature, 1971), pp. 3-6; and Laurence F. X. Brett, "Suggestions for an Analysis of Mark's Arrangement." While it would be possible to interact point by point with these outlines (and others like them), the approach in this book is to present an original outline with arguments for it so that it can be judged on its own merits. The book is not about the structure of Mark per se. Structure is discussed as part of the argument that conversion is of controlling concern to Mark, hence what we have in Mark is a second paradigm for conversion to set alongside the paradigm inherent in Paul's Damascus road experience.

40. V. K. Robbins, using what he calls "three-step progressions," arrives at an outline of Mark that has six major units along with an introduction and a conclusion. However, his divisions are different from the ones proposed here. See *Jesus the Teacher,* p. 27, and pp. 151-55 below for a discussion of Robbins's outline.

41. The following terminology will be used in discussing the outline of Mark's Gospel. The Gospel is divided into two *parts;* these parts are subdivided into six *units;* these units consist of various *sections;* each section is made up of one or more *pericopae.*

that no title is used by "the people" until the unit in which Jesus is revealed to possess that title.

In chapters 7 and 8 the assertion that a new facet of Jesus is revealed in each unit will be discussed and defended in detail. In chapters 9 and 10 the assertion that aspects of conversion provide subthemes in the units will be discussed and defended in detail.

The Two Parts of Mark's Gospel

The opening statement in the Gospel of Mark defines its overall outline: "The beginning of the good news of Jesus Christ, the Son of God." Mark will seek to communicate two main things to his readers: that Jesus is the Messiah (Christ) and that he is also the Son of God. Accordingly, Mark has divided his account into two halves. The first half (which runs from 1:16 to 8:30) culminates in the affirmation by Peter that "You are the *Messiah*" (8:29, italics mine). And the second half (which runs from 8:31 to 15:39) culminates in the affirmation by the centurion that "Surely this man was the *Son of God!*" (15:39 NIV, italics mine).[42] Each half of the Gospel consists of three units (for a total of six units). Each unit is organized around a different title for Jesus. The first half of the Gospel is prefaced by a brief prologue announcing the purpose of the Gospel, while the second half is followed by a brief epilogue which sends the disciples back to Galilee to meet the risen Lord. Mark's main concern (which he expresses in the body of his Gospel) is to convey the good news of Jesus' identity: he is the long-expected Messiah who is the Son of God. The discovery that these two titles define who Jesus is comes primarily through the eyes of the Twelve.

The Prologue

The theme of conversion is introduced immediately by Mark in the prologue (1:1-15) through the choice of terms used, through the words that are repeated, and through the themes that are sounded. The key words in 1:1-15 include "gospel" (good news), "baptism," "repentance," "faith," "kingdom of God," and "Spirit." Each of these terms is related to the idea of conversion. Furthermore, this theme of conversion comes to the forefront in the final two verses of the prologue, in which Mark defines the nature of Jesus' ministry:

42. Rhoads and Michie, pp. 48-49.

"Jesus came to Galilee, proclaiming the *good news* of God, and saying, 'The time is fulfilled, and the *kingdom of God* has come near; *repent,* and believe in the *good news*'" (1:14-15, italics mine). These two verses are programmatic in nature and identify in overview how Mark understands the ministry of Jesus. The language Mark uses in these two verses is the same language used by the first-century church to describe the task of evangelism ("proclaim," "good news" [twice], "repentance," and "faith"). In other words, right from the beginning Mark makes it clear that he will describe the evangelistic activity of Jesus. Jesus is calling for the response of repentance and faith to the good news about the coming kingdom of God. The New Testament equation is that repentance plus faith results in conversion. And indeed, the first act of ministry in the Gospel of Mark involves the selection of four disciples. Jesus immediately engages in calling people into the kingdom.[43]

The Focus of Part I

Part I of the Gospel (1:16–8:30) consists of three major units, each of which focuses on a particular title for Jesus: *teacher* in unit one, *prophet* in unit two, and *Messiah* in unit three. In Part I, therefore, the Twelve move from a contemporary Jewish understanding of who Jesus is (unit one), to a more hopeful and Old Testament view of who he might be (unit two), and end with an accurate (if misunderstood) view of who he actually is (unit three).

Each unit contains at least one passage in particular that identifies clearly the aspect of Jesus that is in focus. In terms of subthemes, in unit one Mark identifies the range of potential responses to Jesus. In unit two Mark discusses the nature of faith, while in unit three Mark discusses the need for repentance (repentance and faith being aspects of this response to Jesus). Each of these subthemes bears directly on the subject of conversion.

43. The assertion has been made, on thematic grounds, that the prologue encompasses 1:1-15. This is not, however, the majority view according to Leander E. Keck, "The Introduction to Mark's Gospel," *New Testament Studies* 12 (1966): 352: "It is widely assumed that Mark's introduction consists of 1:1-13 and that these verses 'introduce' what Mark has to say." Keck has analyzed the conclusions of five scholars who argue for this perspective. He asks: "Does the argument *require* us to view 1:1-13 as the introduction, and do the data on which it is based *permit* us to view 1:1-15 as the introduction instead?" (p. 353). His conclusion is: "The wide-ranging topics and range of material examined support the contention that there is nothing that prevents us from holding, and much that persuades us to believe, that the real introduction of Mark is 1:1-15, and for regarding this entire paragraph as the 'Prologue' to the entire work" (p. 368).

Unit One: Jesus the Teacher[44]

In unit one (1:16–4:34) Mark shows how the disciples initially viewed Jesus. When they first join his band as disciples, it seems clear to them that Jesus is simply a great teacher. The material in 1:16–4:34 provides the baseline view of Jesus, shared by people in general. The title "teacher" is revealed most clearly in 1:22, 27, where Jesus' teaching is singled out as a cause for amazement, and in 4:1-34, in which he is shown in his role as teacher.

In unit one Mark also discusses the range of possible responses to Jesus. He identifies the desired response and sets it in contrast to three inadequate responses. Mark shows that the desired response to Jesus' proclamation of the good news of God (1:14) is that people embrace the word and produce a good crop (4:20). This is what conversion is: the embracing of the word.[45]

Unit Two: Jesus the Prophet

In unit two (4:35–6:30) this comfortable view of Jesus as a gifted teacher is disturbed by an unsettling incident on the Sea of Galilee in which Jesus reveals to his disciples that he has power over the wind and the waves (4:35-41). This incident is then followed by three more incidents, each of which shows that Jesus has power far in excess of what can be expected in a teacher. Jesus has power over chronic evil as he casts out not one but thousands of demons (5:1-20). Jesus can cure even chronic illnesses (5:24b-34). And Jesus even has power over death, which is revealed when he brings a young girl back to life (5:21-24a, 35-43). As a result of these four power incidents, the disciples come to realize that Jesus is no mere teacher. In fact, the title that suits him better is "prophet." And indeed, in the very next pericope Jesus uses the title "prophet" in reference to himself (in 6:4, the only time he does so in the Gospel of Mark). Then in 6:14-15 Mark connects the idea of power to the title of prophet as King Herod muses about the identity of Jesus: "Some were saying, 'John the baptizer has been raised from the dead; and *for this reason these powers are at work in him.'* But others said, 'It is Elijah.' And others said, *'It is a prophet, like one of the prophets of old'*" (italics mine). Since it is the disciples who have witnessed each act of power in this unit, it is fair to say that this as-

---

44. The assertion that unit one portrays Jesus as a teacher will be argued in some detail in chap. 7, as will the assertions made about how he is portrayed in units two and three.

45. The assertion that the subtheme in unit one deals with responses to Jesus and that this theme bears on the larger topic of conversion will be argued in some detail in chap. 9, as will the assertions made about the conversion themes in units two and three.

sertion about how people in general view Jesus corresponds to their own revised view of him.

An important subtheme runs through most of unit two: What is the nature of faith? Jesus raises the question in the first pericope: "Why are you
afraid? Have you still no faith?" (4:40). In the third and fourth pericopae, faith
is a central issue. Jesus asserts that it is the faith of the woman that healed her
(5:34), and he encourages Jairus, the synagogue leader, to have faith when
news reaches him that his daughter has died (5:36). In the fifth pericope it is
the lack of faith of the people of Nazareth that is discussed (6:6), while in the
sixth pericope the faith of the disciples is seen via their willingness to go out
and minister even though they are not allowed to take much of anything with
them. So it is clear that faith is a key issue in unit two. And of course, faith is a
key component in conversion. Without faith a person cannot (or will not)
turn to Jesus.

Unit Three: Jesus the Messiah

In unit three (6:31–8:30), by means of metaphor, it is revealed to the Twelve
that Jesus is, in actual fact, not just a teacher and a prophet but the Messiah.
In the same way that the deaf and dumb man (7:32-37) and the blind man are
healed (8:22-26), so too are the disciples. Their eyes, ears, and tongues are
opened, and they discover that Jesus is the Messiah. The climax of the unit is
the confession at Caesarea Philippi that this is who they know Jesus to be
(8:27-30).[46] The understanding of the disciples about who Jesus is has moved
forward another notch.

An important subtheme runs through most of this section as well: the
need for repentance. The disciples need to turn around in their views of Jesus.
They simply do not grasp what his actions reveal about who he is. They see
but they do not understand. They hear but they do not comprehend. Jesus
points this out in 8:17-21. They have failed altogether to grasp the meaning of
the two feedings which reveal him as the Messiah. It requires a healing touch
from the Lord in order for insight to come that allows them to turn around in
their views. This lack of understanding is traced to hardness of heart (6:52;
8:17) and extends to the disciples' own awareness of who they are. They are in
danger of becoming like the Pharisees, who follow the traditions of men

---

46. "It hardly needs to be proved again that Caesarea Philippi stands as a central and
pivotal event in the Marcan narrative. What is important at this point is the fact that it
comes as a climax to the three sea crossings, the latter two of which stand as a clear sequel
to two occasions during which Jesus works the great miracle of feeding the multitude."
Meye, p. 71.

rather than the commands of God (7:8), unless they understand their own hardness of heart and repent. Repentance is not possible without insight. In the previous unit Jesus challenged them about their lack of faith (4:40); in this unit he challenges them about their need for repentance (8:17b-21). Repentance and faith are the two necessary components if they are to turn to Jesus and so be converted. Units two and three make clear that the disciples have not yet reached the point of conversion. They are still in process.

The Focus of Part II

Part II of the Gospel of Mark (8:31–15:39) also consists of three major units in which the disciples discover what kind of Messiah Jesus is. They discover, in turn, that he is the *Son of Man* who gives his life for the many; the *Son of David*, the messianic king; and the *Son of God*. This discovery concludes Part II of Mark's Gospel. Part II moves from Jesus' prediction of what lies ahead (unit four), to his deliberate triggering of the events he predicted (unit five), and ends with the events themselves (unit six) — each unit revealing a different facet of his messiahship. Again, all this is seen primarily through the eyes of the Twelve.

Once again, in each unit at least one passage in particular identifies clearly the aspect of Jesus that is in focus. In terms of subthemes, in unit four the disciples learn about the nature of discipleship (as well as about their own personal failures). In units five and six the disciples are mainly observers of the events in the final week of Jesus' life (and so receive the rest of the information they need in order to respond fully to him). But from these events they come to see their own lack of commitment to Jesus, which is the basis from which their own repentance comes.

Unit Four: Jesus the Son of Man[47]

In unit four (8:31–10:45) there are four cycles of stories. Each cycle contains three elements: (1) a prediction by Jesus that he will suffer, die, and rise again; (2) some failure on the part of the disciples that reveals their lack of understanding; and (3) teaching by Jesus in the light of this failure on the subject of discipleship. The prediction component provides new insight into who Jesus

47. The assertion that in unit four Jesus is presented as the Son of Man will be argued in some detail in chap. 8, as well as the assertions about how he is presented in units five and six.

is; the misunderstanding section provides new insight for the disciples into themselves; and the teaching section provides new insight into the nature of discipleship. Each component, therefore, touches upon a key aspect of conversion. The first provides the information necessary for the next step in the growing understanding on the part of the Twelve as to who Jesus is. The second gives insight into the need of the disciples to repent and believe. And the third defines what it means to follow Jesus. The major feature of this unit, when it comes to conversion, is the teaching of Jesus about discipleship.[48] Discipleship and conversion are clearly connected. Conversion launches people into a life of discipleship. Christian conversion is the act of becoming a disciple of Jesus.

Unit Five: Jesus the Son of David

In unit five (10:46–13:37) the Twelve discover another important aspect about what it means to be the Messiah. The Messiah is not only the Son of Man who gives his life for the many (unit four), he is also the Son of David. He is the long-expected king who returns to judge those who have been left in charge of his kingdom but who have grown corrupt. Three pericopae reveal that the focus in this unit is on the title Son of David. In 10:46-52 blind Bartimaeus twice calls Jesus "Son of David" (the first time this title is used in Mark). In 11:1-10 explicit reference is made to the "coming kingdom of our ancestor David." And in 12:35-37 Jesus raises the question of how the Messiah can also be the Son of David.

This unit also deals with the question of repentance, an issue which is raised here via the accusations made by Jesus against the religious leaders. The disciples are confronted with men who have clearly corrupted their calling and yet, even when shown this, remain in their hardness of heart. Because they refuse to see or hear, they will be judged. The religious leaders are a negative example for the disciples. The Twelve have already been warned that they, too, show signs of this same hardness of heart (6:52; 7:17-21).

Unit Six: Jesus the Son of God

In unit six (14:1–15:39) there is a shift from Jesus as the one who judges to Jesus as the one being judged, from Jesus in control (he guides the events and triggers the responses) to Jesus being controlled (he is arrested, tried, killed).

---

48. The assertion that the subtheme in unit four is discipleship will be argued in detail in chap. 10, as will the assertions made about subthemes in units five and six.

As a result of his passion, however, the final insight into his true identity emerges. He is revealed to be the Son of God (15:39). In 14:61-62 Jesus confirms to the high priest that he is the Son of God ("the Son of the Blessed One"), and in 15:39 the unit ends with the declaration by the centurion that "Truly this man was God's Son!"

Here the theme of repentance (which has been developing from unit three) reaches its climax. In unit three the lack of understanding and the hardness of heart on the part of the disciples were noted. In unit four their blindness and their moral failure became evident. In unit five it was the sin of the religious leaders that was revealed — almost as a foil against which the disciples could see themselves. Here in unit six the failure of the disciples is complete. The three disciples closest to Jesus fall asleep when he asks them to keep watch with him in the Garden of Gethsemane (14:32-42). One of the disciples actually betrays Jesus (14:10-11, 17-21, 43-46). All of the disciples desert him (14:27, 50). Despite strenuous protestations to the contrary (14:29), even Peter denies Jesus (14:30-31, 66-71) by means of conscious, outright lies. That they have reached the bottom and started to turn around (in repentance over who they have discovered themselves to be) is seen in the tears of Peter (14:72). Once again, Peter functions in the role of representing the disciples.

The Epilogue

The epilogue (15:40–16:8) completes the story of Jesus and ties the whole book together. In terms of who Jesus is, the epilogue provides the final pieces of information that the disciples need in order to understand Jesus. Two important statements are made here. First, Jesus is buried. The fact of his burial (15:42-47) makes the point that Jesus was truly dead. Second, Jesus has risen (16:1-8). The fact of his resurrection means that he overcame death. He is, indeed, the Messiah, the Son of God. Knowing who he is makes it possible for the Twelve to complete their turning to him.[49]

In terms of the theme of conversion, the death and the resurrection of Jesus provides the paradigm for conversion. In the death and resurrection of Jesus the disciples see what must happen to them. They must die to sin (repent) and reach out to Jesus for new life (faith). It is this twofold movement that facilitates (and defines) conversion. The disciples knew about repentance already (even if they were blind to their own need to repent). John preached

---

49. The question of the "lost ending" will be touched upon in chap. 6.

this (1:4). Even they preached repentance (6:12). Now they learn where their faith is to be directed (to the resurrected Jesus who is the Messiah, the Son of God). This is what Mark's whole Gospel has been about: an amplification of his opening definition of Jesus' message: "The kingdom of God is near. Repent and believe the good news!" (1:15 NIV).

A Complete Outline of Mark's Gospel

What follows is an outline of Mark's Gospel based on the analysis that has just been described.[50] It takes into account the entire Gospel and seeks to fit together all the parts of the Gospel into a coherent whole.

Prologue: The preparation of Jesus for ministry (1:1-15)

    A. The focus of the Gospel (1:1)

    B. The forerunner: John the Baptist (1:2-8)

    C. The baptism and temptation of Jesus (1:9-13)

    D. The definition of Jesus' ministry (1:14-15)

Part I: The discovery that Jesus is the Messiah (1:16–8:30)

Unit One. *Jesus the teacher* (1:16–4:34)

    A. Those who are for him: the crowds (1:16-45)

    B. Those who are against him: the religious leaders (2:1–3:6)

    C. For and against Jesus: the range of reactions (3:7-35)

    D. The reactions explained: the parable of the four soils (4:1-34)

Unit Two. *Jesus the prophet* (4:35–6:30)

    A. His power over nature (4:35-41)

    B. His power over evil (5:1-20)

    C. His power over illness and death (5:21-43)

    D. Responses to his power (6:1-13)

        1. Negative: his childhood friends (6:1-6)

        2. Positive: his disciples (6:7-13, 30)

---

50. This outline, which is original, summarizes the analysis of Mark found in this chapter. Its viability is further demonstrated in chaps. 6 through 10.

E. Contrasts to his power (6:14-29)

Unit Three. *Jesus the Messiah* (6:31–8:30)

A. Cycle one: curing the deaf and dumb (6:31–7:37)

1. Feeding the five thousand: the situation (6:31-44)

2. Crossing the sea and landing (6:45-56)

3. Conflict with the Pharisees: their deafness (7:1-23)

4. Conversations about bread: a Gentile's insight (7:24-30)

5. Healing a deaf mute: Jesus' response (7:31-37)

B. Cycle two: curing the blind (8:1-26)

1. Feeding the four thousand: the situation (8:1-9a)

2. Crossing the sea and landing (8:9b-10)

3. Conflict with the Pharisees: their blindness (8:11-13)

4. Conversations about bread: the disciples' blindness (8:14-21)

5. Healing a blind man: Jesus' two-part cure (8:22-26)

C. Confessing him as Messiah (8:27-30)

Part II: The discovery that Jesus is the Son of God (8:31–15:39)

Unit Four. *Jesus the Son of Man* (8:31–10:45)

A. The first prediction (8:31–9:1)

B. The second prediction (9:2-29)

C. The third prediction (9:30–10:31)

D. The fourth prediction (10:32-45)

Unit Five. *Jesus the Son of David* (10:46–13:37)

A. Jesus acts: the Son of David comes to Jerusalem (10:46–11:26)

1. His identity declared: the healing of blind Bartimaeus (10:46-52)

2. His arrival takes place: the triumphal entry (11:1-11)

3. His judgment announced: the clearing of the temple (11:12-26)

B. The religious leaders react: the question of authority (11:27-33)

C. Jesus responds: parable of the tenants (12:1-12)

D. The religious leaders respond: three questions (12:13-34)

E. Jesus responds: the Son of David question (12:35-44)

F. Jesus summarizes: the coming judgment (13:1-37)

Unit Six. *Jesus the Son of God* (14:1–15:39)

A. The anointing at Bethany (14:1-11)

B. The Last Supper (14:12-31)

C. The Garden of Gethsemane (14:32-42)

D. The arrest (14:43-52)

E. The trial (14:53–15:20)

F. The crucifixion (15:21-39)

Epilogue: The conclusion of Jesus' ministry (15:40–16:8)

A. The burial (15:40-47)

B. The resurrection (16:1-8)

CHAPTER SIX

An Analysis of the Structure of Mark

I t has already been argued on the basis of theme that the outline in the previous chapter is an accurate reconstruction of Mark's intentions in writing his Gospel. Four additional considerations support this assertion: (1) each unit is organized in a way that is distinct, thus setting it apart from the other units from a structural point of view; (2) the transitions between the units are similar from a stylistic point of view, indicating that Mark was conscious that he was switching topics; (3) each unit is deliberately bracketed, indicating that the author was consciously packaging together material with a common theme; and (4) no title is used by "the people" prior to the unit in which Jesus is revealed to have such a title, showing that Mark intended that there be an unfolding understanding of Jesus.

The Organization of Each Unit

The first indication, from a structural point of view, that Mark is consciously dividing his material into six units (with a prologue and epilogue) is found in the way he organizes the material within each individual unit. The theme of each unit is different (as would be expected), but the structure of each unit is also different (which is not necessarily to be expected). By structuring each unit around a different organizing principle, each unit stands out from its neighbors.[1]

1. V. K. Robbins (whose six-point outline is the closest of any to the one proposed here) identifies the various divisions on the basis of three-step progressions of a specific

Unit one (1:16–4:34), for example, is organized around polarities: those who are for Jesus and those who are against him. Four responses on a spectrum between these two poles are identified and explained in this unit. In contrast, unit two (4:35–6:30) is organized around similarity and contrast. Four similar pericopae establish the fact of Jesus' power, then three contrasting responses to this power are given. Unit three (6:31–8:30) is organized completely differently from either of the two previous units. Here two parallel cycles of stories are used metaphorically. In unit four (8:31–10:45) the material is organized around the repetition of four predictions on Jesus' part that he will die and rise again; four examples of failure by the Twelve to understand this; and four sections of teaching by Jesus on discipleship. Unit five (10:46–13:37) is organized around the principle of action and reaction. Jesus acts; the religious leaders react; Jesus responds — and so the pattern is established. Unit six (14:1–15:39), in contrast to all the others, is the most strictly sequential of the units. It is organized chronologically around the unfolding events during the last week of Jesus' life. Finally, the prologue and the epilogue are alike structurally. Strong parallels between the two units mark them out as similar to one another in both function (one introduces, the other concludes) and theme (parallel concepts), and as different from all the other units.

These differing organizing principles mark out nicely the individual nature of each unit. What follows is a detailed examination of the structure of each unit that seeks to show that Mark was consciously and intentionally organizing the data in each unit in a unique way so as to set it apart from the others and thereby to assist the reader in following his unfolding argument about the nature of Jesus.

Unit One: Polarities

Unit one is organized around the concept of *polarities.* The issue in this unit is how people respond to Jesus: who is for Jesus and who is against Jesus. First Mark defines the one pole: the wildly enthusiastic crowds who are *for Jesus* without reservation (1:16-45). The language in this section shows the extravagance of this response. Next Mark defines the other pole (2:1–3:6): the dislike of Jesus on the part of the religious leaders who are *against Jesus.* Again

---

kind, as shown in the final section of this chapter. This book posits not *one* way of organizing units but *six:* each unit is structured in its own way so as to accomplish its individual goal.

this hatred is expressed in extreme terms (they want to kill Jesus; 3:6). Thus Mark defines the range within which response to Jesus will fall. Having done this, Mark then differentiates the response more carefully. It is not just a matter of loving Jesus uncritically or hating him unthinkingly. Four responses are noted in the next four pericopae (3:7-35): the self-interested enthusiasm of the crowds who want healing and exorcism (3:7-12) is contrasted to the disciples who now come out from the crowds and give Jesus a new level of commitment that moves beyond self-interest to service (3:13-19). In contrast to these two positive responses are two negative responses which Mark communicates via his first intercalated pericope (3:20-35).[2] By means of this literary device Mark makes it clear that the response from the two quite different sources (Jesus' family and the teachers of the law) is actually similar. Both oppose Jesus, both think he is possessed, both would have him withdraw from ministry. However, the family's response is much milder than that of the scribes. The family is worried that Jesus may be "out of his mind" (3:21), while the scribes conclude that Jesus is evil (3:22). Furthermore, the family's reaction arises out of concern for Jesus, while the scribes are deeply hostile to him. In this way Mark enlarges the spectrum of responses to Jesus. It now remains for Mark to interpret the meaning of these various responses in terms of the kingdom of God. This he does in the concluding section of unit one (4:1-34). In the parable of the sower (4:1-20), the four types of soil correspond to the four types of response to Jesus that have just been described. Thus it is clear that Mark has structured his first unit around a series of four responses which arrange themselves along a spectrum defined by two extreme positions.

Unit Two: Similarity/Contrast

Unit two is organized around the concept of similarity and contrast. The organizing theme is power. The unit begins with four similar stories that demonstrate that Jesus has power over those realities in life that most deeply afflict human beings: the elements, evil, chronic illness, and death (4:35–5:43). In each story the power of Jesus is able to overcome that which threatens the well-being of the people involved. The fact of Jesus' power is then set in sharp relief by means of two sets of contrast. In the first set Mark contrasts the re-

---

2. Mark uses this literary device a total of five times in his Gospel: 3:20-35; 5:21-43; 6:7-30; 11:12-25; and 14:1-11. It generally indicates that the two pericopae must be interpreted together somehow. The one amplifies the theme of the other.

sponse of people of Nazareth (6:1-6a) to Jesus' power (disbelief) with the response of the Twelve (6:6b-13) to that same power (the willingness to use it in their own ministry). The second set of contrasts is between the power of Jesus on the one hand and the power of Herod on the other hand (6:14-29). Thus it is that Mark arranges his second unit of material around two different types of contrast that relate to the fact of Jesus' power which he has established in the four parallel stories that begin unit two.

Unit Three: Metaphoric Cycles

Unit three is organized around two parallel cycles of stories which are used metaphorically. To demonstrate that this is the organizing principle of unit three, it is necessary to show, first, that the two sections are parallel, and second, that they are used in a metaphoric way.[3]

The parallelism is seen in the fact that both cycles of stories unfold in the same manner. In addition to the obvious fact that both cycles begin with a feeding and end with an unusual healing, careful observation shows an identical progression in between, as the following table (developed by Lane) demonstrates:[4]

Cycle One		Cycle Two
6:31-44	Feeding of the Multitude	8:1-9a
6:45-56	Crossing the Sea and Landing	8:9b-10
7:1-23	Conflict with the Pharisees	8:11-13
7:24-30	Conversation about Bread	8:14-21
7:31-36	Healing	8:22-26
7:37	Confession of Faith	8:27-30

But does Mark intend these stories to be understood metaphorically? Is there another meaning beyond the meaning of the stories themselves? The clearest indicator of the metaphoric nature of these stories is the fact that

3. "H. J. Held sees this composition of Mark as made up of two cycles, building respectively to the opening of ears (7:31-37) and eyes (8:22-26); consequently a 'clear theological composition.' . . ." Quentin Quesnell, *The Mind of Mark: Interpretation and Method through the Exegesis of Mark 6:52*, Analecta Biblica 38 (Rome: Pontifical Biblical Institute, 1969), p. 28. On pp. 28-36 Quesnell summarizes a whole series of suggestions as to the structure of this unit.

4. William L. Lane, *The Gospel according to Mark* (Grand Rapids: Wm. B. Eerdmans Publishing Co., 1974), p. 269.

there are *two* cycles of stories. It would not be necessary for Mark to develop a second cycle of stories if his sole interest was in telling yet more stories about the miracles and teaching of Jesus. That point is made by the first cycle of stories. No new information is found in the second cycle.[5]

A second indicator is seen when the two feedings are compared. Both pericopae describe the same type of event. They differ, however, in the numbers that are used, and Jesus makes the point that these numbers are important (8:17-21). In the feeding of the five thousand, both the number five (the five loaves) and the number twelve (the twelve baskets of fragments) are associated with Israel;[6] whereas in the feeding of the four thousand, the number seven (the seven loaves and seven baskets) is associated with the Gentiles.[7] One feeding points to Jesus' role with the Jews; the other to his role with the Gentiles. Furthermore, in the first feeding in particular, the language used alludes to both Moses and David. It reveals that Jesus is the long-expected king of Israel, i.e., the Messiah.[8] The symbolic character of these details points to the symbolic character of the whole unit.

A third indication is seen in the repeated emphasis on understanding (6:52; 7:14; 8:17, 21).[9] Mark seems to be saying "Pay attention. Make sure you

---

5. Larry W. Hurtado, *Mark: A Good News Commentary* (San Francisco: Harper & Row, 1983), p. 87, makes this point in regard to the stories that introduce each cycle: "The fact that Mark has two feeding accounts is evidence that he considered the two miracles as important events, and that the accounts are intended to convey more than the simple point that Jesus could perform such a miracle; one feeding account would have been adequate to make that point."

6. The five loaves remind the reader of the teaching of Moses in the first five books of the OT. This strengthens the connection Mark is making between Jesus and Moses. The twelve baskets seem to represent the twelve tribes of Israel. Taken together, along with other symbolic hints in this pericope, "this feeding account presents Jesus as fulfilling the role of Moses and David. . . . The twelve baskets of fragments are meant to assist the reader in seeing Jesus as supplying the divine provision for Israel promised in the OT." Hurtado, pp. 89-90.

7. On the other hand, the numbers in the feeding of the four thousand point in a different direction. The number seven (loaves and baskets) was associated in the OT with the Gentiles. "These observations about the narrative context of this feeding account and its details allow us to see the purpose for two feeding accounts in Mark: The feeding of the five thousand shows Jesus bringing salvation to Israel. The feeding of the four thousand anticipates that his salvation will reach others (Gentiles) as well." Hurtado, p. 110.

8. "The way the event is described is intended to show Jesus as Messiah, the divinely sent provision for Israel and the fulfillment of OT prophecies of a future salvation. Jesus' action is here 'dressed' in OT imagery, so to speak, to make the point." Hurtado, p. 88.

9. Apart from 4:12 (where he is quoting Isa. 6:9-10), these are the only places in the Gospel that Mark uses *syniēmi* = understand.

have got the meaning." After the crossing of the sea and the discussion about bread in 8:14-21, "Jesus makes it quite clear that both the feeding of the five thousand and that of the four thousand *were* signs which the disciples should have understood but did not."[10] This is what Jesus was trying to communicate to the disciples when he told the parable of the sower (4:9-13). To understand parables the hearer has to pay attention and look carefully. The same is true here. Mark urges his readers to make sure they understand. Clearly these two cycles of stories function like parables in that they have a hidden meaning.

Finally, the metaphoric nature of the two cycles is shown in the concluding pericope of this unit. In 8:27-30 the disciples (through Peter, their spokesman) declare that they know that Jesus is the Messiah. How can this be? Throughout both cycles of stories the point is made that the disciples are deaf, dumb, and blind (just like the Pharisees). In contrast, a Gentile woman engages in rather subtle wordplay that shows she understands Jesus (7:24-30). Furthermore, in both cycles of stories the hardness of heart of the disciples is emphasized (6:52; 8:17). How, then, are the disciples able to understand that Jesus is the Messiah? The fact is, they must have experienced some sort of miracle of healing similar to that experienced by the deaf-mute (7:31-37) and by the blind man (8:22-26). The declaration they make is proof that this has indeed happened. In other words, in the same way that the feedings convey symbolically who Jesus is, the healings convey symbolically what has happened to the disciples.

Thus the third unit is structured around two parallel collections of stories which function primarily on the level of symbol. The structure of this unit is quite unlike that of the previous two units. Furthermore, this manner of organization will not be repeated in any of the final three units.

Unit Four: Repetition

Unit four is organized around the fourfold repetition of Jesus' prediction that he will die and then rise again. The structure of this unit is similar to that of the previous unit, in that Mark uses cycles of stories (i.e., parallel collections of pericopae that unfold in an identical fashion). Each cycle in this unit begins in a similar fashion (with a prediction), is followed by an identical response on the part of the Twelve (misunderstanding), and concludes with the same response by Jesus (teaching on discipleship).

10. Lamar Williamson, "An Exposition of Mark 6:30-44," *Interpretation* 30 (1976): 171.

The parallel nature of the four cycles of stories can be seen in the following chart:

Topic	Cycle One	Cycle Two	Cycle Three	Cycle Four
Prediction	8:31	9:2-13	9:30-31	10:32-34
Misunderstanding	8:32-33	9:14-27	9:32-34	10:35-41
Teaching	8:34–9:1	9:28-29	9:35–10:31	10:42-45[11]

The four predictions (which are virtually identical in content) concern the coming fate of Jesus the Messiah. What Jesus predicts is not what the disciples expect. He says the Messiah will suffer, die, and then rise again. The Twelve cannot imagine such a fate for the Messiah. So strong are their cultural assumptions about the Messiah that they seem literally unable to hear what Jesus has said. In each instance, following Jesus' prediction of what will happen to him, the Twelve do or say something that demonstrates their misunderstanding. In cycle one Peter rebukes Jesus for teaching in this manner about the Messiah (8:32). In cycle two, three of the disciples puzzle over what rising from the dead could mean (9:10) while the other nine are arguing with the scribes after having failed to heal a boy (9:14-18). In cycle three the disciples still do not understand and are afraid to ask, so instead they argue about which of them is the greatest (9:32-34). And in cycle four James and John seek the places of honor in the coming kingdom (10:35-40), which angers the rest of the disciples (10:41).

In each case Jesus uses this misunderstanding to teach the disciples something of importance. In cycle one he teaches that the way of discipleship involves giving up one's life for the sake of the gospel. In cycle two he teaches about faith and prayer. In cycle three, in a long section, he teaches about relationships between disciples. In cycle four he teaches about the use of authority by his disciples. Taken together, the teaching in this unit all relates to the subject of discipleship. There is a coherence to the teaching that indicates that this is indeed a single unit.[12]

Clearly the anomaly in this unit comes in cycle two. Although all three elements are present (prediction, misunderstanding, teaching), they are pre-

---

11. See John F. O'Grady, "The Passion in Mark," *Biblical Theology Bulletin* 10 (April 1980): 83-87. He proposes the same threefold pattern of prediction/misunderstanding/teaching. However, he identifies three, not four, such cycles.

12. Another indicator that this is a coherent unit comes in the fact that the first teaching unit begins with the assertion that those who want to follow Jesus must deny themselves (8:34-38) and the last teaching unit ends with the statement that Jesus has come to give his life as a ransom for many (10:45). The teaching theme that is defined is thus completed.

sented in a different form. Furthermore, the division between the elements is not as clear-cut as in the other three cycles. Within the prediction section (9:2-13) are both misunderstanding (9:10-11) and teaching (9:12-13), and within the misunderstanding section (9:14-27) is teaching (9:19, 23 especially, though the whole section is used as a teaching vehicle). This has led many exegetes to posit three, not four, predictions in this unit.[13] As Swartley points out: "It is . . . recognized that the teaching is presented via a careful structural pattern: three passion predictions (8:31; 9:31; 10:32f), followed by three failures of the disciples to understand (8:32-33; 9:32; 10:35-41), followed in turn by three sessions where Jesus teaches discipleship (8:34-38)."[14] What is foundational to this threefold hypothesis is the threefold prediction of the passion in virtually identical fashion (8:31; 9:31; 10:33-34). "The units repeat three basic actions: the Son of man will be publicly mistreated; he will be killed; and after three days he will rise."[15] However, these same three actions, including the title "Son of Man," *are* present in the transfiguration prediction, though in a different order. So it is not out of line to posit four (not three) predictions of the passion in 8:31–10:45. When this unit is divided into three sections, not four as proposed here, it fails to take into account how the material in 9:2-29 fits into what most scholars consider a single literary unit. The above outline, though not as neat as one might like, does account for all the material in a consistent fashion.[16]

Unit Five: Action/Reaction

Unit five is organized around a chain of events that are connected to one another by the action of one party and the reaction of the other. Generally, it is the

---

13. It is, however, widely recognized that 8:27–10:52 is a coherent unit — with some variation as to whether the Caesarea Philippi pronouncement belongs with this unit or the previous unit and whether the Bartimaeus story belongs with this unit or the next. The disagreement has to do with where to place the initial and the final pericopae. See, for example, Willard M. Swartley, "The Structural Function of the Term 'Way' *(Hodos)* in Mark's Gospel," in *The New Way of Jesus: Essays Presented to Howard Charles,* ed. William Klassen (Newton, Kans.: Faith and Life Press, 1980), p. 74; C. E. B. Cranfield, *The Gospel according to Saint Mark* (Cambridge: University Press, 1959), p. 266; Vincent Taylor, *The Gospel according to St. Mark* (New York: St. Martin's Press, 1966), p. 109; and Lane, pp. 30, 292.

14. Swartley, p. 74.

15. Vernon K. Robbins, *Jesus the Teacher: A Socio-Rhetorical Interpretation of Mark* (Philadelphia: Fortress, 1984), p. 23.

16. Another structural feature of material in unit four deserves comment: Mark's uses of *hodos* = way. As Swartley, p. 76, notes: "The statistical data indicates that *hodos* is a distinctive Markan feature in 8:27–10:52."

actions of Jesus in his role as messianic king that launch and fuel the various *re-actions* by the leadership in Jerusalem. The first section in this unit (10:46–11:26) consists of three pericopae, all of which deal with the arrival of the Son of David in Jerusalem. In the second and third of these pericopae (11:1-26), Mark makes it quite clear that it was Jesus who arranged the events (the entry into Jerusalem and the cleansing of the temple) so as to make a statement. In the cleansing of the temple, in particular, Jesus throws down the gauntlet to the religious leadership. He goes right into the heart of their domain (the temple) and issues his challenge to their leadership. The leaders are not long in reacting, as the next pericope demonstrates (11:27-33). They approach Jesus and come right to the point: "By what authority are you doing these things?" (11:28). Jesus responds by telling a story in which he clearly accuses the leaders of betraying God's trust (12:1-12). And so the cycle of action and reaction unfolds. The leaders counterattack with three questions (12:13-34), the first two of which are designed to trap Jesus. The third question allows Jesus to articulate the Great Commandment (12:28-34). Unit five concludes where it started: with the question of the Son of David (compare 10:46-52 with 12:35-37) and the issue of judgment (compare 11:12-21 with 12:38–13:37), adding more support to the contention that this is an independent unit of thought with a coherent focus.

Unit Six: Chronology

In the final unit the reaction Jesus launched in the previous unit produces a series of events that unfold one after the other in sequence. In unit five it was clear that Jesus controlled the unfolding events. In unit six Jesus is no longer in control of the events in the direct way that he was in the previous unit. However, it is he who has set these events in motion by his actions in unit five. Now they proceed under the weight of their own momentum. Mark tells this final part of the story in a straightforward narrative fashion in which he reports on the sequence of events that lead up to Jesus' crucifixion. Chronology is the organizing principle. Mark relates the events in the order in which they occur.[17] This is the first time Mark has told stories in strict sequence.[18]

---

17. "Most of the pericopae found in the account [14:1–15:47] cannot be isolated from their framework without serious loss. They acquire significance from the context in which they are located. Indications of time and place, which occur more frequently than in earlier chapters, are usually so securely woven into the fabric of the narrative that they cannot be regarded as editorial links inserted by the evangelist in order to unite originally independent units of tradition." Lane, pp. 485-86.

18. There are sections in which stories are placed in chronological order (e.g., 1:2-

Chapter 14 opens with the statement that the leadership is "looking for a way to arrest Jesus by stealth and kill him" (v. 1). This defines the structure of the unit. Mark shows how this intention is fulfilled. He presents in chronological sequence the anointing of Jesus in preparation for his death (14:3-9); the betrayal of Jesus by Judas (14:10-11); the Last Supper, in which Jesus connects his coming death with the institution of the promised new covenant with Israel (14:12-26); the prediction that all the disciples will leave him (14:27-31); the agony of the Garden of Gethsemane (14:32-42); the arrest of Jesus (14:43-52); the trial of Jesus before the Sanhedrin (14:53-65); the betrayal of Jesus by Peter (14:66-72); the trial of Jesus before Pilate (15:1-15); the mockery of Jesus (15:16-20); and the crucifixion of Jesus (15:21-39).

Prologue and Epilogue

The prologue and the epilogue are parallel both in purpose and content. By comparing them, their uniqueness is seen (over against the six units) and they are understood to be independent literary structures with a specific function in the story. When the prologue and the epilogue are taken together, they give a sense of completion to the story. The drama is announced in the prologue and completed in the epilogue. In the prologue the reader learns about the *preparation* for Jesus' coming ministry: his baptism and temptation. In the epilogue the reader learns how Jesus' ministry is *completed and climaxed:* he is buried, but he rises again to new life. In the prologue the nature of Jesus' ministry is announced: he will proclaim the good news of God (1:14). In the epilogue that good news is defined: Jesus has been crucified but has risen from the dead (16:6). The prologue and the epilogue act as parentheses around the story of Jesus — a style of composition much favored by Mark.

Other parallels between the prologue and epilogue also show that they are similar. The prologue opens with the statement that "I am sending my messenger ahead of you" (1:2), and the epilogue concludes with the same

---

13). However, typically Mark sets pericopae alongside each other for thematic rather than chronological reasons (e.g., 2:1–3:6, in which each pericope begins with an intentionally vague time designation). This characteristic of Mark was noted early on in the tradition of the church. Bishop Papias of Hierapolis wrote around A.D. 140, in *Exegesis of the Lord's Oracles,* that "Mark, having become the interpreter of Peter, wrote down accurately whatever he remembered of the things said and done by the Lord, *but not however in order*" (italics mine). Quoted in Lane, p. 8.

phrase: "[Jesus] is going ahead of you to Galilee" (16:7). John the Baptist is the key figure in the prologue. He is the messenger who announces Jesus' coming. In the epilogue the "young man" is the messenger who announces Jesus' resurrection. The events in both sections take place in Judea and involve movement from there into Galilee. The prologue concludes by noting that Jesus has gone into Galilee (1:14). The epilogue concludes by sending the disciples back to Galilee (16:7). The drama has come full circle. "Thus the beginning and end of the gospel are linked up."[19]

These quite different organizational principles in the six units and in the prologue/epilogue enable the careful reader to spot each of the major units. They also support the contention that Mark has deliberately crafted his material into six coherent units surrounded by a brief beginning and ending.

Transitions between Units

A second indicator that the above outline of the Gospel is accurate is found in the way the transitions are effected from unit to unit. If this is indeed the outline Mark had in mind, then it ought to reveal itself at those points where a shift is made from one topic to another.[20] There should be evidence that the redactor was aware of shifting from one subject to another. And indeed, an examination of the transition points reveals that in each instance two things take place: (1) an *abrupt shift in subject* (theme) and (2) an attempt by Mark to provide a *smooth transition* between the two themes so as to lessen the feeling of abruptness in thematic shift. Put another way: (1) when Mark com-

---

19. Augustine Stock, *Call to Discipleship: A Literary Study of Mark's Gospel* (Dublin: Veritas Publications, 1982), p. 34.

20. These are the so-called seams. Ernest Best, *The Temptation and the Passion: The Markan Soteriology* (Cambridge: University Press, 1965), notes: "To single out the Markan contribution we need to look at the phrases by which Mark has joined together the incidents he uses; these appear at the beginnings and ends of pericopae: the Markan seams" (p. ix). He later notes: "The most obvious place to look for Mark's hand is in the words, phrases, sentences which join together the various incidents" (p. 63). N. Perrin, in "Towards an Interpretation of the Gospel of Mark," in *Christology and a Modern Pilgrimage: A Discussion with Norman Perrin,* ed. Hans Dieter Betz (n.p.: Society of Biblical Literature, 1971), using K. L. Schmidt's identification of Mark's "summaries," combines these with a change in geographical locale to identify transitions. However, this methodology does not produce units that account for the themes that are developed by means of various sets of pericopae. Furthermore, Perrin recognizes that "the aids to recognizing divisions we have used so far fail us" when it comes to 11:1–16:8, where he reverts to "common sense" (pp. 3-5).

pletes what he has to say about a topic, he simply stops and goes on to his next subject; (2) but in order to make this less jarring for the reader, he inserts some sort of transitional statement. Thematically Mark is abrupt; stylistically he is smooth.

Several devices are used to effect these transitions. First, the pericope at the end of one unit serves as a bridge into the new unit. It does this by concluding one theme while anticipating the next theme. Second, there is always a piece of narration on one side or the other of the transition (or on both sides) that moves the action forward smoothly. Third, there is some sort of geographical movement in either the pericope that precedes or the one that follows the transition. The shift in topic is mirrored in a shift in locale. Fourth, several other transitional devices are used at specific points.

One of these stylistic devices alone could simply be explained as characteristic of how Mark writes in general, at transitions as well as elsewhere. However, the clustering of these devices at the transitions between units gives evidence that Mark is conscious of the abruptness of thematic shift (as he would be at a genuine transition point) and concerned to smooth out the transition by means of these stylistic techniques. An examination of each transition will indicate that this is the case.

From the Prologue to Unit One

There is an abrupt shift of theme when Mark moves from the prologue (1:1-15) to the first unit of the Gospel (1:16–4:34). Mark begins his Gospel with a brief description of Jesus' preparation for ministry (1:2-13). He describes the role John the Baptist plays. He describes the baptism of Jesus. He describes the temptation of Jesus. And suddenly (in 1:16) it is months later, miles distant, and Jesus is in the process of choosing the first four disciples. The thematic transition is jarring.

What links the prologue to the first unit is the bridging narration in 1:14-15. It does this in two ways. First, in 1:14 the narration looks back at the previous material by reference to John ("after John was arrested") and forward to the new unit by reference to Jesus in this new site ("Jesus came to Galilee"). Then in 1:15 the nature of Jesus' ministry is described. The new unit begins in 1:16, and immediately Jesus is involved in the ministry described in 1:15. Furthermore, he is in Galilee (walking "beside the Sea of Galilee" [NIV]). The shift of geography from Judea to Galilee and the shift in activity (from preparation to ministry) are signaled by the transitional verses, which are clearly a narrator summary.

From Unit One to Unit Two

The same thing happens at the transition point between unit one and unit two (i.e., between 4:34 and 4:35). An abrupt shift of topic is made smoother by several transitional devices.

First, the theme shifts abruptly. Unit one describes a variety of responses to Jesus on the part of various people. Unit two focuses on the power of Jesus and how Jesus deals with situations that are threatening. Unit one displays Jesus as a great teacher and thus concludes with a long teaching section (which explains the various responses to Jesus). Unit two displays Jesus as a mighty prophet and thus begins with four power stories. The opening incident in unit two has nothing to do with Jesus as teacher (although the Twelve call him teacher because they have yet to learn that he is also a prophet). The movement is from teaching to nature miracle.

To smooth out this abrupt shift in topic Mark does four things. First, the narrator offers a brief concluding statement that bridges the gap between the two units (4:33-34). In this statement the narrator looks back to unit one by reference to the parables and how Jesus used them ("With many such parables he spoke the word to them . . ." [4:33]). He looks forward to the next unit with the phrase "he explained everything in private to his disciples" (4:34). The next unit begins with Jesus alone with his disciples, commenting on a puzzling incident they have just been through together. Second, the long teaching section in 4:1-34 is itself, as a whole, a bridge of sorts (and not just the final paragraph).[21] In terms of unit one this teaching section summarizes and explains the various responses to Jesus. In terms of unit two the same teaching section anticipates the variety of responses that will occur in the new unit. For example, compare the response of faith on the part of the woman healed from bleeding (5:34) to the quite different response of disbelief on the part of the townsfolk in Nazareth (6:5). Third, there is a geographic transition. Jesus sails across the Sea of Galilee. Fourth, and most significant, Mark indicates that both the concluding section of unit one and the beginning section of unit two take place on the same day. At the transition point he says: "On that day, when evening had come, he said to them, 'Let us go across to the other side.' And leaving the crowd behind, they took him with them in the boat, just as he was" (4:35-36). The reference to "that day" leads the reader back to 4:1 (the beginning of the concluding section of unit one), where Jesus begins to teach the crowd by the lake. He does so from a boat moored just off-

---

21. Mark 4:1-34 and Mark 13 are the two longest teaching sections in the Gospel. Both also function as bridges between units.

shore. At the end of the day (in 4:35), he simply sails across the lake. Hence, Mark smooths the way from one theme to another by placing the end of one unit and the beginning of the other on the same day. That this is a narrative device is clear from the fact that 4:1-34 is most likely a thematic compilation on the part of Mark of the teaching of Jesus. Matthew and Luke place some of this material in quite different contexts in their accounts.[22]

From Unit Two to Unit Three

This same thematic abruptness coupled with stylistic smoothness is found at the next transition point: 6:30 and 6:31. The abruptness in the shift of topic is clear.[23] Mark moves from the story of King Herod to the story of the feeding of the five thousand. He moves from the question of Jesus' power (in contrast to that of Herod) to the question of Jesus' messiahship (which is displayed via the rich Old Testament allusions in the feeding of the five thousand). The feeding of the five thousand launches the first of two parallel cycles of stories in unit three which are used metaphorically by Mark to describe how the Twelve come to realize that Jesus is the Messiah. Thus Mark turns from Jesus as a powerful prophet in unit two to Jesus the Messiah in unit three.

This thematic transition is smoothed over in three ways. First, both sto-

22. For example, the parable of the sower with Jesus' explanation occurs in Mark 4:1-20; Matt. 13:1 23; and Luke 8:4-15. Luke follows Mark and retains the parable of the lamp on a stand (Luke 8:16-18 parallels Mark 4:21-25), but Matthew puts these materials in four places: Matt. 5:15; 10:26; 7:2; and 13:12. This is not to say that Jesus could not have strung these parables together in this way on this day. Still, one gets the sense of the editorial hand of Mark at work here. Note also that Mark 4:10 and 34 communicate the idea that the day is broken somehow. Jesus does not stay on the lake teaching the whole day. "Cf. Ch. 4:2, 10, 13, 33 where Mark implies that these three parables have been selected from a larger collection." Lane, p. 149 n. 1.

23. Robert P. Meye, *Jesus and the Twelve: Discipleship and Revelation in Mark's Gospel* (Grand Rapids: Wm. B. Eerdmans Publishing Co., 1968), notices the sharp shift in topic: "What is the meaning of the abrupt ending of the apostolic mission at 6:30?" (p. 110). He is struck by how strange it is that Jesus calls the disciples to become fishers of men and then sends them out on only one mission. His answer is that "*the one mission of the Twelve is a point of beginning for Jesus' instruction in the full meaning of their mission. The mission of the Twelve during Jesus' ministry is unique; the time of the Incarnation is rather the time of being with Jesus and being instructed by him. The time of their mission is after Easter. It is the risen Christ who is the decisive originator and the content of their mission*" (pp. 112-13, italics in original). However, while such an explanation gives insights into the overall theme of Mark, the abruptness at this point can be explained by the fact that here Mark shifts to another topic.

ries in the intercalated pericope that ends unit two (the mission of the Twelve, into which has been inserted the story of King Herod) provide a thematic bridge. The banquet of Herod for the leading men of Galilee anticipates the banquet of Jesus for the common people of Galilee (in the first pericope of the new unit). Also, the ministry of the Twelve in unit two is continued in the feeding of the five thousand in unit three (6:37-43). "This is one of those rare instances . . . wherein the disciples are actively involved (as they also were during their mission) in Jesus' ministry."[24] In other words, the disciples are engaged in ministry to the crowds on both sides of the transition. Second, the narration that ends unit two (6:30-31) and begins unit three (6:31-34) flows smoothly together. The return of the Twelve is linked to the feeding of the five thousand by Jesus' decision to take his disciples away for rest: "He said to them, 'Come away to a deserted place all by yourselves and rest a while.' For many were coming and going, and they had no leisure even to eat" (6:31). The crowds note their departure to this place of rest. From experience they know what Jesus and the Twelve are doing (they are escaping; see 4:35-36). So the crowds follow along on the shore, watching where Jesus and his disciples are sailing. As the crowds march along they gather ever more people, and the result is, "five thousand men" (6:44) are waiting for Jesus and the disciples when they land (6:31-34). The end of one experience of ministry (the mission of the Twelve) thus moves naturally into another experience of ministry (the feeding of the five thousand). Thirdly, there is geographical movement. Once again this involves a boat trip across the Sea of Galilee (6:32).

From Unit Three to Unit Four

The fourth transition occurs between 8:30 and 8:31. Thematically there is a shift from the disciples' confession of Jesus as the Messiah to Jesus' teaching about the Messiah. Though there is a common theme at this point (the Messiah), what Jesus says about the Messiah is shocking to the Twelve, and they react strongly to it (8:32). The reader is moved abruptly into consideration of a whole new issue. Part I has concluded (in which Jesus is revealed to be the Messiah) and Part II begins (in which Jesus will be revealed to be quite a different Messiah from what anyone expected).

The transition is smoothed out in several ways. There is a thematic bridge. In the pericope that concludes unit three, the disciples confess that Jesus is the Messiah. This confession sets the stage for the teaching about the

24. Meye, p. 111.

nature of messiahship in unit four. There is a shift between the two units from dialogue with the disciples (unit three) to teaching of the disciples (unit four). The narration in 8:31-32 (which this time is found at the beginning of the new section) describes what Jesus taught about the Messiah. The physical movement this time takes place in the end pericope of unit three, where it is reported that "Jesus and his disciples went on to the villages around Caesarea Philippi" (8:27 NIV). In fact, these two units blend together so smoothly that were it not for the introduction in 8:31 of the first of four predictions about the fate of Jesus (which define the structure of unit four), it might be argued that 8:27–9:1 belongs together.

From Unit Four to Unit Five

The fifth transition occurs between 10:45 and 10:46. There is an abrupt shift in action at that point from teaching about discipleship and messiahship (directed at the Twelve) to healing a blind man (in the midst of the crowds). There is also an abrupt shift of theme from unit four to unit five.[25] In unit four Mark has organized the material around four predictions that define what kind of Messiah Jesus is. Jesus concludes this teaching with the definitive statement in 10:45 about the role of the Messiah. In unit five Jesus does not teach about the Messiah; he functions as the Messiah. Specifically, he conducts himself as the messianic king who has returned to judge his erring people. There is also a shift in title, from the suffering Son of Man in the final pericope of unit four to the Son of David in the opening pericope of unit five. "The story of blind Bartimaeus introduces a transition in christological nomenclature concerning Jesus' activity. A transition is made from the disciples' following 'in the way of the Son of Man' (8:27–10:45) toward Jerusalem to following 'in the way of the Son of David' (10:46–12:44) into Jerusalem."[26]

The thematic transition between these two different emphases is smoothed out in several ways. First, the story of blind Bartimaeus provides the thematic bridge from one unit to the next. His confession that Jesus is the Son of David (which parallels the confession of Peter in the pericope that concludes unit three) sums up what Jesus has been trying to teach the disciples in unit three. He is different from the Messiah of popular imagination,

---

25. Meye comments on the way Jesus' teaching about discipleship ends: "This course of instruction clearly extends to the latter part of chapter ten, where it abruptly ends" (p. 111).

26. Vernon K. Robbins, "The Healing of Blind Bartimaeus (10:46-52) in the Marcan Theology," *Journal of Biblical Literature* 92 (1973): 241.

and Bartimaeus's cry defines part of that difference. He is not a conquering hero but the returning king. This confession not only points backward to sum up unit four; it also points forward to unit five, in which Jesus functions as the king who has returned. Second, the Bartimaeus story also sums up the teaching about discipleship in that most of the elements of discipleship are present in this pericope. In this way it connects back to unit four even while it opens unit five. Third, the brief narrative statement in 10:46 notes the movement that is characteristic of transition points. Here Jesus and the disciples enter and leave Jericho en route to Jerusalem. The sense of continuous movement along the road that takes Jesus to the gateway of Jerusalem ties these two pericopae together, although thematically they are different.

From Unit Five to Unit Six

The transition between unit five and unit six occurs at 13:37 and 14:1. There is a dramatic shift in theme between unit five and unit six. In unit five Jesus is the king who returns in judgment; in unit six Jesus is the one who is judged. In unit five Jesus is the active agent who arranges events and provokes reactions; in unit six Jesus is the passive victim who is arrested, tried, and killed.

The transition is made in a way that is now familiar. First there is the transitional pericope. Chapter 13 is the longest teaching section in Mark, and it (like the other long teaching section in 4:1-34) serves as a bridge into the next unit. Chapter 13 summarizes the theme of judgment in unit five with its predictions of what lies ahead for the temple (and indeed for Jerusalem). The temple has been the site and sometimes the subject of unit five. Chapter 13 also alerts the readers as to what they (and the disciples) must do: watch carefully and interpret accurately the coming events. Throughout chapter 13 it has been emphasized that Jesus' disciples need to be vigilant; they must pay attention to what is happening and understand it rightly (13:5, 21-23, 33-37). The last word in the chapter is the injunction to "Watch!" (NIV). This is precisely what the reader is asked to do in the new section: "Watch the events unfold." The narrative section in unit six (14:1-2) begins by noting that the religious leaders are seeking to arrest and kill Jesus. (The first thing the readers see as they "watch" is the plotting of the religious leaders.) From then on, events unfold one after the other until the actual death of Jesus.

Chapter 13 anticipates unit six in yet another way. This discourse points out the way that lies ahead for the disciples. It is almost a farewell address to them, warning them what to expect and telling them how to act in the face of this coming suffering. Thus it forms a bridge between the end of Jesus' public ministry and the beginning of those events which culminate in his death. Finally, the physical movement in this section is found at the beginning of chapter 13, where it is reported that Jesus leaves the temple (13:1) and moves to the Mount of Olives (13:3), where he gives his address.

From Unit Six to the Epilogue

The theme of unit six is the suffering, trial, and death of Jesus. The focus of the epilogue is on the burial and resurrection, which are different events (although they are part of the passion). It might be argued that the epilogue (15:40–16:8) belongs to the previous unit. Certainly Jesus predicts not only rejection, suffering, and death (all of which are found in unit six) but also resurrection (which has been placed in the epilogue). However, two factors indicate that this a transition point. First, the culminating statement of the centurion completes the outline Mark provides in 1:1. In the same way that 8:29 with its affirmation of Jesus as the Messiah draws unit three (and Part I) to a close, so too 15:39 and its affirmation of Jesus as the Son of God draws unit six (and Part II) to a close. Second, all along Mark's focus has been on the death of Jesus. Little is said about the resurrection; indeed, only a few verses are allocated to describing it (16:1-8). With Jesus' death, Mark's story has been completed. It remains only for him to note the fact of the resurrection. Third, there is a balance to the document when 15:40–16:8 is considered an epilogue. It is approximately as long as the prologue which begins the Gospel. Such bracketing is characteristic of Mark's style.

Once again, there is an abrupt transition from 15:39 to 15:40, as Nineham recognizes. He comments on 15:40: "The women, who have not hitherto played much part in the Gospel, appear somewhat abruptly. . . ."[27] This abruptness is smoothed over in the usual ways. First, narration connects the two incidents together. In this case it consists of noting that the women were watching all this happen from a distance. Second, there is the typical geographical mention. In 15:40-41 Mark notes that the women came from Galilee to Jerusalem so as to care for Jesus' needs. The narrative here also identifies the women who will figure in the events of the burial and resurrection, thus preparing the reader for the epilogue.

27. D. E. Nineham, *The Gospel of St. Mark* (London: Adam & Charles Black, 1968), p. 431.

From the Epilogue to the Conclusion

The last verse (16:8) is the final (and perhaps most notorious) example of abruptness in the Gospel of Mark. At the end of Mark's very brief statement of the resurrection, the angel instructs the women to tell the disciples to return to Galilee, where they will meet the resurrected Jesus. The Gospel ends with the women trembling as they flee from the empty tomb. Period. The Gospel concludes. The abruptness of this ending has often been noted. Early on, probably because of the unusual nature of the ending, some scribe felt the need to append Mark 16:9-20 (which is quite clearly not part of the original manuscript).[28] Likewise, scholars have ruminated on the so-called "lost ending of Mark."[29] However, there is no need to hypothesize any concluding verses. This abruptness is quite in line with Mark's style. He has finished what he wanted to say, so he simply stops. This time, because there is no more material on the other side of the transition point, he has no need of a narrative to smooth out the reading of the text. It just ends.

Transitional Passages as Freestanding Pericopae

It should also be noted that at certain transition points it is difficult to decide whether a pericope belongs with one unit or with the other. The decision as to where to place the material must be made, firstly, in terms of theme (which, after all, is the key organizing principle of a unit) and secondarily in terms of internal structure of the unit (which unites the various pericopae in the unit). It is only after these two considerations are taken into account that Mark's transition style can be called in to help place a pericope in one unit or the other. The very difficulty of knowing where to place particular material — from the point of view of transitional techniques — is evidence of the skill of the redactor in effecting these transitions. There is a smoothness to the reading of the text that facilitates the abrupt shift of topic.

---

28. "It is unnecessary to examine in detail the almost universally held conclusion that xvi.9-20 is not an original part of Mk. Both the external and the internal evidence are decisive." Taylor, p. 610. However, William R. Farmer would dispute this blanket judgment on the part of Taylor. See *The Last Twelve Verses of Mark* (Cambridge: Cambridge University Press, 1974), p. 109.

29. "How the original ending disappeared is . . . obscure. The mutilation of the original papyrus MS., Mark's premature death, and deliberate suppression have been conjectured." Taylor, p. 610.

In fact, it might be argued that the transitional sections should be separated out from the units and allowed to stand on their own since they bridge the gap between two units and are, therefore, connected to both units (and not to one unit only). In fact, in almost every case an argument can be made (and often has been) that the material is connected to the other unit (and not the unit in this outline). For example, in terms of the transition between the prologue and unit one, for a long time the consensus of scholars was that 1:14-15 was connected to the material beginning at 1:16. Likewise, the long teaching section that concludes unit one (4:1-34) could stand alone, both summarizing unit one and anticipating unit two. The same is true of the other long teaching section, Mark 13. It could stand alone, summarizing unit five while anticipating unit six. This is also true of the transition from unit two to unit three. The mission of the Twelve, with the intercalated story of King Herod, could stand alone. Both are unique events. Likewise, the statement about the women that begins the epilogue (15:40-41) could stand alone.

The difficulty of placing a transitional pericope in one unit or the other is perhaps best demonstrated in the long section from 8:27 to 10:52, material which encompasses unit four and the transitional passages on either side of it. The first issue has to do with 8:27-30. Does it belong with unit three or with unit four? Clearly this pericope climaxes unit three. Equally clearly this incident launches the four predictions that make up unit four. Furthermore, the presence in 8:27 of the phrase *en tē hodō* (which figures so importantly in unit four) would tend to make 8:27-30 part of that unit. The transition at the other end of unit four is equally ambiguous. The Bartimaeus story (10:46-52) clearly initiates the Son of David theme in unit five; but it also functions symbolically (in a way parallel to 8:22-26) as an indication that the disciples have received a second touch of healing, and so it climaxes unit four. Furthermore, the phrase *en tē hodō* in 10:52 would tend to make this pericope part of unit four. In fact, scholars have placed it on both sides of the divide.[30] It is clearly a transitional passage and could even be set apart from either unit and labeled as such. However, the decision to place 8:27-30 as the conclusion of unit three and 10:46-52 as the start of unit five was made on the basis of the christological titles used in the two pericopae. The christological development in Mark is taken as the primary organizing motif. Furthermore, the Bartimaeus incident is connected with unit five because geographically Jesus and his disciples have finally reached Judea. Jericho is just fifteen miles from

---

30. Robbins notes the scholars on either side of the issue in "Blind Bartimaeus," pp. 237-38.

Jerusalem.[31] It is the gateway to Jerusalem and the momentous events of the final week of Jesus' life.[32]

The difficulty of choosing whether to connect the transitional material with one unit or the other, rather than being a problem, is a demonstration that this material is transitional in nature.

The Use of Parentheses

Mention has already been made of Mark's tendency to enclose materials in parentheses. This stylistic trait is found in sections as small as a pair of pericopae and as long as a unit. Indeed, it has already been pointed out that the whole Gospel is bracketed by a prologue and an epilogue.

Each unit is bracketed in some way. Since Mark uses brackets to define material that is connected together (and which should be interpreted together), this is a strong indication that the units are meant by Mark to be interpreted as a connected set of materials. Brackets are, therefore, the third structural indicator that the units as they have been defined above are indeed structures created by Mark.

Bracketing a Pericope

First, note must be made of those places where Mark has intercalated a pericope between the beginning and the end of another pericope. The use of this technique on the micro-level gives a clear indication of how Mark intends bracketed material on all levels to be interpreted. In the case of two pericopae, each pericope interprets the other. The two stories are connected in meaning, and by placing them together in this way Mark helps the reader understand the intention of each story.[33] So too, by extension, longer sections of material that are bracketed together are meant to be interpreted together. This is, in fact, the definition of a unit: material that is meant to be interpreted together.

31. Taylor, p. 447.

32. "The unity of 10:46–11:11 has often been overlooked because of the chapter division that was imposed between the healing of blind Bartimaeus and the sending of the two disciples to bring the colt. There is actually no narrative break between 10:46-52 and 11:11." V. K. Robbins, "Summons and Outline in Mark: The Three-Step Progression," *Novum Testamentum* 23 (April 1981): 109.

33. Lane, p. 28.

There are five instances in the Second Gospel where two pericopae are intercalated. The first example is found in 3:20-35, where the Beelzebub incident is sandwiched between the expression of intention on the part of Jesus' family to "restrain him" (3:20-21) and their actual arrival at the place where he was teaching (3:31-35). By interconnecting the two stories, the point is made that the assessments of Jesus made by his family and by the scribes are similar ("He has gone out of his mind" versus "He has Beelzebul, and by the ruler of the demons he casts out demons"). The fact that the conclusions about Jesus on the part of two quite different groups are similar would not be so obvious (since it is so unexpected) were not the two stories intercalated.

The same sort of mutual interpretation is seen in the other four instances of intercalation. In 5:21-43 Mark sandwiches together the stories of two women whom Jesus heals by his power. The two stories are connected not only because healing takes place in both instances but also by the fact that each story is connected to the question of faith (in contrast to the next pericope, 6:1-6a, in which there is no faith and so no healing). In 6:7-30 Mark sandwiches the story of King Herod between the beginning and end of the mission of the Twelve. In this way he shows the nature of genuine authority (power). Herod, theoretically, has the most power in the land, but he is actually controlled by those around him (his wife, his officials, his stepdaughter), while Jesus, who has no official power, is able to empower those around him to do his work (the Twelve are able to duplicate his ministry of preaching, healing, and exorcism). In 11:12-21 the cleansing of the temple is placed between the beginning and end of the story of the cursing of the fig tree. The two stories are similar in that both are acted-out parables of judgment and both point to the future judgment which is coming on the temple. Furthermore, by intercalating the two stories, the meaning of the otherwise puzzling cursing of the fig tree is made clear. Finally, in 14:1-11 the anointing of Jesus is placed between the story of the desire by the officials to arrest Jesus without provoking a riot and the action of Judas that enables them to accomplish their wishes. Both stories concern the death of Jesus. The act of the woman foretells what will happen to Jesus as the result of his coming arrest. In other words, each time one story is intercalated into another, this enriches the readers' understanding of both stories.

Bracketing Units

The same thing happens when a wider range of material is bracketed. The brackets enclose material that is connected together, material that deals with the same theme or themes, and material which is meant to be interpreted together to give a deeper meaning than if it were not so connected. Thus each unit is bracketed.

First, the prologue is bracketed by a summary statement at the beginning (1:1) and at the end (1:14-15). The first statement defines the nature of what Mark is writing ("the good news"), and the second statement defines how Jesus will go about announcing this "good news." This unit is all about the "good news" (or gospel). (Mark does not use the word "gospel" again until 8:35.) The first verse defines the outline for the whole manuscript (the first part is about Jesus the Messiah, the second part is about Jesus the Son of God), and 1:14-15 describes how these two facts will be presented (by the proclamation of Jesus). Mark 1:15 also amplifies the statement in 1:1 by describing the desired response to the gospel (repentance and faith). This is an example of bracketing in which both halves of the bracketing materials are part of the unit itself.

The bracketing in unit one is conceptual in nature and has to do with the kingdom of God. In 1:15 the theme of Jesus' message is defined. It has to do with the kingdom of God. At this point unit one begins. Unit one ends with the long teaching section in 4:1-34 consisting of the parables about the kingdom of God. The whole unit, it turns out, is about responding to the kingdom of God — though this is not made clear until the final section of the unit (4:1-34). In this case the use of brackets makes clear Mark's thematic concern, which might otherwise go unnoticed.[34]

Unit two is also bracketed by the concept of kingdoms. On the one side is the teaching about the kingdom of God (4:1-34), and on the other side is a discussion of the kingdom of Herod (6:14-29). In between is a discussion of authority or power. True authority is the mark of the genuine king. The kingdom of God which Jesus brings is a kingdom of genuine power; the kingdom of man which Herod rules is a kingdom of illusory power. Unit two is also bracketed by sea journeys. The unit begins with a journey across the lake to flee the crowds (4:35-36). The first pericope of unit three involves a similar flight across the lake to get away from the crowds, except this time this ploy does not work (6:30-34).

Unit three is bracketed on either side by statements concerning who the people think Jesus is (6:14-15 and 8:27-28). In the one case this report is made to Herod, in the other to Jesus. In between the true identity of Jesus as Messiah is made known.

Unit four is also bracketed. The final pericope of unit three (8:27-30) is

---

34. Indeed, few if any outlines identify the material from 1:16 to 4:34 as a single unit which deals with responses to the kingdom.

characterized by two elements: a christological declaration ("You are the Messiah") and the phrase "on the way" (in 8:27). The first pericope of unit five (10:46-52) contains the same two elements: a christological declaration (the twice-repeated cry of Bartimaeus, "Jesus, Son of David," in 10:47 and 48) and the phrase "on the way" in 10:52. Swartley argues persuasively for the "redactional intention in Mark's use of *hodos* in 8:27–10:52."[35] In between, the material has to do with what kind of Messiah Jesus is (he suffers and dies) in what kind of kingdom (a place where true power involves giving your life for others).

Unit five is bracketed on both ends by incidents which take place on the Mount of Olives (11:1 and 13:3). The Mount of Olives has to do with judgment, and in between Jesus is shown acting as the rightful judge over his kingdom.

Unit six is bracketed by incidents involving women. The story of the anointing begins the unit (14:3-9), and on the other end mention is made of the women who watched Jesus die. Both stories have to do with the death of Jesus. In between, of course, is the story of his death at the hands of the kingdoms of this world (the religious kingdom and the secular kingdom). The epilogue is bracketed on both ends by accounts of the same three women (15:40-41 and 16:1-8) who are witnesses to Jesus' death and Jesus' resurrection. It is they who serve to point the way back to Galilee, where the story will start all over again, except this time the crucified Savior will reign as the living Lord.

In other words, what is seen on a small scale in intercalated pericopae (stories that are meant to be interpreted together) is seen on a larger scale (units of material that belong together). The bracketing technique of Mark is yet another indication of the validity of the units derived above.

The Use of Titles

Mark's careful use of titles for Jesus is yet another indication that he consciously divided his material into six major units, each of which focuses on a different aspect of Jesus. This is seen, first of all, in the fact that the titles for Jesus build upon one another so that there is an unfolding of insight on the part of the Twelve as to who Jesus is. No title is used by "the people" (the Twelve, the religious leaders, the crowds)[36] prior to the unit in which Jesus is

---

35. Swartley, pp. 75-77.

36. According to David Rhoads and Donald Michie, *Mark as Story: An Introduction to the Narrative of a Gospel* (Philadelphia: Fortress, 1982), p. 101, in their analysis of Mark as a piece of narrative writing, the three major sets of characters against which Jesus is set are the disciples, the crowds, and the authorities.

revealed to have such a title. The titles the people use for Jesus at any one point in time are only those they have discovered apply to him. So, for example, he is not called the Son of David until unit five when he is discovered to be such.

Once Jesus is established in a role, he continues thereafter to be seen by the people in that role and/or to function in that role. So, in unit one it is established that he is a teacher. Thereafter he continues in his role as teacher. He is seen as a teacher in unit two (4:38; 5:35; 6:2, 6b), in unit three (6:34; 7:1-23; 8:14-21), in unit four (8:31–9:1; 9:9-13, 17, 31; 9:35–10:34 [esp. 9:38; 10:17, 20]; 10:35, 42-45), in unit five (11:12-25; 12:1-12, 14, 16-17, 19; 12:24–13:37 [esp. 12:32; 13:1]), and in unit six (14:3-31 [esp. 14:14], 45). In unit two Jesus is shown to be a prophet with great power. He continues in that role in unit three (6:39-44, 48-51; 8:6-9), in unit four (9:25-27), in unit five (13:1-37), and in unit six (14:17-21, 27-31). In unit three Jesus is shown to be the Messiah. He continues in that role in unit four (8:31; 9:2-13, 31; 10:33-34, 45), in unit five (11:1-33; 13:1-37), and in unit six (14:22-25, 61-62). In unit four Jesus is shown to be Son of Man. That title continues to be applied to him in unit five (13:26) and in unit six (14:21, 41, 62). Finally, he is shown to be the Son of David in unit five. He continues in that role in unit six (14:62; 15:2-3, 16-20, 26, 32).

While it is true that the understanding of the people (the three groups struggling to know who Jesus is) emerges over time, those that stand "above" the action (the narrator and the supernatural characters) already know who Jesus is. Thus, while the title Messiah is not used of Jesus by the people prior to unit three, the narrator calls him this in 1:1. Likewise, Jesus twice calls himself the Son of Man prior to unit four (in one pericope; see 2:10, 28). Furthermore, the title Son of God is used prior to unit six: by the narrator (1:1), by God (1:11; 9:7), and by the evil spirits (3:11; 5:7), all of whom possess after-the-fact or supernatural insight.

It must also be noted that it is by means of these titles that Mark's view of Jesus is made evident. As E. Best has pointed out, an author's choice of titles reveals his theology.[37] Matthew and Luke use different titles for Jesus. They drop out certain titles (e.g., they do not use "king of the Jews/Israel" as frequently as Mark). They alter other titles (e.g., Matthew tends to change "teacher" to "Lord"). They add titles to those in Mark (e.g., Matthew adds to Peter's confession that Jesus is the Messiah the phrase "the Son of the living God" [Matt. 16:16]). At other times all three synoptics preserve the same title (e.g., "Son" in the words of the Voice at the baptism and transfiguration).

37. Best, p. 160.

Thus, by noting the progression of titles it is possible to track the unfolding view of Jesus that *Mark* wants to present. This is an accurate way of getting at his particular viewpoint.

Finally, it is important to note the difference in understanding on the part of the Twelve in Part I of the Gospel of Mark over against that in Part II. In Part I their understanding grows as to who Jesus is until they grasp that he is the Messiah (8:29). In Part II, where Jesus attempts to describe the nature of his messiahship, they do not give evidence of having understood his teaching. The Twelve never refer to Jesus as the Son of Man, the Son of David, or the Son of God. At the end of Part II it is the centurion, not one of the disciples, who declares Jesus to be the Son of God (15:39). Their failure to understand what it means for Jesus to be the Messiah is related to their failure to understand themselves. They must repent before they can know who Jesus is. They have all the data. It remains for them to act upon it. The process of their repentance and belief will be tracked in chapters 9 and 10.

Another Outline: A Comparison

It would be desirable, though not possible, to compare the outline for Mark presented in this book to the other outlines that exist, responding to the differences between each construction. Such a process would lead the discussion too far astray from its main point, which is to understand the two main paradigms for conversion in the New Testament. However, consideration will be given to one other outline, namely, that of V. K. Robbins in *Jesus the Teacher: A Socio-Rhetorical Interpretation of Mark.*[38] This outline has been selected because it is a fairly recent piece of work (and therefore reflects current scholarly views about Mark); because it is remarkably close to the outline proposed above (and therefore adds weight to the contentions in this book); and because pointing out the differences between the two outlines yields interesting insights into Mark's intention (and is another form of verification of the outline proposed in the previous chapter).

In his book (and in his previously published paper "Summons and Outline in Mark: The Three-Step Progression"),[39] Robbins develops an outline for Mark based on a stylistic characteristic of Mark called the three-step progression. The outline described in chapter 5 above and the comments in this chapter on structure, though developed independently, bear some strik-

38. Philadelphia: Fortress, 1984.
39. *Novum Testamentum* 23 (April 1981): 97-114.

ing similarities to the conclusions of Robbins — as well as some notable differences — so that comparison is in order.

How, then, did Robbins derive his outline? Robbins's methodology is based upon the observation that Mark makes frequent use of threefold repetition of actions and events.[40] Robbins illustrates this three-step progression by means of the triple repetition of the passion predictions.[41] His conclusion is: "The kind of three-step progression that provides the framework for each passion prediction leads to the formal structure, or outline, of Mark."[42] Specifically, he argues that the transition points between units of narration are indicated by the presence of a three-step repetition, during the third section of which Jesus issues a summons to his disciples. Robbins identifies six such transitional sections: 1:14-20; 3:7-19; 6:1-13; 8:27–9:1; 10:46–11:11; and 13:1-37.

> Characteristically, these units begin with explicit reference to the presence of the disciples with Jesus as he travels out (exerchomai, ekporeuomai) of one place to another. The second part, then, involves Jesus in interaction that sets the stage for the third part which begins with a narrational comment that Jesus summons (proskaleomai), calls (kaleō, phōneō), or sends (apostellō) his disciples.[43]

Four of the six transition points noted by Robbins correspond to transitions in the outline presented in this book. Specifically, his transition in 1:14-20 encompasses the material at the end of the prologue (1:14-15) and the beginning of unit one (1:16-20); his transition in 8:27–9:1 encompasses the material at the end of unit three (8:27-30) and the beginning of unit four (8:31–9:1); his transition in 10:46–11:11 is the beginning of unit five (11:1-11); and his transition at 13:1-37 concludes the material in unit five. Robbins's remaining two transitions at 3:7-19 and 6:1-13 fall within units as defined above.

Obviously, Robbins has pinpointed a genuine stylistic pattern used by Mark at several places to move from one set of materials into a new set of materials. The three-step transition with summons does indeed identify the beginning and the end of Part I of Mark's Gospel. It does distinguish between

40. This is a stylistic characteristic noted in Rhoads and Michie, pp. 52-53, and in Frans Neirynck, *Duality in Mark: Contributions to the Study of the Markan Redaction*, Bibliotheca Ephemeridum Theologicarum Lovanienses 31 (Leuven: Leuven University Press, 1972), pp. 110-12.

41. Robbins, *Jesus the Teacher*, pp. 22-25.

42. Robbins, *Jesus the Teacher*, p. 25.

43. Robbins, "Summons and Outline in Mark," p. 113.

the three units in Part II. It does not, however, identify the three units within Part I, nor does it identify the epilogue. What can be said about these differences?

First, it must be noted that one further three-step transition with summons is not noted by Robbins. This occurs in the epilogue (15:40–16:8). This three-step progression does not quite conform to Robbins's definition in that Jesus is not the initiator and the Twelve are not the secondary characters against which the scene is played out. However, in all other ways it bears the same marks of a three-step transition. In the first step (15:40-41) the key figures are the women. There is the requisite movement in step one: "These used to follow him and provided for him when he was in Galilee; and there were many other women who had come up with him to Jerusalem" (15:41). In step two (15:42-47) Joseph and Pilate are introduced, along with two of the women from the previous step. Here the centurion (of 15:39) is the one summoned *(proskalesamenos)*. In step three (16:1-8) the three women are central once again (16:1). There is a summons given to the disciples. They are to go to Galilee. This command does come from Jesus, though it is relayed via the "young man." Although this is not quite as neat as the other transitions, by definition it cannot be since Jesus is dead and the disciples have fled. However, all the essential characteristics are there. But what is this a transition to? Mark's account has ended. But clearly, Mark intends to tie the end of the story back to the beginning. This three-step progression links the end back to the beginning. The sense is that the story is about to begin again, but this time the Twelve will journey with the risen Lord with their eyes and ears open, their hearts soft, and with understanding. In the new journey, in their new state, they will now in fact be the fishers of men that Jesus promised he would make of them when he first called them to be his disciples. The result will be the establishment of the church.

What about the transitions at 3:7-19 and 6:1-13 which do not fit into the outline in this book? For one thing, not all three-step transitions with summons signal a major transition. Robbins demonstrates this himself when he uses the three passion predictions as an example of this stylistic characteristic (though he does not draw attention to this fact).[44] He identifies 8:27–9:1 (which contains the first passion prediction) as a transition into a new unit of material. However, as he shows, 9:30-50 (which contains the second passion prediction) bears all the marks of a transition but is not used as such. The same is true of 10:32-45 (which contains the third passion prediction). It too has the right characteristics but is not identified as a major transition. In fact,

44. Robbins, *Jesus the Teacher*, pp. 22-25.

Robbins contends that the next major transition follows on immediately after the conclusion of the material with the third prediction (10:46–11:11).

The fact of the matter is that the boundaries of the major units in Mark cannot be determined on the basis of one stylistic characteristic alone. Mark makes use of a variety of narrational techniques: repetition, two-step progression, questions, framing, episodes in concentric patterns, as well as episodes in a series of three.[45] In addition, he develops characters, establishes settings, and lets a complex plot play itself out.[46] It is not one of these storytelling techniques alone that Mark uses to move from one unit to the next; it is several (although three-step progressions seem most frequently used). In any case, it is not transitions that determine units; it is thematic content (as argued above).

Back to 3:7-19 and 6:1-13. What is the function of the three-step progression in these two instances if not to point out a major transition? In the case of 3:7-19, the progression serves to tie together the two pericopae which identify the nature of the positive response to Jesus. They then stand as a joined pair in opposition to the next pair of pericopae, which register the negative response to Jesus and are tied together by means of intercalation. In the case of 6:1-13, the three-step progression once again joins pericopae that function in opposition to one another: 6:1-6a describes those who refuse to accept the fact of Jesus' authority, while 6:6b-13 describes those who not only accept the fact of his authority but are given it to use to minister in the same way Jesus did. The three-step progression ensures that the readers make the connection. In any case, it is unlikely that 6:1-13 was meant as a major thematic transition, since it would split the two halves of an intercalated pericope into two different units. Mark 6:6b-13 and 6:30 clearly belong in the same unit.

With the differences between Robbins's outline and the one presented in this book having thus been analyzed, it is interesting to note the similarities. Apart from four common transition points, there is also a common understanding of overall theme. Robbins's view of Mark is as follows:

> My outline of the Gospel of Mark suggests that repetitive forms are the vehicle for the portrayal of a qualitative progression in the identity of Jesus. A qualitative progression . . . does not advance step by step like a perfectly conducted argument, but presents one quality as preparation for the introduction of another. In Mark, repetitive forms containing three units are the

45. Rhoads and Michie, pp. 45-55.
46. Rhoads and Michie, pp. 63-136.

means for unfolding attributes of Jesus and the implications of those attributes for discipleship.[47]

Thus Robbins affirms that what Mark is presenting is an unfolding view of who Jesus is and that this is seen primarily through the eyes of the disciples. "The three-step progressions that end with a summons by Jesus unfold the identity of Jesus and reveal the means by which Jesus' system of thought and action is transmitted to disciple-companions."[48]

Summary of the Structural Argument

Two main arguments support the contention that Mark deliberately organized his story of Jesus into six individual units with a prologue and an epilogue. The first is the thematic argument. Each unit has been shown to have a different perspective on Jesus. Each presents him with a different "title," as it were. Each title for Jesus is accurate but incomplete until the final unit. Mark invites his readers to watch how the disciples move, in six stages, from a cultural view of Jesus to an accurate view of Jesus. In addition to presenting Jesus in different ways, each unit also has a variety of subthemes related to the question of conversion.

The second is the structural argument with its four parts. In part one, it is noted that each unit is designed around a different organizing principle. Two outcomes emanate from noting the structure of each unit. For one thing, the coherence of a unit is seen. The thematic unity of the unit is given structural form. For another, the independence of each unit is made visible. The differences between units are clearly seen. Each unit is seen to stand on its own even as it connects with other units and carries forth the argument. Part two of the structural argument concerns the nature of transitions. Mark carries out each transition between units in a similar fashion. Specifically, he abruptly ends one theme and then launches right into a new theme, blending the two diverse units together by means of various literary devices that smooth out the otherwise rough conceptual transition. Part three of the structural argument deals with the question of bracketing. In the same way that Mark sometimes inserts one pericope into the middle of another and so forces the reader to hear the two stories together, he also brackets each unit (as well as the prologue and epilogue) and so causes the reader to notice the

47. Robbins, *Jesus the Teacher*, p. 20.
48. Robbins, *Jesus the Teacher*, p. 45.

common theme that runs through the material in the unit in question. Part four focuses on the careful use by Mark of the titles for Jesus so that no title is used in a unit prior to its discovery by the Twelve to be an accurate title for Jesus.

This argument can be described another way. It must first be noted that what determines the boundaries of any particular unit is theme. A unit is defined primarily by its content. This is an important point since a fair amount of the analysis of the structure of Mark has involved an examination of stylistic characteristics, with theme as a secondary consideration — as if style were Mark's prime concern.[49] In fact, what Mark is concerned about is telling the story of Jesus, not playing stylistic games. Style is very much in service to story. Theme must be the primary determinant of structure. Having noted the primacy of theme, one may undertake an examination of style. If the units have been properly defined in terms of theme, the stylistic traits will confirm the rightness of the division. Thus a second-level indicator of the integrity of a given unit is the internal structure of that unit. As has been argued, there is a different structural pattern to each unit and this internal pattern is able to account for all the pieces of the unit.[50] A third indicator of the genuineness of the boundaries for a particular unit is the evidence of an attempt on the part of the redactor to smooth out the abrupt thematic transition between units. The fourth evidence of unit coherence is found in the conscious bracketing by the redactor of the material in each unit. The final piece of evidence has to do with the titles for Jesus, which are often different from those used in other Gospels in parallel pericopae but which fit with the concept of an unfolding understanding of Jesus by the Twelve.

---

49. See, for example, Laurence F. X. Brett, "Suggestions for an Analysis of Mark's Arrangement," in *Mark: A New Translation with Introduction and Commentary*, by C. S. Mann (Garden City, N.Y.: Doubleday, 1986), pp. 174-90.

50. This is an important consideration since virtually none of the proposed outlines for Mark can account for all the pieces of the document.

CHAPTER SEVEN

Jesus the Messiah

Thus far the case for the outline of Mark described in this book has been argued in general terms. The material in the Second Gospel has been examined in overview, and various assertions have been made about individual pericopae and units. It is now time to look carefully at the details of the text. The purpose of this examination is twofold: (1) to give more substance to the argument that this is in fact Mark's outline by looking at how his description of Jesus unfolds via the pericopae in each unit, and (2) to dig out details of text that will be of value in the ministry of evangelism (which will be discussed in Part III).

So in chapters 7 and 8 each of the six main titles for Jesus will be discussed, including background material that defines the meaning of each title. In chapters 9 and 10 the four main subthemes that bear upon the theme of conversion (response, faith, repentance, and discipleship) will be examined.

The Terms Defined: An Analysis of the Prologue (Mark 1:1-15)

In the prologue to his account Mark identifies exactly who Jesus is: he is the Messiah, the Son of God (1:1). This verse is the first of an ongoing series of comments by Mark in his role as narrator, in which he stands back from the action and reports on what is happening and what it means. This is also the first indication that Mark's story will unfold on two levels. On one level he is telling the story to people who already know it (in part or in full). In any case, the readers of the Gospel are never left in doubt about the identity of Jesus. They are told the outcome of the story right from the beginning.

157

On another level, however, Mark will tell his story by describing the un-folding discovery on the part of the actual characters in the story that Jesus is the Messiah who is the Son of God. The characters do not know the outcome of this account beforehand. Each person responds to the central figure, Jesus, out of his or her own background, bias, need, and willingness and/or ability to be open. It is by watching these responses by "the people" (the Twelve, the crowds, the religious leaders, the family) that the readers come to understand themselves better; in particular, their own response (or lack of response) to Jesus. Throughout his account Mark is inviting readers to hear the good news and respond to it so as to produce good fruit in their own lives, just as the Twelve (in particular) hear it and respond to it. Mark is preaching the gospel to his readers and not just simply relating the facts of the gospel.[1]

The opening statement in the Gospel of Mark defines the overall aim of the Gospel: to tell the story of Jesus the Messiah, the Son of God. Then the two main sections in the prologue amplify this statement. In 1:2-8 Jesus is identified by John the Baptist to be the one whose coming was foretold in Scripture. He is the long-expected Messiah. In 1:9-13 Jesus is identified by God as God's beloved Son. He is the Son of God. The final two verses (1:14-15) describe how this information about Jesus will be made known to others: it will be transmitted via the ministry of Jesus.

All this is open and plainly stated. The prologue is for the readers of the Gospel. The unfolding understanding of Jesus on the part of the disciples (the main characters in the story apart from Jesus) begins in unit one. Only at the end of the whole account, in the epilogue, will the disciples understand what the readers already know: that Jesus is the Messiah, the Son of God.

Mark 1:2-8: The Messiah

In the first section of the prologue (1:2-8), Mark provides three pieces of in-formation about Jesus: (1) he is the Messiah who was foretold, (2) he is pow-erful, and (3) he will baptize with the Holy Spirit.

The first piece of information is communicated in 1:2-4. Mark starts his account with a quotation attributed to Isaiah that draws attention to two key

1. H. C. Kee, "Mark's Gospel in Recent Research," *Interpretation* 32 (October 1978): 355, in commenting on Willi Marxsen's book *Mark the Evangelist: Studies on the Redaction History of the Gospel* (Nashville: Abingdon, 1969), states: "The enduring insight of Marxsen was that Mark's Gospel is what he calls 'a representation' of Jesus; the Gospel confronts Mark's readers with the reality of Jesus. It is not a report about Jesus, but an en-counter with the Risen Lord."

facts: there is someone coming ("the Lord"),[2] and his way will be prepared by a messenger.[3] Immediately after this is stated, John is introduced: "John the baptizer appeared . . ." (1:4). John is this messenger. He is the Elijah-like figure who was expected to precede the coming of the Messiah.[4] Furthermore, by means of the quotation from the Old Testament, Mark conveys that the coming of Jesus was not a happenstance event. His coming had been predicted. What God promised via his prophets is now unfolding. The age of salvation is about to dawn via the coming of the Lord. Thus Mark sets the coming of Jesus squarely in the midst of messianic expectations. He establishes the first category by which Jesus is to be understood. He is the Messiah.[5]

The second piece of information is communicated in 1:5-7. First, the

2. This is not a title that Mark uses as a central description of Jesus. "Lord" = *kurios* is used fifteen times in the Gospel but only twice in direct reference to Jesus: once in 7:28 where it is a form of address and has the force of "sir," and once in 11:3 where it probably is messianic in tone. In contrast, it is used as a title, "Lord Jesus," in the spurious ending (16:19-20). See C. S. Mann, *Mark: A New Translation with Introduction and Commentary* (Garden City, N.Y.: Doubleday, 1986), p. 195.

3. "The citation . . . is a composite quotation from Ex. 23:20; Mal. 3:1 and Isa. 40:3, passages which evoke the image of the forerunner Elijah. . . . The blended citation functions to draw attention to three factors which are significant to the evangelist in the prologue: the herald, the Lord and the wilderness." William L. Lane, *The Gospel according to Mark* (Grand Rapids: Wm. B. Eerdmans Publishing Co., 1974), pp. 45-46.

4. C. E. B. Cranfield, *The Gospel according to Saint Mark* (Cambridge: University Press, 1959), p. 39, identifies three views that existed in first-century Judaism concerning Elijah. "In the view of some Rabbis he is a messianic figure preparing the way for God himself and restoring Israel. According to another view which is more widely spread he is the forerunner not of God but of the Messiah. It is this view that is behind Mk i.2. (Cf. the ancient prayer preserved in *Sopherim* xix.9: 'May Elijah the prophet come to us soon; and King Messiah come forth in our days.')" As Mark 6:15 indicates, Elijah was on the minds of the people. The connection between Elijah and John the Baptist is made clear by the description of John in Mark 1:6, which is a close parallel of 2 Kings 1:8, where Elijah is described. The link between the two men is made explicit in Mark 9:12-13 during the transfiguration. See D. E. Nineham, *The Gospel of St. Mark* (London: Adam & Charles Black, 1968), pp. 58-59, for a discussion of contemporary Jewish belief in the time of Jesus about the coming Messiah. He quotes two sources from the *Testament of the Twelve Patriarchs*.

5. See Robert A. Guelich, *Mark 1–8:26*, Word Biblical Commentary, vol. 34a (Dallas: Word, 1989), p. 12:

> The composite citation of Exod 23:20; Mal 3:1; and Isa 40:3 in 1:2b-3 set the stage for John's and Jesus' appearance against the background of redemptive history. Not only does God's promise to his people during the exodus (Exod 20:23) find its expression in the promise to God's people of a messenger to prepare the way for the age of salvation (Mal 3:1-2; 4:5-6), but both texts now combine with Isa 40:3 to identify the Baptist's coming and ministry in the wilderness as the fulfillment of that promise for the coming of the "Lord."
>
> Isaiah's promise of the coming of the Lord clearly applies to Jesus.

impact of John the Baptist's ministry is described (1:5). Enormous crowds of people are drawn to John. To make this point Mark uses the first of a number of hyperboles that will characterize his account. Literally translated, 1:5 reads: "*all* the Judean countryside and *all* the people of Jerusalem went out to him." Such a response was not unexpected. For over three hundred years Israel had been without a prophet. Now suddenly here is a man who looks and sounds like a prophet, and thus huge numbers of people make the somewhat difficult journey out to the Jordan River to see him. Second, Mark uses John's enormous popularity as a foil against which to measure Jesus. In 1:7 this man to whom the whole country is flocking says: "The one who is more powerful than I is coming after me." In other words, the Coming One will be far more powerful than the powerful John. The Coming One will be, in fact, a man of power. To make the comparison even more striking, the Baptist adds the statement: "I am not worthy to stoop down and untie the thong of his sandals" (1:7). The job of removing the sandals of the master was so lowly that not even a Hebrew slave was forced to do it.[6] Thus the comparison between John the Baptist and the Coming One (the Messiah) is the comparison between a person who is lower even than a slave and a person who is a great master. In this way the preeminence of the Messiah is established.

The final piece of information about the Messiah has to do with his role. He will baptize with the Holy Spirit (1:8). "The outpouring of the Spirit was a well-known feature of speculation about the end-time," as C. S. Mann points out.[7] "Through Jesus' life (ministry) and death, one receives the 'baptism with the Holy Spirit,' i.e., the salvation promised for the new age (1:14-15; 1:16-18)."[8]

Thus, right from the start of his account Mark tells his readers that Jesus is the Messiah. He also tells them something about the role of the Messiah.

Mark 1:9-13: The Son of God

But this is not all Mark has to say about the Coming One. In the next section of the prologue (1:9-13), Mark provides three more pieces of information:

---

6. Lane, p. 52.

7. Mann, p. 197. Mann also points out that nowhere is the Messiah described as bestowing the Spirit. But this is not a necessary connection. The connection with the end times is sufficient. In any case, Mark is involved in refining cultural expectations about the Messiah and redefining who the Messiah is (e.g., 8:31–10:45).

8. Guelich, p. 25.

(1) he gives the name of the one who was foretold, (2) he reveals his full identity, and (3) he foreshadows the nature of his ministry.

Mark communicates the first piece of information in the same way he revealed in the previous section that John was the messenger who had been foretold. There Mark recited the prophecy about the forerunner and then stated, "John the baptizer appeared. . . ." Mark's sentence structure indicates that the Baptist is the forerunner. Here he follows up John's testimony about the Coming One with the statement: "In those days Jesus came. . . ." Once again the sentence structure makes the point. Jesus is the Coming One, the Messiah who was foretold.

The second piece of information is communicated via the baptism of Jesus. The Holy Spirit comes upon Jesus (1:10) and the voice of God declares: "You are my Son" (1:11). Jesus is also the Son of God.

The final piece of information is revealed via the activity of the Holy Spirit, who sends Jesus into the wilderness to do battle with Satan (1:12-13). This foreshadows what is to come: Jesus in conflict with Satan. Jesus will cast out demons, undo illness, soften hardened hearts, open blinded eyes. In other words, he will undo the works of Satan.

There is no mystery in the prologue. The Messiah who has been prophesied has come. John the Baptist, the Elijah figure, clearly pointed him out and declared his power. His baptism shows that Jesus the Messiah is also the Son of God. The reader is given all this information. However, the people in the story do not know all this about Jesus. It will take time for them to discover who Jesus is. This is what Mark's story will be about: how these insights into his true identity came to be understood.

Mark 1:14-15: How the Gospel Is Made Known

The final two verses in the prologue may at first glance seem to be connected to unit one rather than to the prologue. In 1:14-15 the narrator tells his readers that Jesus has come into Galilee and is busy proclaiming the gospel. And in the next pericope (1:16-20) he shows Jesus doing this very thing as he calls four fishermen to follow him.

However, a closer look reveals that 1:14-15 not only describes what is taking place as Jesus begins his ministry. It also describes the whole of his ministry in all six units. It is similar to the overview statement with which Mark begins his Gospel (1:1). Mark 1:14-15 is also an overview statement which describes how the "good news about Jesus Christ, the Son of God," will be communicated. It will be via the ministry of Jesus himself. He who is the message (1:1) is also the messenger (1:14-15). Clearly 1:14-15 is connected to the prologue and is a fitting summary to what has been said in that prologue.[9]

And what is this "good news of God" that Jesus proclaims? Mark has already given the core content of it in his first thirteen verses. The "good news of God" is about Jesus, the powerful one, who has come in fulfillment of prophecy; it is Jesus, the bearer of the Holy Spirit, who confronts Satan; it is Jesus who proclaims this news of the kingdom and calls for response to it.

The Titles of Jesus

One further observation remains to be made about the prologue of the Second Gospel. Each of the six titles by which the Twelve gradually come to know Jesus is expressed, in one way or another, in the prologue. First, the role of Jesus as teacher is seen in the fact that when he comes into Galilee, his work is described as "proclamation" (1:14). The word used here is *kērussōn,* from which *kērugma* is derived. Kerygma (the Anglicized version of the word) is used "as a technical term for the early Christian preaching."[10] Second, Jesus' role as prophet is shown in two ways. For one thing, John the Baptist is clearly a prophet (1:6) and Jesus is described in terms similar to him — only Jesus will be greater (1:7-8). For another thing, the phrase the Baptist uses in making this comparison is: "The one who is more powerful than I." In Mark's Gospel a prophet is a person of power, capable of mighty deeds. Third, the role of Jesus as Messiah is identified in the opening statement of the prologue. Also, the descent of the dove is a picture of "anointing," which is the root idea of the concept of Messiah. In this way he is shown to be, literally, the Anointed One of God. Fourth, his role as Son of Man is implied in his baptism by John. For Mark's readers, baptism was a symbol of dying and rising again (Rom. 6:3-10), and death and resurrection come to define the role of the Son of Man. Fifth, Jesus' role as Son of David is the least obvious in the prologue. However, it is implied in the opening quotation from the Old Testament (Mark 1:2-3). Jesus is "to be understood in the context of the prophecies regarded by ancient Jews and Christians as holy Scripture and divine revelation of God's purposes."[11] Thus, in connecting Jesus with the coming

9. Although some scholars feel that the prologue ends at 1:13, as Guelich notes: "The recent trend has been to include 1:14-15 within the opening section" (p. 4).

10. Michael Green, *Evangelism in the Early Church* (London: Hodder & Stoughton, 1970), p. 58.

11. Larry W. Hurtado, *Mark: A Good News Commentary* (San Francisco: Harper & Row, 1983), p. 2.

redemptive work of God on behalf of his people and in identifying him as the Messiah, the overtones of Davidic sonship are there for those familiar with the characteristics of the coming Messiah. Finally, the title Son of God is mentioned twice in the prologue (1:1, 11). Thus to the knowledgeable reader (i.e., one who already knows who Jesus is), all the correct titles are found in the prologue. These will, then, unfold through the eyes of the disciples throughout the remainder of the Gospel.

Jesus the Teacher: An Analysis of Unit One (Mark 1:16–4:34)

In the opening pericope of unit one Jesus says to Simon and Andrew: "Follow me" (1:17). Immediately the two fishermen drop their nets and follow him. Soon after this Jesus meets James and John. He calls them, and they too immediately follow him. The questions one must ask are: What did these men imagine themselves to be doing when they agreed to follow Jesus? Whom did they think they were following? What were the cultural categories available to them in first-century Israel by which they would understand who Jesus was and agree to follow him?

Jewish Rabbis and Greek Teachers

The traditional view is that these four men understood themselves to be joining a rabbi as his disciples.

> It is customary to presuppose that the teacher/disciple relation in Mark derives from the rabbi/disciple relation in first-century c.e. Judaism. In four stories in Mark, Jesus is addressed either as *rabbi* or *rabbouni* (9:5; 10:51; 11:21; 14:45), and in many other stories Jesus' dialogue with his disciples follows patterns akin to patterns in rabbinic accounts.
>
> Moreover, the phrases *akolouthein opisō* and *erchesthai opisō* (to follow after or to come after) are to be compared not only with the biblical phrases but with rabbinic accounts where disciples are featured in a position of following behind. In addition, in four settings in Mark Jesus sits as he teaches (4:1; 9:35; 12:41; 13:3), and this position is characteristic of the rabbinic teacher.[12]

---

12. Vernon K. Robbins, *Jesus the Teacher: A Socio-Rhetorical Interpretation of Mark* (Philadelphia: Fortress, 1984), p. 101.

The four fisherman (as well as the other eight men who would soon join Jesus' band) would have been aware of other bands of disciples who followed religious figures. Mark makes a point of mentioning this fact. In 2:18 he twice identifies the disciples of John and the disciples of the Pharisees. The question at issue in that particular pericope (2:18-22) is why the disciples of Jesus do not fast when the disciples of John and the disciples of the Pharisees do fast. This comparison would not have been made had there not been similarities between all three bands. It would appear that Mark himself is drawing attention to this commonality since this is the only time he refers to other disciples, with the exception of 6:29 where it is noted that John's disciples carried away the body of their master.

However, Jesus and the Twelve are not fully comparable to a rabbi and his disciples. There are important differences. For one thing, rabbis did not seek out disciples. Disciples sought out rabbis. "A student had to try to gain admittance into the circle of a respected teacher and to engage in the study of Scripture and tradition in this fellowship."[13] "There are no rabbinical stories of 'calling' and 'following after' analogous to the pericopae in Mark and Q, nor did the summons 'follow me' resound from any rabbinical teacher in respect of entry into a teacher-pupil relationship."[14] For another thing, rabbis were not, in general, itinerant. They had schools. They remained in one place. "Mark presupposes an itinerant tradition, while rabbinic literature presupposes a school tradition."[15] In the rabbinic tradition "the student travels, but the teacher does not travel."[16]

And in fact, at first the disciples seem to assume that Jesus would remain in Capernaum to teach. After all, when he called them, they did not go off elsewhere immediately. Mark reports that they go from the lake where they are fishing to nearby Capernaum, where they stayed until the Sabbath (1:21). Mark then reports on a twenty-four-hour period of ministry in Capernaum (1:21-34). Early in the morning after this day of ministry, Jesus goes off on his own to pray (1:35). "Simon and his companions hunted for him. When they found him, they said to him, 'Everyone is searching for you'" (1:36-37). The assumption on the part of the disciples seems to be that Jesus will return to Capernaum and resume his ministry there. This, after all, would fit in with how they understood the ministry of a rabbi. However, Jesus

13. Eduard Lohse, "Rabbi," in *Theological Dictionary of the New Testament* (1968), vol. 6, p. 962.

14. Martin Hengel, *The Charismatic Leader and His Followers*, trans. James C. G. Grieg, ed. John Riches (Edinburgh: T. & T. Clark, 1981), pp. 50-51.

15. Robbins, p. 105.

16. Robbins, p. 102.

insists that they leave and go on to other villages, and hence they travel together throughout Galilee (1:38-39).

The purpose of the rabbinic schools was different from what Jesus had in mind. Rabbinic schools were established so that young men could study Scripture and tradition in order to become teachers and be themselves called rabbi. The title of rabbi "gradually became the exclusive term for those who had completed their studies and been ordained as teachers of the Law."[17] In contrast, "Jesus' aim was not to form tradition or to nurture exegetical or apocalyptic scholarship but to proclaim the nearness of God in word and deed, to call to repentance, and to proclaim the will of God . . . ; similarly, 'following after' him and 'discipleship' were oriented to this one great aim."[18]

So, while in some senses the disciples were attaching themselves to a rabbi-type figure, in other senses this did not fully define the nature of their relationship to Jesus. In fact, a second model was operating in the first century that helps to define the relationship between Jesus and his disciples: that of the itinerant Greek teacher. W. D. Davies notes the differences between Jesus and a rabbi and comments "that in many ways Jesus was like a wandering Cynic-Stoic preacher rather than a rabbi. . . ."[19] Robbins adds: "It was a common practice of sophists to travel from city to city in order to gather disciples who would seek to embody wisdom and virtue by associating with them, receiving instruction from them, and imitating them."[20] This model was known in first-century Jewish culture. As Robbins notes: "When Israelite tradition began to be transmitted within Hellenistic culture, it was natural for the teacher/disciple pattern to make inroads into Jewish thought."[21]

The Concept of Teacher in Mark's Gospel

So, when Jesus calls Simon, Andrew, James, and John to follow him, they would have understood him to be inviting them to become part of a band of disciples attached to a religious teacher. They may not have accurately understood all the details of their relationship to Jesus, but they would have been clear about whom they were following: Jesus was a rabbi/teacher. This was the only category available to them at that time by which to understand Jesus.

17. Lohse, pp. 962-63.
18. Hengel, p. 53.
19. W. D. Davies, *The Setting of the Sermon on the Mount* (Cambridge: Cambridge University Press, 1964), p. 422.
20. Robbins, p. 88.
21. Robbins, p. 94.

And in unit one, according to Mark's account, this is how they thought about Jesus.

In unit one Mark presents Jesus as an itinerant teacher. He does this in three ways: (1) by how he structures his initial pericopae to reveal that Jesus is a teacher of exceptional power; (2) by showing Jesus engaged in those activities associated with first-century Jewish teachers; and (3) by the titles given to Jesus in this unit.[22]

The Opening Pericope: The Disciples Discover That Jesus Is a Great Teacher

Yet another characteristic of Mark's writing style is important to mention. The opening pericope in each unit contains the same three characteristics: (1) a misunderstanding on the part of the Twelve (and sometimes others) about who Jesus is, related to the title that is the focus of that unit, or a discovery of something new about Jesus, again related to the focus of the unit;[23] (2) a strong emotional response related to this discovery, usually on the part of (or including) the Twelve; and (3) the idea of rebuke. This consistent stylistic characteristic is yet another indication that the units as described in this book are the units that Mark intended, and that Mark focused on a different title for Jesus in each.

In Mark 1:16-28 the disciples discover that Jesus is an exceptional teacher.[24] They could not have anticipated his skill as a teacher/healer/exorcist. Jesus had no formal training to equip him to be a rabbi, nor had he been the disciple of a famous rabbi. But here in these opening stories they discover, along with the crowd, that he teaches with authority. This fact is commented upon because the teaching of Jesus is so different from the teaching of the scribes (1:22). Furthermore, Jesus is able to command evil spirits because of

---

22. "The repeated use of the term *didache* in Mark 1:21, a pericope describing Jesus' first appearance in a synagogue, as well as Jesus' first 'public' appearance, is most striking." Robert P. Meye, *Jesus and the Twelve: Discipleship and Revelation in Mark's Gospel* (Grand Rapids: Wm. B. Eerdmans Publishing Co., 1968), p. 45.

23. In fact, these are two facets of the same issue. To say that the Twelve discover a new facet of Jesus is also to say that prior to that point they had misunderstood Jesus. Or put the opposite way, failure to have understood who Jesus is, is seen in the new discovery they make about him. Sometimes the emphasis is on misunderstanding, at other times it is on discovery.

24. This section is different from the other five opening sections in that two pericopae are combined together to produce this insight into Jesus. However, the pericopae are not distinct from one another; rather, the second follows directly from the first in subject matter and time sequence.

this authority (1:27). And, like other teachers, he has disciples who follow him (1:16-21). In these stories Jesus is compared to the teachers of the law because in the minds of the people this is the group he most closely resembles (1:22).

The emotional response found in the opening pericope of each unit is expressed by the crowd. They are "amazed" at Jesus. This response is repeated twice in the pericope (1:22 = *exeplēssonto*, 1:27 = *ethambēthēsan*). The response of the disciples is probably reflected in the response of the crowd. The disciples have not yet been differentiated from the crowd in terms of how they view Jesus. (They will, however, be called out from among the crowd in 3:13-19.) The rebuke found in the opening pericope of unit one comes from Jesus and is directed at the evil spirit (1:25).[25] Thus the reader is informed that the primary role of Jesus in unit one will be that of a great teacher.

The Activities of a Teacher

This impression is reinforced by the activities of Jesus that Mark describes in unit one. These are the activities of a teacher. First, Jesus gathers disciples. As the unit begins, Jesus' first act is to call to himself four disciples (1:16-20). Soon he calls a fifth disciple (2:13-14). Then in 3:13-19 he appoints twelve men to be "apostles" (including the five whose call has already been described). Jesus defines the role of these twelve in two ways: they are "to be with him" as disciple-companions, and they are to extend his ministry as they go out to preach and cast out demons (3:14-15). In no other unit does Jesus call specific individuals to follow him, nor does he appoint any other people to be his emissaries. As noted above, this sort of summons of disciples is characteristic of an itinerant teacher in the first-century Mediterranean culture. "From the fifth century B.C.E. through the second century C.E., a wide variety of itinerant teachers was active throughout the Mediterranean world, producing a well-established cultural tradition of the traveling preacher-teacher who gathered disciples."[26]

Second, Jesus does what other first-century Jewish teachers did: he teaches/preaches, he casts out demons, and he heals. After the call of the four disciples, Mark then describes a twenty-four-hour day of ministry for Jesus (1:21-34). The day begins with Jesus going to a synagogue and teaching

25. In four of the six opening pericopae the word "rebuke" (from *epitimaō*) is used: in 1:25 (unit one), 4:39 (unit two), 8:32-33 (twice) (unit four), and 10:48 (unit five). In unit six the word *enebrimōnto* is used, meaning "they were indignant" or "they rebuked harshly," while in unit three the disciples respond to Jesus in a rebuking sort of way (6:37).

26. Meye, p. 88.

(1:21). His teaching is a source of amazement to the congregation "because he taught them as one who had authority, not as the teachers of the law" (1:22 NIV).[27] He is not just any teacher, he is a powerful teacher. His teaching, however, is interrupted by a demon-possessed man. Jesus confronts the demon and casts him from the man. This exorcism is understood to be a part of his teaching: "They were all amazed, and they kept on asking one another, 'What is this? A new teaching — with authority! He commands even the unclean spirits, and they obey him'" (1:27).[28] After his ministry in the synagogue, Jesus goes to Peter's home and heals Peter's mother-in-law (1:30-31). Later in the day he casts out demons and heals others from the town (1:32-34).

It might be asked whether healing and exorcism were part of a teaching ministry. But in the first century the role of healer-exorcist was not incompatible with the role of teacher. Exorcism was undertaken by Pharisees (Matt. 12:27) as well as by rabbis. As D. Daube points out: "A great Rabbi was expected to be prominent in both fields, or rather, the two fields were not kept strictly separate."[29] Likewise, healing was undertaken by priests and prophets.[30] Robbins points out that both healing and exorcism were activities undertaken by teachers.

> In first-century Greco-Roman culture, not only physicians but also political leaders, prophets, magicians, and philosophers-teachers were known for healing people of physical ailments. The important consideration was not whether a person performed healings but the social identity in which he performed them. *In Mark, both exorcisms and healings are part of Jesus' role as teacher.* Both his words and his actions attack spiritual forces that afflict people and offer an alternative approach to life.[31]

In unit one the emphasis is on the teaching ministry of Jesus. This is seen in the activities of Jesus that Mark describes. He gives seven specific examples of Jesus' teaching (2:8-11, 17, 19-22, 25-28; 3:4, 23-29, 33-35). In addition, the longest section in the unit (4:1-34) is devoted entirely to his teaching. Mark also mentions Jesus' teaching and preaching in general terms nine times (1:21-22,

---

27. David Daube, *The New Testament and Rabbinic Judaism* (London: University of London, The Athlone Press, 1956), p. 206, argues that this phrase means that he taught not like those who were unordained but like a learned rabbi.

28. "What is particularly remarkable is that the emphatic reference to 'a new teaching' follows the exorcism, not the notice that Jesus taught." Daube, p. 206.

29. Daube, p. 206.

30. Geza Vermes, *Jesus the Jew: A Historian's Reading of the Gospels* (London: Collins, 1973), p. 59.

31. Robbins, p. 114 (italics mine).

27, 38, 39; 2:2, 13; 3:14; 4:1-2, 33-34). In addition, there are four healings: Peter's mother-in-law (1:30-31), the leper (1:40-45), the paralytic (2:1-12), and the man with the shriveled hand (3:1-6). The healing ministry of Jesus is mentioned twice in general terms (1:32-34; 3:10). And there is the one exorcism: the man in the synagogue (1:23-28). However, his ministry of exorcism is mentioned four times in general terms (1:32-34, 39; 3:11-12, 15).

The Title "Teacher"

The title that best defines who Jesus is portrayed as in unit one is not found in unit one at all but in the first incident in unit two (4:35-41).[32] The way the disciples have come to view Jesus during their early days with him is expressed during the storm that overtakes them while crossing the Sea of Galilee. In the moment of crisis the disciples call Jesus "Teacher" (4:38). It is clear that Mark has used this title on purpose. In the parallel account in Matthew the term used is "Lord" (Matt. 8:25), while in the parallel account in Luke the term is "Master" (Luke 8:24). But for Mark the term "teacher" best describes who Jesus is to the disciples up to this point. It acts as a summation of their experience of Jesus.[33]

After their cry for help (they probably want Jesus to assist them in bailing out the boat), Jesus stills the storm with a word of power. Clearly this is not the act of a teacher, no matter how exceptional he might be. Teachers do not have this kind of power. The inadequacy of this title is evident to the Twelve. They no longer know who he is: "Who then is this?" they cry. "Even the wind and the sea obey him" (Mark 4:41). The title "teacher" is no longer adequate. In unit two the disciples will discover a whole new facet of Jesus. However, the title "teacher" does sum up the disciples' view of Jesus in unit one, prior to the new insight into Jesus which they will soon be given.

The Twelve do not again call Jesus "teacher" until 9:38, and then in a sit-

---

32. Only two titles are used of Jesus within the unit itself. He is twice called the Son of God by the demons (in 1:24, "the Holy One of God," and in 3:11, "the Son of God"). He twice calls himself the Son of Man (2:10, 28). Neither title is definitive for the disciples (or anyone else for that matter). The cries by the demons are never noticed and never commented upon (neither here nor elsewhere in the Gospel). It is not until unit six that the title Son of God is mentioned by any person. As to the title Son of Man, it is far too vague for it yet to have much significance, probably meaning to those who heard it the equivalent of "a man" or "the man," as Vermes points out on pp. 162-63.

33. Meye notes that Mark uses the term "teacher" while Matthew and Luke use other titles. He attributes this to Mark's particular interest in the teaching ministry of Jesus. See Meye, pp. 36-37.

uation in which Jesus is actually engaged in teaching them.[34] They call him "teacher" a second time in 13:1, at the start of the longest teaching section in the Gospel. Once again, the title defines the role he is playing at that moment. There is one further example when he is called "teacher." James and John address him in this way when they want a favor from him (10:35). This particular use of the title parallels the way it was used by the rich young man (10:17, 20) and by the religious leaders (12:14), namely, as a preface to a request. This was an insincere form of flattery, as Mark points out in 12:15, and it has this ring when spoken by James and John in 10:35. They are buttering him up, trying to get him to do something they know he will not be keen on doing. In other words, the title "teacher" drops into the background as far as the Twelve are concerned. He is a great teacher, but they come to understand that he is more than this.

In contrast, the crowds continue to perceive Jesus as a teacher. The title "teacher" may become inadequate for the disciples, but it does define how those outside the Twelve view him. So in 5:35 the friends of Jairus call him "teacher"; in 9:17 the man with the epileptic son calls him "teacher"; and (as noted) in 10:17, 20 the rich young ruler calls Jesus "teacher."[35]

It must be remembered that Mark does not simply introduce a title for Jesus, discuss it, and then drop it.[36] Once Jesus is identified in a certain way, he continues to be shown functioning in accord with that ability. Mark does not define six *independent* aspects of Jesus. He presents an *unfolding* view of Jesus in which each vision of him is correct but incomplete until the final vision. All the titles are accurate, but they must be taken together if one is to have a full picture of Jesus. Thus in unit one Mark introduces Jesus as a teacher. Jesus will continue to function as a teacher for the remainder of the Gospel. It has long been noted that Jesus as teacher is a major emphasis in

34. This statement is found in 9:35-50, one of the major sections of teaching in the Second Gospel. Here Mark collects together various sayings of Jesus (as seen by the fact that the materials here are found in various contexts in Matthew and Luke), and by means of various "catchwords" crafts them into an integrated unit having to do with relationships (specifically, how to move from argument — 9:35 — to peace with one another — 9:50). This section of teaching is parallel in structure to the way Mark has crafted an earlier unit of teaching, 4:1-34. Hence, the most accurate term to use for Jesus in this context is "teacher."

35. Jesus once refers to himself as teacher. When he sends two of his disciples out to find the room where they will eat the Passover, he instructs them to say to the owner of the house: "The Teacher asks, Where is my guest room where I may eat the Passover with my disciples?" (14:14). Apparently this is how the owner of the house would have viewed Jesus.

36. See above, p. 150.

Mark.[37] One of the reasons for this is perhaps that, being the first title introduced, it has the most space to develop. And certainly, "the title *didaskale* is the most common form of address to Jesus in Mark. . . ."[38]

So it is that the Twelve begin their relationship with Jesus by viewing him as a powerful and effective teacher. This is not unexpected given the cultural and theological categories available to them. But they need to move beyond this limited view.

Jesus the Prophet: An Analysis of Unit Two (Mark 4:35–6:30)

The rather comfortable assessment on the part of the disciples that Jesus is a teacher is about to be challenged. While the title "teacher" accurately describes Jesus, it does not do him full justice. It captures only one part of who he is. In unit two the disciples learn that Jesus is not just an exceptional teacher, but he is also a prophet of great power.

The Power of Jesus

The Stilling of the Storm: Mark 4:35-41

In the first pericope of unit two (4:35-41), the Twelve discover that Jesus is not just a teacher. The story begins with Jesus' decision to sail across the lake at the end of a day of teaching. Jesus has been addressing the crowd from a boat moored offshore. Rather than landing and having to deal with the crowds, he and the disciples simply set sail for the other side (4:35-36). A "great windstorm" comes up. This is not an unusual event for the bowl-shaped Sea of Galilee, where the combination of a deep lake and winds blowing down off the ridges creates the conditions for serious storms. However, this particular storm proves to be especially fierce. Even the fishermen-disci-

37. "The comparative brevity of the Marcan narrative makes it obvious that Mark uses the didactic designation of Jesus with a relatively greater frequency [than the other Synoptics]" (Meye, p. 36). "Matthew and Luke were not as obviously and consciously concerned to depict Jesus *as a teacher* as was Mark." Meye, p. 39. See also R. T. France, "Mark and the Teaching of Jesus," in *Gospel Perspectives: Studies of History and Tradition in the Four Gospels*, ed. R. T. France and David Wenham, vol. 1 (Sheffield: University of Sheffield, 1980), p. 102, and Ralph Martin, *Mark: Evangelist and Theologian* (Grand Rapids: Zondervan, 1973), pp. 111-17.

38. France, p. 104.

ples are worried, although this lake with all its tricks is familiar to them. We are told that the boat is about to be swamped (4:37). The disciples are afraid. They wake up Jesus. "Teacher," they say with some anger, "do you not care that we are perishing?" Jesus "woke up and rebuked the wind, and said to the sea, 'Peace! Be still!'" The elements obey. "Then the wind ceased, and there was a dead calm" (4:39). The disciples are aghast. This is not at all what they had expected.

Three details make this evident. First, the reason they wake Jesus is to get his help in bailing out the boat. This is implied by Mark's explicit statement in verse 37 that the problem was that "the waves beat into the boat, so that the boat was already being swamped." They needed to get the water out of the boat, lest they sink. At this point in their experience of Jesus (as described by Mark) the disciples have no reason to expect that he can or will do anything miraculous to save them.[39] Second, the title by which they address Jesus indicates their view of him at that time (4:38). He is a "teacher" to them — and while teachers might be able to heal and cast out demons, the disciples would not have expected him to have power beyond such acts.[40] Finally, their reaction after he calms the storm shows that they were not expecting a miracle from him. Their fear turns into terror. This would not have been their response had they anticipated a miracle of this sort. They ask: "Who is this?"

39. Thus far *in Mark's account* they have had no experience of Jesus' great power. However, in the parallel account in Luke 8:22-25 the Twelve already know that Jesus can raise people from the dead (Luke 7:11-17). In fact, they already know he is a powerful prophet. The title given Jesus in this incident is "great prophet" (Luke 7:16). This raises the whole question of multiple Gospels and the fact that pericopae are used in different ways by different Gospel writers for different purposes. It has long been recognized that each Gospel writer tells his story with his own theological intentions. As was pointed out in chapter 5, the concern in this book is to look at how Mark tells his story in accord with his particular theological intentions. And one of his intentions is to tell the story of the unfolding understanding of the Twelve. It is important to hear Mark's story the way he tells it. His story has a unity to it that must be taken seriously so that the integrity of the account is maintained. Thus in this book, when the experience of the Twelve is described, it is discussed as it unfolds in Mark's account and in accord with his and only his literary intentions. The question of the chronology of events and how different writers use pericopae to tell their own stories is another issue, beyond the scope of this book.

40. Moule's comment that "modern readers find even the most startling accounts of the cure of disease less hard to believe than this control over the elements" applies to the disciples as well. They would have witnessed healings and exorcism prior to joining up with Jesus — such things would not have been rare in first-century Israel. But "who can believe that the weather will obey personal commands?" They would not have anticipated such an outcome to their dilemma. C. F. D. Moule, *The Gospel according to Mark* (Cambridge: University Press, 1965), p. 41.

Their old categories no longer prove adequate. "The change from relatively calm teaching discourse [4:1-34] to a violent storm and the display of Jesus' awesome authority over the forces of nature is intended to jolt the reader with a reminder that Jesus is more than a religious teacher."[41]

A teacher, no matter how great, cannot control the elements. Teachers don't do that sort of thing. So the disciples' fear for their physical safety is turned into the kind of terror one feels in the face of the numinous (to use Rudolf Otto's category).[42] And the Twelve learn that Jesus is no mere teacher. But if Jesus is not a teacher, then who is he? Who is this man they thought they knew but who turns out to have such great power? Thus Mark poses the question which will be answered over the course of the next few pericopae.

This opening pericope in unit two bears the same three characteristics one finds in the opening pericopae in the other units. First, a new facet of Jesus is revealed. His ability to calm the storm forces the disciples to recognize that Jesus has power beyond that of a teacher. To put this another way, when they woke him they had not understood what he could and would do in light of their peril. Second, the disciples have an overwhelming emotional experience. At first they are afraid (*deiloi* = cowardly, timid,[43] and the context shows that this fear is due to the physical danger they face — they might drown). This physical fear, however, turns into "a feeling of reverential awe, a sense of the uncanny"[44] (*ephobēthēsan phobon* = lit. "they feared fear"). Third, there is the element of rebuke: "He woke up and rebuked the wind . . ." (4:39).

The Exorcism of Legion: Mark 5:1-20

Mark's next story is even more terrifying for the Twelve. After the storm Jesus and the disciples continue across the lake and land somewhere on the eastern shore in a largely Gentile region.[45] It is probably still night. (They left as evening came; it is not more than two hours across the lake under normal conditions;[46] the storm blew them off course, but chances are they landed well be-

---

41. Hurtado, p. 67.

42. See above, pp. 77-79.

43. William F. Arndt and F. Wilbur Gingrich, *A Greek-English Lexicon of the New Testament and Other Early Christian Literature* (Chicago: University of Chicago Press, 1957), p. 173.

44. Vincent Taylor, *The Gospel according to St. Mark* (New York: St. Martin's Press, 1966), p. 277.

45. The exact location of "the region of the Gerasenes" is not known. See Eduard Schweizer, *The Good News according to Mark,* trans. Donald H. Madvig (London: SPCK, 1971), p. 113, and Nineham, p. 153.

fore dawn.)[47] After their terrifying experience the disciples must have been glad to be on land again. However, what greeted them was the equivalent of a living nightmare. A man possessed by demons comes shrieking out of the tombs. It turns out they have landed in a cemetery — the worst place to be at night because this is where demons were said to be found.[48] The demon-possessed man is a frightening sight to behold: he is naked; he is unkempt; he has gashes on his body; perhaps he still has chains hanging from his feet and hands (5:3-4). It is no wonder that the presence of the disciples is not reported at all in this incident, though they are there by implication. They are in the boat that has crossed the lake (5:1), and the boat is still there when the story ends (5:18).

In this incident the Twelve learn about a different kind of power in Jesus: the ability to overcome the most severe form of evil. They already knew Jesus had power over demons, but this was something else. In this man he faced not one demon but a legion of demons. (A Roman legion was about six thousand strong.[49] When the demons came out of the man, they entered a herd of about two thousand pigs — 5:13.) The term "legion" indicates not only the large number of these demons but their power. A Roman legion was the most formidable fighting machine of that era. The term also suggests that what is going on between Jesus and this man is akin to warfare. Yet, as it turns out, it is no contest. Jesus easily dominates the demons. They beg his indulgence (5:12). He is their master. Jesus has amazing power.

The residents of the region recognize this power. After viewing the disaster that has taken place (from their point of view), they beg Jesus to leave (5:16-17). Being Gentiles (they kept pigs), they probably understood Jesus to be a powerful magician.[50] As such, he was not to be trusted. He had to leave. Who knew where he might direct his power? After all, he had already destroyed the town's herd of pigs.

---

46. Lane, p. 181.

47. The objection might be raised that were it still night, it would not have been possible for the demoniac to see Jesus from a distance (5:6). However, if there had been a full moon, this would not have been a problem. In any case, something other than pure sensory observation is going on in this account. The demoniac already knows who Jesus is. He falls at his feet and addresses him as "Jesus, Son of the Most High God" (5:7).

48. William Barclay, *The Gospel of Mark,* rev. ed. (Philadelphia: Westminster, 1975), pp. 34-35. Guelich, p. 278.

49. Hurtado, p. 71.

50. See discussion below, pp. 178-79.

The Healing of Chronic Illness: Mark 5:24b-34

The next two stories reveal yet more about the power of Jesus. For the second time in his account Mark sandwiches two pericopae together. Both have to do with women; both women are unclean in a ritual sense (the one due to her vaginal discharge, the other because she was dead); both women are healed by the power of Jesus. The first story focuses on a woman with a chronic illness. She had been ill twelve years (5:25). No one had been able to heal her. On the contrary, "she had endured much under many physicians, and had spent all that she had; and she was no better, but rather grew worse" (5:26). This unnamed woman approaches Jesus secretly. She is forced to do this since her particular illness made her ritually impure, which meant she could not come in contact with others lest she make them impure (Lev. 15:19). In fact, she should not even have been in the crowd. As a result, she cannot approach Jesus directly. All she can hope to do is touch his cloak (Mark 5:27).[51] But amazingly she is healed (5:29). Jesus, for his part, is aware that power has left him (5:30), and he forces her to reveal herself (so that her healing will be complete).[52]

This passage reveals three additional facts about Jesus. First, it shows that no disease is beyond his power to heal. He cures even chronic illness. Second, it defines what these four stories are all about: the power of Jesus. For the first time Mark uses the word "power" (*dynamis*, 5:30). Third, this power resides in Jesus. It is part of him. It goes forth out of him at the woman's touch (5:30). "Fundamentally *dynamis* is the power of the living personal God . . . or a 'mighty work' which manifests His power. In the present passage *tēn ex autou dynamin* is the divine healing power which dwells in Jesus . . . and proceeds from Him. . . ."[53]

The Raising of a Dead Child: Mark 5:21-24a, 35-43

The story into which this pericope was intercalated further amplifies the concept of the power of Jesus. Jesus is en route to a sick child when news reaches

---

51. "The person of a healer was in former times regarded as sacrosanct, and objects associated with the healer's person were held to be potent as in some way partaking of the healer's power (cf. Acts 5:15, 19:12)." Mann, p. 285.

52. Her healing would not be complete without this public disclosure, since her disease had not only physical but social consequences. In the same way that Jesus insisted that the leper go through the cleansing ritual and thus be admitted back into society (1:44), here Jesus makes it publicly known that she has been healed so that she can once again have a normal social life. In other words, he healed her physically, spiritually, and socially.

53. Taylor, p. 291.

his traveling party that the girl has died (5:35). Jesus counsels faith, not fear (5:36), and they continue on to her home. When they get there the presence of professional mourners signals that by all normal criteria of the first century the girl had died (5:38). But Jesus denies that this is so: "The child is not dead but sleeping" (5:39). Jesus does not mean that she has not really died or that she is in some sort of coma. This is said to reassure the father. But the girl is dead, as the presence of the mourners, the report of the messengers, the laughter that greeted this statement all indicate. Besides, Jesus had not yet seen the child and so was in no position to render an opinion on her medical condition. Furthermore, Jesus uses this same expression in reference to Lazarus when he was so dead that he stank (John 11:11-15). Jesus, the parents, and three disciples go in to the child (Mark 5:40). Jesus reaches down, takes the girl by the hand, speaks to her, and she gets up (5:41-42). He has power even over death itself.

Thus in these four pericopae the Twelve learn that Jesus has power over all the forces that afflict humankind: natural disaster, evil, incurable illness, and even the ultimate enemy, death. His power is of an overwhelming kind.

The Role of the Prophet

In the first story of this series the disciples ask, "Who is this?" Who has the power to tame the elements? By implication they would have asked the same question at the end of each of the next three pericopae. Who has the power to defeat overwhelming evil? Who has the ability to heal chronic illness? Who has the power to raise the dead? Who indeed?

But the Twelve could have answered their own question simply by recalling Scripture. In the Old Testament, prophets had this kind of power. They were able to do nature miracles. The prophet Jonah prays, and "the sea ceased from its raging" (Jon. 1:15). Elijah provides a widow with a jar of meal and a jug of oil that did not empty (1 Kings 17:8-16). The prophets confronted evil and overcame it. For example, Moses faced down the sorcerers in the court of the pharaoh, showing that the power of God was superior to the power of the magicians (Exod. 7–9).[54] The prophets healed. Elisha healed

---

54. "Considering the widely held belief in the existence of evil spirits and also in the efficacy of the magicians to dispose of them, it is surprising that the OT maintains complete silence about this branch of magical practice. . . . The absence of any direct reference to exorcism in the OT is particularly remarkable, since the postbiblical literature relates the activities of the exorcists as a matter of incontestable fact." I. Mendelsohn, "Exorcism," in *The Interpreter's Dictionary of the Bible*, vol. 2 (Nashville: Abingdon, 1962), p. 199.

Naaman of his leprosy (2 Kings 5), and Isaiah healed Hezekiah (2 Kings 20).[55] And, most striking of all, the prophets were able to raise the dead. In 1 Kings 17:17-24 Elijah restores the life of a boy who has died, and in 2 Kings 4:18-37 Elisha raises the son of the Shunammite from the dead.[56]

But it is Jesus himself who provides the correct title for the Twelve. In the pericope which follows the four power stories, Jesus refers to himself as a prophet. He says: "Prophets are not without honor, except in their hometown, and among their own kin, and in their own house" (Mark 6:4). This is the only time in the Second Gospel that Jesus uses the title "prophet" in reference to himself. Other people describe him as a prophet (6:15; 8:28), but here this title functions as a definition of the aspect of Jesus that Mark is portraying in unit two.

That it is Mark's intention to so describe Jesus is reinforced by the final pericope of the unit. In 6:14-16 Mark summarizes the prevailing views at that time as to who Jesus might be. "Some were saying, 'John the baptizer has been raised from the dead; and for this reason these powers are at work in him.' But others said, 'It is Elijah.' And others said, 'It is a prophet, like one of the prophets of old'" (6:14-15). People may not be exactly sure who Jesus is, but the best guess is that he is some sort of prophet. This is the definition of Jesus in this unit. He is a wonder-working prophet. This is the new aspect of Jesus about which the disciples learn in unit two.

They learn about Jesus' power, however, not just from the rumors (6:14-16) nor from watching him in action (4:35–5:43). They learn about his power by experiencing this power for themselves (6:6b-13, 30). Jesus transfers his power to them for ministry. He gives them authority over evil spirits (6:7). And the Twelve go out into the villages, two by two, and actually drive out demons and cure the sick (6:13). Thus they experience the power of Jesus working through themselves. What more convincing way is there for them to realize that Jesus is not just a teacher but a prophet of great power?

So each pericope in unit two is related in some way to Jesus' role as a prophet and to the power that a prophet possesses. The first four pericopae (4:35–5:43) reveal Jesus' power and hence his role as prophet. In the next pericope (6:1-6a) Jesus refers to himself as a prophet, thus providing the new

---

55. However, as Howard Clark Kee, *Medicine, Miracle, and Magic in New Testament Times* (Cambridge: Cambridge University Press, 1986), p. 9, states: "Stories of healing are relatively rare in the Old Testament."

56. There is a difference, however, between Jesus and the OT prophets. The prophets call upon God to perform these mighty acts, whereas Jesus himself possesses the power to bring about these outcomes. He is like a prophet but greater than the prophets, as will subsequently be revealed in Mark's account.

title by which the Twelve come to know him. In the penultimate pericope (6:6b-13, 30) Jesus transfers his power to the Twelve so that they experience firsthand the reality of his power. And in the final pericope (6:14-29), not only is Jesus once again referred to as a prophet, but his true power (which is from God) is contrasted to Herod's muted power (which is from the state).

Jesus as Magician?

In first-century Judaism there was a fervent hope that God would once again send prophets to the people of Israel. In particular, Jews hoped Elijah would return.[57] When John the Baptist appeared there was great excitement. Perhaps he was a genuine prophet sent by God. With all the conversation sparked by the Baptist, it was not much of a stretch of imagination for the Twelve to consider Jesus a prophet. Nor were they alone in that assessment. That Jesus was a prophet is what the crowds came to believe (6:15; 8:27-28).

But the Jewish understanding of prophets was not the only tradition from which the disciples could draw in order to understand Jesus. Greek culture would explain his power in a different manner. According to Morton Smith, both Jesus' disciples and others viewed Jesus as a magician.[58] Smith argues that in Galilee in particular, given its mixed population and history of exposure to various cultures, the figure of the magician would be well known. And certainly, at one point the scribes charged Jesus with being a magician (3:22).

However, to call Jesus a magician and see him only as such is a misreading of the text. As E. P. Sanders notes (after interacting with Smith's hypothesis):

> Even if Jesus, in performing miracles, sometimes employed some of the devices of a magician . . . and thus may be said to have practiced "magic," we cannot, from that possibility, conclude that he *was* a magician. The Essenes, Josephus informs us, were adept at magical practice (*BJ* II.159), but we do not understand them adequately by calling them "magicians." Nor do we understand Jesus by calling him "a magician." . . . I propose that Smith presses beyond what is helpful in categorizing Jesus as "a magician." "Prophet," at least thus far, is probably to be regarded as the better term.[59]

57. Ferdinand Hahn, *The Titles of Jesus in Christology* (London: Lutterworth Press, 1969), pp. 352-55.
58. Morton Smith, *Jesus the Magician* (San Francisco: Harper & Row, 1978), pp. 20, 67-68.
59. E. P. Sanders, *Jesus and Judaism* (London: SCM Press, 1985), p. 170.

Aune amplifies this point:

> The wonderworking activities of Jesus cannot be considered magical simply because his healing and exorcistic techniques have parallels in Graeco-Roman magic (though they in fact do), neither can they be considered non-magical because such traits are relatively infrequent. . . . However, it does not seem appropriate to regard Jesus as a magician. While magical activities may constitute important aspects of the role of such figures as the shaman, the sage (both Graeco-Roman and rabbinic), the prophet and the messiah, each of these socio-religious roles involves different collections of specializations. Sociologically, . . . it would be problematic to categorize Jesus as a magician, since those magical activities which he used can be more appropriately subsumed under the role of messianic prophet.[60]

The disciples may have been aware of the existence of magicians, but they never used that title for Jesus. According to Mark, in unit two they came to understand Jesus to be a prophet. This is what replaced the idea of Jesus as teacher when that title proved unable to explain the power of Jesus.[61]

Thus the disciples have taken the second step in their journey to a full understanding of who Jesus is.

Jesus the Messiah: An Analysis of Unit Three (Mark 6:31–8:30)

Is this, then, all there is to Jesus? Is his role that of a powerful prophet sent by God? Does this title define him? Certainly to know that Jesus was a prophet from God had to be exciting news to a people starved for a word from God.[62] The disciples would have shared this longing for a prophet that first-century Jews had. And certainly, fresh from their great success at ministry, they must have found their new understanding of Jesus to be quite exhilarating (6:12-13, 30). They now knew Jesus to be not only a great teacher but a powerful prophet. How wonderful to be his disciples.

But the Twelve are not allowed to stop at this point in their understanding of Jesus. In unit three that understanding takes a quantum leap forward as

60. David E. Aune, "Magic in Early Christianity," in *Aufstieg und Niedergang der römischen Welt* II.23.2 (1980), p. 1539.

61. "After his appearance Jesus was first regarded mainly as a rabbi. Certain of his traits, however, did not harmonize with the figure of a scribe and recalled rather the appearance of a prophet." Hahn, p. 372.

62. This was amply demonstrated by the enthusiasm which the arrival of John the Baptist engendered in the whole population (Mark 1:5).

they learn that Jesus is not just one of many teachers and many prophets, albeit the best of the lot. He is unique. He is the Messiah. He is the One whom God has sent to rescue the nation.

Mark introduces this unit in the same way he introduced the previous two units: with an affect-laden story containing rebuke that shows that the disciples have not understood fully who Jesus is (6:31-44). In terms of new understanding about Jesus, in unit one the disciples had no way of knowing what a good teacher Jesus was; in unit two they do not anticipate that he can do anything about the storm; here in unit three they do not understand that Jesus can feed five thousand people. In terms of emotional response, in unit one there was amazement at Jesus' authoritative teaching; in unit two there was physical fear which turned into numinous terror; and in unit three the emotional response of the disciples is one of annoyance that Jesus should worry about feeding all these people and that he should expect them to do something about the problem. In terms of rebuke, in unit one Jesus rebuked the demon, in unit two he rebuked the storm, but here in unit three it is the disciples who rebuke Jesus! They are put out that Jesus should suggest that they feed the crowd when this was clearly undesirable (they would have to spend a lot of money to do so), and besides, it was probably impossible (given that it was late in the day). Their response is, in essence, one of rebuke toward Jesus for his outrageous suggestion.[63] But in this unit they are about to learn that Jesus can "feed the people" in ways they could not even imagine.

Though there are parallels to the way in which other units begin, this unit is quite different from the previous two when it comes to revealing who Jesus is. In unit one the disciples discover what an amazing teacher Jesus is by hearing him preach and teach and by watching him cast out demons and heal the sick. In unit two they learn that he is a prophet of great power by observing his acts of power and then being allowed to share in the experience of that power. But here in unit three their discovery that Jesus is the Messiah comes by means of reading the symbolic meaning of his acts, which they are enabled to do because Jesus opens their eyes to see, their ears to hear, and their tongues to speak with a miracle of healing. Mark presents the material in this unit in the form of two cycles of stories, which are to be interpreted symbolically, climaxed by a confession that reveals the change that has taken place in the disciples. Each of these two cycles begins with a feeding miracle and ends with an unusual healing miracle.

---

63. There is a "tone of astonishment, amounting to reproof" in their question. Taylor, p. 323.

The Two Feeding Stories

The two feeding stories reveal, via a series of symbolic references, who Jesus is. First, the feedings themselves have a symbolic character. They allude to what Moses did when he fed the multitudes in the wilderness with bread from heaven (Exod. 16; Num. 11). Thus they reveal Jesus to be a Moses-like figure. The disciples "should have recognized in him [Jesus] the 'prophet like unto Moses' (Deut. 18:15ff.) whom God would raise up — 'the prophet that cometh into the world' (John 6:14)."[64] They also allude to David.[65] The setting is described as the desert or wilderness *(erēmon)* (Mark 6:32), and Jesus likens himself to a shepherd of the flock (6:34). Two Old Testament texts connect the two themes of desert and shepherd: Numbers 27:15-17 and Ezekiel 34:5, 23. "With these Old Testament links between the themes of the shepherd and desert in the background, v. 34 implies that the prophecy concerning the prophet like Moses and the new David was fulfilled in Jesus."[66]

Second, the two feedings reveal that Jesus, in his role as the new Moses and the new David, has come for all peoples — both Jew and Gentile. In the feeding of the five thousand (Mark 6:35-44) the focus is on the Jews, whereas in the feeding of the four thousand (8:1-9a) the focus is on the Gentiles.

> [In the feeding of the five thousand] [t]he crowd is a Jewish crowd and the scene is Galilee; the five loaves possibly represent the five books of the Law; the twelve baskets of fragments clearly represent the twelve tribes of Israel. The word used for "baskets" represents a distinctly Jewish kind of basket. When we come to the second Feeding Miracle, the Four Thousand, the scene has changed, and the crowd is a Gentile multitude, drawn from the mixed population of the Decapolis. . . . The second story symbolizes the offering of the bread of life to the Gentiles. Again, the numbers may well be significant; four is a number symbolic of universality — the four corners of the earth and the four winds of heaven; the seven baskets of fragments doubtless represent the seventy nations into which the Jews traditionally divided the Gentiles. . . . Furthermore the word for "baskets" is now significantly altered to the ordinary Greek word for a basket *(spuris)*.[67]

64. Alan Richardson, "The Feeding of the Five Thousand," *Interpretation* 9 (1955): 145.

65. See below, pp. 204-7, for the discussion of the role of David in the expectations of the people.

66. Sanae Masuda, "The Good News of the Miracle of the Bread: The Tradition and Its Markan Redaction," *New Testament Studies* 28 (1982): 209.

67. Richardson, p. 146. See also Masuda, pp. 208-11 (for the symbolic value of the elements of these stories); E. G. Parrinder, "The Feeding of the Four Thousand: Mark 8:1-

Masuda comments on the expectations in the first century that a Moses-like figure would come:

> In Judaism at the time of Jesus the expectation was growing for the one who would liberate them from Roman oppression. They were waiting for a mediator of salvation like Moses. What they were expecting was not the return of Moses, but a prophet similar to Moses who would accomplish an eschatological role in salvation history. We can assume an expectation for the recurrence of Exodus including the miracle of the manna. For the Jews, the miracle of the manna was the sign of the one who brings eschatological salvation.[68]

At least three layers of meaning are found in these feeding stories. The first level has to do with the miracles themselves and what they demonstrate about Jesus: he has power to multiply food. This is another great nature miracle. Unit two begins with a nature miracle (the stilling of the storm). Likewise, unit three begins with an equally spectacular miracle that reveals the depths of Jesus' power. The second level of meaning has to do with the Old Testament allusions that the disciples, as first-century Jews, ought to understand. They show Jesus to be the new Moses and the new David.

The third level of meaning relates to the readers of Mark's Gospel. On this level it seems clear that Mark intends his readers to recall the Eucharist in the two feeding stories. At 6:41 the words he uses parallel the words of institution which are later given in 14:22. Mark 6:41 states: "Taking the five loaves and the two fish, he looked up to heaven, and blessed and broke the loaves, and gave them to his disciples . . . ," and 14:22 reads: "While they were eating, he took a loaf of bread, and after blessing it he broke it, gave it to them. . . ." Furthermore, in 8:6 the same sequence of giving thanks and breaking the bread is repeated, but in addition the word *eucharistēsas* is actually used (lest Mark's readers missed the point the first time?). In this way the readers would understand two things: (1) Jesus is himself the bread of life, and (2) Jesus will give his life for the sake of the world as the paschal lamb.[69]

10," *Expository Times* 51 (May 1940): 397-98; and D. Hawkins, "The Symbolism and Structure of the Marcan Redaction," *Evangelical Quarterly* 49 (1977): 103.

68. Masuda, p. 207.

69. Richardson, pp. 146-47. Quentin Quesnell, in his exhaustive examination of Mark 6:52, concludes that the only thing known for sure about what the disciples did not understand about the bread is that this was "a comment on the eucharistic implications of the story of the feedings in the wilderness" intended for readers of this document. Nothing can be known about the original event. Nothing can be known about the Evangelist's personal opinion about what happened. Quesnell's comment is: "The full meaning of the Eu-

The Two Healings

There is a problem, however, when it comes to the feeding stories. The disciples do not seem to have grasped their meaning! In the stories that follow each feeding, the point is made by Mark that the Twelve do not understand.[70] And yet at Caesarea Philippi they are able to answer correctly when Jesus asks who they think he is. How did they receive such insight? How did they move from no understanding to new understanding? The answer is that their eyes, ears, and mouths have been opened in the same way the deaf-and-dumb man and the blind man were healed: by the miracle of Jesus' healing touch. In the same way that the two feeding stories function on a symbolic level, so too do the two healing stories (which end each cycle of stories). Mark does not show the Twelve being healed. There is no account in which Jesus is said to lay his hands on the disciples. Instead, Mark conveys the fact that they know Jesus is the Messiah because they, like the two men, have been healed.[71]

The incident at Caesarea Philippi is not only the climax of unit three, it is the climax of Part I of the Gospel. In this pericope (8:27-30) Jesus first asks his disciples who the crowds think him to be. The popular assessment of Jesus continues to be that, as Herod learned (6:14-15), he is a prophet. While this is accurate, it is an incomplete assessment. He is more than that. Jesus next asks Peter who they, the Twelve, think he is. Peter gives a more accurate description. The disciples have discovered that he is not just a prophet; he is the Messiah. This is the last passage in Mark in which the title "prophet" is applied to Jesus. From this point on the disciples (who are the only ones who have come to this new understanding) will be involved in the process of discovering just what kind of Messiah Jesus is.

First-Century Views of the Messiah

When Peter declared "You are the Messiah," what did he mean? How did he and the other disciples understand the Messiah? Who was the Messiah to them? In order to answer this question it is necessary to examine the cultural assumptions about the Messiah that were operative in the first-century world inhabited by the disciples.

---

charist is the full meaning of Christianity." See Quentin Quesnell, *The Mind of Mark: Interpretation and Method through the Exegesis of Mark 6:52,* Analecta Biblica 38 (Rome: Pontifical Biblical Institute, 1969), pp. 275-77.

70. The lack of understanding of the disciples will be analyzed in chap. 9.

71. The two healing miracles will also be discussed in chap. 9.

Basic to the religious ideas of first-century Jews was the assumption that God had chosen Israel as God's special people. God had selected them out from all the nations and set them apart. They would be God's people; God would be their God.[72] A second basic assumption was that God would bless them as a nation. And yet, for many years they had been a subject people without a land of their own. Where was the blessing of God? Perhaps, they reasoned, their blessing would come in the future messianic age. The longer they lived in bondage to others, the more their hope turned to the future.[73] So, in the first century there was a lot of speculation about the future and the role of the Messiah in that future.

The way first-century Jews thought about the future was shaped by both the Old Testament and the intertestamental literature. While there was some variety in the speculation about the future, there were common strands of thought.[74]

The roots of this speculation are found in the Old Testament prophets.

The hope of the pre-exilic prophets was that the community would be morally purified and cleansed of all its bad elements; that it would flourish unmolested and be respected in the midst of the Gentile world, its enemies either destroyed or forced to acknowledge Israel and its God; that it would be ruled by a just, wise and powerful king of the house of David, so that internal justice, peace and joy would prevail; and even that all natural evils would be annihilated and a condition of unclouded bliss come into being. This vision was however substantially modified in later ages, partly during the time of the later prophets, but particularly in the post-biblical period.[75]

One of the earliest glimmerings of a messianic idea is found in the visions of Daniel.[76] The author prophesies a future in which God will sit in

---

72. Emil Schürer, *The History of the Jewish People in the Age of Jesus Christ (175 B.C.–A.D. 135)*, ed. Geza Vermes and Fergus Millar, rev. ed., 3 vols. (Edinburgh: T. & T. Clark, 1975), 2:492.

73. "[God] also gave them a law and thereby bound himself to grant his blessings provided that law was obeyed. . . . Yet it was obvious that in actual experience the reward came neither to the people as a whole, nor to individuals, in the proportion anticipated. Accordingly, the more deeply this awareness penetrated into the mind of the nation and the individual, the more they were forced to turn their eyes to the future; and of course, the worse their present state, the more lively their hope." Schürer, 2:492.

74. Schürer, 2:493.

75. Schürer, 2:493.

76. Schürer, 2:497, feels Daniel was written about 167 to 165 B.C., though other scholars would date it earlier.

judgment on the nations, the saints will receive the kingdom and possess it forever, and the nations will serve God even though their kingdoms will be destroyed.[77] However, it is not clear whether Daniel envisions a Messiah who will serve as king.

The hope of a Messiah emerges most clearly in the pseudepigrapha.[78] According to J. Klausner, it was this literature that shaped the messianic sensibilities during the time of Jesus:

> Great numbers of people found in the Pseudepigraphical apocalyptic literature divine consolation in their severe tribulations. The marvelous expectations and the glorious hopes, filled with the flowers of imagination, were as dew to the souls of the majority of the cultured persons in the nation who were not inclined toward Halakhah even though they observed strictly the ceremonial laws. These wonderful promises were balm to the broken hearts of the educated in the nation and food for the marvel-seeking imagination of the common people. Not without reason did the Pseudepigraphical books influence the first Christians, and perhaps also Je-

---

77. Dan. 7:9-27; 2:44.

78. The Book of Enoch (second century B.C.) talks about the Messiah. He comes as a white bull, but he appears after God has judged the nations. He has no functional part in bringing about this end. The Sibylline Oracles (ca. 140 B.C.) is rich in messianic prophecy. The emphasis here is on the establishment of an everlasting kingdom over all people.

However, in the Psalms of Solomon the figure of the Messiah is etched in sharper detail. This is a pseudepigraphical work composed most likely in the mid first century B.C. (though not earlier than the second century B.C.). J. Oswalt, "Psalms of Solomon," in *Zondervan Pictorial Encyclopedia of the Bible* (1975 ed.), summarizes the content of the seventeenth psalm:

> The Messiah is clearly an individual. He is a son of David, in special fulfillment of God's promise after the apparent destruction of that kingship. While there is no clear statement of his divinity, he is called "the Lord Messiah." (Although commentators believe that this should be read "the Lord's messiah," there is no example of such a reading in these psalms.) Since "the Lord" refers to God only, the implication is clear. Beyond this, it is clear that the kingdom which will be set up will be no ordinary human one, but a supernatural one wherein all wrongs and all inequities will be conclusively righted. He will purify Jerusalem, destroy the ungodly nations and convict the sinners. He will give the earth to the tribes of Israel and free them from the heathen in their midst. Yet all this was to be done without implements of war. He would smite the earth with His word and purify the nations with His righteousness. He would care for His people as a shepherd cares for his flocks. This picture is not different from that which may be gained from a reading of canonical Messianic passages, but it is more complete and coherent. Interestingly enough, it perpetuates that ambiguity between conqueror and redeemer which was to confuse so many during Jesus' lifetime.

sus himself. For from the common people *(amme ha-arets)* came most of the believers in the new Messianism.[79]

The fullest picture of the expected messianic kingdom is not developed until the final decades following the destruction of the temple. The Apocalypses of Baruch and Ezra describe this era in great detail. The pattern that emerges from these two works is as follows:[80] (1) There will be a time of great chaos and suffering. All of nature will be in great turmoil: "The sun shall suddenly shine forth at night, and the moon during the day; blood shall drip from wood, and the stone shall utter its voice; the peoples shall be troubled and the stars shall fall."[81] (2) Elijah will return to prepare the way for the Messiah. It will be his task to restore order and bring peace. (3) Then the Messiah will come. He was expected to be "a fully human individual, a royal figure descended from the house of David."[82] However, as this idea evolved he became a superhuman figure. "In 4 Ezra and the Parables of Enoch, his appearance is raised to the level of the supernatural and he is credited with pre-existence."[83] (4) After his appearance, the Gentile nations come together to wage war on him. (5) These forces will be destroyed by God through the agency of the Messiah. (6) A new and glorified Jerusalem will descend from heaven in place of the old Jerusalem. (7) Jews who have been dispersed around the world will be regathered into the Holy Land. (8) The kingdom of God will be established with the Messiah at its head. This will be a time of great blessedness. (9) The world will be renewed. (10) There will be a general resurrection of the dead. (11) The final judgment will take place with some consigned to hell and others to paradise.

Not all of these elements were in place during the time of Jesus and the disciples. Furthermore, it is difficult to pin down the exact contours of belief in the Messiah during the early part of the first century.[84] Perhaps there was no one view but only a collection of expectations gleaned from both Old Testament and intertestamental sources, or perhaps there were schools of thought.[85]

---

79. Joseph Klausner, *The Messianic Idea in Israel from Its Beginning to the Completion of the Mishnah* (London: George Allen & Unwin, 1956), p. 385.

80. This outline follows Schürer, 2:514-47.

81. 4 Ezra (Charlesworth, ed.), vol. 1, p. 532.

82. Schürer, 2:518-19.

83. Schürer, 2:519.

84. In fact, the whole subject is an enormous one, with a literature all its own. Given the space limitations in a book of this sort, it is not possible to do justice to the issues involved here, except to attempt to identify those conclusions that seem to have a certain consensus and apply them to the particular issue at hand.

85. M. de Jonge, "The Use of the Word 'Anointed' in the Time of Jesus," *Novum Testamentum* 8 (1966), and Schürer, 2:497.

Still, no matter how it might be expressed, during the time of Jesus the expectation was strong that Messiah would come and that he would rescue the nation.[86] God would act to bring to pass the salvation that had been promised to the people of God, and God would act through a Messiah. The details of the messianic age were debated, but the general sense was that the Messiah would come as a conquering hero to establish God's kingdom.

These, then, were the common views held during the time in which the Twelve lived. It can be assumed that the Twelve held such views. They give no evidence of being original thinkers who would have novel religious ideas. So, when Peter declares that Jesus is the Messiah, what he has in mind is a conquering hero who will wage war on the Gentile nations and then establish the kingdom of God on earth. But Jesus is not that kind of Messiah. Part II of the Gospel of Mark is the story of how the Twelve come to understand what kind of Messiah Jesus actually is. The pilgrimage of the Twelve in their understanding of Jesus has brought them to the point of realizing that Jesus is the Messiah. This is a major discovery. They have gotten half his identity right. In the next part of their pilgrimage they will discover the other half of that identity. They will discover that he is the Son of God.

---

86. Schürer, 2:497.

CHAPTER EIGHT

Jesus the Son of God

A new note is struck in unit four. Up to this point the disciples have been on familiar ground in their understanding of Jesus. They know about teachers; they understand about prophets; they expected the Messiah. But now they enter an arena that is unfamiliar. In the next three units the Twelve will be pushed beyond their cultural categories into a whole new understanding of God's work in and through Jesus. They will first be told that the Messiah is a suffering servant, not a conquering hero (unit four). They will then learn that in his role as the Son of David, he stands in judgment against the corruption of the temple and the religious leaders of Israel (unit five). Finally, they will discover that he is not just David's son but God's Son (unit six). In other words, Jesus is in a category all by himself. There has been, is, and will be no one like him — past, present, and future. Unit four launches this inquiry into these new and somewhat mysterious (from the disciples' point of view) aspects of Jesus.

Jesus the Son of Man: An Analysis of Unit Four
(Mark 8:31–10:45)

The Meaning of Messiahship

Unit four begins much as do the previous units: with a story in which there are strong emotion, rebuke, and lack of understanding about Jesus. In this case, all these elements emerge in the encounter between Jesus and Peter over the definition of messiahship. Peter takes great offense at Jesus' teaching that the Messiah will suffer, die, and then rise again (8:31). This is not how he understands messiahship. Thus Peter "rebukes" Jesus (8:32). Jesus in turn "rebukes" Peter, saying, in essence, that Peter is acting like Satan (8:33)! Once again, by this stylistic mark Mark tips his hand that this is the start of yet another step in the disciples' ongoing discovery of the identity of Jesus.

Unlike unit three, in which it was not clear until the final pericope just what title of Jesus was being revealed, in unit four there is no mystery. Mark identifies Jesus as the Son of Man in the first pericope, and then restates this title six more times throughout the course of the unit. Not only is the title itself stated in the first pericope, so too is its content. The reader learns that the Son of Man is one who, in his role as Messiah, must suffer, be rejected, be killed, and then rise again (8:31).

On four separate occasions in unit four Jesus predicts his passion.[1] It is worth comparing these four statements in order to see just what Jesus says. In each statement Jesus identifies himself as the Son of Man; in each his dying is mentioned; in each his suffering is mentioned (in the first two sayings the fact that he will suffer is noted, in the third the suffering is identified as betrayal, while in the fourth his betrayal is again noted as well as the fact that he will be mocked, spit upon, and flogged); his rejection is noted in the first two sayings; the identity of his persecutors is made known in the first and fourth statements; and each statement predicts that he will rise again.

The culmination of Jesus' teaching about the Son of Man is found in 10:45. Here Mark identifies the *meaning* of the events which Jesus predicts. As Lane points out, each phrase of this pivotal verse is laden with content.

> The formulation "The Son of man came . . ." places the entire statement in the context of Jesus' messianic mission. . . . In a Jewish frame of reference this expression was characteristically used of the death of the martyrs (e.g. I Macc. 2:50; 6:44; Mekilta to Ex. 12:1). In this context it expresses the element of voluntariness or self-sacrifice in the death of Jesus who offers himself in obedience to the will of God. His death has infinite value because he dies not as a mere martyr but as the transcendent Son of Man.

> The ransom metaphor sums up the purpose for which Jesus gave his life

---

1. It is not necessary to answer the question of whether the four predictions are variants of a single saying (e.g., E. Lohmeyer) or multiple statements on the part of Jesus. The important thing is the way Mark uses these statements to structure this unit and so communicate new information about who Jesus is. However, as Vincent Taylor, *The Gospel according to St. Mark* (New York: St. Martin's Press, 1966), p. 377, states, each statement "is distinctive in its setting, and it is probable that Jesus made several attempts to familiarize His disciples with the idea of Messianic suffering. . . ."

and defines the complete expression of his service. The prevailing notion behind the metaphor is that of deliverance by purchase, whether a prisoner of war, a slave, or a forfeited life is the object to be delivered. Because the idea of equivalence, or substitution, was proper to the concept of a ransom, it became an integral element in the vocabulary of redemption in the OT. . . .

The thought of substitution is reinforced by the qualifying phrase "a ransom *for the many*." The Son of Man takes *the place* of the many and there happens to him what would have happened to them (cf. Ch. 8:37: what no man can do, Jesus, as the unique Son of Man, achieves). The many had forfeited their lives, and what Jesus gives in their place is his life. In his death, Jesus pays the price that sets men free.[2]

Many writers have questioned the genuineness of this saying in 10:45, tracing it to Pauline influence. J. Wellhausen "claims that it is out of harmony with the context."[3] However, it makes perfect sense when taken as the explanation of why the Messiah must suffer and die. As Taylor comments: "It is wise never to forget that *lutron* [= ransom] is used metaphorically, but it is equally wise to remember that a metaphor is used to convey an arresting thought. Jesus died to fulfill the Servant's destiny and His service is that of vicarious and representative suffering. We are ill-advised if we seek to erect a theory upon 10:45 alone, but equally so if we dismiss it as a product of later theological construction."[4]

After Jesus' first prediction of what lies ahead for him as the Messiah, Peter takes Jesus aside and rebukes him. Mark does not identify what, in particular, is so offensive to Peter. Perhaps it was each of the four aspects of his prediction that troubled Peter. However, it is interesting that in the teaching by Jesus that follows (8:34–9:1), the focus is on dying. It is likely that this element of the prediction stands out as the most offensive.[5] That Jesus should die, now that they know him to be the Messiah, is literally beyond the imagination of the disciples. Messiahs don't die.

But this is not the only element of Jesus' prediction that is baffling to the disciples. On the second occasion in which there is mention of what lies ahead for Jesus, Mark notes that Peter, James, and John were not at all sure

---

2. William L. Lane, *The Gospel according to Mark* (Grand Rapids: Wm. B. Eerdmans Publishing Co., 1974), pp. 383-84.

3. Taylor, p. 445.

4. Taylor, p. 446.

5. "Peter would hardly have objected to Jesus being raised!" Ernest Best, *Following Jesus: Discipleship in the Gospel of Mark* (Sheffield: JSOT Press, 1981), p. 25.

"what this rising from the dead could mean" (9:10). It is not that the concept of resurrection was new to the disciples. Certain of the first-century religious groups (like the Pharisees) believed in the resurrection. Furthermore, the disciples had seen Jesus raise a young woman from the dead (5:35-43). Their problem was in understanding the connection between the Messiah and resurrection. Only dead men need to rise, and they cannot imagine that Jesus, as Messiah, will die. At the time of the third prediction, Mark notes that "they did not understand what he was saying and were afraid to ask him" (9:32). The whole of Jesus' teaching about the Son of Man was baffling to them.

How was it possible for the disciples not to understand what Jesus was saying? He was not speaking in parables. Mark makes a point of noting this fact after the first prediction: "He said all this quite openly" (8:32). Furthermore, Jesus has made this prediction more than once. The disciples were already aware of the hostility of the religious leadership toward Jesus (2:1–3:6). So the whole question of rejection was not a new one; suffering was a distinct possibility given this opposition; even death was not out of the question. And yet, when Jesus predicts what lies ahead for him, it is as if the disciples do not even hear the words. The problem, it seems, has to do with their expectations concerning the Messiah.

The Messiah that the disciples expected, as portrayed by the intertestamental literature, would be a warrior-king. This is made clear in the seventeenth Psalm of Solomon. According to this psalm,

> a Davidic Messiah, raised up by God, would overthrow the Gentile over-lords, restore Israel's glory, gather the dispersion, reign from Jerusalem and bring the Gentiles under his sway as he acts as God's vice-regent on earth.
>
> This was the hope most widely shared, no doubt: a political Messiah of David's stock, wielding the weapons primarily of spiritual power, but nevertheless ridding the holy soil of Israel from foreign domination, and ushering in the days of glory of which the prophets had spoken.[6]

In other words, in the popular view of things, when the Messiah came it would be to win, not to lose. No one anticipated that the Messiah would or could die. There are some references in rabbinic literature to a slain Messiah, but these are late, dating from A.D. 135 and after.[7] In other words, by defining

---

6. Michael Green, *Evangelism in the Early Church* (London: Hodder & Stoughton, 1970), p. 88. See also M. de Jonge, "The Use of the Word 'Anointed' in the Time of Jesus," *Novum Testamentum* 8 (1966): 136.

7. Geza Vermes, *Jesus the Jew: A Historian's Reading of the Gospels* (London: Collins, 1973), pp. 139-40.

his messiahship in terms of death and resurrection, Jesus is forging new theological ground.

The same problem that the disciples had with the idea of suffering and dying persisted even after these events actually took place. This was one of the issues that early Christian missionaries had to confront in evangelizing the Jews.[8] According to Deuteronomy 21:22-23, anyone hanged on a cross is under God's curse. That Jesus, who was crucified, could be the Messiah was therefore impossible in the view of many first-century Jews. First-century Gentiles had a similar problem. To them Jesus was simply a state criminal. That he was crucified meant he must have been a rebellious subject of the Roman Empire. Furthermore, his death pointed to his inherent weakness. The all-powerful God could not possibly work through such a person.[9] "Indeed, 'Christ crucified' is a contradiction in terms, of the same category as 'fried ice.' One may have a Messiah, or one may have a crucifixion; but one may not have both — at least not from the perspective of merely human understanding. *Messiah* meant power, splendor, triumph; *crucifixion* meant weakness, humiliation, defeat. Little wonder that both Jew and Greek were scandalized by the Christian message."[10]

Of course, the idea of the suffering servant *is* found in the Old Testament. However, in the pre-Christian era rabbis failed to connect the figure in Isaiah 53 with the Messiah of their expectations. In fact, the authoritative Targum Jonathan, although making the connection between the Messiah and Isaiah 53, "interprets the very verses which deal with the suffering of the Servant of God as *not* referring to the Messiah."[11] "It must be emphasized that nowhere before the New Testament is the Servant identified with the Messiah. . . . There is no evidence that Jewish eschatology anticipated that a righteous man would come to suffer vicariously in order to atone for the sins of his people."[12]

If the disciples cannot understand the meaning of his messiahship — and they of all people had the best view of who Jesus was — who then could grasp the true identity of Jesus? The fact is, it seems no one was capable of un-

---

8. Green, pp. 29-32.

9. Gordon D. Fee, *The First Epistle to the Corinthians* (Grand Rapids: Wm. B. Eerdmans Publishing Co., 1987), pp. 75-76.

10. Fee, p. 75.

11. Emil Schürer, *The History of the Jewish People in the Age of Jesus Christ (175 B.C.– A.D. 135)*, ed. Geza Vermes and Fergus Millar, rev. ed., 3 vols. (Edinburgh: T. & T. Clark, 1975), 2:549.

12. Donald E. Gowan, *Bridge between the Testaments: A Reappraisal of Judaism from the Exile to the Birth of Christianity* (Pittsburgh: Pickwick Press, 1976), p. 499.

derstanding Jesus, given the cultural presuppositions in play. This is one explanation of why Jesus constantly enjoined secrecy when it came to revealing who he was.[13] To preach openly that he was the Messiah would have been to court misunderstanding. "Jesus' purpose, however, is not to precipitate a messianic uprising. . . ."[14] Hence the response of Jesus is to warn the disciples to be silent after Peter's affirmation that he is the Christ. One day they will be able to declare who he is. But, as Mark notes in 9:9, this will be possible only after his resurrection.[15]

The Meaning of the Title "Son of Man"

This general sense of misunderstanding may also explain why Jesus refers to himself as the "Son of Man." In using this rather nondescript title — yet one possibly tinged with messianic content — he is able to identify who he is without using other titles that have too much cultural baggage attached to them. To call himself the Messiah would have been to generate a false expectation that he had come to rid Israel of her Roman enemies, thus obscuring his real mission. But to call himself the Son of Man and then go on to give content to this somewhat vague title was another matter.[16]

Two points need to be made about the title Son of Man. First, this is the title Mark uses in this unit to describe Jesus. There are seven references to the Son of Man in unit four compared to seven other references scattered throughout the other units.[17] The reason for this is that here Jesus departs

13. See Ralph Martin, *Mark: Evangelist and Theologian* (Grand Rapids: Zondervan, 1973), pp. 91-97, for a discussion of Wrede and the idea of the messianic secret.

14. Morna D. Hooker, *The Son of Man in Mark* (London: SPCK, 1967), p. 107.

15. Joseph Tyson, "The Blindness of the Disciples in Mark," *Journal of Biblical Literature* 80 (1961): 261-68.

16. "It is generally assumed by those who accept the Marcan narrative as historical that Jesus introduced the teaching about the sufferings of the Son of man at this point as an explanation or qualification of the meaning of his Messiahship: his idea of the Messiah did not coincide with theirs, and it was therefore necessary to change their ideas as to what is involved. . . . Mark's narrative suggests that this teaching not only was not but could not be given until after the recognition of Jesus as Messiah: it appears as if the messiahship of Jesus and the sufferings of the Son of man are so vitally related that the second cannot be understood until the first is acknowledged." Hooker, p. 111.

17. "Son of Man" is used twice in unit one (2:10, 28), once in unit five (13:26), and four times in unit six (14:21 [twice], 41, 62), compared to seven times in unit four (8:31, 38; 9:9, 12, 31; 10:33, 45). The two uses prior to unit four carry with them the idea of the divine nature of Jesus. In 2:10 he claims to forgive sin — something only God can do; and in 2:28 he declares the Son of Man to be the Lord of the Sabbath — again a role reserved to

from traditional titles or, at least, from the generally accepted interpretation of these titles. He is in the process of redefining the meaning of messiahship, and the title Son of Man gives him the way to do it. "Jesus, therefore, might well prefer the term 'Son of man' as a self-designation, not because of any opposition between this and 'Messiah,' but because it could define and explain the nature of his Messiahship."[18] Second, this is Jesus' title for himself. No one else refers to him by it. In fact, "no one ever asks him what he means by it (except in John 12:34; not answered)."[19] Furthermore, the early church used this title only infrequently to describe Jesus.[20] This is clearly a self-designation with a temporary value. It was an interim title, used only up to the time of his death and resurrection, after which the proper Old Testament titles could be applied to him with understanding.

In many ways this was the ideal title to use. It was a familiar phrase to his hearers. It was used in ordinary conversation as a way of referring to an individual human being. "It is now accepted by every expert that the phrase was in general use as a noun ('a man,' 'the man') at all stages of the Palestinian Aramaic dialect, and as a substitute for the indefinite pronoun ('one,' 'someone')."[21] The title "son of man" is used in the Old Testament as a way of referring to certain people, as in the book of Ezekiel, where God regularly addresses the prophet by this title (e.g., Ezek. 2:1; see also Ps. 8:4). So people hearing this title would think little of it.

However, at one point in the Old Testament this title was used in a different way. Daniel 7:13 refers to "one like a son of man, coming with the clouds of heaven" (NIV).[22] The one "like a son of man" approached God ("the Ancient One")

> and was presented before him.
> To him was given dominion
> and glory and kingship,
> that all peoples, nations, and languages
> should serve him.

God. The use of this title in the remaining units is connected either with his betrayal (14:21, 41) or with the second coming (13:26; 14:62; cf. 8:38) — this latter being an event connected to God and his purposes.

18. Hooker, p. 113.

19. Gowan, p. 498.

20. The only uses of "Son of Man" outside the Gospels are in Acts 7:56; Rev. 1:13; 14:14. Gowan, p. 498.

21. Vermes, pp. 162-63.

22. The NRSV translates this: "one like a human being coming with the clouds of heaven."

His dominion is an everlasting dominion
    that shall not pass away,
and his kingship is one
    that shall never be destroyed.   (Dan. 7:13-14)

So, lurking in the background of this common title was a messianic usage.

Who this "son of man" in Daniel is and how this phrase was understood in the first century are the subject of much debate. Some, like G. Vermes, insist: "The phrase is no more employed as a title here than it is in any other text. Indeed, the derivation from Daniel 7:13 of such Messianic names as *Anani* or *bar nephele* proves that son of man was never understood as a title."[23] Others, such as A. J. B. Higgins, assert: "A majority of recent writers continue to support the view that there existed in pre-Christian apocalyptic Judaism a concept of the eschatological Son of man, a transcendent and preexistent being whose primary function in the End-time would be that of a judge, delivering the righteous and punishing the wicked."[24] Which view is correct cannot easily be determined due to the lack of materials from the era in question. However, by at least the time of the second century A.D. (and probably by mid–first century A.D.), Daniel 7:9-14 was recognized "as a Messianic text depicting the coming of the new, glorious, and exalted David."[25]

---

23. Vermes, p. 172.

24. A. J. B. Higgins, *The Son of Man in the Teaching of Jesus* (Cambridge: Cambridge University Press, 1980), p. 3.

25. Vermes, p. 172. The basis on which this is asserted has to do with the use of the phrase "Son of Man" in the Similitudes of Enoch and in 4 Ezra. "Chapter 13 of the Fourth Book of Ezra is . . . concerned with a dream. The pseudonymous author saw 'as it were the form of a man' rising from the sea and flying 'with the clouds of heaven.' A multitude of men assembled to fight him, but he annihilated them with his mouth. God then explains the meaning of the vision. The 'man' is the preserved, hidden, heavenly Messiah, the son of God. In other words, the dream is modeled on Daniel 7; its flying hero, the pre-existent royal Messiah, is Daniel's 'one like a son of man.'"

Fourth Ezra is definitely dated later than A.D. 70. Vermes, p. 173. B. M. Metzger dates the book at about A.D. 100 in *The Old Testament Pseudepigrapha*, ed. James H. Charlesworth, (Garden City, N.Y.: Doubleday, 1983), vol. 1, p. 520.

Despite an early dating for the Similitudes of Enoch by R. H. Charles (94-64 B.C.), it is now the consensus that it should be dated after the Gospels though still in the first century. "Still one of the most vexed and disputed matters in biblical studies is the question of the origin and date of I Enoch, chapters 37–71, the so-called Similitudes or Parables of Enoch. . . . Dates as widely apart as the second century B.C. (J. B. Frey), and A.D. 270 (J. T. Milik) have been proposed for the Similitudes." Christopher L. Mearns, "Dating the Similitudes of Enoch," *New Testament Studies* 25 (1979): 360. See also M. A. Knibb, "The Date of the Parables of Enoch: A Critical Review," *New Testament Studies* 25 (1979): 345-57. Current scholarly consensus seems to be that they were written by a Jewish author during the first century A.D.

The question is still open as to whether there were other pre-Christian uses of this title (and hence other meanings attached to it in the first century).[26]

What is clear in the midst of all the questions about this title[27] is that "Son of Man" was, on one level, a well-known, rather nondescript way of talking about oneself. Whether it had messianic overtones, and whether these were recognized by Jesus' hearers, is impossible to establish. Either way it does not matter, since it is Jesus who fills this title with what will later be recognized as messianic content. It is clear that both in Christian sources (such as the synoptic Gospels) and in mainstream Jewish tradition, by the mid–first century the title Son of Man, as derived from Daniel 7, was recognized to be messianic in nature.

So "Son of Man" was the kind of title Jesus could use without arousing unrealistic expectations; yet it has a hint of the supernatural to it. Thus he can take a rather neutral phrase and redefine it (as he does here in unit four) so as to give it new meaning.[28]

> My hypothesis . . . supposes that Jesus took up the term "son of man" just because it was not yet a definite title. It was a term stimulating the hearer to reflect and to answer the question, put by its usage, who Jesus really was. It described, first of all, the earthly "man" in his humiliation and coming suffering. It depicted the messenger of God suffering for his people and calling it to repentance. It declared that this very "man" would confront his hearers in the last judgment, so that their yes or no to the earthly Jesus would then decide their vindication or condemnation.[29]

26. See Arthur J. Ferch, *The Son of Man in Daniel 7*, Andrews University Seminary Doctoral Dissertation Series, vol. 6 (Berrien Springs, Mich.: Andrews University Press, 1979), for a survey of the materials related to this inquiry.

27. In the same way that the study of the Messiah involves a vast literature, so too does the study of the title Son of Man. As Ferdinand Hahn states at the beginning of his *The Titles of Jesus in Christology* (London: Lutterworth Press, 1969), p. 15: "Of all Christological titles, that of the Son of man has been the most thoroughly investigated." Despite this fact, as G. Vermes comments (in what is surely an overstatement): "Shortly before his death, Paul Winter remarked stoically that the literature on the *son of man* was becoming more and more impenetrable with no two people agreeing on anything." Vermes, p. 160. Needless to say, it is not possible within the limits of this book to do more than touch upon some of the issues connected with this enigmatic title.

28. "Jesus may well have used 'The Man' [Son of Man] to define his own interpretation of messiahship. . . ." C. S. Mann, *Mark: A New Translation with Introduction and Commentary* (Garden City, N.Y.: Doubleday, 1986), p. 354.

29. Eduard Schweizer, "The Son of Man Again," *New Testament Studies* 10 (1963): 259.

In unit four Mark completes his description of what Jesus directly taught his disciples about himself. They began by viewing him as a teacher; they move to understanding him to be a prophet; they come to discover that he is the Messiah; and in unit four they are taught that, as the Messiah, he will suffer, die for the sins of others, and rise again. But now the time for teaching the disciples is over. At this point in the story Jesus and the Twelve have journeyed to Jericho, the gateway to Jerusalem. During the last week of his life, Jesus will set in motion the events that culminate in his predicted death and resurrection. The disciples have only small roles to play in the drama from this point on. Their main role is simply to watch and remember.

Jesus the Son of David: An Analysis of Unit Five (Mark 10:46–13:37)

Once again Mark leaves the reader in no doubt as to which aspect of Jesus he will focus on in the new unit. As he did in the previous unit, Mark defines the key title for Jesus in the first pericope. Unit five opens with blind Bartimaeus twice calling out to Jesus as the "Son of David."[30] This is a whole new side of

---

30. Paul J. Achtemeier, "'And He Followed Him': Miracles and Discipleship in Mark 10:46-52," *Semeia* 11 (1978): 118, argues that "the title 'son of David' is not significant for Mark's understanding of Jesus." His reason for saying this is that Mark would have made the title explicit in the next pericope (the entry into Jerusalem) — as Matthew does in Matt. 21:9 — had it been of major redactional interest to Mark. As will be argued in this section of the book, this is to miss the whole point of the unit. The double mention of the title in the opening pericope, the fact that six of the seven mentions of David occur in this unit, and the fact that Jesus is presented acting in the role of one who is king all argue against Achtemeier's assertion. Frank J. Matera, *The Kingship of Jesus: Composition and Theology in Mark 15,* SBL Dissertation Series 66 (Chico, Calif.: Scholars Press, 1982), argues against Achtemeier's "negative trajectory of the Davidic ancestry of Jesus" (p. 115) by interpreting 12:35-37 in its larger context. He concludes: "He is David's son inasmuch as he inherits the divine promises (1:11; 9:7; 12:6), but the origin of his sonship necessarily goes beyond physical descent because Jesus, the Messiah, is the Father's only Son. In other words, Jesus' sonship is a unique sonship which the scribal messianic doctrine cannot comprehend" (p. 87). Mark, it seems, is very interested in the title Son of David even though he does not use it explicitly in the second pericope of the unit.

Achtemeier makes this same point a second time in his paper when he discusses 2:23-27 and 6:1-3 (pp. 127-28). He contends that Mark could have asserted Jesus' Davidic ancestry in both places had this been important to him. The argument of this book is that Mark did not (and would not) make this point at those places in the text because his focus was not yet on the Davidic nature of Jesus.

Jesus, one that has not yet been considered but one that is crucial if the Twelve are to understand the nature of Jesus' messiahship.

This unit begins, as do the others, with a pericope in which there is new insight into Jesus in the context of strong emotion and rebuke. The new insight has to do with the title Son of David, which is used for the first time in the Gospel.[31] Bartimaeus shouts out this title not once but twice.[32] The strong emotional context is also generated by Bartimaeus. For one thing, he calls out to Jesus over and over again (10:47). He shouts at him, in fact (10:48). The crowd gets caught up in his outburst. They try to stop him, but Bartimaeus is not to be restrained. For another thing, when Jesus calls him over, Bartimaeus comes to him with an energetic flourish: "So throwing off his cloak, he sprang up and came to Jesus" (10:50). The rebuke comes from the crowds, who try to calm down Bartimaeus: "Many sternly ordered him to be quiet" (10:48).[33]

The King Returns

Bartimaeus declares that Jesus is the Son of David, and in the very next pericope Jesus is portrayed as the returning king (11:1-10 — the so-called triumphal entry). Four factors indicate this. First, it is clear that Jesus himself arranges to ride into Jerusalem as the Davidic king.[34] It is he who sends the two disciples to get the colt (11:1-3). Jesus must have previously made arrangements for the use of the colt, including the establishment of a code word to be used by his disciples (11:3, 6). Otherwise the disciples would not have been allowed simply to walk off with the animal (11:4-6). Alternatively, he could have been exercising the royal right of impression (*angareia*), as Derrett

31. Robbins notes that "It is customary now to interpret the Bartimaeus story as solely a discipleship story. . . . While there can be no doubt that the Bartimaeus story is oriented to discipleship, we must recognize that the story also produces a poignant christological statement pertaining to Jesus' activity." Vernon K. Robbins, "The Healing of Blind Bartimaeus (10:46-52) in the Marcan Theology," *Journal of Biblical Literature* 92 (1973): 225-26.

32. There are other places in the Gospel where Mark repeats a statement in order to make sure that the readers realize that this is where his emphasis lies. The most notable example is in unit three where there are two feedings and two healings, both with symbolic meaning. In unit one he twice repeats the fact that the people were amazed at the teaching of Jesus (1:22, 27).

33. Although Mark does not say so explicitly, chances are the disciples joined in this rebuking. They did this sort of thing on other occasions (see 9:38; 10:13).

34. Lane, p. 365.

argues. "A typical royal impression would take place by sending messengers ahead to arrange for the next stage. . . . The method in general would be to seize the object impressed . . . and to explain the action by such words as 'I, or the army, or the ruler (as the case may be) require(s) this.'"[35] In either case, by arranging for the loan of the animal beforehand or by exercising his right as king to use the animal, Jesus is seen to be stage-managing his entrance into Jerusalem. He comes not as an ordinary pilgrim but as returning royalty.

Second, the way in which Mark describes Jesus' entry into Jerusalem is rich with allusion to his royal character. The healing of blind Bartimaeus sets the stage for this event. Isaiah 29:18-19 (a passage connected with the messianic age) states:

> On that day the deaf shall hear
>   the words of a scroll,
> and out of their gloom and darkness
>   the eyes of the blind shall see.
> The meek shall obtain fresh joy in the LORD,
>   and the neediest people shall exult in the Holy One of Israel.[36]

The colt also has symbolic significance. According to Zechariah 9:9, the king would come riding on a colt:

> Rejoice greatly, O daughter Zion!
>   Shout aloud, O daughter Jerusalem!
> Lo, your king comes to you;
>   triumphant and victorious is he,
> humble and riding on a donkey,
>   on a colt, the foal of a donkey.

In fact, this prophecy contains "the three essential elements of the Marcan account: the entry ('See, your king comes'), the messianic animal ('riding upon an ass, even upon a colt, the foal of an ass'), and the jubilation of the people ('Rejoice greatly, O daughter of Zion')."[37] Furthermore, Genesis 49:8-12 speaks of a tethered colt, and this was understood by many to be a prophecy of the Messiah.[38] "The description of the animal as one that had never been

---

35. J. Duncan M. Derrett, "Law in the New Testament: The Palm Sunday Colt," *Novum Testamentum* 13 (1971): 246.

36. See Lane, pp. 392-93.

37. Lane, p. 393.

38. Larry W. Hurtado, *Mark: A Good News Commentary* (San Francisco: Harper & Row, 1983), p. 167. Lane cites rabbinical evidence that attests to this. See Lane, p. 395.

ridden is significant in light of the ancient rule that only animals that had not been put to ordinary use were appropriate for sacred purposes (cf. Num. 19:2; Deut. 21:3; 1Sa. 6:7)."[39] In addition, the spreading of garments in front of the animal "is similar to the royal salute given to Jehu (II Kings 9:12f.), or the gesture of profound respect to Cato of Utica when he was about to leave his soldiers (Plutarch, *Cato Minor* 7)."[40]

Third, the site from which this entry is launched is significant (Mark 11:1). The Mount of Olives was associated in popular understanding with the coming of the Messiah.[41] According to Zechariah 14:4f., this is the place where God will commence the final judgment of Israel's enemies.[42] "On the basis of this citation, it appears that there existed a tradition that the Messiah would come from this place. . . . The tradition is also alive in Acts 1:6 where the apostles, while on the Mount of Olives, ask the Risen Lord if he will establish the Kingdom of Israel at this time."[43]

Fourth, the chanting of the Hallel Psalms adds to the overwhelming impression in this passage that the king has returned. The cry "Hosanna!" (lit. "Save Now") is taken from Psalm 118:25f., which was understood by the rabbis to be a messianic psalm referring to King David and the final redemption.[44] These shouts of joy were not unusual. They were typical of pilgrims en route to Jerusalem for a feast. However, Mark gives the reader the sense that this is not just business as usual. Something highly unusual and most significant is taking place in the midst of the normal celebration during a religious feast. Mark tips the reader off to this by the quotation "Blessed is the coming kingdom of our ancestor David!" (Mark 11:10). This is exactly what is happening. The real king is, indeed, arriving in the Holy City. Jesus enters Jerusalem as the prophesied Davidic king.

The first action by the returned king is to cleanse the temple. This is recounted in the third pericope of this unit (11:15-19). This story, as with the

---

39. Hurtado, p. 173.

40. Lane, p. 396. Matera, p. 70, comments: "The story is reminiscent of the royal enthronements of Solomon (I Kg. 1:38-40) and Jehu (II Kg. 9:13). In the first, Solomon rides David's mule to Gihon where Zadok anoints him and the people shout 'Long live the King.' In the second, the people take off their garments and proclaim 'Jehu is king.' Neither reference has formed the present story but both point to the intimations of kingship which are present."

41. T. A. Burkill, "Strain on the Secret: An Examination of Mark 11:1–13:37," *Zeitschrift für die neutestamentliche Wissenschaft* (1960): 34-45.

42. Lane, p. 394.

43. Matera, p. 69.

44. Lane, p. 398.

previous one, is laden with Old Testament references.[45] There is a direct quotation from Isaiah 56:7 and Jeremiah 7:11 (Mark 11:17). "Perhaps the evangelist has other Old Testament passages in mind, such as Hos. 9:15; Zech. 14:21; Mal. 3:1ff. For it is St. Mark's conviction that the cleansing of the temple occurs in fulfillment of the scriptures and as an integral part of the Messiah's earthly mission."[46]

The specific nature of the problem which Jesus attacked in the temple is difficult to determine. It is hard to know exactly what the merchants were doing wrong in the temple. Perhaps the problem had to do with "swindling and extortion practiced in the Temple mart and by the money changers."[47] Or it may have had to do with the fact that the Court of the Gentiles had been turned into "an oriental bazaar and a cattle mart."[48] Geddert argues that "the real problem was that the Jewish religious leaders were robbing *God*."[49] Whatever the specifics of the problem, the root issue is that the temple had been corrupted from its original purpose. And Jesus, in his action against these traders (and the religious leaders who sanction their presence), is acting in judgment against the temple. What he does here is symbolic of the actual judgment that is coming.[50] The important point to note is that Jesus' first act as the Davidic king is one of judgment against the temple. Such action on his part is clearly consonant with this role.

This same note of judgment is also sounded in the story of the fig tree into which the pericope concerning the cleansing of the temple is intercalated. On the Mount of Olives fig trees are in leaf by early April but would not have ripe fruit until June, long after the Passover. Thus it would appear that Jesus was cursing a fig tree for not doing what it could not do. One explanation of this action by Jesus is that he is teaching his disciples a vital lesson during the final week of his life by doing something so out of character that they cannot help but notice. Since there is no obvious reason for his action

45. See Howard Clark Kee, "The Function of Scriptural Quotations and Allusions in Mark 11–16," in *Jesus und Paulus,* ed. E. Earle Ellis and Erich Grässer (Göttingen: Vandenhoeck & Ruprecht, 1975), pp. 165-88, for a discussion of this feature of unit five.

46. Burkill, p. 39.

47. C. E. B. Cranfield, *The Gospel according to Saint Mark* (Cambridge: University Press, 1959), p. 358.

48. Lane, p. 406.

49. Timothy J. Geddert, "Mark 13 in Its Markan Interpretative Context" (Ph.D. diss., University of Aberdeen, 1986), p. 250. See also pp. 247-50 for a summary of suggested explanations as to the meaning of "den of robbers."

50. "A clear majority of scholars hold that Mark's 'cleansing' account is more a disqualification than a purification, more a prophecy of destruction than a reform movement." Geddert, p. 246.

(Mark has taken care to point out that "it was not the season for figs"), they are forced to ponder why he did this.[51] In doing so they would come to understand the meaning of the fig tree.

W. Telford, in his exhaustive study of this pericope, has shown that in the Old Testament the fig was an emblem of peace, security, and prosperity that was connected to the golden ages of Israel's history. The blossoming of the fig tree was used to describe God's blessing on his people. But the fig was also a symbol of judgment. The withering of the fig tree described God's judgment. "Very often the reason given for God's wrathful visitation is cultic aberration on the part of Israel, her condemnation for a *corrupt Temple cultus and sacrificial system*."[52] Furthermore, in reviewing the later Jewish writing, this understanding is strengthened so that he concludes that "we find it difficult to believe that Mark and his readers would not have attached a similar allegorical significance to Jesus' visit to Jerusalem and his search, in that context, for figs from the fig-tree."[53] The sandwiching together of these two pericopae strengthens the note of judgment.

Jesus continues in his role as judge in Mark 12:1-12. Here he tells the parable of the wicked tenants. This parable is directly connected with the cleansing of the temple in that it is directed at the religious leaders (as they themselves understand [12:12]).[54] Jesus' parable is based on a parable in Isaiah 5:1-7 (continuing the use of the Old Testament in this unit). However, there are clear differences between the original parable and Jesus' use of it here. As Geddert points out:

> In both parables God is the owner, Israel is the vineyard, and the owner fails to get from the vineyard the fruit he had a right to expect. However, the reason why he failed in his quest for fruit is the crucial point of divergence. In the Isaiah parable, the owner did not get a harvest commensurate with his careful gardening because the vineyard itself did not produce an adequate one. In the Markan parable, the vineyard produced fruit just as desired and expected, but a blockage, the wicked tenants, prevented the owner from re-

---

51. Mark continues his allusion to the Old Testament. Such acted-out parables were very much a part of how the OT prophets communicated. For example, at the command of God, Isaiah went around naked for three years to make his point (Isa. 20) and Ezekiel acted out a complex tableau to show what would happen to Israel (Ezek. 4 and 5).

52. William R. Telford, *The Barren Temple and the Withered Tree,* Journal for the Study of the New Testament Supplement Series 1 (Sheffield: JSOT Press, 1980), pp. 161-62.

53. Telford, p. 194.

54. John R. Donahue, *Are You the Christ? The Trial Narrative in the Gospel of Mark,* SBL Dissertation Series 10 (Missoula, Mont.: Scholars Press, 1973), pp. 122-27.

ceiving good fruit. In Isaiah judgment falls on the vineyard; in Mark it falls on the tenants. . . .

It is unmistakably Israel's leadership, not Israel itself, that stands under condemnation in Mark 12:1-12.[55]

Jesus concludes his parable by citing Psalm 118:22-23 (Mark 12:10-11). Here "he suggests that the Messiah, despised and rejected on earth, will be finally exalted to a position of pre-eminence through a marvelous manifestation of God's supernatural power."[56] The use of Psalm 118 for the second time is significant. "Mark has employed the psalm to interpret what has taken place. In the first instance, the crowds greet Jesus as the one who brings David's Kingdom (11:9b-10) whereas in the second, Jesus points to the only son as the rejected stone which has become the cornerstone."[57]

Matera argues that there is a connection between the only son in this parable and the only son in the baptism (1:11) and the transfiguration (9:7) and that Mark understands the only son to be a royal figure.[58] Clearly Psalm 118 has a royal tone to it. Furthermore, this psalm was understood in the first century to have been written by David. "It is precisely this royal imagery and the prophetic voice of David which lends itself so well to a messianic interpretation. Psalms 'composed' by King David become prophecies for his royal descendant."[59] The significance of all this is "that the rejected stone refers to the rejected son/king."[60] Thus Mark connects the theme of unit four (the rejected Son of Man) and the theme of unit five (the Son of David who is rejected by the religious leadership).

The emphasis on the Son of David climaxes in Mark 12:35-37. Jesus has been asked three questions following his parable of the tenants. Then he himself asks a question: How is it that the Messiah can be both the Son of David and David's Lord? A father does not refer to his son as his master. The answer is, as Mark's readers know, that the Messiah is David's son in that he fulfills the promise that God will one day raise up a successor to David and that this successor will usher in a new age for Israel (see Isa. 9:6-7; 16:5; Jer. 23:5; 30:8-9; Ezek. 34:23-24; 37:24; Hos. 3:5; Amos 9:11). But, according to the psalm quoted here, the Messiah is more than a mere descendant. He is more than a second David. He is above David. "The divinely inspired David is quoted as

55. Geddert, p. 253.
56. Burkill, p. 41.
57. Matera, p. 68.
58. Matera, pp. 75-79.
59. Matera, p. 82.
60. Matera, p. 83.

connecting the Messiah with the throne of God ('at my right side,' v. 36), suggesting that the true Messiah is to be understood as bearing not only Davidic, but also divine, significance."[61] Thus Mark hints at what lies ahead in the next unit where the full identity of Jesus is finally made clear.

Finally, it is important to note that by means of the question Jesus asks in Mark 12:35, the intention of Mark in Part II of his Gospel is made clear. Jesus asks: "How can the scribes say that the Messiah is the son of David?" (12:35). At the end of Part I the Twelve learn that Jesus is the Messiah. In Part II they learn what kind of Messiah he is. In unit four they learn that the Messiah is the Son of Man. Here in this unit they learn that he is the Son of David. In unit six they will learn that he is the Son of God (14:61).

The Son of David in First-Century Debate

From Jesus' comments in 12:35-37 it is clear that the connection between the Messiah and the Son of David was the subject of theological debate in the first century. Certainly the Old Testament gave the hope that one day a descendant of David would establish the throne of David forever (e.g., 2 Sam. 7:12-16). This idea was expanded upon in the Hellenistic period in the Psalms of Solomon (first century B.C.),[62] which state that the Son of David will rule over Israel (17:21), will "purge Jerusalem from gentiles" (17:22), will gather a holy people (17:26) which he will judge (17:26), and that "their king will be the Lord Messiah" (17:32). "The writer appears to hope, not for God-fearing kings in general of the house of David, but for a single Messiah endowed by God with miraculous powers, holy and free from sin (17:41, 46), one made mighty and wise by God through the holy spirit (17:42), who will therefore smite his enemies not with external weapons but by the word of his mouth (17:39 after Isa. 11:4)."[63] It is interesting that at two places Psalm of Solomon 17 explicitly states that the coming Davidic king will judge (vv. 26, 29). Mark's description in unit five of the Son of David contains both the idea of royalty and the idea of judgment.

De Jonge comments on the expectation that lay behind the Psalm of Solomon:

> Just because no son of David has been king over Israel for a long time, the
> return of the Davidic kingship was expected with so much fervour. In the

61. Hurtado, p. 192.
62. See, in particular, Pss. Sol. 17:4, 21-32.
63. Schürer, 2:504.

glorious future promised by God His promises connected with David will become a reality. Therefore a number of O.T. prophecies concerning David's offspring clearly influenced the description of the kingship of this son of David and he is depicted as an ideal figure like the king in the so-called "royal psalms" in the O.T., where a number of the O.T. occurrences of the term "Anointed of the Lord" are found.[64]

Thus "some scholars have understood the title 'son of David' in the NT to be largely a political designation, referring to the nationalistic hopes of a conquered Israel."[65]

The context of this debate had to do with how God would bring about the salvation God had promised. The question was not if God would rescue the Jews from their oppressor, but how God would accomplish this. There were two predominant views on this subject at the time. "Some Jews looked for an anointed eschatological figure from the tribe of Levi while others expected a king in the line of David."[66] The Pharisees came down on the side of the Davidic line. They were expecting a figure of royalty. Thus in Mark 12:35-37 Jesus was not disputing the view held by the Pharisees as much as he was attempting to get them to broaden it. "The clear meaning of the passage is that the Jewish conceptions of the day were inadequate vehicles for containing the full role and person of the Messiah, and the full sweep of God's plan of redemption. At best, they only hinted at the scope of the Messiah's significance."[67] That this expectation of a royal redeemer was shared by the general population is shown in John's account of the feeding of the five thousand. The people attempt to make Jesus *king* by force (John 6:15). Although the various groups might not agree on who exactly would rescue the people of God, there was a general sense that someone would. "All the groups were united in the belief that Israel's hope would be realized in individual figures who would usher in the eschatological salvation. It was in the time of most

64. De Jonge, p. 135.

65. Achtemeier, p. 125. Achtemeier also mentions two other interpretations of this title. The first is the suggestion of K. L. Berger that in the NT the title is connected to the traditions about Solomon as a healer and exorcist. E. S. Johnson asserts that the probable second-century date for Berger's main rabbinic source as well as "the likelihood that it has been influenced by NT phraseology, its similarity to Hellenistic miracle stories . . . cast considerable doubts on the value of this passage as a demonstration of the antiquity of the Jewish expectation of a healing Messiah." Achtemeier, p. 195 n. 24. The second interpretation is that this title is a postresurrection Christian reflection and not a part of Jewish tradition.

66. Gowan, p. 496.

67. Hurtado, p. 192.

extreme need that people hoped that God would make himself known to them, and lead them out of their obscurity and ambiguity."[68]

The disciples, of course, would have been exposed to this crosscurrent of opinion about the coming redeemer. Thus they probably would have greeted enthusiastically this new revelation that Jesus was the Son of David. It fitted in with their assumptions. "Ancient Jewish prayer and Bible interpretation demonstrate unequivocally that if in the inter-Testamental era a man claimed, or was proclaimed, to be 'the Messiah,' his listeners would as a matter of course have assumed that he was referring to the Davidic Redeemer and would have expected to find before them a person endowed with the combined talents of soldierly prowess, righteousness and holiness."[69] That Jesus was the Son of David was a much more congenial concept for the Twelve than the idea of Jesus as the Son of Man who suffers and dies.

If all this is true, why is Mark not more forthright in asserting Jesus' royal character in unit five? A blind beggar shouts out the title, but he is not taken seriously by the crowds. Jesus rides into the city amidst the cries of the pilgrim crowds, but it is doubtful that many understand the significance of their acclamation. Jesus simply raises the question of the connection between the Son of David and the Messiah; he does not claim it directly at this point in the story. Nor is there a direct assumption on his part of the role of the returning Son in Mark 13. As Lane puts it: "The Marcan account of the entry into Jerusalem is characterized by vivid detail and yet is remarkably restrained in its messianic assertion."[70] Matera explains this as follows: "Mark has not explicitly employed the title 'king' because he carefully reserves it for the moment when there can be no misunderstanding the nature of Jesus' kingship. That moment, of course, is the passion when the accusations of the priests, the inscription and the mockeries will proclaim Jesus a suffering, rejected king according to the pattern of Ps. 118."[71]

By developing the theme of Jesus' royal messiahship in the context of the temple and the coming judgment, Mark prepares his readers for the next and final unit. "There, the passersby and religious authorities ridicule Jesus as the temple-destroyer and the Messiah, the King of Israel. Here Mark has prepared for both themes that will dominate that scene. He will show Jesus as breaking with the old temple and pointing to the new. He will raise the ques-

68. R. Mayer, "Israel," in *The New International Dictionary of New Testament Theology*, ed. Colin Brown, vol. 2, p. 313.

69. Vermes, p. 134.

70. Lane, p. 393.

71. Matera, p. 91.

tion of royal messiahship and indicate in what ways old titles have become inadequate and must be reinterpreted."[72]

Jesus the Son of God: An Analysis of Unit Six
(Mark 14:1–15:39)

Thus Mark comes to the final unit. The central event in unit six is, of course, the crucifixion of Jesus. This is the event toward which the whole Gospel has been pointing. This is the event that reveals the full identity of Jesus. It is during the events of the crucifixion that Jesus is positively and publicly connected with the title that sums up best who he is, namely, Son of God. This is the final piece in the puzzle needed by the disciples in order to make sense out of Jesus.

Unit six begins with a pair of intercalated pericopae, which taken together bear all the marks of the other five leadoff pericopae. In the first of the two pericopae (the betrayal by Judas — 14:1-2, 10-11), it is clear that Jesus is misunderstood. Had Judas really believed him to be the Messiah, he would not have betrayed Jesus to the officials. Had the religious authorities really believed Jesus to be the Messiah, they would not have sought to arrest him. Judas's act is also a rebuke of Jesus and all that he has stood for. In the same way, the desire to arrest Jesus is a rebuke on the part of the officials. And clearly the emotion was running high at this point in time. Jesus had so angered the leaders that they want to kill him (14:1). The people also had strong feelings about Jesus so that there would have been a riot were the officials to arrest him (14:2). And who can guess at the torture in the soul of Judas (as his subsequent suicide demonstrates) as he agrees to betray Jesus? In addition, there is the delight the leaders must have felt now that they had found a way to arrest Jesus without provoking a riot.

The same elements can be found in the second story of the intercalated pair (14:3-9). Strong emotion permeates the story as Jesus is anointed with costly ointment. There is the complex of feelings (i.e., love, honor, devotion) that lead the woman to pour expensive perfume over Jesus (14:3). And there is the strong reaction on the part of the disciples: "some were there who said to one another in *anger* . . ." (14:4, italics mine) and "they rebuked her *harshly*" (14:5 NIV, italics mine). Equally strong is the reaction of Jesus to the disciples: "Let her alone; why do you trouble her?" (14:6). And of course, the people in this story rebuke one another: the disciples rebuke the woman

---

72. Matera, p. 69.

(14:5) and Jesus rebukes the disciples (14:6). None of this would have gone on had the disciples really understood the identity of Jesus.

The new title here — the one at the center of the unit — is Son of God. This title is "generally recognized" to be "the most important of the titles of Jesus in Mark."[73] Yet this title is used sparingly by Mark in his Gospel. Mark uses it in his prologue (1:1); twice the voice from heaven refers to Jesus as the beloved Son (1:11; 9:7); twice the demons call Jesus the Son of God (3:11; 5:7). And here in unit six Jesus is publicly identified twice by this title. The high priest identifies Jesus as the Son of God in 14:61, and the centurion does the same in the closing verse of the unit (15:39).

It must be noted that while Son of God is the key title in unit six, it is set in the context of all the other major titles that have been applied to Jesus in this Gospel. Each of the six titles is found here in unit six (in one form or another): teacher (14:14), rabbi (14:45), prophet (14:65), Messiah (14:61; 15:32), Son of Man (14:21 [twice], 41, 62), king (15:2, 9, 12, 18, 26, 32), as well as Son of God (14:61; 15:39). Jesus refers to himself as "Teacher" in the coded message that identifies the disciples to the owner of the house where they will eat the Passover.[74] This is probably how this man thought of Jesus at this point in time: as a wise teacher of Israel. The related title "Rabbi" is used by Judas. This may well be how Judas finally made sense out of Jesus: he is merely a rabbi who is in conflict with other rabbis. This view of Jesus would make it possible for him to betray Jesus. The idea of Jesus as a prophet comes from the Sanhedrin. During their torment of Jesus they taunt him by urging him to prophesy if he really is sent from God (not expecting that he can or will). The title Son of Man continues on the lips of Jesus in reference to his coming betrayal (14:21, 41) and enthronement/ return (14:62). The title of king (of the Jews) is what "Son of David" becomes in this unit. In each instance when "King of the Jews (Israel)" is used of Jesus, it is applied to him by others in an accusatory way. The title Messiah is coupled with the titles Son of God and Son of Man during the accusation by the high priest. This is the only unit in which all the titles are

---

73. Ernest Best, *The Temptation and the Passion: The Markan Soteriology* (Cambridge: University Press, 1965), p. 167. So too N. Perrin, "Creative Use of Son of Man Traditions in Mark," *Union Seminary Quarterly Review* (1968): 358, as noted by Donald Juel, *Messiah and Temple: The Trial of Jesus in the Gospel of Mark,* SBL Dissertation Series 31 (Missoula, Mont.: Scholars Press, 1977), p. 80 n. 14.

74. J. Duncan M. Derrett, *The Making of Mark: The Scriptural Bases of the Earliest Gospel,* 2 vols. (Shipston-on-Stour: P. Drinkwater, 1985), 2:234-35, refers to the prior arrangement that Jesus must have made to secure a room as well as a properly slaughtered lamb for thirteen people.

found. They are used here because at this point in his account Mark is summing up the full identity of Jesus.

The Declaration by the High Priest

The first person who calls Jesus "Son of God" is the high priest when challenging Jesus about his identity (14:61-62). In fact, in this climactic confrontation all four of the major titles are used: "Again the high priest asked him, 'Are you the *Messiah*, the *Son of the Blessed One* [Son of God]?' Jesus said, 'I am; and "you will see the *Son of Man / seated at the right hand of the Power* [the King]," / and *"coming with the clouds of heaven* [as the returning messianic King]."'"[75] This question by the high priest will be examined in some detail.

First, it must be noticed that the high priest addresses Jesus with the dual titles Messiah and Son of the Blessed One. (The phrase "Blessed One" is a "reverential circumlocution . . . used to avoid speaking directly of God.")[76] These are the same two titles used by Mark in the opening sentence of the Gospel to define the two parts of Jesus' identity about which he will write. Here both titles finally come together as one and are focused on Jesus.

The question must be asked, however, as to what the high priest meant when he called Jesus the Son of God. What weight attached to this title in his mind? Lane states that "in Jewish sources contemporary with the NT, 'son of God' is understood solely in a messianic sense. The question of the high priest cannot have referred to Jesus' deity, but was limited to a single issue: do you claim to be the Messiah?"[77] Thus the high priest was, in fact, attaching to Jesus a single title (Messiah) which he phrased in two ways. However, for Mark the distinction between the two titles is signifi-

75. The italics and other notations are my insertions.
76. D. E. Nineham, *The Gospel of St. Mark* (London: Adam & Charles Black, 1968), p. 407. See Juel, pp. 77-79, for a discussion of this circumlocution. He argues that this expression is "a pseudo-Jewish expression created by the author as appropriate in the mouth of the high priest" (p. 79).
77. Lane, p. 535. Lane, p. 135 n. 133, contends that Ps. 2 and 2 Sam. 7:14 "are interpreted messianically in 1QSa 2:1ff. and 4QFlorilegium. In 4QFlorilegium 1:10f. the scroll reads 'I will be to him as a father and he will be to me as a son. He is the shoot of David . . . ,' providing evidence of a sonship being predicated of the Davidic Messiah." See Juel, pp. 79-80, 108-14, for a discussion of this issue. His conclusion is similar to that of Lane: "There is evidence both in pre-Markan Christianity as well as in pre-Christian Judaism that the title was used with clear awareness of its scriptural (= royal) origin" (p. 114).

cant. It is not enough to call Jesus "Messiah" and think that this captures who he is. As the second half of the Gospel demonstrates, once Jesus' messiahship is affirmed then it must be stated what kind of Messiah he is, which is what the title Son of God does.

Thus this title must be understood not merely in terms of cultural assumptions (i.e., how the high priest understood it) but in terms of how Mark uses it in the whole of the Gospel. First, Mark uses this title to define the unique relationship that Jesus has with God. The title Son occurs at both the baptism and the transfiguration, both times uttered by the voice from heaven. "Mark is not as clear as Luke or John about the precise character of the relationship, but the importance of this unique sonship is unquestionable."[78]

Second, this title is used by the demons (3:11; 5:7). Juel suggests that in these instances the term might be used by Mark to mean "divine man."[79] These supernatural beings (in this case evil ones) understand the special connection Jesus has with God.

Third, this is the first time in Mark that another person publicly addresses Jesus by the title Son of God. Hitherto only those with special knowledge (the author and supernatural beings) know that this is who he is. It is only the second time in Mark that Jesus has been directly addressed by the title Messiah *(Christos)*. When Peter first addressed him this way in 8:29, Jesus made no response. Instead, he urged his disciples to be silent about their discovery. Throughout the Gospel Jesus has carefully avoided calling himself, or allowing others to call him, "Messiah." "It was not his desire to arouse the nationalistic and political hopes which clustered around the figure of the Messiah in popular thinking."[80] But now the time for silence is past. Here in this public setting Jesus accepts these titles as an accurate designation of who he is. When asked if this is who he is, he responds with a simple affirmative. He is, in fact, the Anointed One sent by God.[81]

Fourth, neither title used by the high priest (Christ, Son of the Blessed One) appears in Jesus' response. Rather, his answer both amplifies and defines the meaning of these two titles. Such amplification and definition was necessary because (as has been shown above) the title Messiah was likely to be misunderstood if used without qualification. Likewise, the title Son of God

78. Juel, p. 81.
79. Juel, p. 81.
80. Lane, p. 536.
81. "That his reply was an affirmative reply, and not a pronouncing of the theophanic formula 'I am he' is evident from the structure of verses 61-62. The question 'Are you . . . ?' demands and receives the response 'I am.' . . ." Lane, p. 536.

was also capable of being misunderstood (as Donahue has shown, using the work of Weeden).[82]

It is important to examine carefully what Jesus says about these two titles in 14:62. First, he describes himself as the Son of Man. "Jesus publicly accepts the title Son of the Blessed, but he qualifies it in reference to the future Son of Man. The true meaning of Jesus as Son of God will be known only when he returns in glory as the victorious Son of Man. Therefore, Son of Man serves to give a correct understanding of not only the earthly ministry of Jesus, and his suffering, but also of his status as Son of God."[83] How does the title Son of Man define what it means to be the Messiah, the Son of God? For one thing, the title Son of Man is connected with the concept of suffering and death. This lies at the heart of both offices. The connection between the Son of Man and dying is made in unit four via Jesus' predictions of what lies ahead for him (see 8:31; 9:9-10, 31; 10:33-34). The connection between sonship and dying is made in unit five in the parable of the vineyard, where it is the son who is put to death (12:6-8). E. Best suggests yet another link between sonship and death. It is via the word *agapētos* = "beloved." As C. H. Turner has shown, it is probable that the "meaning of the word is 'only' rather than 'beloved.'"[84] This phrase was used by the Voice at the baptism and at the transfiguration as the qualifier attached to the word "son." The same word is used of Isaac in Genesis 22:2, 12, 16. In the same way that Isaac was an only son who was a sacrifice, so too was Jesus. Best argues from both apocalyptic and New Testament sources that Jesus was understood to be the new Isaac. He shows that "in Rabbinic teaching the sacrifice of Isaac, though no blood was shed, came to be accepted as the one perfect sacrifice by which the sins of the people of Israel were forgiven."[85]

> We may view him [Jesus] in Mark's picture as an only (1:11; 9:7) and obedient (14:32ff.) son who goes willingly to his death like Isaac, and whose death is a sacrifice for the sins of men. If this interpretation is accepted, sonship is fulfilled in willing sacrifice, which is for others, and sonship is recognized in the moment of death (cf. 15:39). Thus taking Jesus to be the new Isaac we find that the theme of sonship is linked to the sacrifice of the Cross, with the underlying conception, as in Judaism, of a sacrifice for others (cf. Rom 8:32).[86]

82. Donahue, p. 180.
83. Donahue, p. 180.
84. Best, *The Temptation and the Passion,* pp. 169-70, citing C. H. Turner, *Journal of Theological Studies* 27 (1926): 113-29; and 28 (1927): 152.
85. Best, *The Temptation and the Passion,* p. 171.
86. Best, *The Temptation and the Passion,* pp. 172-73.

For another thing, the title Son of Man is connected with the idea of royalty. The allusion to Psalm 110:1 (in Mark 14:62) points to the coming resurrection and exaltation of Jesus to the right hand of God. The phrase "sitting at the right hand of God" was a common idiom which meant that he sat in the highest place of honor in God's court.[87] Furthermore, Psalm 110 is a royal psalm. As Donahue points out, "the imagery of the psalm suggests the enthronement of the king surrounded by his enemies, but vindicated in the face of them and judging them. Such a scene corresponds directly to the trial scene, so that in many respects the trial is a 'midrash' on the psalm."[88] Thus the concept of the Son of David, the promised royal successor, is connected to the concept of the Son of Man. The allusion to Daniel 7:13 (also found in Mark 14:62) extends the image to include the second coming. The Messiah/Son of God will return again to gather the elect.[89] Both quotations are connected with Jesus' role as judge, which in turn is connected to his title Son of David. "Jesus thus spoke without reserve of his exaltation and coming as the eschatological Judge."[90] There is some precedent for linking these two texts around the terms "Son" and "Messiah," as C. S. Mann shows: "Ps 2:7 links the terms 'Son' and 'the anointed one,' and the Midrash on that psalm uses both Psalm 110 and Daniel 7 in explaining it."[91]

Thus it is that all the titles attached to Jesus come together here in the statement by the high priest and are connected to his coming death.[92] This is who Jesus is according to Mark. He is the Messiah, the successor to David's throne who is more than David because he is God's only Son. In this role he has come to die. One day he will return again in judgment. Up to this point in the Gospel it has not been clear — to the disciples or to anyone else who did not already know the whole story — just who Jesus is. But now his full identity is out in the open.

87. Lane, p. 537.

88. Donahue, pp. 174-75.

89. There has been much discussion between Glasson (*The Second Advent,* 3rd rev. ed. [London: Epworth Press, 1963]), J. A. T. Robinson (*Jesus and His Coming* [London: SCM Press, 1957] and "The Second Coming — Mark 14:62," *Expository Times* 67 [1956]: 336-40), and McArthur ("Mark 14:62," *New Testament Studies* 4 [1958]: 156-58) as to whether 14:62 refers to Jesus' exaltation to heaven through the resurrection or to his return again at the second coming. Donahue rightly contends that both senses are meant to be conveyed by 14:62. It is not a matter of either/or. See Donahue, pp. 142-43.

90. Lane, p. 537.

91. Mann, p. 625.

92. Donahue, p. 95; Juel, p. 86.

The Confession of the Centurion

The second response to Jesus as the Son of God comes at the end of unit six with the declaration by the centurion that "Truly this man was God's Son!" Several aspects of this confession need to be highlighted. First, the context of the declaration is important. Mark makes the point that the centurion made his declaration when he "heard his cry and saw how he died" (15:39 NIV). The cry referred to was Jesus' death cry ("With a loud cry, Jesus breathed his last" [15:37 NIV]). Somehow it was Jesus' death that revealed who he was. "In the view of Mark, nobody can understand Jesus . . . until he has learned that Jesus' divine sonship reveals itself primarily in his rejection, his suffering, and his dying."[93]

Second, there is some question as to whether the centurion referred to Jesus as "the Son of God" or "a Son of God." The problem is grammatical in nature. The statement by the centurion is *alēthōs houtos ho anthrōpos huios theou ēn*. There is no definite article before *huios*. However, as Moule and others have pointed out, according to Colwell's rule, the omission of the article does not necessitate the translation "a Son of God."[94]

Third, the important question is: What did the centurion mean by his statement? Two lines of argument seem to have been followed. This "has been understood (1) as an admission that the dying man on the Cross was an extraordinary man, a hero, and (2) as a Christian confession of faith in Jesus as the Son of God."[95] Bratcher argues (on grammatical and textual grounds) that the second meaning is intended. This is a "full-fledged confession of Jesus as the Son of God."[96] So too Nineham: "So what we have here is not simply a case of an executioner being won over to the side of a martyr (something which often occurs in the martyrologies and is all that Luke sees here — Luke 23:47), but a much greater miracle, the conversion of an unbeliever by the dying Saviour."[97]

---

93. Eduard Schweizer, "The Portrayal of the Life of Faith in the Gospel of Mark," *Interpretation* 32 (October 1978): 390.

94. See Robert G. Bratcher, "A Note on *Huios Theou* (Mark 15:39)," *Expository Times* 68 (October 1956): 27, and "Mark 15:39: The Son of God," *Expository Times* 80 (June 1969): 286; Philip H. Bligh, "A Note on *Huios Theou* in Mark 15:39," *Expository Times* 80 (November 1968): 51-53; T. Francis Glasson, "Mark 15:39: The Son of God," *Expository Times* 80 (June 1969): 286; and Harold A. Guy, "Son of God in Mark 15:39," *Expository Times* 81 (February 1970): 151.

95. Bratcher, "A Note on *Huios Theou*," p. 27.

96. Bratcher, "A Note on *Huios Theou*," p. 28. So too Bligh, "A Note on *Huios Theou*."

97. Nineham, p. 430.

But the question remains: What content was attached by the centurion to the title Son of God? What information did the centurion have on which to base his assertion? First, it is likely that he knew of the events surrounding Jesus' trial before Pilate (Mark 15:1-20). This would include information about the charges laid against Jesus ("'Are you the king of the Jews?' asked Pilate. 'Yes, it is as you say,' Jesus replied" [15:2 NIV; see also 15:9]) and the mocking of Jesus by the soldiers (during which they call him the "King of the Jews" [15:18]). Second, he witnessed the events involved in the crucifixion of Jesus (15:21-37). He would have seen the notice attached to the cross: "The King of the Jews" (15:26); heard the insults (that connected Jesus with the destruction of the temple — 15:29); heard the mocking of the Jewish leaders (that connected Jesus to the salvation of others and that named him as Messiah and king of Israel — 15:31-32); and heard Jesus' cry of despair to God (15:34). Third, he witnessed the actual death of Jesus, as Mark notes (15:37, 39), which was itself the final source of revelation. Thus, when the centurion made his confession, there was content to what he said. Most clearly, Jesus was connected for him to the royal theme that is so dominant in chapters 14 and 15. It is not inconceivable that the centurion understood the title Son of God in ways similar to how it is defined in 14:61-62. He would understand that Jesus was the Messiah-King.[98]

Certainly Mark gives the centurion's confession its full christological weight. Mark's point is that the death of Jesus reveals him to be the Son of God. This is, of course, the final bit of information needed by the disciples in order to understand Jesus. It is significant that prior to his death they did not (nor could not, Mark seems to be saying) know that he was the Son of God. The first time the title is attached to Jesus by a person (the high priest), it is done in the context of unbelief (and out of the hearing of the disciples). The second time it is uttered as a faith statement (by the centurion). It is Jesus' death that makes such faith possible. "Mark clearly intended this as a recognition of Jesus' messiahship, concluding the account of Jesus' earthly life on the note with which he had begun it in 1:1. The climax of his narrative is the acknowledgment of this on the lips of a Roman."[99] "Thus the Gospel beginning with the divine testimony to the sonship of Jesus ends with the same human

---

98. Juel writes: "Can we assume that when, according to Mark, the Centurion witnesses the death of the 'King of the Jews,' who has been mocked by soldiers as 'King of the Jews' and by his Jewish enemies as 'the Christ, the King of Israel,' his use of the title *huios theou* is unrelated to the use in 14:61? At least from the perspective of the author it seems highly probable that the relationship is intended, that the confession of the Centurion belongs with the royal motif as well" (p. 83).

99. Guy, "Son of God in Mark 15:39," p. 151.

testimony; Jesus is the Son of God, and he is this, not despite, but because of his death."[100]

Summary

Thus it is evident that Mark organizes his Gospel around the unfolding view of who Jesus is on the part of disciples. Such an understanding provides a coherent view of the whole Gospel and accounts for all of the materials. In the first half of the Gospel Jesus is seen first as a teacher, then as a prophet, then as the Messiah. In the second half of the Gospel the nature of his messiahship is defined. He is not the Messiah of cultural expectation; rather he is the Son of Man, the Son of David, and the Son of God. In the same way that the title Messiah includes the concepts of teacher and prophet, so too the title Son of God includes the concepts of Son of Man and Son of David.

The first three titles (teacher, prophet, Messiah) define Jesus in terms of what he does (activity); the second three (Son of Man, Son of David, Son of God) define him in terms of who he is (being). The first three titles focus on his acceptance within first-century Judaism; the second three focus on his rejection by first-century Judaism. That is, first-century Jews were comfortable with (and excited about) Jesus as a teacher (e.g., 1:22, 27, 28, 45; 3:7-12) and Jesus as prophet (e.g., 6:14-16; 8:27-28). If the disciples' reaction is a fair measure, the people would have been equally excited about him as the Messiah (though they, like the disciples, would have understood him in terms of cultural categories). However, when it came to the three titles which define what kind of Messiah Jesus is, there was rejection. The disciples reject the concept of the Son of Man suffering, dying, and rising (as unit four shows). The religious leaders reject Jesus in his role as the returned Son of David (as unit five shows). The leaders and the disciples both reject him as the Son of God (as unit six shows).

Who, then, is Jesus? As Mark indicates in his introductory statement (1:1), the dual title Messiah/Son of God is needed to define him. Mark's Gospel is the account of how the disciples came, step-by-step, to know him as such. With this information they become able to respond to him in repentance and faith and so experience conversion. It is this process that is described in chapters 9 and 10.

---

100. Best, *The Temptation and the Passion*, p. 168.

CHAPTER NINE

Conversion Themes in Mark's Gospel: Response, Faith, Repentance

M ark is not only concerned that his readers understand who Jesus is. He is also concerned that they know how to respond to Jesus. Conversion begins with understanding but moves to response. So it is that in each unit Mark discusses not only a particular title for Jesus but also certain aspects of conversion. Thus in unit one he defines a range of possible responses to Jesus. In unit two he discusses faith, while in unit three he raises the question of repentance. Unit four focuses on discipleship. And in units five and six the disciples learn the final lesson about repentance. Taken together, repentance, faith, and discipleship define conversion.

Interestingly, the information the disciples have about repentance, faith, and discipleship remains merely theoretical for them while they are with Jesus. They simply do not understand the meaning of what Jesus is saying. They are taught but they do not comprehend. Right up to the very end, to that moment when Jesus is taken away from them, they display a lack of understanding of both him and his teaching as well as a lack of adequate commitment to Jesus. The fact is, however (as shown in chapter 8), they could *not* have understood what all this meant prior to Jesus' death. It was his death that revealed who he really was and thus unlocked the meaning of his teaching. Furthermore, as the analysis of Paul's conversion demonstrates, it is the resurrected Lord they must meet in order to be converted. New Testament conversion involves repentance and faith that is focused on the Jesus who died for one's sins and lives again as the Lord who brings new life. It is only after they, like Paul, meet the resurrected Jesus that it all makes sense for them and the response of conversion is possible.

In the next two chapters, therefore, the conversion themes in Mark will be analyzed. In each case the theme in question will be traced within a particular unit. Then detailed attention will be given to selected pericopae in that unit that bear upon the theme.

Conversion: The Theme Defined in the Prologue
(Mark 1:1-15)

Two portions of the prologue in particular are important in understanding the theme of conversion in Mark. In 1:1 the author defines the kind of document he is writing, and in so doing makes his evangelistic purpose clear. And in 1:14-15 he defines the nature of Jesus' ministry and further clarifies the evangelistic intent of the book. In between these two sections (1:2-13), Mark points to his concern for evangelism by means of the vocabulary he uses.

The Gospel: Mark 1:1

Mark begins his manuscript by stating that what he is writing is "the good news" (lit. "gospel"). But what is the nature of "the gospel"? What, therefore, is this book all about? Lane defines this term as follows:

> In Ch. 1:1 "gospel" is the technical term for Christian preaching, and the words which qualify it should be understood objectively, "the good news concerning Jesus the Messiah, the Son of God." Mark's Gospel as a whole gives an interpretive account of the historical appearance of Jesus. . . . Consistent with this, "Jesus the Messiah, the Son of God" in verse 1 should be understood as the content of Christian proclamation. The superscription indicates that Mark's primary concern is to delineate the historical content of the primitive Christian message of salvation.[1]

What Mark is doing, according to Marxsen, is preaching a sermon.[2] Commenting on this, Best says: "It is a sermon in the sense of 'a proclamation of the word'; Mark gives God's word to his people; a sermon is the directing of God's word to a particular people in a particular situation; this is what

---

1. William L. Lane, *The Gospel according to Mark* (Grand Rapids: Wm. B. Eerdmans Publishing Co., 1974), pp. 44-45.
2. W. Marxsen, *Introduction to the New Testament: An Approach to Its Problems*, trans. G. Buswell (Oxford: Basil Blackwell, 1968), p. 144.

Mark is doing."[3] This "preaching of the gospel" via the writing of a Gospel has long been recognized as one of the functions of the four Gospels. What does not seem to have been noted is that, at least in the case of the Gospel of Mark, this is not just preaching to the reader. It is that primarily, but it is also an account of how the gospel was preached to the Twelve. How the Twelve came to faith becomes a model for how the reader can come to faith.[4]

There is some question as to the interpretation of the phrase "the good news of Jesus Christ" in 1:1. The question is whether this is an objective genitive or a subjective genitive. If it is an objective genitive, then the focus is on Jesus as the person who is proclaimed (the good news "about Jesus Christ," as the NIV renders this phrase). If it is a subjective genitive, the focus is on Jesus as the one who proclaims the gospel (the good news "of Jesus Christ," as the NRSV renders the phrase). Either rendering is possible. "In fact there is a sense in which both are true; Christ is both a figure of the past in the book of Mark and he speaks in and through it as living Lord."[5] Christ is both the message and the messenger. Either way Mark's intention is clear. The content of the gospel message he is about to communicate in his book focuses on Jesus.[6]

The Vocabulary of Conversion: Mark 1:2-13

In the section that follows this opening statement (i.e., 1:2-13), Mark continues to stress the evangelistic nature of his literary work by means of the vocabulary he uses. John the Baptist is introduced. The first thing said about John is that his twofold ministry involves "baptizing" (which in the early church was the outward sign of conversion) and "preaching a baptism of re-

---

3. Ernest Best, *Mark: The Gospel as Story* (Edinburgh: T. & T. Clark, 1983), p. 41.

4. Once again the issue of chronology presents itself. Suffice it to say that the important issue is how Mark tells his story. His Gospel consists of a series of interconnected pericopae, each of which relates a historical event accurately, translated from an oral format that made the story easy to remember and relate. These independent stories are then crafted together by Mark on the basis of themes (and not chronology) so as to make the theological point which is his reason for writing. We cannot tell, therefore, how the coming to faith took place in time for each of the eleven who remained disciples of Jesus after his death. We can know, on the basis of what Mark tells us, that they grew in their understanding of who Jesus was and how to respond to him.

5. Best, *Mark*, p. 39.

6. "That its content is Christ appears through its paralleling with him in 8:35; 10:29 ('for my sake and the Gospel's'). The two are again associated in 13:9, 10." Ernest Best, *The Temptation and the Passion: The Markan Soteriology* (Cambridge: University Press, 1965), p. 63.

pentance" (*metanoeō* — one of the key terms in conversion) (1:4 NIV). Jesus, who is defined by John as "one more powerful than I" (1:7 NIV), is said also to come to baptize, but he will baptize not with water but with the Holy Spirit (1:8). The Holy Spirit is a key agent in conversion.[7] And indeed, Jesus is immediately shown receiving the Holy Spirit (1:10) and then being guided by that Spirit (1:12). The theme of conversion, in other words, is suggested in the body of the prologue. It will be defined clearly, however, in the final two verses of the prologue, which launch the story of Jesus' ministry.

The Message of Conversion: Mark 1:14-15

That repentance and faith (i.e., conversion) are to be central themes in Mark's Gospel is seen in the final statement of the prologue. In 1:14-15 Mark defines for his readers the nature of Jesus' ministry. He does so by using terms that the early church used to describe both the process of evangelism and the nature of the response to it. These words are "proclaiming," "good news" (twice), and the phrase "repent and believe."

Mark 1:14-15 begins by specifying time ("after John was arrested")[8] and place ("Jesus came to Galilee"). Then Mark makes four statements that define the nature of Jesus' ministry. He says: (1) Jesus came "proclaiming the good news of God." Specifically, this meant proclaiming that (2) "the time is fulfilled" and (3) "the kingdom of God has come near." The appropriate response to this good news is for men and women to (4) "repent, and believe in the good news." Each of these four phrases needs comment.

First, Jesus came "proclaiming the good news of God." The word translated "proclaiming" is *kērussō*, which was used in Hellenistic Greek to describe an announcement of great importance made by a herald who drew attention to his message by blowing a trumpet.[9] *Kērussein* (the root word from which *kērussō* is derived) is "one of the three great words used for proclaiming the Christian message, the other two being *euaggelizesthai* (to 'tell good

---

7. "However we may define the new birth, it clearly occurs in the human soul through the action of the Spirit of the living God. . . . The Spirit who regenerates the individual and who creates the new people of God is the same Spirit who came upon (and remains upon) Jesus the Messiah." Peter Toon, *Born Again: A Biblical and Theological Study of Regeneration* (Grand Rapids: Baker, 1987), p. 16.

8. That is, there is a significant time gap between the events in the lower Jordan described in 1:2-13 and the start of Jesus' ministry in Galilee.

9. C. S. Mann, *Mark: A New Translation with Introduction and Commentary* (Garden City, N.Y.: Doubleday, 1986), p. 205.

news') and *marturein* (to 'bear witness')."[10] While it is true that *kērussō* is used in the New Testament to describe the heralding of messages other than the gospel (e.g., Luke 12:3), most of the time (and certainly here with an accusative denoting that the content of the proclamation is "the good news of God") "*kērussō* means precisely the same as *euaggelizomai*."[11] The second part of this phrase is *euangelion tou theou* = the good news of God. The word *euangelion* means "good news" and was used in Greek literature to describe an event of great importance, as for example, the birth of a royal son or the winning of a great battle. "The phrase [the good news of God] was widely used in the early Church (cf. 1 Thess. 2:2, 8-9, Rom. 1:1, 15:16, 2 Cor. 11:7) to describe the Christian message of salvation. . . ."[12] Specifically, this was "the announcement of the climax of history, the divine intervention into the affairs of men brought about by the incarnation, life, death, resurrection and heavenly session of Jesus of Nazareth."[13] In other words, *kērussō* and *euangelion* are both words used to describe the process of calling men and women into the kingdom. Thus it is clear that Jesus comes as the evangelist.[14] This is what Mark will show Jesus doing in the remainder of his account.

Second, the phrase "the time is fulfilled" reiterates what Mark drew attention to in 1:2-3, namely, that a historic moment was unfolding at that mo-

10. Michael Green, *Evangelism in the Early Church* (London: Hodder & Stoughton, 1970), p. 48.

11. Green, p. 59.

12. D. E. Nineham, *The Gospel of St. Mark* (London: Adam & Charles Black, 1968), p. 69. See also Larry W. Hurtado, *Mark: A Good News Commentary* (San Francisco: Harper & Row, 1983), p. 8: "Good News is a term in Greek *(euangelion)* . . . that seems to have acquired a special significance for early Christians as a technical term for the message of salvation through Jesus." See as well Lane, p. 44.

13. Green, p. 60.

14. Robert P. Meye, *Jesus and the Twelve: Discipleship and Revelation in Mark's Gospel* (Grand Rapids: Wm. B. Eerdmans Publishing Co., 1968), p. 52, comments: "If Mark 1:14f. is a summary statement as many scholars believe, then it would seem that Mark has cast Jesus at the very outset in the role of a 'Proclaimer.' *But a problem arises in that there is not a single instance in the remaining chapters of Mark where Jesus' work is described with kerygmatic terminology.*" And indeed this is the case. Instead, Mark shows Jesus in his role as proclaimer of the gospel without using the terms that are used in the Epistles to describe such activity. Thus in Mark, to see how Jesus goes about the work of proclaiming the kingdom, one must look at the relationship between Jesus and the Twelve in the whole of the Gospel. Mark does not isolate certain instances in which Jesus is shown as the proclaimer because the whole of his work is proclamation. As Meye further points out: "Mark uses kerygmatic terminology of Jesus only in the first chapter; from that point he shifts over to the use of didactic terminology" (p. 60). The intention of Jesus is to evangelize; he does it, however, via his teaching.

ment in time. Prophecy was being fulfilled. This phrase, "the time is fulfilled," means that at that point in history God was acting to fulfill the prophetic promises. "That which for the O.T. was in the future, the object of hope, is now present."[15] But what is this new thing God is doing?

The new thing God is doing is defined in the third phrase: "the kingdom of God is near" (NIV). What is happening is that God is asserting God's kingly rule.[16] The "kingdom of God" is a phrase that has Old Testament roots, referring to two main things: (1) that God was even then the King of Israel, and indeed, of the whole world; and (2) that this divine kingship was something that had yet to be realized.[17] In the first century these two meanings mingled in the assessment of the political reality under which the people of Israel lived. God was their king, and so it was an offense to them that Caesar should, in fact, be reigning over them. Not surprisingly, in the midst of their suffering and frustration as a captive people there were great emphasis on and interest in how God would make manifest and unambiguous the reality of that kingship (the future sense of the phrase).[18] But while it is true that Jesus used this phrase in the sense that was commonly understood, Schweizer notes that, on another level, "Jesus' manner of speaking distinguishes him from the Judaism of his day. He rarely spoke of God as king, nor did he ever speak of the establishment of God's sovereignty over Israel or over the world. Instead, he spoke frequently of one's entering the kingdom. Therefore, the kingdom is more like an area or a sphere of authority into which one can enter, so 'realm' would be a better translation. . . ."[19] With this emphasis on "the realm of God" and "entering" it (which is picked up in the next part of Jesus' proclamation), it is clear that Mark is concerned with how Jesus will go about the work of evangelism.

Fourth, the final sentence in this summary statement makes it clear that conversion (seen as coming into the kingdom) is a key theme of Mark's Gospel.[20] Jesus defines what the response to the kingdom of God is meant to be.

15. C. E. B. Cranfield, *The Gospel according to Saint Mark* (Cambridge: University Press, 1959), p. 65.

16. "Corresponding to the Aramaic *malkuth*, the phrase means 'the kingly rule' of God, His 'reign' or 'sovereignty.' . . . It is held that, while 'the rule of God' is the primary emphasis, the thought of a community is necessarily implied." Vincent Taylor, *The Gospel according to St. Mark* (New York: St. Martin's Press, 1966), p. 166.

17. Cranfield, p. 65.

18. Cranfield, p. 65.

19. Eduard Schweizer, *The Good News according to Mark*, trans. Donald H. Madvig (London: SPCK, 1971), pp. 45-46.

20. See William J. Abraham, *The Logic of Evangelism* (Grand Rapids: Wm. B. Eerdmans Publishing Co., 1989), for a perceptive discussion of evangelism as initiating people into the kingdom of God.

Men and women are called on to "repent and believe the good news" (NIV). As has been demonstrated, in the New Testament these are the two terms that combine together to produce the experience of conversion. Repentance speaks about coming to a new understanding of what God is doing and changing one's life in accord with this fact. Then, having come to a new understanding of what God is doing, one reaches out in faith (trust) to embrace this new thing and make it the central reality in one's life.

What, specifically, is Jesus calling men and women to when he says, "Repent, and believe in the good news"? In terms of Jesus' own ministry, the sense is that he is calling men and women to change their minds about their understanding of what God is doing in their midst. Instead, they are to turn around and accept by faith the new thing God is doing. "They are to believe the good news that the hoped for kingdom of God has come near."[21] Furthermore:

> In this passage Jesus himself speaks of the gospel as the object to be believed in. That corresponds to the character of the early Christian missionary proclamation found in its earliest NT form in Paul. Later on the author of the Gospel of John has Jesus say directly, "Believe in me" (John 14:1). Mark also probably means believe in Jesus with his challenge to believe in 1:15, since in Mark's Gospel Jesus himself is present as its real content.
>
> Mark thus takes up the key word "gospel" from early Christian missionary language.[22]

So Mark invites his readers to watch as Jesus' ministry unfolds; he encourages them to notice the various ways in which Jesus proclaims the good news; he urges them to pay attention to how Jesus went about the work of evangelism. "The rest of the Gospel, it might be said, consists of illustrations of the way in which the deeds and words and character of Jesus himself brought this sovereignty of God to bear on his people. Wherever he was, there people found themselves confronted with the 'kingdom of God.' . . ."[23]

The ministry of Jesus described in Mark 1:14-15 will be seen unfolding during the remainder of the Gospel.[24] Structurally, therefore, these two verses

21. Cranfield, p. 68.

22. Karl Kertelge, "The Epiphany of Jesus in the Gospel (Mark)," in *The Interpretation of Mark*, ed. William Telford (Philadelphia: Fortress, 1985), p. 79.

23. C. F. D. Moule, *The Gospel according to Mark* (Cambridge: University Press, 1965), p. 14.

24. Vincent Taylor (p. 165) states (though he does not demonstrate) that the summary statement in 1:14-15 is intended to cover the period up through 3:6. However, it is more likely that 1:14-15 defines the nature of Jesus' entire ministry. Certainly it defines his

perform the same function as 1:1; that is, they are a summation of what lies ahead in the Gospel. If 1:1 describes the overview of the whole Gospel (the first half involves the discovery that Jesus is the Messiah, and the second half describes the discovery of him as the Son of God), then 1:14-15 describes the ministry of Jesus out of which the discovery of his true nature emerges. Mark 1:1 defines what is to be discovered; 1:14-15 describes how that discovery comes about. In other words, Mark informs his readers right at the start of his Gospel that entry into the kingdom of God via repentance and faith in the gospel (Jesus) is the outcome of hearing and responding to this story. The component parts of this process of response will be made clear as each unit unfolds with its special emphasis.

Responding to Jesus: An Analysis of Unit One
(Mark 1:16–4:34)

If evangelism is a key theme for Mark, then these questions must be asked: How are people meant to respond to this "kingdom of God" that Jesus is proclaiming? What does the outcome of repentance and faith look like in the lives of individuals? In unit one Mark identifies a range of possible responses to Jesus. Three responses are identified as inadequate (for varying reasons); one response is identified as correct. Mark spells out all of this in the four sections of material that make up unit one. In sections one and two he identifies the two polar responses: those who are for Jesus (1:16-45) and those who are against Jesus (2:1–3:6). In section three he differentiates this response into a spectrum along which four types of responses are identified (3:7-35). Finally, in the concluding section he explains the meaning of these four responses via the parable of the sower (4:1-34). In this way he clearly identifies the nature of the desired response to Jesus and warns against less-than-adequate responses.

---

whole ministry in Galilee (which would include the material up to 9:50). It probably covers his ministry up to and including his death and resurrection since the "good news of God" (1:14) is not complete until these events. D. E. Nineham, pp. 67-68, understands the phrase in this way: "These verses are extremely important because they seem to be intended by St. Mark as a sort of manifesto which sums up the substance and essential meaning of the whole public ministry."

The First Response to Jesus:
Enthusiasm from the Crowds (Mark 1:16-45)

Overview of the Section

Mark begins by pointing out the overwhelmingly positive response to Jesus on the part of the ordinary people in Israel. In the first pericope in this section, Simon, Andrew, James, and John are shown gladly leaving behind occupation and family to join Jesus' band (1:16-20). Jesus now has four disciples in tow, and Mark next describes a typical twenty-four-hour period of ministry by Jesus in Capernaum which demonstrates this same positive response (1:21-39). This "typical" day begins with preaching in the synagogue and casting out a demon (1:21-28). It moves to the private healing of Peter's mother-in-law (1:29-31). The day ends with the whole town gathered at his door, where he heals the sick and casts out demons (1:32-34). The twenty-four-hour period concludes the next morning with Jesus up early and alone in prayer, much to the distress of the crowds who are still clamoring after him. Finally, this section ends with a pericope in which Jesus heals that most dread disease in the first century, leprosy, thus drawing even more crowds to himself (1:40-45). Structurally, this first section of unit one has as its core the twenty-four-hour period of ministry, surrounded (and balanced) by one pericope at the beginning and one pericope at the end.[25]

Mark makes it very clear in this section that the crowds are genuinely enthusiastic about Jesus. His language expresses both the positive nature of the response to Jesus and how widespread it is. The four fishermen (who are at this point in the story typical of the crowds in general and not yet differentiated from them) are so drawn to Jesus that they act in an uncharacteristic way for their era and social class. They drop everything and become Jesus' disciples. Similarly, the people in the synagogue are "amazed" at Jesus' teaching (1:22, 27) and "amazed" at his authority over evil spirits (1:27). "At once his fame began to spread throughout the surrounding region of Galilee" (1:28). "The whole city" of Capernaum gathers at his door in the evening (1:33). The next morning the townsfolk continue to seek him out (1:37). After the healing of the leper, the crowds make it impossible for Jesus to minister in the towns (1:45). The language Mark uses is quite extravagant in describing the overwhelmingly positive response to Jesus on the part of the crowds. Thus it is that Mark defines the first type of response to Jesus: the uncritical acclaim of the ordinary people who are drawn to Jesus for what he can

25. This is yet another example of Mark's use of brackets.

do, namely, preach and teach with authority, heal effectively, and cast out demons with authority.

The Calling of the Four: Mark 1:16-20

The first pericope in this section (1:16-20) requires special attention because it is the first of three pericopae in the Second Gospel that focus on the calling and ministry of the Twelve.[26] In addition, the evangelistic intent of the Gospel as defined in 1:1 and 1:14-15 is further amplified in this pericope. First, it is significant that the initial act of Jesus in the Gospel of Mark is the calling of four men to be his disciples. This is what his ministry is all about: disciple making.[27] This act also shows where Mark's attention is focused: on this process of drawing men and women into the kingdom of God. This again reinforces the idea that Mark's intention in his Gospel is to show how people are drawn into the kingdom and to invite his readers, likewise, to become disciples. The very language used in this pericope is evangelistic in nature. It is all about following Jesus, about becoming his disciples. He calls; they follow.

However, as Mark will eventually make clear, the initial response of these four men is not the whole story. What they experience is not "conversion." There is no repentance; the faith response, while substantial, is based more on assumptions about Jesus than insight into him; there is little content to their commitment at this point in time.[28] This is not, as some commentators seem to feel, a step of full and sufficient faith.[29] What these four men are doing is mirroring the uncritical enthusiasm of the crowds for this "amazing" teacher. They want to be part of this new thing that is happening in their midst. This is the beginning of the process for these four men, not the culmination of it. However, the important thing is that they have taken the first step in following Jesus.

Second, by the way in which Jesus defines the task of the disciples in 1:16-20, Mark's emphasis on evangelism is further clarified. What Jesus says

---

26. See also 3:13-19 and 6:6b-13, 30.

27. This will become clearer in unit four (8:31–10:45) when the subject of discipleship is the focus. See below, chap. 10.

28. All this will become abundantly evident by the end of the Gospel.

29. For example, Cranfield, p. 69: "In this section we have the first of a series of incidents that illustrate the authority of Jesus. His word lays hold on men's lives, and asserts his right to their whole-hearted and total allegiance, a right that takes priority even over the claims of kinship." While it is true that they leave their families to follow Jesus, Mark will demonstrate that they have not yet given him "total allegiance." See, for example, Mark 14:27-31.

when he invites James and John to follow him is: "I will make you fishers of men" (NIV). Meye argues against interpreting the expression "fishers of men" *(halieis anthrōpōn)* to mean, as some have claimed, "agents of judgment" (based on the use of the phrase in Jer. 16:16).[30] Instead, he feels that the reference is to the occupation of the four disciples. By means of this fishing imagery they would understand Jesus to mean that they are "to be concerned with the men they encounter in their ministry in a positive way. As fishers, they are ministers to the needs of men."[31] This definition of ministry is evangelistic in orientation. "The fisherman, it is true, catches fish in order to eat them; but the evangelist catches men for their own salvation as well as the good of others."[32] In other words, Jesus promises that he will teach his disciples how to call others into the kingdom.

Third, it should also be noted that the phrase *poiēsō humas genesthai halieis anthrōpōn* should be translated "I will make you *become* fishers of men." In other words, they are about to embark on a training course in which they will be taught how to be "fishers of men." The emphasis is on the *process* they are to undergo. How they become fishers of men will be revealed by Mark in the rest of his Gospel. As Meye comments:

> There could not be a clearer statement of Jesus' deliberate intention to work a *creative* work in the persons of those called to follow him. It is strange that so few commentators have looked beyond Mark 1:16-20 with any seriousness, asking the question, Where in the evangelistic narrative is this creative activity of Jesus to be found? The preceding discussion has already suggested that the command to follow ascribes a comprehensive scope to Jesus' creative activity, i.e. it refers to the totality of the disciples' exposure to Jesus.[33]

V. K. Robbins echoes this same idea:

> When Jesus tells the first two fishermen that he will make them "become fishers of men" (Mark 1:17), he introduces logical progressive form into the narrative. The reader now expects Jesus to engage in the interaction necessary to equip these disciple-companions with the ability to "fish men." The reader may or may not know exactly what such a function will entail, although it is likely that a member of a first-century Mediterranean culture would recognize the use of fishing imagery to describe the dynamics of

30. Meye, pp. 100-102.
31. Meye, p. 104.
32. Moule, p. 14.
33. Meye, pp. 104-5.

teaching people a special system of thought and action. The assertion by Jesus raises the conventional expectation, from Greek heritage, that the disciples will be "made into" people who are able to gain other people's attention and teach them the system of thought and action that the teacher transmits to them.[34]

How will they learn to become fishers of men? *Will they not learn this lesson as they themselves are evangelized by Jesus?* Is it not out of their own experience of repentance and faith that they will learn how to lead others to repentance and faith? "Mark 1:17 so clearly points to Jesus' future work with the disciples that one cannot help wondering how it is that exegetes have so often failed to use this text as a clue to the recovery of the Marcan intention in the developing narrative."[35]

The Second Response to Jesus: Accusations by the Religious Leaders (Mark 2:1–3:6)

In contrast to this positive response from the people, Mark sets the negative response from the religious leaders (2:1–3:6). There are five pericopae in this second section.[36] They show a growing negative reaction to Jesus, so that by the end of the section the religious leaders conclude that Jesus must be killed (3:6). This response is as starkly negative as the response of the common people is starkly positive.

In the first pericope (2:1-12) Jesus directly confronts the scribes with a claim to deity. Instead of saying to the paralytic, "Stand up, take your mat and go to your home" (as would have been expected from a healer and which Jesus eventually does say in 2:11), he says, "Son, your sins are forgiven" (2:5). This is immediately perceived by the scribes to be blasphemy, since they know

---

34. Vernon K. Robbins, *Jesus the Teacher: A Socio-Rhetorical Interpretation of Mark* (Philadelphia: Fortress, 1984), p. 85.

35. Meye, p. 107.

36. That this is, in fact, a separate section is shown in several ways. First, there is a sharp break between the editorial comment by Mark in 1:45 and the action in 2:1. Second, in familiar fashion, Mark frames this section between the statement in 1:45 that Jesus "stayed out in the country; and people came to him from every quarter" and the parallel statement in 3:7 that "Jesus departed . . . and a great multitude from Galilee followed him. . . ." The narrative could have proceeded without pause from 1:45 to 3:7 had 2:1–3:6 not been inserted. Furthermore, Joanna Dewey, "The Literary Structure of the Controversy Stories in Mark 2:1–3:6," in *The Interpretation of Mark,* ed. William Telford (Philadelphia: Fortress, 1985), p. 109, shows that 2:1–3:6 has a definite chiastic (concentric) pattern: A, B, C, B', A'.

that only God can forgive sins (2:6-7). Therefore, in claiming this prerogative Jesus is claiming to be qualified to act like God. Jesus compounds the problem by demonstrating (on the basis of their own theological assumptions) that he has, indeed, forgiven the man's sins and does therefore have "authority on earth to forgive sins" (2:10).[37] Hence, right from the start of his confrontation with the religious leaders, Jesus refuses to equivocate about who he is and what he has come to accomplish. Though no further reaction from the scribes is noted by Mark, clearly they must have perceived Jesus as someone dangerous. After all, from their point of view he quite openly committed blasphemy. It would be clear to them that Jesus is not their ally.

This feeling of hostility continues to grow through the next four pericopae.[38] In the second pericope (2:13-17) Mark relates how Jesus calls Levi, the tax collector, to follow him (even though tax collectors were despised as traitors to Israel). Then Jesus compounds this indiscretion by going to dinner at Levi's house and "eating with sinners and tax collectors" (2:16). All this disturbs the scribes, who know this to be a breach of ritual law. They would never eat with such people, nor should Jesus if he is indeed a teacher who is true to their teachings. His clever response might satisfy them for the moment: "Those who are well have no need of a physician, but those who are sick; I have come to call not the righteous but sinners" (2:17). However, upon reflection they will hear the irony in Jesus' voice and wonder just who he considers the "sick" to be (is he referring to them?). In the final three pericopae the issue of ceremonial law becomes central. Jesus does not require his disciples to fast (2:18-22); he allows them to harvest grain on the Sabbath (2:23-28); and he even heals on the Sabbath (3:1-6). Such actions clearly set Jesus in opposition to the religious leadership. Their conclusion that he should die — reached by the unlikely combination of two traditional enemies, the Pharisees and the Herodians — is therefore not surprising.

In other words, Mark has, in this section, defined a second, contrasting

---

37. The connection between sin and sickness in first-century Judaism is well established. In the OT sickness is connected with sin (e.g., Deut. 28:21-22; Ps. 38:1-8). The same connection is made in Ecclesiasticus (18:19f.), in the *Testaments of the Twelve Patriarchs*, and in the Babylonian Talmud (e.g., *Nedarim* 40a: "No sick person is cured of his disease until all his sins are forgiven him"). This connection is also found in the NT in John 5:14. See Sophie Laws, *A Commentary on the Epistle of James* (London: Adam & Charles Black, 1980), p. 229. Therefore, when Jesus healed the paralytic, he demonstrated that he had, indeed, forgiven his sin.

38. "Along with the chiastic structure of the five sub-units, there exists also a linear development of hostility in the opponents from silent criticism to the questioning of Jesus' disciples, to the questioning of Jesus himself, to watching him, finally to plotting to destroy him." Dewey, p. 113.

response to Jesus and his ministry. Therefore, in the first two sections of unit one he has defined the two polar responses to Jesus: uncritical acclaim by the crowds versus critical condemnation by the religious leadership. These responses will be further refined and explained in the final two sections of this unit.[39]

The Range of Responses to Jesus: The Spectrum Defined (Mark 3:7-35)

Overview of the Section

Mark next differentiates the nature of the positive and the negative response to Jesus. In 3:7-35 he presents four distinct responses to Jesus: that of the crowd, that of the Twelve, that of Jesus' family, and that of the scribes. The response of the crowd and of the Twelve is positive (though in differing ways), while the response of the family and of the scribes is negative (though to differing extents).

In the first pericope of section three (3:7-12), Mark makes the point that the crowds are no longer drawn just from Galilee. They are coming from a wide radius: from the deep south (Idumea), from the north (Tyre and Sidon), from the west (Judea), and from the east (the Perea). They are coming from both rural regions (Galilee) and from the religious center of Israel (Jerusalem). Both Jews and, presumably, Gentiles from Tyre and Sidon are drawn to Jesus. Mark makes clear the reason for their coming: they want Jesus to heal and to cast out demons (3:10-11). There is no evidence of any commitment to Jesus beyond that of self-interest.[40]

In contrast, the Twelve are selected out of the crowd (they are "called to him" [3:13], "appointed" [3:14, 16], and "named" [3:14]). They are taken by Jesus from the lake (where the crowds are) to the mountain (where they are, presumably, alone). There they are given a twofold task: (1) "to be with him"

---

39. It becomes clear in this section that Mark is, in fact, organizing his material thematically and not chronologically. In each case the pericope is introduced by an indefinite time reference (seen most clearly in the NIV rendering): "a few days later" (2:1), "once again" (2:13), "Now John's disciples and the Pharisees were fasting . . ." (2:18), "one Sabbath" (2:23), and "another time" (3:1). This is important to note. Mark is using some criterion for selecting and setting pericopae alongside one another. He is functioning, consciously, as an editor who shapes his materials to make his point.

40. Jesus gives them what they seek, namely, healing and exorcism. He does not push them away nor demand anything from them before he will respond to their need.

and (2) "to be sent out" to minister in his name (3:14-15). This ministry involves preaching and casting out demons (3:14-15). Jesus also gives them a title. They are designated apostles (3:14). They accept this appointment ("they came to him" [3:13]), and in so doing differentiate themselves from the crowd because of their commitment. The response of the crowds and the Twelve is essentially positive, though the response of the Twelve involves commitment while that of the crowd reflects enthusiasm (what people would have for someone with genuine ability to heal and cast out demons). In terms of the actual commitment on the part of the Twelve, this is parallel to what Peter, Andrew, James, John, and Levi have already agreed to (1:16-20; 2:13-14). Now, however, their call to follow is given more definition. It involves being part of a special band and engaging in ministry.

The third and fourth pericopae define the nature of the negative response to Jesus. Those who oppose him include the scribes (which is not surprising in the light of 2:1–3:6) and Jesus' family (which is unexpected). The connection and essential similarity between the responses of these two groups are indicated by Mark's (first) use of the stylistic technique of intercalating one pericope inside another. So as to make it clear to the reader that these are essentially the same types of responses, Mark sandwiches the Beelzebub story into the story of the visit of Jesus' family. Both groups think Jesus is "possessed." The family feels "he has gone out of his mind" (3:21), while the scribes say "he has Beelzebul" (3:22). Both the family and the leaders seek to stop Jesus' ministry. The family wants to take him home; the Pharisees try to undercut his ministry by claiming it has an evil origin. The difference between these responses is that the family is genuinely concerned for Jesus' well-being (the crowds so press in upon him that he and his disciples "could not even eat" [3:20]). The scribes, however, see him as standing for the opposite of what they stand for. (This seems to be the logic of their assertion that he is empowered by evil. They understand themselves to be God's servants, and Jesus is clearly not one of them. Since they represent God, and Satan is the only other power that could generate the acts of wonder performed by Jesus, it is "logical" from their point of view to assume that Jesus is possessed by an evil spirit.)

Thus in this section Mark defines a range of responses between the two poles identified in the first two sections of the unit. But just what do these responses mean and how do they differ? Mark defines this in the final section of unit one: the four responses in 3:7-35 are explained as four types of soil in the parable Jesus tells and interprets in 4:1-20.

The Calling of the Twelve (Mark 3:13-19)

One pericope in this section requires additional comment: 3:13-19, in which Jesus calls and names the disciples. This is the second of three pericopae by which the mission of the Twelve is defined. It follows on from the calling of five disciples: Simon, Andrew, James, and John in 1:16-20 and Levi in 2:13-14. In this pericope the other seven apostles are named. This naming of the Twelve is the first problem which needs to be addressed. There are four lists in the New Testament in which the Twelve are named (Mark 3:16-19; Matt. 10:2-4; Luke 6:14-16; Acts 1:13). These are notable for their similarity; however, there is also some variation in the names. Two issues arise when these four lists are compared: (1) Is Levi one of the Twelve, as his name does not appear on any list? (2) Are Thaddaeus and Judas the son of James the same person? The solution to both questions is connected to the use of multiple names for the same person in the New Testament. For example, Peter is referred to by four names in the New Testament: Simeon, his Hebrew name (Acts 15:14); Simon, a Greek name (e.g., Mark 1:16; 3:16; John 1:42); Peter, the name Jesus gave him (Mark 3:16; John 1:42); and Cephas, which is the Aramaic version of Peter (John 1:42). Mark draws attention to multiple names in 3:16 ("Simon [to whom he gave the name Peter]") and to nicknames in 3:17 ("James son of Zebedee and John the brother of James [to whom he gave the name Boanerges, that is, Sons of Thunder]").[41] Thus, because multiple names were used regularly, it would seem likely that (1) Levi is indeed Matthew, whose name appears in all four lists, since he is identified as a tax collector in Matthew 10:3 (see also Mark 2:13-14; Matt. 9:1-12); and (2) Thaddaeus and Judas the son of James are the same person.

A second issue has to do with the connection between the three terms by which Jesus' colleagues are known: "disciples," "the Twelve," and "the apostles." The question is: Do these three terms delineate the same group of individuals or different groups? Meye states: "In a number of instances (cf. 6:35; 9:31, 35; 10:32; 11:11 & 14; esp. 14:32 & 14:17, 20), the term *dodeka* = twelve is used interchangeably with *mathetai* = disciples. This makes it clear that the Twelve were disciples in the Marcan conception."[42] On the other hand, Best concludes that "Mark distinguishes to some extent between the twelve and the disciples, the latter being the wider group. Thus the twelve together with those about Jesus (4:10) are identical with the disciples (4:34) and the twelve

41. Meye, p. 202.
42. Meye, p. 98. See pp. 137-72 for his detailed argument that "discipleship and Twelveship are identical for Mark" (p. 137).

are part of a smaller group than those who received secret instruction in 9:33-35 and 10:32. . . ."[43] It is clear, therefore, that a select band of twelve men did exist and that they were indeed Jesus' disciples (in the narrow sense). However, it is also clear that while Jesus does not appear to expand his core band beyond twelve, he does issue a general call to follow him (8:34), and that those who come after him in this way are disciples (in the broad sense).[44]

The third question has to do with the relationship of the Twelve to the apostles.[45] The traditional view is that the Twelve in Mark are the twelve apostles. They are called *apostoloi* in 6:30. (The phrase used here in 3:14, "named apostles," is a disputed text and will not be considered.)[46] Others, such as G. Klein, would argue that to view "the *Marcan* Twelve as apostles is historically and conceptually unacceptable."[47] Meye examines the arguments on both sides and concludes: "The term *apostoloi* in Mark 6:30 should be viewed as more than an innocent participle. Rather, by it Mark both designates the Twelve as missionaries and assigns to them a function exercised by only a few in the early Church."[48]

By exploring the various questions of the identity of the Twelve, of whether the disciples are equivalent to the Twelve, and of whether the Twelve are equivalent to the apostles, one can better understand the second most prominent characters in Mark (Jesus is the clearly the central character). However, the resolution of these issues does not impact the thesis of this book. The fact is that a special group called the Twelve are singled out by Mark to be the focus of his account. Whether they are the only disciples or part of a larger group of disciples makes no difference in terms of the argument. All the instruction of and interaction with the "disciples" would include the Twelve. "Mark makes little distinction in the way in which he uses the twelve and the disciples; the same role is attributed to them; the sole exception is in relation to the twelve depicted as missionaries."[49] Since they are, in any case, an example or case study of how people in general should come to Jesus, their specific identity does not matter. Since Mark is not concerned to draw sharp lines between the two groups (if there are two), the reader is not required to do so either. Thus in this book the terms "the disciples" and

---

43. Ernest Best, *Disciples and Discipleship: Studies in the Gospel according to Mark* (Edinburgh: T. & T. Clark, 1986), p. 157.

44. See chap. 10.

45. See Taylor, pp. 619-27.

46. Meye, pp. 189-90.

47. Meye, p. 176. His summary of Klein's view is found on pp. 175-76.

48. Meye, pp. 190-91; see his discussion of the issues on pp. 173-91.

49. Best, *Disciples and Discipleship*, p. 157.

"the Twelve" are used interchangeably as a way of referring to the core group of men most intimately involved with Jesus, i.e., those individuals whose conversion Mark is describing as a model for all who would be disciples. The issue is not who they are but how they come to faith.

The Meaning of the Four Responses to Jesus: The Parables (Mark 4:1-34)

The Parable of the Sower

In 4:1-20 the meaning of these four responses to Jesus is interpreted via a lengthy parable. In the shorter parables that follow in 4:21-34, the context for these responses is defined and amplified.

The final section of unit one begins with the so-called parable of the sower. (It should actually be called the parable of the soils.) The four soils are interpreted by Jesus to represent four responses to the word ("some people are like . . ." [4:15 NIV]). The word is the word of the kingdom which Jesus has been preaching (see 1:14-15).[50] The four soils interpret the four types of responses to Jesus and his word seen in 3:7-35 (and anticipated in 1:16–3:6).

Thus the hardened soil is like the hardened hearts of the scribes (see 3:22-30). The fact that Jesus is from God and is speaking God's word does not even penetrate their consciousness. Hence, it is possible for them to come to the quite erroneous conclusion that he is possessed by Beelzebub. They will never be forgiven — though not because they are beyond the pale of forgiveness for making such a statement (Jesus says, "Truly I tell you, people will be forgiven for their sins and whatever blasphemies they utter . . . ," in 3:28). The problem is that to be forgiven they have to ask for forgiveness. To ask for forgiveness they must see the need for forgiveness. But the word never penetrates their hearts. They are unaware of their blasphemy, and being unaware, they will never ask (and therefore never receive) forgiveness. Thus their response of total misunderstanding stands at one end of the spectrum of possible responses to Jesus.

If the one pole is defined by soil in which the seed never even penetrated, the other pole of the spectrum is defined by soil that produces an astonishing yield: "growing up and increasing and yielding thirty and sixty and a hundredfold" (4:8). This is most probably the response of the Twelve (as

---

50. Jesus defines "the kingdom of God" as the interpretive key to these parables in 4:11.

against the religious leaders, the crowds, or the family — the other key characters in Mark's account to this point). Or at least, this is the kind of response they will one day make. At the moment, they are on the path which points toward this kind of fruit-bearing commitment. The goal has now been clearly defined: to allow the word to produce fruit.

New insight is given into the response of the crowd by understanding that it is like seed sown on rocky ground. At first they are enthusiastic ("they immediately receive it with joy" [4:16]). And indeed, as 3:7-12 shows, the crowds flocked to Jesus in ever increasing numbers. This was not a surprising response in a day with little effective medicine and in an era that believed strongly that demons could possess a person. Jesus had the answer to two of their major problems in life. The prediction is, however, that this enthusiasm will not last ("when trouble or persecution arises on account of the word, immediately they fall away" [4:17]). And indeed, trouble will come, as the second half of the Gospel shows. In other words, enthusiasm over what Jesus can do for them does not automatically translate into discipleship (to anticipate a concept Mark will develop in 8:31–10:45).

There is an equally interesting insight into Jesus' family when their response is understood to be like seed sown among the thorns. The worries of the world, wealth,[51] and the desire for other things[52] choke off the growth of the seed. And indeed, it is precisely because of their worry over Jesus and what is happening to him that the family attempt to "restrain him" and thus limit his ministry (3:21). It is interesting that in the context of the parable this seed does not die out; it simply never bears fruit (4:19). The sense is that one day the weeds could be pruned away and his family can then bear kingdom fruit (as eventually did happen).

Thus it is that Mark identifies a range of possible responses to Jesus. Reading the parable one way, one sees only two responses: those that bear fruit and those that do not. Looking at it another way, one sees one positive response and three types of negative responses. It is clear, however, that when it comes to Jesus and the kingdom, the goal is to bear fruit. The sense is that it will be the Twelve who do so. And yet they have a long way to go. From this point on in his account, Mark will tell the story of how they come to bear fruit. He will show them turning away from these inadequate responses and turning instead to Jesus and his way.

51. Jesus will amplify this statement in 10:17-31.
52. Perhaps this is the temptation that the disciples have to avoid. Their desire for greatness (9:33-34) and for a place of authority in the kingdom (10:35-37) could choke off fruitfulness.

The Crucial Role of Understanding

Two more things need to be said about 4:1-20. First, it is here that Mark establishes who will be the cast of characters against which the story of Jesus will be set. The three major "players" will be the disciples, the crowds, and the authorities.[53] His family will also appear on several occasions, as will other characters, but they are "bit players" (to continue the metaphor) whose story Mark is not going to tell.[54]

Second, the comments of Jesus in 4:9-13 about "understanding" shed light on the problem of entering the kingdom. Understanding, it seems, is crucial in order to enter the kingdom. This concept is repeated in various ways in these verses. In verse 9 Jesus urges people to "listen." This is not just hearing the sound of the words, but listening so as to understand them. In verse 10 the Twelve indicate that they do not understand, so Jesus explains his parable in verses 14-20. His explanation makes it clear that "understanding" involves "hearing" his words in terms of the kingdom. The kingdom is the interpretive principle. In verses 11 and 12 he contrasts those to whom the "secret of the kingdom of God" has been given with those on the outside. This simply confirms what the parable of the soils is saying: not all respond properly to Jesus. The Twelve, however, give no evidence of understanding — as Jesus notes in verse 13. His saying in verse 11 anticipates what will happen in unit three when their eyes, ears, and tongues are opened by the miracle of healing.[55]

Verse 12 seems at first glance to be saying: "No matter how hard you try, you will never be given understanding, but instead you will perish unforgiven." However, it is better taken simply as a description of the way things are: "Some people just never seem to get the point, which is so sad because if they understood, they too would turn to God and be forgiven." This interpretation fits the context. In 3:28 Jesus said that "people will be forgiven for their sins and whatever blasphemies they utter." However, in 3:29 he seems to con-

---

53. "In Mark's story Jesus is of course the dominant character. In addition, the authorities can be treated together as a single character, because the different groups which oppose Jesus share similar traits and carry on a continuing role in the plot in relationship to each other. For the same reasons, the disciples also can be treated as a character. And although Peter, James and John have individual roles, they typify the disciples as a whole. The minor characters, whom we call the 'little people,' can also be treated together because of their similar traits." David Rhoads and Donald Michie, *Mark as Story: An Introduction to the Narrative of a Gospel* (Philadelphia: Fortress, 1982), p. 101.

54. The chief of these minor characters is John the Baptist, who appears in the prologue (1:2-11) and then in the pericope intercalated between the sending out and return of the Twelve at the conclusion of the second unit (i.e., 6:14-29).

55. See below, pp. 249-51, for discussion of this issue.

tradict himself by saying, "but whoever blasphemes against the Holy Spirit can never have forgiveness, but is guilty of an eternal sin." But this must be understood in the context of this statement. The scribes have just charged him with being empowered by an evil spirit. This comment by the scribes is an illustration of the blindness of some people. They see but do not perceive. They hear but do not understand. And thus they cannot be forgiven because they will never ask for forgiveness. They will not ask because they do not understand. Once again, understanding is the key to the kingdom. Mark reiterates this idea twice more in chapter 4. In verse 23 Jesus says a second time, "Pay attention to what you hear." And in verses 33-34 Mark comments on the difficulty the Twelve have in understanding.

The point of all this is made clear in Jesus' quotation in verse 12. The desired response to the kingdom is that people "turn again and be forgiven." Here is Mark's only direct use of the word "conversion" *(epistrephō)*. It comes at a crucial place in that it defines clearly what unit one is all about: turning to God, which is seen to mean responding properly to Jesus. This, in turn, has to do with understanding. If people do not understand, they will not (cannot) turn. *Understanding is the key to conversion.* If people do not understand, they will not (cannot) decide to turn around in terms of their view of God and their response to Jesus (i.e., repent). Without repentance, faith becomes irrelevant. Faith has no focus, context, direction, or motivation without understanding. There is no will to turn. This is, of course, the same conclusion that was reached in the analysis of Paul's conversion. Insight (understanding) is the first step in conversion.

Unit one is thus seen to be an outline for what lies ahead in the Gospel of Mark. It defines the lines of growth of the major characters in the Gospel. First, there are the religious leaders. In 2:1–3:6 they have moved from interest in Jesus to the decision to kill him. In 3:22-30 they rationalize their decision to reject Jesus and his teaching on the basis of (faulty) theological reasoning. In 4:15 their condition is defined as hardness of heart, which is shown to have Satan behind it. It seems clear that they as a group will not grow beyond this position. Their hardened hearts mean they will never see, never understand, and thus never repent and reach out in faith. They will remain outside the kingdom. Second, it also becomes clear that the crowds will move in a similar direction. Despite their uncritical enthusiasm for Jesus (1:21-45) which grows and spreads (3:7-12), the prophecy here is that this enthusiasm will wither away (as indeed it does in 15:6-15). Third, the family will remain on the periphery of Jesus' ministry. And indeed, they emerge only twice more in the Gospel, both times hidden in the background. In 6:1-6a it is probably they who are behind the lack of faith of the people in Nazareth; and in 15:40-41 it is quite possible that Mary the mother of Jesus is amongst the "other women" who had come up to Jerusalem from Galilee. The genuine care on the part of the family has been choked off by other cares. Still, the potential is there for them to "bloom" when they shed these impediments. (This is what repentance will mean for them.) Finally, for the Twelve it will be a different road. The seed has been planted. It is good soil. In due course it will blossom and produce a miraculous harvest. However, for the duration of Mark's Gospel it will be silent growth. The seed is hidden; the seed is alive; the seed is at work; but the grain will not be seen for some time yet (4:26-32). The uncritical enthusiasm they show in 1:16-20 has already grown into commitment to ministry. It will continue its growth in the days ahead.

Faith: An Analysis of Unit Two (Mark 4:35–6:30)

Having established that response to Jesus is key to becoming an effective (i.e., fruitful) part of the kingdom of God, Mark now begins to probe the dynamics of this response. He has already defined the nature of the desired response to the kingdom of God. It is repentance and faith (1:15). But what is faith? What is repentance? What does it look like in the lives of people? What does it look like in the lives of the Twelve? In unit two Mark focuses on the dynamic of faith.[56] In unit three he will probe the nature of repentance.

The Connection between Faith and Fear (Mark 4:35–5:43)

The first four pericopae in unit two all touch upon the question of faith (4:35–5:43). In each of these stories there is also fear of some sort. In the first story the disciples are afraid for their lives when they are caught in the storm, and even more afraid of Jesus when they discover that he has power over the elements (4:40-41). In the second story the response of the townspeople when they see the healed demoniac is one of fear (5:15). (The disciples by their absence from this story give evidence of the fact that they are still afraid.) In the third story the woman with the problem of bleeding trembles with fear when she is forced to identify herself in the crowd (5:33). And in the

---

56. Ralph Martin, *Mark: Evangelist and Theologian* (Grand Rapids: Zondervan, 1973), in commenting on special emphases in Mark's Christology, notes that "Mark's Gospel is rich in the importance it gives to faith. It is a religious attitude which Jesus calls forth and praises. Negatively this is shown by Jesus' rebuke of 'unbelief' . . ." (p. 108).

fourth story Jairus is told by Jesus not to be afraid when news reaches him that his daughter has died (5:36). In this way a polarity is set up between faith on the one side and fear on the other. Jesus makes this connection between fear and faith twice in these four stories. In the first pericope Jesus says to the disciples: "Why are you afraid? Have you still no faith?" (4:40). And in the last of the four pericopae Jesus says to the grieving father: "Do not fear, only believe" (5:36).[57]

This connection between faith and fear yields insights into the nature of faith. For one thing, fear and faith are opposed. Fear is the enemy; faith is the solution. Fear paralyzes one in the face of a problem, while faith frees one from that problem. It seems that faith needs an environment in which to operate. It is fear (in these stories) that energizes (or gives rise to the need of) faith. Fear forces people to recognize their true state. It opens eyes. It demands a response.

However, fear alone is insufficient to generate properly directed faith. Fear can cause people to look in the wrong direction for an answer, as the first two stories demonstrate. The disciples are afraid of drowning, but they do not come to Jesus in faith. They come in resentment. (He is sleeping when they need his help.) In the second story the townspeople sense how powerful Jesus is. And fearing that power, they ask him to leave. In the third and fourth stories, however, fear brings people to Jesus as the one who can solve the overwhelming problems they face. Both Jairus and the woman fall at the feet of Jesus — he out of fear for his daughter, and she out of fear of what she has done (5:22, 33). They both turn to Jesus and not away from Jesus. By contrast, in the fifth pericope in this unit (6:1-6a) there is no fear as such, only resentment directed at Jesus (as was the case with the disciples in the first pericope in this unit). And the lack of fear (i.e., the lack of awareness of their need) is one of the elements that produce the lack of faith of the people in Nazareth.

However, it is not fear as such that opens the eyes of faith. Fear is merely one example of a powerful emotion that triggers faith. For the woman who was bleeding, it is not fear that brings her to Jesus in the first place (her fear is provoked as a result of the secret way she came to Jesus). It is suffering that motivated her. The word "suffering" is twice mentioned in this pericope — once to describe what she had gone through (5:26) and once to describe what she had been freed from (5:34).[58] The point is not that in order to have faith

---

57. Another example of bracketing. In this way Mark connects together these four stories which are a single section and focus on the power of Jesus.

58. The NRSV translates this as "disease." It is more properly rendered "suffering," as in the NIV.

one must experience fear or suffering (or some other problem, for that matter). The point is that one will not reach out in faith unless a strong sense of need drives one to do so.

The Nature of Faith (Mark 5:34)

It is via Jesus' response to the woman who was bleeding that the nature of faith is defined. Jesus says to her: "Daughter, your faith has healed you. Go in peace and be freed from your suffering" (5:34 NIV). This statement has a paradigmatic quality to it. The issue for the woman was that of "suffering." Her suffering was, on one level, physical. She was ill with an incurable disease. But because of the nature of her affliction, she also suffered on an even deeper level. Her illness had cut her off from normal human contact. She was "unclean" and so could not be involved with her husband (no sexual relations were possible given the Levitical code), her family, and her community. "Her existence was wretched because she was in a constant state of uncleanness and would be generally shunned by people since contact with her rendered others unclean."[59] She was like a leper, cut off from human contact. She had no one to whom she could turn. So on another, more profound level, her suffering was emotional.

Her healing comes as the result of her faith, the reader is told. But what elements of faith bring about this healing? For one thing, the woman redirects her confidence from the physicians to Jesus. The physicians have failed her repeatedly, as Mark notes. That was a path that made her worse, not better. She realizes this. So she turns from them to one who can actually help her. This turning is, of course, akin to the turning of repentance. Second, she believes that Jesus can heal her. "If I but touch his clothes, I will be made well" (5:28), not "I might be healed" or "Maybe it will help" or "It can't hurt." She believes in the power of Jesus. Third, the woman acted on the basis of her beliefs. She sought out Jesus. She hid herself in the crowd although she ought not have been there. She figured out how to reach out to Jesus despite the severe restrictions placed on her because of her uncleanness (she could not call out, she could not identify herself, she could not directly ask Jesus for healing). Then she acts by pushing forward to him and touching his cloak from behind. In other words, she behaves in a certain way as a result of her faith. Her cognitive conviction that Jesus can heal is translated into action. It is not that her action magically releases the power of Jesus. Rather, it is that her action demonstrates the reality of her faith. So, while it is the power of Jesus that

59. Lane, pp. 192-93.

heals (5:30), it is her faith that causes her to call upon that power. Jesus makes this clear: "Daughter, your faith has made you well."

The outcome of her faith is described by Jesus in a threefold way in 5:34: she is healed, she is freed from suffering, and she goes in peace. The word used to describe her healing is *sesōkev* (from the root *sōzō*, which means either "heal" or "save"). What is Jesus proclaiming here? That she has been made well or that she has been saved? Probably both meanings are intended. If healing was the only concern, two other Greek words could have been used that mean only that.[60] As Nineham states: "It is . . . no accident that the Greek of v. 34 is ambiguous and can equally well be translated: 'Your faith *has brought you salvation*. Go in peace and be whole of your plague.' What happened to the woman is thus an example of 'salvation by faith.' . . . [It is] a model for those who want to enter into relationship with Jesus and win from him the affectionate address 'Son' or 'Daughter' (v. 34)."[61]

The blessing by Jesus, "Go in peace," gives useful insights into what has happened. Jesus did not mean, simply, "Be free from worry." This phrase means "Be complete, be whole." The word *eirēnēn* corresponds to the Hebrew word *shalōm*, which carries this meaning.[62] Furthermore, "the word 'peace' is synonymous with 'salvation.' It does not indicate peace of mind, but the objective standing of a man who, although he may be in the midst of storm and strife, has been restored to a proper relationship with God."[63] Each of the first four incidents in unit two portrays an extreme situation in which there is no hope, humanly speaking, and yet each ends in peace as the result of the power of Jesus (see 4:39; 5:15; 5:34; 5:42). The disciples do not drown, the demoniac is freed, the woman is cured, and the child is raised from the dead.

Finally, it is important to note that Jesus forces the woman to reveal who she is, there in the midst of the crowd (5:31-32). She does so with great fear and trembling (5:33). This seems at first glance to be an insensitive act on Jesus' part (forcing her to admit that she was where she should not have been, i.e., in the crowd, and forcing her to reveal this rather sensitive medical problem in public). Yet on reflection, the call of Jesus is seen to have two vital purposes. For one thing, it is part of the healing process. By publicly acknowledging her physical healing, Jesus makes it possible for her to reenter society. She is no longer unclean and everyone knows it. Thus her relationships are also healed. For another thing, the acknowledgment of what she has done and

---

60. Schweizer, p. 118.
61. Nineham, pp. 158-59.
62. Mann, p. 286.
63. Schweizer, p. 118.

why (she "told him the whole truth," v. 33) is the last step in the faith process. In this way she is made to understand what has happened to her. This corresponds to the public confession of faith that was vital to salvation in the early church (e.g., see Rom. 10:9-10).

Those Lacking Faith (Mark 6:1-6a)

In the fifth story in this unit, Mark deliberately contrasts the two examples of faith that precede it (the woman and Jairus) with the lack of faith by those living in Nazareth. He also contrasts the great power of Jesus (as seen in the first four stories) to his relative powerlessness in Nazareth ("he could do no deed of power there, except that he laid his hands on a few sick people and cured them" [6:5]). Jesus is powerful. This has just been convincingly demonstrated. Why, then, can he not do miracles in Nazareth? The missing element, Mark states, is faith. Verse 6 makes this clear: Jesus "was amazed at their unbelief." It is faith that makes it possible for people to link into the power of Jesus. Why do the townspeople have no faith? The reason is that they are offended by him (6:3). They think he is trying to be someone he is not (6:2-3). After all, they know of his suspicious birth. ("It was contrary to Jewish usage to describe a man as the son of his mother, even when she was a widow, except in insulting terms. Rumors to the effect that Jesus was illegitimate appear to have circulated in his own lifetime.")[64] And they know him as a tradesman. In their eyes he is a carpenter, not a teacher. Furthermore, they know him as a boy who grew up in town and has brothers and sisters still there. He is just like them, and yet (in their mind) he pretends to be a teacher and comes to town with a band of disciples following after him. "Who does he think he is?" is the sense that is conveyed here, in reading between the lines. Feeling this way about him, they do not recognize who Jesus really is. In not recognizing his true nature[65] and his enormous power, they do not ask for healing. Thus they are not healed. In other words, informed faith that motivates action is necessary in order to come into contact with the power of God that is found in Jesus.

---

64. Lane, p. 203.
65. This is, of course, the central issue in Mark: the need on the part of the Twelve to recognize who Jesus really is.

Faith and the Twelve

What does all this say about the pilgrimage of the Twelve to conversion? Apart from anything else, it makes it clear that faith is the issue for the disciples. As Jesus states in 4:40: "Have you still no faith?" This gives an interesting insight into the condition of the disciples. They may be following Jesus, but they do not yet have faith in the way in which Jesus requires. In fact, they will not display the requisite faith for the duration of this Gospel. "This is the first of a series of rebukes of the disciples by Jesus for their lack of faith and understanding (cf. 7:18; 8:17f., 21, 32f.; 9:19)."[66] At no point in the Gospel are they commended for their faith.

Interestingly, the scribe who penned the long ending to Mark picked up on the fact that this is how the disciples are portrayed in the Second Gospel. In 16:11-14 he says: "But when they [the disciples] heard that he was alive and had been seen by her, *they would not believe it.* After this he appeared in another form to two of them, as they were walking into the country. And they went back and told the rest, but *they did not believe them.* Later he appeared to the eleven themselves as they were sitting at the table; and *he upbraided them for their lack of faith and stubbornness,* because *they had not believed* those who saw him after he had risen" (italics mine). This anonymous writer then goes on in 16:15-18 to juxtapose those who believe (and all the wonderful things they will do) with those who do not believe (and what will happen to them). While not a part of the Gospel itself, this material reflects an early tradition as well as a thoughtful reading of the Gospel. Faith is the issue for the disciples throughout their years with Jesus. It is an issue that is not resolved until they meet the resurrected Jesus.

However, there is progress in the lives of the Twelve in terms of this issue of faith. In the first pericope in this unit they are said to have no faith. In the intervening four pericopae they are in the background, listening and watching. And then in the final pericope in unit two (6:6b-13, 30), they are described as acting with some faith. For one thing, they go out on their mission with a minimum of provisions (6:8-11). To survive (i.e., to find food and shelter) they will have to trust in God (which seems to be the intention of Jesus in forbidding the taking of food, money, or blankets). For another thing, they actually engage in ministry: they preach, they cast out demons, and they heal. Interestingly, their message is repentance (6:12) and not repentance and faith. In this regard they are more akin to John the Baptist (1:4) than to Jesus (1:15). They are not yet ready to preach faith.

66. Cranfield, p. 175.

What, then, is this faith *(pistis)* that Jesus demands? "It denotes a confident trust in Jesus and in his power to help."[67] The disciples had no faith that Jesus could help in the storm. The townspeople of Nazareth had no faith that Jesus could heal. In contrast, both Jairus and the woman had faith that Jesus could heal, so they came and asked. Schniewind takes this argument a step further by commenting (on 4:40): "Thus faith in Jesus coincides with faith in God."[68] This is the connection that yet needs to be made by the disciples. They need to understand that it is God working in and through Jesus; and then they themselves must put their trust in God through Jesus.

Thus in unit two Mark defines the faith aspect of conversion. In order to turn to Jesus and so become a fruitful part of the kingdom of God, there must be faith. In summary, four things can be said about faith, based on the material in unit two. First, faith begins with an awareness of need. It is a sense of need that drives one to faith. Need (be it fear, suffering, or something else) is the motivation behind faith. Second, this faith needs to be focused. It is not faith in general that is important. It is faith in Jesus (and in God, who is working through him) that counts. Fear (and other needs) not only motivates one to turn to Jesus; it can also cause one to turn away from Jesus. Thus it is necessary to be informed about Jesus. The disciples were not aware that he had power over the elements, so it was literally impossible for them to have asked for his help in this way. Hence, before they can turn to Jesus in full faith, they must walk the path that will lead them to understand who he truly is. The townsfolk in the region of the Gerasenes looked at Jesus and saw only a dangerous magician and so turned away. They needed more information about what kind of person he was. This is what the healed demoniac will provide for them when he tells about all that happened to him and how the Lord had mercy on him (5:19-20). Information about Jesus is the basis on which confidence in him is possible. As the townspeople of Nazareth demonstrate, people will not come to Jesus unless they see him rightly. People will not come unless they think he has the power to help them.[69] Third, it is not enough just to know Jesus can help. It is necessary to ask. Faith requires a reaching out to Jesus. Jairus falls at his feet to plead for his daughter. The woman reaches out to touch his cloak. Finally, it is not the faith that brings the results (as if it were some sort of magical entity); it is the power of Jesus that effects the change. Faith reaches out; Jesus responds. All this is, recognizably, the paradigm for

67. Taylor, p. 194.

68. Quoted in Cranfield, p. 174.

69. "It is clear that 'understanding' is closely associated with 'faith' in defining the religious attitude Mark advocates." James M. Robinson, *The Problem of History in Mark and Other Markan Studies* (Philadelphia: Fortress, 1982), p. 122.

conversion: a sense of need, insight into who Jesus is, and a reaching out to him in faith.

Repentance: An Analysis of Unit Three
(Mark 6:31–8:30)

This theme of "understanding" is picked up and amplified in unit three. In unit two the difference between those who have faith and those who do not is shown to be a matter of understanding. The two people who have faith in unit two (the woman who was bleeding and Jairus) understand that Jesus can help them; the three groups that do not have faith (the disciples, the people in the region of the Gerasenes, and the people of Nazareth) fail to realize who Jesus is and what he can do. The one group *understands* that Jesus has power and can (and will) heal (save); the other group *does not understand* that he has such power.

The question that presents itself at the end of unit two, therefore, is how one gets beyond bias, beyond blindness, and beyond assumptions to a new understanding of Jesus. What enables a person to move from old, inadequate ideas to new, accurate ideas? Here in unit three Mark points out how it is possible to move beyond misunderstanding to new understanding. Thus the discussion in this unit is really one of repentance (the second component in Jesus' definition of the gospel — 1:15). Or, more accurately, it is a discussion of the condition that underlies repentance (i.e., understanding). One cannot repent unless one understands. A "change of mind in regard to religious realities" (the definition of repentance) is not possible unless there is insight into the truth of the new concept and the inadequacy of the old concept. Once there is understanding, repentance becomes possible. Repentance is the choice one makes concerning this new understanding; specifically, the choice to turn away from the old understanding and embrace, instead, the new truth. Repentance is a turning around in one's thinking. But without understanding there can be no such turning of repentance. And without repentance there can be no response of faith. And without faith one cannot (will not) come to Jesus. However, when there is understanding, both repentance and faith become possible.

The pertinent material in this unit is found at three points: (1) in Mark's use of the word "understand," (2) in the discussion of hearts that are hardened, and (3) in the metaphoric use of the two major healings in this unit.

The Concept of Understanding

The whole concept of understanding permeates this unit. Of the twelve uses in the Gospel of Mark of words that mean "understand" or "understanding," five occur in this unit, three occur in the parables section in chapter 4 (which is directly related to the material in this unit), while the remaining four uses are scattered throughout the rest of the Gospel.[70]

The question of understanding (or the lack of it) is central to the first cycle of stories in unit three (6:31–7:37). In the first pericope (6:31-44) Jesus asks the disciples to do something that seems clearly impossible and/or undesirable to them (feed the five thousand). How can they get enough bread for a crowd like that? Why should they do so (6:37)? They do not understand. In the second pericope (6:45-56) they do not understand who is walking across the water (6:49-50). Mark comments that their amazement is due to the fact that they "did not understand about the loaves" (6:52). In the third story (7:1-23) it becomes evident that the disciples are not the only ones who do not understand. The Pharisees do not understand why the disciples of Jesus do not follow "the tradition of the elders," and they ask Jesus about this (7:5). The lack of understanding by the religious leaders, as this pericope shows, is due to their failure to understand that they have substituted the traditions of men for the commands of God (7:8). After confronting the Pharisees with their blindness, Jesus then calls the crowd to himself and urges them to avoid this error: "Listen to me, all of you, and understand," he says (7:14), and he then goes on to explain why ritual is not the issue (7:15). Hearing this, the disciples do not understand. Once again they ask him to explain the meaning of what he just said (7:17-18). In the fourth pericope, however, the Syrophoenician woman does understand. She understands that Jesus can cast the demon from her child. She "begs" him to do so in the same way that Jairus begged Jesus to heal his daughter (cf. 5:22-23 and 7:25-26). She also understands Jesus' rather enigmatic response to her and engages in wordplay with him that delights Jesus (7:27-29).

---

70. *Syniēmi* = understand (4:12; 6:52; 7:14; 8:17, 21); *synesis* = understanding (12:33); *asynetos* = without understanding (7:18); *epistamai* = know, understand (14:68); *ginōskō* = know, understand (4:13); *agnoeō* = not understand (9:32); *noeō* = consider, perceive (13:14); *oida* = know (4:13). The five examples of the use of these words in unit three are found at 6:52; 7:14, 18; 8:17, 21. The three examples of use of these words in the parables section in unit one (4:1-34) are 4:12, 13 (twice), while the remaining four uses occur at 9:32; 12:33; 13:14; 14:68. Q. Quesnell notes this fact in *The Mind of Mark: Interpretation and Method through the Exegesis of Mark 6:52*, Analecta Biblica 38 (Rome: Pontifical Biblical Institute, 1969), pp. 70-71.

The second cycle of stories also focuses on the issue of understanding (8:1-26). At the feeding of the four thousand, the disciples still do not understand how they can carry out Jesus' directions to feed so many people. "How can one feed these people with bread here in the desert?" (8:4). Likewise, the Pharisees continue to test Jesus against their own assumptions. But he refuses to allow himself to be judged by these categories (8:11-12). The Pharisees appear incapable of understanding Jesus in any terms other than their own. The disciples are little better. They still do not understand what the two feedings mean (8:16-21). Thus it is that the center section of this second cycle of stories (the material between the feedings and the healings) ends with Jesus' summary statement: "Do you not yet understand?" (8:21).

Metaphors That Explain the Lack of Understanding

This lack of understanding is explained by means of two metaphors. The first has to do with the disciples' *hardness of heart*. Mark twice states that this is the case for the disciples: once in his role as narrator (6:52), once on the lips of Jesus (8:17). In both cases the word used for "hardened" is *pepōrōmenē*, which is derived from *pōroō*. "*Pōros* is a kind of marble."[71] When *pōros* occurs in medical writings, it is used to describe the bony formation on a joint or the ossification which serves to weld broken joints back together. In the wider sense it refers to a hardening of the flesh (a callus). The emphasis in this latter case is not on the hardness of the flesh as much as it is on the deadness or insensibility of the flesh.[72] The idea of *hardness* is a special concern of Mark's. "*Pōroun* and *pōrōsis* occur eight times in the New Testament: four times in St. Paul, three times in St. Mark, and once in St. John."[73]

The concept of the "heart" is Hebraic. The heart was understood to be "the locus of reasoning and decision making."[74] As such, the heart was considered to be the "seat of understanding." Therefore, the phrase "hardness of heart" means "their minds were closed."[75] V. Taylor notes that this hardness of heart is "a failure to perceive akin to moral blindness rather than willful

---

71. J. A. Robinson, *St. Paul's Epistle to the Ephesians*, 2nd ed. (London: Macmillan, 1904), p. 264.

72. The material on hardness is derived from Robinson's excellent essay. See J. A. Robinson, pp. 264-74.

73. J. A. Robinson, p. 265.

74. Mann, p. 224.

75. Mann, pp. 304, 332.

obstinacy."[76] Interestingly, Jesus has used the phrase "hardness of heart" on one prior occasion (3:5). There it was as a description of the Pharisees. (Mann translates *pōrōsei tēs kardias* in 3:5 as "obdurate stupidity.")[77] In other words, the disciples are showing signs of the same inability to understand Jesus that characterizes his opponents.[78]

A second metaphor is used to explain this lack of understanding. The disciples are said to be *blind and deaf.* They hear but do not understand; they see but do not perceive (8:17-18). This image harkens back to 4:1-34 and Jesus' comments on understanding parables. In 4:9, following the parable of the four soils, Jesus states: "Let anyone with ears to hear listen!" When he is alone, the disciples ask Jesus to explain the parable he has just told (4:10). He responds: "To you has been given the secret of the kingdom of God, but for those outside, everything comes in parables; in order that 'they may indeed look, but not perceive, / and may indeed listen, but not understand; / so that they may not turn again and be forgiven'" (4:11-12).[79] The warning about hearing and seeing is given a second time: "Let anyone with ears to hear listen!" (4:23). This whole section in chapter 4 is about understanding. In 4:13 Jesus says: "Do you not understand this parable? Then how will you understand all the parables?" And Mark concludes this section by commenting: "With many such parables he spoke the word to them, as they were able to hear it" (4:33). Thus it becomes clear that here in unit three the reference to not seeing and not hearing is yet another way of discussing the failure to understand. Furthermore, as 4:11-12 shows, all of this is connected to the failure to turn to Jesus.

At two places in unit three the various ways of talking about this lack of understanding are brought together. Mark 6:51-52 states: "they [the disciples] were utterly astounded, for they did not understand about the loaves, but their hearts were hardened." The same point is made in 8:17-21. Jesus makes a reference to the "yeast of the Pharisees and the yeast of Herod" (8:15). The disciples are puzzled by this and, after discussing it with one another, conclude that Jesus was referring to the fact that they had brought no bread along (8:16). This is not what Jesus meant, so he patiently explains

76. Taylor, p. 331.

77. Mann, p. 243.

78. Five of the twelve uses of *kardia* = heart are found in this unit. See 6:52; 7:6, 19, 21; 8:17.

79. The connection between understanding and conversion is made clear by Mark in 4:12 where he quotes Isaiah. This is the one place in his Gospel that he uses *epistrephō* in the theological sense (translated here as "turn"). The statement is quite clear: conversion is made possible by understanding.

about the two feedings (8:17-20). In doing so he uses all three concepts that have been discussed thus far: lack of understanding, hardness of heart, and failure to see or hear. Jesus says: "Why are you talking about having no bread? Do you still *not perceive or understand?* Are your *hearts hardened?* Do you have *eyes, and fail to see?* Do you have *ears, and fail to hear?* And do you not remember?" After reminding them of the leftover bread in each feeding, Jesus concludes: "Do you not yet *understand?*" Thus Mark makes it clear what this unit is all about in terms of the disciples. They do not have faith (unit two) because they do not understand (unit three). Not understanding (because their hearts are hard), they fail to repent (i.e., they fail to turn to Jesus with understanding faith). Clearly, the Twelve are still on the way to Jesus; their conversion is not yet complete.

Two additional comments are in order concerning 8:17-21. First, Jesus twice stresses the "not yet" that characterizes the disciples (8:17, 21). Once again it is made evident that the disciples are in process. Second, it is important to notice what Jesus encourages the disciples to do in the midst of their misunderstanding. He urges them to "remember." "Do you not remember?" he asks (8:18). And then he recounts for them the details of the two feedings. They may not yet understand, but they can and must remember. At the moment, they do not have all the facts. But one day it will all make sense. For the moment, the important thing is that they store away in their memories the details of what Jesus said and did. This emphasis on remembering will be picked up again in units five and six.

What is it, then, that the disciples need to understand about the loaves (6:52)? What do the baskets of leftover bread reveal (8:17-20)? It was suggested in chapter 7 of this book that the feeding of the five thousand revealed that Jesus was the long-expected Messiah. Cranfield agrees with this assessment: "6:52, 8:16-19, indicate that he [Mark] thought of it as a pointer to the secret of the kingdom of God, the secret of the person of Jesus."[80] Had the disciples understood who Jesus was, they would not have been amazed that he walked on the water. They would have understood why no further sign beyond what had been given could be given to the Pharisees and why the viewpoint of the Pharisees and the Herodians is a corrupting element like yeast.[81]

---

80. Cranfield, pp. 221-22.

81. "Leaven is ordinarily used metaphorically in the New Testament, and in a bad sense, of the evil disposition in man (1 Cor. 5:6, 7, 8; Gal. 5:9). It is the evil disposition of the Pharisees that they seek a sign from Jesus when great signs, i.e. the repeated feeding of the multitude, have already been given. Jesus then warns the disciples to rest content with the signs already received, to see in them the full sign of God." Meye, p. 69.

The Healing That Enables Repentance

This raises the question of how one deals with misunderstanding. How does a person turn around in his or her thinking? In fact, is it possible to move beyond misunderstanding? Mark's answer to these questions is found in the final pericope of unit three, where he shows that the Twelve have moved beyond misunderstanding to a new and significant understanding of who Jesus is.

At Caesarea Philippi Jesus asks the disciples two questions to test their understanding. The first has to do with how the crowds understand him. According to the disciples, people in general have not yet moved beyond the realization that Jesus is some sort of prophet (8:27-28). Jesus then asks the disciples who they think he is. This seems a curious question to ask in the light of the emphasis in unit three on their lack of understanding. And yet — contrary to what might have been expected — the disciples answer correctly (via their spokesman Peter). They have come to understand that he is the Messiah (8:29). The reader is forced to ask how such understanding was possible. Nothing in unit three seems to indicate that the disciples had moved beyond their assumptions and presuppositions about Jesus. The answer as to where this new insight came from is found in the two healings which are so prominent in unit three. In the same way that the two feedings reveal in a symbolic way who Jesus is, the two healings reveal in a symbolic way what has happened to the disciples to bring them to this point of new understanding.

It is not by accident that what is cured in the two men in unit three is deafness, dumbness, and blindness. By means of Jesus' healing touch these two men come to hear, speak, and see clearly. These are, of course, the very maladies from which the disciples suffer, as Jesus makes clear in 8:17-18: "Do you still not perceive or understand? Are your hearts hardened? Do you have eyes, and fail to see? Do you have ears, and fail to hear?" Thus in this unit that is largely metaphoric in nature, the two healings become metaphors for how the disciples come to understand. *Their confession of Jesus as Messiah at Caesarea Philippi is due to a miracle of Jesus' healing touch.* There is no other explanation for their new insight. Up to this point the disciples simply do not understand; they are as unseeing as the Pharisees. And yet, they make this amazing confession about who Jesus is. The reason is that their ears have been unblocked and their eyes have been opened. They now understand, and their tongues have been loosened so that they can declare this fact.

When did they receive this healing touch? In fact, Mark relates no incident in which Jesus lays his hands on the disciples (as he did on the two ill men) in order to bring new insight. Such a healing is simply presented as having happened because they are able to make their confession at Caesarea Philippi.

What happened within the Twelve to bring about the realization that Jesus was the Messiah? Again, nothing is said explicitly about the inner dynamics of insight. But the implication is that this revelation of the truth about Jesus was the work of the Holy Spirit. After all, this is how the Holy Spirit was understood in the Old Testament (i.e., prior to Pentecost): as the revealer of truth.[82] And in the prologue where Mark establishes the categories that he will deal with in the body of his Gospel, the Holy Spirit is prominent (see 1:8, 10, 12).[83] In particular, as John the Baptist declares about Jesus, "He will baptize you with the Holy Spirit" (1:8). Furthermore, in the three references to the Holy Spirit following the prologue, the work of the Holy Spirit is to reveal what is true. In 3:29 forgiveness is made impossible because the scribes refuse to accept what the Holy Spirit reveals about Jesus. In 12:36 a statement in the Old Testament is attributed to the Holy Spirit. And in 13:11 Jesus prophesies that when his disciples are brought to trial, the Holy Spirit will give them the words to say. Thus it is not unreasonable to understand that the source of the new insight is the Holy Spirit at work in the disciples, unstopping ears, unblocking tongues, unsealing eyes. This is, after all, what Jesus came to do: to baptize with the Holy Spirit.

A comment is in order about the two-stage healing of the blind man in 8:22-26. Mark is the only writer to recount this miracle.[84] Furthermore, there is no other healing recorded in the Gospels quite like this. The two touches the man needs seem, therefore, to have a metaphoric meaning (like so much else in this unit). At the first touch the man sees dimly. He knows he is looking at people, but they appear to him like trees. This also seems to be the case for the disciples when it comes to their understanding of Jesus. They have received the first touch of healing. They now know that Jesus is the Messiah, but, as they immediately demonstrate, they do not see clearly what kind of Messiah he is (8:31-32). In the story of the healing, at the second touch the man sees clearly. This is a prophecy about what will happen to the disciples. Their eyes will eventually be fully opened. In the context of Mark's account,

---

82. "The sayings of Jesus make very few references to the Spirit, and those we have are in accordance with Old Testament references to the Spirit of God." Mann, p. 519. "In Jewish thought the Holy Spirit had two great functions. First, he revealed God's truth to men; second, he enabled men to recognize that truth when they saw it." William Barclay, *The Gospel of Mark*, rev. ed. (Philadelphia: Westminster, 1975), p. 80.

83. The other three references in Mark to the Holy Spirit are scattered throughout the text (3:29; 12:36; 13:11).

84. E. S. Johnson, "Mark 10:46-52: Blind Bartimaeus," *Catholic Biblical Quarterly* 40 (1978): 201, thinks that Mark includes this miracle because it is so closely related to his presentation of the blindness of the disciples.

this happens when they come to Jerusalem for the final week of Jesus' life. Then they begin to see clearly — a fact which is communicated by the story that launches the final week: the healing of blind Bartimaeus. This is the only other healing of a blind man in Mark (see 10:46-52).

The Concept of Repentance

Thus it is that Mark discusses repentance without using the actual word "repentance." Repentance is, by definition, a cognitive concept. It involves a decision to change one's mind about God and the work of God. It involves new understanding and the ability and willingness to act upon this new understanding. Repentance means to turn away from the old understanding about God and to embrace the new understanding. In this unit Mark has discussed understanding and how hardness of heart prevents a person from embracing new understanding. He has shown that hardened hearts can be changed by the healing touch of Jesus. He ends this unit with a dramatic example of repentance. At Caesarea Philippi the Twelve "turn around" in their thinking about Jesus. They move from considering Jesus simply to be a teacher and a prophet and come, instead, to think of him as the Messiah — which is a staggering assertion given their cultural backgrounds and their seeming hardness of hearts. Thus it is that in unit three Mark gives substance to the category of repentance that was introduced in the prologue.

The material in unit three needs to be set in the context of what else Mark says in the Second Gospel about repentance. First, in the prologue the idea of repentance is established as one of the issues that are basic to Mark's Gospel. Two of the three uses of *metanoia/metanoeō* occur in the prologue. In 1:4 the Baptist's message is said to be one of repentance. Specifically, the repentance he preaches is related to the forgiveness of sins.[85] Likewise, the message of Jesus is about repentance (1:15). Specifically, he calls men and women to repentance and faith in terms of the kingdom of God. Both of these uses of the word "repentance" carry with them the normal New Testament sense of the word, namely, changing one's mind about God and his ways.

Second, the word "repent" is also used in 6:12. Here it defines the message that the disciples preached during their mission. However, what they

---

85. The connection is made in 3:28-29 between the Holy Spirit and forgiveness. The issue there is also that of repentance; specifically, the fact that the scribes will not be forgiven because they will not ask for forgiveness. They do not ask because they do not see their need for forgiveness.

preach is more akin to John's message (repentance) than to the message of Jesus (repentance, faith, and the kingdom of God) — as might be expected. In unit two (where this mission is described) the Twelve come to understand that Jesus is a prophet. Thus they preach a prophetlike message about a prophet.[86] Had their mission occurred after unit three (where they learn that Jesus is the Messiah), they would have preached differently with their newly loosened tongues. It is therefore not surprising that Jesus does not send them out on another mission. He does not want the fact of his messiahship to be declared openly. His response to Peter's declaration is a call to secrecy. They are not to tell anyone what they now know about Jesus (8:30).

In unit three Mark gives more substance to the concept of repentance. Just as unit two amplifies the meaning of Jesus' call to faith in 1:15, so too unit three amplifies the meaning of his call to repentance (also found in 1:15). In summary, Mark says two things here about repentance. First, understanding is foundational to repentance (just as it is to faith, as he demonstrated in unit two). Without understanding, a proper response to Jesus is not possible. Understanding is that which makes it possible to respond to Jesus. It is the motive power. Hence it is not surprising that the whole Gospel of Mark is structured around the unfolding understanding on the part of the disciples as to who Jesus is. They need to understand clearly who he is in order to reorient their thinking. Second, new understanding requires the healing touch of Jesus. It is this that enables a person to go beyond his or her cultural assumptions and religious commitments. In the end, it is the Holy Spirit who opens eyes, unclogs ears, loosens tongues, and softens hearts.

86. Note also that the story of King Herod is intercalated into the mission of the Twelve. There is some confusion amongst interpreters as to why Mark included this story in which Jesus is not central (the only such pericope in his Gospel). V. Taylor, p. 307, goes so far as to suggest that Mark simply recorded a popular story about the death of John to fill in the gap between the mission of the Twelve and their return. However, it is clear that in the Gospel of Mark, when two pericopae are sandwiched together they interpret each other. In this case the parallel is between the mission of the Twelve and the mission of John. That their ministry reproduces Jesus' ministry (as it has been revealed up to this point in the Gospel) is made clear by the description of what the Twelve do. That their ministry is akin to that of John is made clear by the intercalation.

CHAPTER TEN

Conversion Themes in
Mark's Gospel: Discipleship

Following Jesus: An Analysis of Unit Four
(Mark 8:31–10:45)

In unit four Mark discusses discipleship, the final component in conversion to Christ. The outcome of repentance and faith is meant to be discipleship. This is the desired response to Jesus. This is the bountiful harvest that comes from hearing and accepting the word of God. Unit four consists of four cycles of stories. The conclusion of each cycle is a section of teaching by Jesus, and the main focus of this teaching is discipleship: what it means to follow him.

The First Statement: Mark 8:34–9:1

The first and perhaps clearest statement of what is involved in following Jesus is found in 8:34–9:1. This discussion of discipleship is precipitated by Peter's rejection of the prediction by Jesus that he, as Messiah, will suffer, be killed, and rise again. In response, Jesus calls his disciples and the crowds to himself and then states clearly the relationship between dying and following him. He points out a close connection between his fate and the fate of his followers. Jesus will be "rejected." His disciples must "deny themselves" (i.e., reject the natural tendency to assert themselves before all others). Jesus will "be killed." His disciples "must take up their cross" and "lose their life." The implications

253

are clear. As the master, so the disciple. *The pattern which the Son of Man will live out is the same pattern that his disciples must follow.*[1]

It is important to note that Jesus gives this definition of discipleship not simply to the Twelve but to the crowd as well (8:34a).[2] What he defines here is not just the special role of the Twelve but discipleship in general. His remarks are directed at all who would follow him, both the crowds (see 3:7) and the disciples (see 1:17; 2:14). In the context of Mark's account, no one is yet this kind of disciple because no one, including the Twelve, understands that the way of Jesus is the way of suffering and death.

Jesus begins his comments by stating: "If any want to become my followers, let them deny themselves and take up their cross and follow me" (8:34b). This is the key assertion in this passage, and each of the four elements in the verse must be considered: (1) the call to discipleship, (2) self-denial, (3) cross bearing, and (4) following.[3]

First, it must be noted that discipleship is spoken of in two ways in 8:34b. The two phrases by which Jesus invites people to be his disciples are "come after me" (= *opisō mou elthein*) and "follow me" (= *akoloutheitō moi*). Both are virtually identical in meaning, probably deriving from the same Semitic background, and both have as their basic idea "movement after." When used in the Old Testament, they frequently refer to following after a god or God.[4] What it means to "come after" or "follow" after Jesus is made clear by the other two phrases in 8:34b, namely, self-denial and cross bearing.

Second, the idea of self-denial is easily misunderstood, as Best points out:

> Self-denial as it is used in our verse must not be confused, as it regularly is, with the denial of things to the self, i.e. with asceticism or self-discipline. It is not the denial of something to the self but the denial of the self itself. It is the opposite of self-affirmation, of putting value on one's being, one's life, one's position before man or God, of claiming rights and privileges pecu-

---

1. "For Mark, Jesus is himself the model of discipleship." John F. O'Grady, "The Passion in Mark," *Biblical Theology Bulletin* 10 (April 1980): 83. See also p. 86. "The rule of discipleship is: Jesus. As Jesus was, so the disciple must be." Ernest Best, "Discipleship in Mark: Mark 8.22–10.52," *Scottish Journal of Theology* 23 (August 1970): 325.

2. Best, "Discipleship in Mark," p. 329. See Robert P. Meye, *Jesus and the Twelve: Discipleship and Revelation in Mark's Gospel* (Grand Rapids: Wm. B. Eerdmans Publishing Co., 1968), pp. 120-25, where he discusses various explanations for the crowds in 8:34a.

3. Ernest Best, *Following Jesus: Discipleship in the Gospel of Mark* (Sheffield: JSOT Press, 1981), p. 34.

4. Best, *Following Jesus*, p. 33.

liar to one's special position in life or even of those normally believed to belong to the human being as such (e.g. justice, freedom).[5]

Third, the image of taking up a cross supports this definition of self-denial as renouncing self for the sake of Jesus.[6] The cross was not an uncommon sight in the first century. It was used to put criminals to death. It was especially loathed by the Jews because it was the mode of death used by the occupying powers. As such, the image of a cross would evoke a powerful response from Jesus' audience.[7] However, to the Jew of that day a cross was not just a symbol of death; it was also a sign of God's disapproval. Deuteronomy 21:22-23 was understood to mean that the curse of God rested on a person who was so killed. This would have added to the horror of the cross image for Jesus' Jewish audience.[8] To take up a cross voluntarily was denial of self of the most extreme sort. It was to renounce one's very life and to put one under the curse of God.

It might be asked whether it was a literal death to which Jesus was inviting his followers. His own death would certainly be a real death. And some Christians in the first century were indeed martyrs for their faith. But in fact, this statement about cross bearing was never meant to be taken literally, as Best shows. Discipleship is "not just a quick walk in the footsteps of Jesus to the place of execution. . . ." As he points out, apart from anything else "the addition of the clause about self-denial takes away the literal meaning from 'cross-bearing.'"

What, then, do these two descriptive terms say about the nature of discipleship? Best asserts: "Cross-bearing then implies the willingness to make any sacrifice, even life itself, for Christ. Self-denial is the inner attitude; cross-bearing is the outward activity which should accompany the inner attitude.

---

5. Best, *Following Jesus,* p. 37.

6. The idea of bearing a cross would anticipate, of course, Jesus' own manner of dying and would be perceived as such by Mark's readers. For this reason, many scholars take this to be a later Christian insertion.

7. "The Jews had good reason to regard crucifixion with revulsion and horror. They were acquainted with it, all too much so. Although Josephus' assertion that Alexander Jannaeus, himself a Jewish king, had on one occasion crucified eight hundred Pharisees in Jerusalem is probably exaggerated, it reminds us that the Jews had been witnessing crucifixions since the time of Antiochus Epiphanes. It was a mode of death associated with tyrants — in Jesus' day with the hated Roman overlords." Donald R. Fletcher, "Condemned to Die: The Logion on Cross-Bearing: What Does It Mean?" *Interpretation* 18 (1964): 162. See also J. Gwyn Griffiths, "The Disciple's Cross," *New Testament Studies* 16 (1969-70): 360.

8. Fletcher, p. 162.

Both imply a definite action on the part of the disciples, a resolve to adopt a particular course of action."[9]

M. P. Green goes further. He sees cross bearing not just as willingness to sacrifice but as a sign of obedience to God's will. He understands the phrase "take up his cross" to be "a figure of speech derived from the Roman custom requiring a man convicted of rebellion against Rome's sovereign rule to carry the cross-beam *(patibulum)* to his place of execution. . . . Cross-bearing means to submit to the authority or rule one formerly rebelled against, or to obey God's will."[10] He understands the related call to deny oneself in similar terms. The self that is to be denied is the self in rebellion against God. Thus both cross bearing and self-denial are connected with the "inherent sin nature" which results in hostility to God and God's will.[11] Discipleship begins, therefore, with the act of turning from rebellion against God (self-denial) and accepting instead God's will and way (cross bearing). Self-denial is a negative action; it is a rejecting. It is "an initial act without which discipleship is impossible: at the beginning, once and for all, the disciple says No!, and he says it to himself."[12] Cross bearing, on the other hand, is a positive action; it is an accepting. It is the act of saying "Yes!" to the way of the Cross. Thus, this is another way of speaking about repentance (turning from the way of the self) and faith (turning to the way of God).

These two complementary acts enable a person to "follow after" Jesus, i.e., to become a disciple.

> "Come after me" is a general command which specifically links discipleship to Jesus; discipleship is not just the readiness to suffer, howbeit in ever so good a cause; it is a step to fall in behind Jesus, and no other, in the way in which he is going. The call is not one to accept a certain system of teaching, live by it, continue faithfully to interpret it and pass it on, which was in essence the call of a rabbi to his disciples; nor is it a call to accept a philosophical position which will express itself in a certain type of behaviour, as in Stoicism; nor is it the call to devote life to the alleviation of suffering for others; nor is it the call to pass through certain rites as in the Mysteries so as to become an initiate of the God, his companion — the carrying of the cross is no rite! It is a call to fall in behind Jesus and go with him.[13]

9. Best, *Following Jesus,* p. 39.

10. Michael P. Green, "The Meaning of Cross-Bearing," *Bibliotheca Sacra* 140 (1983): 120.

11. Green, p. 121.

12. Best, "Discipleship in Mark," p. 330.

13. Best, "Discipleship in Mark," p. 329.

Best draws attention to the shift in tense that takes place in 8:34b. The first three verbs are in the aorist tense (*elthein* = "come," an aorist infinitive; *aparnēsasthō* = "deny" and *aratō* = "take," both aorist imperatives). The fourth verb is a present imperative (*akoloutheitō* = "follow"). "This suggests an initial act, or set of actions, 'come, deny, take up,' followed by a process, 'keep on following.'"[14] This same pattern is present in other calls in Mark. "We find an initial aorist or aorists followed in most cases by a present imperative, or its equivalent, setting out what lies ahead (cf. 1.16-18, 19f; 2.14; 10.21). The aorist denotes an act which at the moment of discipleship is complete."[15] However, these "acts" of coming, denying, and taking up are not one-time responses. Best points out that "The aorists in 8.34b cannot . . . be punctiliar but denote processes which begin with the decision to follow Jesus and continue right through discipleship."[16] *Discipleship is both act and process.*

Jesus continues his teaching about discipleship in verse 35 by expanding upon the idea of self-denial and cross bearing. He says: "For those who want to save their life will lose it, and those who lose their life for my sake, and for the sake of the gospel, will save it." *Psuchē* = life/soul refers to the essential person: that which makes a person himself or herself.[17] Self-denial and cross bearing, therefore, will result in the saving of the essential person; whereas to refuse this path is to lose one's essential self. In this verse Jesus also defines the focus of discipleship. It is done "for my sake, and for the sake of the gospel," i.e., it involves "adhesion to Christ and to God's plan. . . ."[18]

The Second Statement: Mark 9:14-29

Needless to say, such a demanding call to discipleship raises many questions, not the least of which is, Who can possibly follow such a hard way? To follow Jesus as the teacher/prophet/Messiah of popular imagination is one thing. This has glamour and appeal. Clearly Jesus is in touch with the power of God, and equally clearly he plays a unique and special role in God's scheme of things. But the glamour fades quickly when following Jesus is defined in terms of self-denial and cross bearing. Who would want to follow such a hard way? In fact, how is it possible to turn away from one's own needs in this self-

14. Best, *Following Jesus*, p. 32. See also Best, "Discipleship in Mark," p. 329.
15. Best, *Following Jesus*, pp. 32-33.
16. Best, *Following Jesus*, p. 33.
17. Best, *Following Jesus*, p. 41.
18. Best, *Following Jesus*, p. 40.

denying way? In this section Mark describes how it is possible to live such a life. In essence he says that to be a disciple of Jesus requires resurrection from our old, dead life to the new life of discipleship, and this comes by the power of Jesus.

The key information about discipleship in the second section is found within the story of the healing of the demon-possessed/epileptic boy.[19] Three issues need to be considered: (1) the climate of unbelief that pervades this incident, (2) the symbolic nature of this pericope, and (3) Jesus' comment about prayer.

First, this is a story about unbelief. It begins with the three disciples who are with Jesus on the mountain during his transfiguration. They are baffled by the whole experience, and in their fear they grope for an adequate way to respond (9:5-6). And they still do not understand what Jesus means when he talks about rising from the dead (9:10). (In fact, as it turns out, it is the issue of resurrection that is the central focus of this section.) The other nine disciples are no better. While Jesus is away on the mountain, they try to cast out a demon but are unsuccessful (9:19). This leads to an argument with the scribes (9:14). The crowd for its part is just standing around and watching. Jesus lumps all these groups together and calls them a "faithless generation," thus defining the character of the situation (9:19). That this is the case is further amplified when Jesus encounters the father of the boy, who asks him to heal his son: "If you are able to do anything, have pity on us and help us" (9:22). This is yet another example of unbelief — to which Jesus responds, with some force: "If you are able! — All things can be done for the one who believes." The father then confesses both his belief and his unbelief (9:24).[20] Jesus is surrounded by a climate of unbelief that encompasses the disciples (both the three and the nine), the religious leaders, the crowd, and even the father of the boy. Once again the question (first raised in unit three) is asked: How can a person move from unbelief to belief?

Second, the answer to this question can be discerned when the story is understood not just as an account of another exorcism/healing but as a meta-

---

19. Best, "Discipleship in Mark," p. 325, thinks this incident fits into the unit on discipleship, "because it tells the early church how to exorcise, and exorcism is one of the tasks of a disciple (3:15, 6:7)." However, as is argued above, there is a much more direct connection with the theme of discipleship than just the idea of exorcism.

20. The problem for the father is one of *doubt* (being of two minds about an issue), not one of *disbelief* (certainty that something is not true). The father did not disbelieve. After all, he had brought his son to Jesus to be healed (9:17). His faith has been shaken, however, by the failure of the disciples to heal his son (9:18), so that even though he desperately wants his child to be free of this demon, he wonders if it is possible (9:22).

phor. Two factors point to a symbolic (as well as literal) interpretation of this pericope. For one thing, there is precedent in Mark for healings to be used in a symbolic way. In the previous unit the two healings were seen to have symbolic content (7:31-37; 8:22-25).[21] For another thing, the close parallels between this story and the account of the raising of Jairus's daughter (5:21-23, 35-43) point in the direction of another level of meaning than the literal.

The parallels between the two stories are striking: (1) in both cases the father comes to Jesus to ask for his help (cf. 5:22-23 and 9:17); (2) both incidents involve children; (3) both children are thought by the crowds to be dead (cf. 5:35, 39-40; and 9:26); (4) in both healings the concerned parents (or parent) are present at the healing (cf. 5:40 and 9:24); (5) in both cases Jesus lifts the "dead" child by the hand (cf. 5:41 and 9:27); (6) in both cases the child stands up (cf. 5:42 and 9:27); and (7) both healings involve the faith of a parent (cf. 5:36 and 9:24). Furthermore, so the reader does not miss what is being said, the boy is described as looking like a corpse (9:26). Coming as this incident does after a discussion of the meaning of resurrection (9:9-10), and given the close parallels with the only incident in Mark where Jesus raises someone from the dead, it seems clear that Mark intends the reader to see this as a reference to resurrection.[22] Thus it seems that this incident is used by Mark in a symbolic way to describe how people can be raised from the dead. As O'Grady suggests: "When Jesus healed him [the boy], Mark may have been symbolizing that Jesus will enable others to rise from the dead and be with God just as he will rise and is with God. The only condition is that of faith. Since Mark uses the healing of the blind men for symbolic purposes, he may be attempting the same thing in this pericope."[23]

What, then, is the metaphoric meaning of this pericope? *The implication is that to move from unbelief (the context of the story) to new life (the experience of the boy) requires the power of Jesus.* Thus this story provides a needed piece of information about how to achieve the kind of discipleship to which Jesus is calling men and women. To turn one's back on oneself even to the point of death is too hard a way for mere mortals. But the healing touch of Je-

---

21. Later in the chapter the healing of blind Bartimaeus in 10:46-52 will also be shown to have symbolic content.

22. The focus in this section on resurrection may also explain the somewhat different structure of this section as compared to the other three sections which are structurally very similar to one another (see pp. 132-33). The other three sections are concerned primarily with the death of Jesus (i.e., his suffering and death are what the disciples seem not to grasp in these sections), whereas this is the only section that focuses on his resurrection (and the inability of the disciples to understand it).

23. O'Grady, p. 86.

sus can bring new life to the one who wishes to be Jesus' disciple, just as it did to Jairus's daughter and to the boy.

And indeed, the disciples need this new life. Clearly they are part of the "faithless generation" (9:19) which is also spoken of as an "adulterous and sinful generation" a few verses earlier (8:38). They too are possessed by a type of evil: cultural blindness (which prevents them from seeing who Jesus is) and a concern for self (which is brought out clearly in unit four). Both conditions prevent true discipleship. A person possessed by this sort of evil force is not free to follow Jesus. In order to move away from commitment to false gods[24] — from misunderstanding, from unbelief, and from sin — a miracle is needed. And indeed, this is what Jesus provides. He casts out the demon in the child. The boy is brought back to "life." So too, for those from the adulterous, sinful, and faithless generation, the healing touch of Jesus can release them from their captivity. It will be like rising from the dead when one is released from the power of evil. Thus they will be enabled to become the self-denying, cross-bearing disciples Jesus wants.

Third, one further statement by Jesus requires comment. At the end of the pericope (and section) he states, in answer to his disciples' question as to why they were unable to cast out the demon: "This kind can come out only through prayer" (9:29). Gundry feels that Mark is here using the disciples' inability and failure as a foil against which is seen the great power of Jesus, who did not need to pray when he cast out the demon.[25] As such, it is a reminder once again of the necessity of opening oneself by faith to the power of Jesus. To be a disciple is impossible on one's own. Prayer is an essential feature of discipleship. "The disciples are reminded of the necessity of prayer for discipleship. The person who is called to discipleship realizes his own inability to exorcise the demons. Only by the power of prayer can the most difficult demons be cast out. Surrender to God is what matters most. Self emptiness is essential to discipleship, a lesson learned only in the gesture of openness to Another which characterizes prayer."[26]

Thus, in section two the reader learns that to be a disciple of Jesus ne-

---

24. "The description of a community as 'adulterous' and 'sinful' is influenced by OT teaching; cf. Hos. 2:2(4)ff., Isa. 1:4, Ezek. 16:32ff.; also Isa. 1:21, Jer. 3:3." Vincent Taylor, *The Gospel according to St. Mark* (New York: St. Martin's Press, 1966), p. 383. These references portray Israel as a nation which has left the true God and taken up with false gods. Possession by an evil spirit would be a fitting way to describe such a state of affairs.

25. Robert H. Gundry, *Mark: A Commentary on His Apology for the Cross* (Grand Rapids: Wm. B. Eerdmans Publishing Co., 1993), p. 493.

26. Daniel Malone, "Riches and Discipleship: Mark 10:27-31," *Biblical Theology Bulletin* 9 (April 1979): 86.

cessitates the kind of faith in Jesus that opens one to the power of Jesus. Only Jesus can bring the new life that makes discipleship possible.

The Third Statement: Mark 9:35–10:31

In the third section of teaching (9:35–10:31) the focus is on the kingdom of God. Two issues in particular are dealt with here. The primary issue has to do with membership in the kingdom, especially how one enters into the kingdom. The secondary issue has to do with the nature of relationships within the kingdom. Both issues shed light on the ongoing discussion in this unit about discipleship.[27]

Misunderstanding on the part of the Twelve launches this teaching section.[28] Once again Jesus predicts his betrayal, death, and resurrection (9:31). Once again the disciples fail to understand what he means (9:32). They misunderstand because what they have in mind is an earthly kingdom in which the Messiah reigns and the whole world is subject to him. So they argue about who will be greatest in that kingdom (9:33-34). But the kingdom that Jesus has in mind is all about giving your life for others and being in relationship to others. So in this section Jesus teaches them about the actual character of the kingdom of God over against their cultural understanding of that kingdom.

27. There is a tight structure to this third teaching section. This section begins with a pericope in which Jesus teaches and the disciples do not understand what he is saying (9:30-32; pericope A). The section ends with a second example of Jesus teaching and the Twelve misunderstanding (10:23-31; pericope A'), except this time they ask Jesus about what they do not understand (cf. 9:32 and 10:28). The second pericope in the section involves a discussion of what it means to be great (9:33-34; pericope B). And in parallel fashion the penultimate pericope deals with a great person (10:17-22; pericope B'). The third pericope in the section focuses on a child as an example of kingdom realities (9:36-37; pericope C), while the third pericope from the end also focuses on a child used as an example (10:13-16; pericope C'). The pericopae in between (9:38–10:12) focus on kingdom relationships.

28. By comparison with where this material appears in Matthew and Luke, it would appear that once again (as he did in 4:1-34) Mark has collected together into one section teaching given by Jesus on various occasions. However, Best, *Following Jesus*, p. 75, states: "There are good reasons for supposing that most of this section (9:33-50) came to Mark in the tradition as a unit: (i) It is held together, not by any logical development of thought but by catch-words; their use is typical of oral speech rather than of written materials." In either case, the important thing is that Mark has brought together this material (in whole or as parts) so as to move the discussion of discipleship forward in light of the latest misunderstanding of the disciples.

The focus on membership in the kingdom emerges in the first pericope (9:33-37). The Twelve conceive of the kingdom as a place of hierarchy in which some are great and others are not (9:34). Jesus immediately reverses their thinking. Those who wish to be first in his kingdom will become such by serving others, he says, thus answering the question about which the disciples were arguing (9:35). Then Jesus takes a child into his arms and announces that in his kingdom even children (who were amongst the lowest on the first-century social scale) are welcome. In fact, receiving even a single child is equal to receiving Jesus. And receiving Jesus is equivalent to receiving the God who sent him (9:37).

The next pericope (9:38-41) makes the same point. A freelance exorcist is to be welcomed into the kingdom (9:38-40), as is the one who does deeds of kindness in the name of Christ (9:41). In other words, the boundaries of Jesus' kingdom are wider than the disciples imagined. Harmony is maintained in that kingdom by a welcoming attitude rather than a rejecting attitude.

The issue of kingdom relationships is raised in another way via the material in 9:33-50. The disciples are urged to move from argument (9:33) to peace (9:50) in the community of Jesus. The topic with which the teaching section begins (the disciples arguing with each other) is resolved at the end of the first subsection (with the injunction in 9:50 to "be at peace with each other"). Mark then moves to the related subject of marriage (10:1-12) in his second subsection. The connection between the first two subsections seems to arise from the fact that marriage can be a place of strife, leading to divorce, if peace is not gained.

Jesus' teaching about kingdom relationships was initiated by taking a child into his arms and using that child as an example of those relationships (9:36-37). Here, for a second time, Jesus takes a child into his arms and once again uses that child as an example (10:15-16). This time Jesus' point is that to enter his kingdom one must become "as a little child." It is not enough just to welcome a child into the kingdom (9:37); one must become like that child to be a disciple of Jesus.[29] Lane states: "Entrance into the Kingdom is defined as the gift of God bestowed upon those who acknowledge their helplessness

---

29. Best, *Following Jesus*, p. 108, summarizes the meaning of 10:13-16 as follows: "We conclude that the kingdom is to be received in the way children receive. . . . Just as a child trusts an adult and receives from him what he offers, so the disciple is to trust God and receive from him the kingdom. But the kingdom is not a 'thing'; it is God's active rule; the disciple has therefore to allow God to rule in his life. He does not achieve this all at once when he becomes a disciple; it is a gradual process; hence our pericope fits appropriately into a discussion of the nature of discipleship."

in relationship to the Kingdom."[30] Once again (as in 9:19-29) there is a stress on the work of God.

This leads into a story about one of the "great" people (a wealthy man).[31] Once again Mark is pairing a child with a "great" person (see 9:33-37). The Twelve want to be great (9:34), but the point of this story is that the very thing that puts this man on top of the social scale (his wealth) is the impediment that keeps him from the kingdom (10:21-22). The story of the so-called "rich young ruler" (10:17-31) consists of three parts: the encounter with the young man (10:17-22); the interpretation of the incident by Jesus to the disciples with comments about wealth and discipleship (10:23-27); and the response to Peter's statement about having left all (10:28-31).[32] Taken together, this is an account concerned "almost exclusively" with discipleship.[33] This whole section is permeated with words and phrases related to the kingdom of God and how one enters it. These terms include: "eternal life" (vv. 17, 30); "follow me" (v. 21); "enter the kingdom of God" (vv. 23, 24, 25); "saved" (v. 26); "for my sake and for the sake of the good news" (v. 29); "this age" (v. 30); and "the age to come" (v. 30).

The first question the young man asks Jesus concerns eternal life and how to obtain it (10:17). This is a new form of the question that controls the focus of the passage (i.e., how to enter the kingdom). Jesus' first response seems oblique and unrelated to the young man's question about eternal life. It has to do with the goodness of God and the commandments given by this God who is good (10:18-19). However, by responding to his question in this

30. William L. Lane, *The Gospel according to Mark* (Grand Rapids: Wm. B. Eerdmans Publishing Co., 1974), p. 363.

31. In contrast, Jeremias — and Best after him — asserts that the material from 10:1-31 deals with marriage, children, and possessions, in that order, and so is connected together thematically. See Best, *Following Jesus*, p. 99. While this is true — and indeed, the whole of this third teaching section touches in some way upon the ordering of life within the kingdom of God — Mark gives two signals that he has a different division in mind. First, he parallels 9:33-37 with 10:13-16. In both cases a child is used as an illustration, and in both cases what he says about the child launches a new (though related) line of teaching. Mark has done this before. In unit three he used a parallel story (the second feeding account) to signal the start of a new (though related) topic. Second, the topic of the first set of stories is relationships in the kingdom, introduced by using the child as an illustration of the fact that all people are welcome in the kingdom. The topic of the second set of stories is also introduced by what Jesus says about children. Now the focus is on entering the kingdom.

32. Paul S. Minear, "The Needle's Eye," *Journal of Biblical Literature* 61 (1942): 160, and Ernest Best, "The Camel and the Needle's Eye (Mark 10:25)," *Expository Times* 82 (1970-71): 83.

33. Best, "The Camel," p. 83.

manner, Jesus raises the fundamental issue of sin and righteousness. He makes it clear that no one but God is truly good — not even those who keep the commandments.[34] Thus, it is made evident that there is in every person something that must be turned away from (repentance) before that person can turn to God and obtain eternal life. In 10:21-22 Jesus pinpoints exactly what this is for this young man. His "god," it seems, is his wealth. Being unable to turn away from that, the young man instead turns away from Jesus (10:22).[35] His action demonstrates, in a literal way, the nature of repentance. Repentance is making a choice about the direction one's life should take; it is deciding whom to serve. The young man illustrates the choice *not* to follow Jesus (the first such example in Mark; Judas also will choose this path).

It is useful to examine exactly what Jesus says to the young man. He issues five commands: "go," "sell," "give," "come," "follow" (10:21). The first three imperatives — "go," "sell," "give" — appear to be prerequisites to "coming" and "following." They parallel 8:34b where Jesus describes these actions as self-denial and cross bearing. As the broader terms in 8:34b indicate, this is not a general call to reduce oneself to poverty in order to follow Jesus. It is not a statement that it is by works of righteousness that one obtains eternal life (i.e., entrance into the kingdom of God).[36] As 10:15 made clear, the kingdom is received (as a child), not earned (by good deeds of any sort). Likewise, in 10:27 where Jesus answers the disciples' question about how to be saved, nothing is said about works. The emphasis in 10:27 is on the miracle of God that makes it possible to enter the kingdom.

However, what is prerequisite to entrance into the kingdom (and has been all along) is repentance[37] — the voluntary turning away from whatever functions as the motivating center of one's life, be it the tradition of the elders, as in the case of the Pharisees (7:1-23); unbelief (9:14-27); or in this case, wealth. Jesus makes this clear in his definitional statement in 1:15 ("Repent, and believe in the good news"). The need for repentance is reinforced

---

34. Minear, p. 160.

35. "'One thing you lack.' That phrase echoes like a haunting refrain, for we all lack at least one thing.... The call to repentance is clear if one's wealth stands in the way of true discipleship." William J. Carl III, "Mark 10:17-27 (28-31)," *Interpretation* 33 (1979): 285.

36. "The demand of Jesus is not for any specific act, but for an attitude of abandonment to loyalty to his ministry and person." C. S. Mann, *Mark: A New Translation with Introduction and Commentary* (Garden City, N.Y.: Doubleday, 1986), p. 401.

37. "In Jesus' words to him [in 10:21] many things are combined, the sharp probe that will show the man his self-deception, the summons to repentance, the gracious offer of himself as the way, the command and the promise of eternal life about which he inquired." C. E. B. Cranfield, *The Gospel according to Saint Mark* (Cambridge: University Press, 1959), p. 329.

by the negative example of the teachers of the law in 3:23-30 (see especially vv. 28-29), and it is at the root of the discussion of the hardness of heart of the disciples in unit three (see especially 6:51-52; 8:14-21).

The kingdom of God is spoken of in various ways in this pericope. The young man thinks of it in terms of "eternal life." (This is the only place in Mark where the idea of eternal life appears, though the equivalent term, "life," is used in 9:43 and 45.) As Jesus' response in 10:23 to the question of the young man in 10:17 indicates, eternal life is related to the concept of the kingdom of God. The young man asks: "What must I do to inherit eternal life?" and Jesus responds to the disciples: "How hard it will be for those who have wealth to enter the kingdom of God!" To inherit eternal life (10:17) or receive eternal life (10:30) is equivalent to entering the kingdom of God. The word "kingdom" refers not just to the rule of God but to the domain in which this rule is experienced. The word "life" refers to "the kind of life which belongs to this domain, that is, the rule of God in human experience" in both the present and future.[38] There is yet another way of speaking about entering the kingdom. The disciples think of entering the kingdom as being "saved" (10:26).[39] Jesus states: "'It is easier for a camel to go through the eye of a needle than for someone who is rich to enter the kingdom of God.' They [the disciples] were greatly astounded and said to one another, 'Then who can be saved?'" (10:25-26). According to V. Taylor, what they are asking in 10:26 is: "Who will finally be found within the *basileia?*"[40] (Prior to this Jesus has spoken of "receiv[ing] the kingdom of God as a little child" [10:15].)

The nature of the kingdom of God is further described in 10:29-30 when Jesus discusses the reward for renunciation of wealth and family. He points out that the kingdom of God is expressed both in the here and now and in the eschatological future. More importantly, Jesus notes here that such renunciation is done "for my sake and for the sake of the good news." This same link is found in the first teaching section where Jesus echoes this phrase ("those who lose their life for my sake, and for the sake of the gospel, will save it" [8:35]). Thus he makes it clear that he himself is the focus of discipleship, and that there is a connection between him and the gospel. As V. Taylor notes, in the early church there was "an identification of Jesus Himself with the 'Gospel' and the 'Kingdom.'. . ."[41] Thus, the object of faith is identified. In 1:15 Jesus said, "The kingdom of God is near. Repent and

---

38. Taylor, p. 412.
39. Mann, p. 402.
40. Taylor, p. 432.
41. Taylor, p. 434.

believe the good news!" (NIV). Now the nature of that good news has been defined. It is Jesus.[42]

The logion in 10:27 plays an important role in understanding the process of becoming a disciple. It is not just a matter of keeping the commandments, forsaking wealth, leaving family, career, or anything else. It is the grace of God which makes it possible to leave behind whatever binds one and so follow Jesus.[43] For the third time in unit four Mark makes this point. That which lies behind repentance and faith (and makes each possible) is the power of God. "'Eternal life,' 'salvation,' or 'entrance into the Kingdom' describe a single reality which must be bestowed as [God's] gift to men."[44]

Thus in the story of the rich young man the nature of Jesus' ministry (as defined in 1:15) is clarified. To repent is to turn away from that which functions as the "god" of one's life, be it wealth, religious commitments, or cultural assumptions. To believe the gospel is to trust in Jesus. Such a response is made possible by the power (grace) of God. The fruit of repentance and faith is entrance into the kingdom of God. It is how one inherits or receives eternal life. It is how one is saved.

This account provides a negative and a positive illustration of discipleship. The young man is the negative illustration; the disciples are the positive example.[45] The young man will not turn from that which possesses him; the disciples have begun their turning. They have left family and career (1:16-20; 10:28). They have yet to turn from personal ambition, as the pericopae on either side of this account show (see 9:33-34 and 10:35-37). Their turning will climax at the cross (14:27-31, 66-72). In sum, then, what Mark says about discipleship (following the story of the rich young man) is: (1) that a conscious decision is necessary in order to follow Jesus (10:28; cf. 1:16-20); (2) that it takes the work of God for a person to make this turn to Jesus (10:27); and (3) that although repentance is required, any renunciation is compensated in this world by the community of Christians and in the next world by eternal life (10:29-30).

The Fourth Statement: Mark 10:42-45

The disciples still do not understand. Two of them (James and John) come to Jesus privately with a request (10:35). They want a commitment from Jesus

---

42. Ralph Martin, *Mark: Evangelist and Theologian* (Grand Rapids: Zondervan, 1973), p. 110.

43. Best, "The Camel," p. 84.

44. Lane, p. 370.

45. Minear, p. 168.

that when he comes into his kingdom they will be his chief assistants (10:37). Their desire is to be preeminent. When the other ten hear about this, they are angry (10:41) — probably because James and John presume to think they have the right to such key positions. Nobody seems to get the point that Jesus' kingdom will not be that kind of place. All of them are still thinking in terms of an earthly, messianic kingdom. The issue of greatness is still on their minds.

So in the final section of teaching in unit four (10:42-45), Jesus returns to a theme he has already discussed: what constitutes greatness in his kingdom. As he did in the previous section, Jesus calls those who would be his disciples to a life of service to others. To be first in his kingdom, as he has already taught them (9:35), is to become a "servant" (10:43). In fact, and here his language grows even more demanding, "you must be slave of all" (10:44). This, apparently, is what it means to deny self and take up a cross. His kingdom is a kingdom in which all serve the needs of others.

Once again he reiterates that he himself is the model upon which their lifestyle is to be based. It is not the Gentile rulers who are to be copied. They "lord it over" others. They are "tyrants." Their "great ones" do not define greatness in his kingdom (10:42-43).[46] Instead, they are to model their lives on the example of the Son of Man: "For the Son of Man came not to be served but to serve, and to give his life a ransom for many" (10:45). In this way teaching about the Son of Man and teaching about following Jesus (Christology and discipleship) are tied together. "Verse 45b offers a suitable ending to the long section on discipleship which commenced at 8:27, for it brings the death of Christ back into the centre of the picture; the discussion began from the first prediction of that death (8:31). Moreover in providing an interpretation of the death it opens up the way for the final journey to Jerusalem and the passion itself."[47]

In the final verse of this section, it also becomes clear that to be a disciple of Jesus is not merely a matter of imitating him.

> Mark leaves us in no doubt that the Christian disciple cannot imitate Christ. At every stage where it seems that the disciple goes after Jesus and does what he does, Mark clearly distinguishes between the disciples and Jesus. It is not just that Jesus was the first to walk along the way of humble service to the cross and that men must follow, for Jesus is set in a much more unique position. This comes out in the final programmatic statement with its distinction: all minister to others, only Jesus gives his life a ransom

46. Best, *Following Jesus*, p. 128.
47. Best, *Following Jesus*, p. 127.

for many, and the many include the disciple who is moved to follow and minister.[48]

Discipleship: A Summary

"On the Way"

The threefold pattern of prediction/misunderstanding/teaching ties unit four together. However, another feature runs through the whole of the unit as well. It is the use of the word *hodos* = "way," and in particular, the phrase *en tē hodō* = "on the way." Mark uses the term *hodos* some seven times in 8:27–10:52 (8:27; 9:33, 34; 10:17, 32, 46, 52).[49] By using the phrase *en tē hodō* in this way, Mark conveys the fact that to be a disciple is, literally, to follow Jesus. He deliberately sets the discussion of discipleship in unit four in the context of an actual journey — from Caesarea Philippi to Jerusalem. Best comments on this feature by calling Mark's Gospel the "gospel of the Way."[50]

The Twelve are well along on the Way. At this point in the account they have most of the information they need in order to become disciples in the way Jesus intends. They know about faith; they know about repentance. They know about self-denying, cross-bearing discipleship. They have grown in their understanding of Jesus and know that he is the Messiah. But they do not yet understand. This is the missing piece of the puzzle. In particular, they

48. Best, "Discipleship in Mark," p. 335.

49. Note that *hodos* is found not only in unit four but also in the transitional sections on either side of unit four, once again giving evidence of Mark's use of bracketing. The phrase *en tē hodō* occurs in 8:27 (the first verse of the pericope that brackets unit four on its front side) and in 10:52 (the final verse in the pericope that brackets unit four on the other side). W. M. Swartley, "The Structural Function of the Term 'Way' *(Hodos)* in Mark's Gospel," in *The New Way of Jesus: Essays Presented to Howard Charles,* ed. William Klassen (Newton, Kans.: Faith and Life Press, 1980), pp. 73-86, argues persuasively for Mark's redactional use of this term in 8:27–10:52.

50. Mark "used verbs of motion more frequently than any of the other evangelists. In our section [8:22–10:52] this sense of motion is brought out by his use of the phrase 'on the way' *(en tē hodō);* it is found at the end of the second prediction of the Passion when the question of greatness arises (9:33); when Jesus makes the third prediction they are 'on the way' going up to Jerusalem (10:32); lastly when Bartimaeus receives his sight it is said that he follows him 'on the way' (10:52). If we go back to the beginnings of the Gospel and the only formal quotation of Scripture that Mark makes in the whole Gospel we find it again: 'Behold, I send my messenger before thy face, who shall prepare thy *way;* the voice of one crying in the wilderness: Prepare the *way* of the Lord, make his paths straight.' Mark's Gospel is the gospel of the Way." Best, "Discipleship in Mark," pp. 326-27.

have yet to understand about his death and resurrection. "Part of discipleship is acceptance of the strange idea that Jesus the Lord should die, and acceptance takes time; even at the end of the journey to Jerusalem the disciples do not fully understand; and if they do not fully understand the death of Jesus, still less do they understand what this means for themselves."[51] So the journey has more steps to it. But as unit five begins they enter into the final stage of the journey. In Jericho they stand at the gateway to Jerusalem, where the final part of the drama is about to begin.

"Watch, Therefore": An Analysis of Units Five and Six (Mark 10:46–15:39)

In units five and six the disciples fade somewhat into the background. Jesus comes to center stage as events unfold in the final week of his life. In unit five Jesus asserts his identity in such a way that the religious officials have no choice but to act. They must either accept his claims or put an end to him. In unit six the events which he set in motion unfold and culminate in his death. Through all this the disciples are present, though not at the center of events as they often have been in previous units. However, at certain points they do play an important supporting role. In 11:1-7 they secure the donkey on which Jesus rides into the city. In 11:12-14, 20-25; 13:1-37 they are the recipients of his teaching about the coming judgment. And in 14:1-52, 66-72 they take part in the events that led up to Jesus' betrayal.

However, even though the question of the pilgrimage of the Twelve moves to the background now that Mark has finished with his main discussion of repentance, faith, and discipleship, there are several incidents that bear on the question of their conversion. These incidents serve to round off the themes Mark developed in previous units. Three sections in particular will be examined: the healing of blind Bartimaeus (10:46-52), the Olivet Discourse (chap. 13), and the betrayal of Jesus (14:1-11, 27-52, 66-72).

Blind Bartimaeus: Mark 10:46-52

Mark uses the story of blind Bartimaeus in two ways as he tells the story of the conversion of the Twelve. First, it sums up what discipleship is all about and what the Twelve need to grasp. In unit four the elements of discipleship

---

51. Best, "Discipleship in Mark," pp. 328-29.

are described, and here in the opening pericope of unit five the reader sees these come together (for the most part) in the experience of one man. Second, the story of Bartimaeus symbolically describes how the Twelve will come into the full understanding of Jesus needed to complete their turning to Jesus.

When it comes to the discipleship issue, the key verse in this pericope is the final one: "Jesus said to him, 'Go; your faith has made you well.' Immediately he regained his sight and followed him on the way" (10:52). Here Mark expresses the relationship between faith, salvation, and discipleship.[52] In terms of faith, the response of Bartimaeus stands in sharp contrast to the responses of both the disciples and the father of the epileptic boy in unit four (cf. 9:14-29). "In these passages Mark looks at faith from three different perspectives, the tentative faith of the father, the powerless unbelief of the disciples and the exuberant *pistis* of Bartimaeus."[53] Thus Mark points ahead to what must come for the Twelve: an "exuberant faith" that responds to Jesus in full understanding of who he is.

In terms of salvation, Best points out the double meaning of *sesōken*, which can be rendered either heal or save.[54] "The story is then a symbol of the unbeliever who as such is blind but who is saved when his 'eyes' are opened. Salvation and sight are, of course, closely related. . . ."[55] The "salvation" is, of necessity, proleptic. Jesus has not yet given himself as a ransom for the many (10:45). Once again the experience of Bartimaeus has important implications for the Twelve. Their eyes are being opened so that by the end of the coming week they too will understand and be able to reach out in repentance and faith for the salvation that comes via Jesus' death on the cross.

In terms of discipleship, Mark shows that Bartimaeus has started the process of becoming a disciple by following Jesus along the way. But as R. Meye points out, the term "*akolouthein* [following] is not a univocal characterization of discipleship for Mark. Though it may indeed represent a response to the mighty words and works of Jesus, following does not automatically signify the will to abide with Jesus and learn from him, factors that ordinarily denote discipleship in Mark."[56] Rather, the word "follow" is used for those who start on the path after Jesus. Bartimaeus is not yet a disciple in the full sense of the word because he, like everyone else, must first go to the

52. E. S. Johnson, "Mark 10:46-52: Blind Bartimaeus," *Catholic Biblical Quarterly* 40 (1978): 199.

53. E. S. Johnson, p. 200.

54. Ernest Best, *The Temptation and the Passion: The Markan Soteriology* (Cambridge: University Press, 1965), pp. 109-10, and Best, *Following Jesus*, pp. 141-42.

55. Best, *Following Jesus*, p. 141.

56. Meye, pp. 121-22.

cross. So too the Twelve. If anyone can be said to be followers of Jesus at this stage, it is the disciples. Yet they too must demonstrate the will to follow Jesus to the cross and beyond, and one of them will fail.

Here, then, in this pericope in a symbolic way are many of the elements of discipleship: the christological declaration (even though it is of necessity incomplete since Christ has yet to die [10:47, 48]), the call of Jesus to a person (10:49), the request for healing/salvation (10:51), faith (10:52), the healing work of Jesus (10:52), the experience of healing/salvation by Bartimaeus (10:52), and the beginning of discipleship (10:52). The healing of Bartimaeus functions on a symbolic level, therefore, as a statement of what discipleship is.

The story of Bartimaeus also functions on a symbolic level when it comes to the unfolding understanding of the Twelve as to who Jesus is. Two blind men are healed in the Gospel of Mark. In both instances Mark uses these healings in a symbolic way.[57] The first blind man to be healed requires two touches from Jesus (8:22-26). Mark uses the healing of this blind man at Bethsaida to indicate that the Twelve have also been cured of their blindness. Immediately following this healing, the Twelve confess for the first time that they understand that Jesus is the Messiah. However, they then go on to indicate that they do not know what kind of Messiah Jesus is. The Twelve, like the blind man at Bethsaida, need a second touch of healing, and it is this second touch that comes here in 10:46-52.

The Twelve need this second touch of healing so that they can understand what kind of Messiah Jesus is. That they do not yet understand is stressed repeatedly in unit four. But now, as they stand at the threshold of the events that will take place in Jesus' last week of life, their eyes are opened so that they can understand the meaning of these events. "Just as the confession of faith (Mk 8:29) and the first passion prediction (8:31) were preceded by a restoration of sight (8:22-26), so this last orientation towards the passion is followed by the healing of blind Bartimaeus (10:46-52), and thereafter Jesus rides into Jerusalem and the whole train of events leading up to the cross has begun."[58]

However, there is a difference between the first touch of healing and the second touch of healing. The impact of the first touch is indicated via the confession at Caesarea Philippi that Jesus is the Messiah at the conclusion of Part I of the Gospel. However, there is no comparable confession by the Twelve that they now understand Jesus to be the Son of God at the conclusion

---

57. "Blindness is a common symbol for lack of understanding and its recovery for the opening of the mind." Best, *Following Jesus*, p. 134.

58. Barnabas Lindars, "Salvation Proclaimed VII. Mark 10:45: A Ransom for Many," *Expository Times* 93 (1981-82): 295.

of Part II (with all that such a confession implies about his messiahship). That confession is given by the centurion. As for the Twelve, "[t]hey never attain full sight within the Gospel. . . ."[59] But perhaps the understanding of the Twelve is contained within the confession of the centurion. Certainly Mark seems to hint in the Bartimaeus story that they now have the ability to discern fully who Jesus is. And Mark's readers know that this was the outcome of their story. The readers know that the disciples did indeed come to full insight and faithful obedience to the mission of Jesus.

Watchfulness: Mark 13

Chapter 13 stands between units five and six. It is a transitional section that sums up unit five and launches unit six. It also defines what is expected of the disciples during the final week of Jesus' life: they are to "watch." This note of watchfulness is sounded in three ways in this passage. First, the command *blepete* = "see" or "take heed" is repeated four times (13:5, 9, 23, 33). This is a call for vigilance so that they will not be deceived by false prophets or by the events that are taking place.[60] In 13:33 a second command is coupled with *blepete*, namely, *agrupneite* = "be wakeful." A third command, *grēgoreite* = "watch," is added in 13:35, 37. All three commands are given in the context of the parousia and in light of the fact that no one knows when this will take place. The chapter ends with the imperative *grēgoreite*.

Although set in the context of the last days, the call to watchfulness is actually broader than this. Lane notes: "The stress upon vigilance sustained throughout the discourse suggests that the final call to watchfulness in verse 37 is not focused exclusively upon the last day, but like the previous admonitions, has bearing upon the continuing life of the church. . . ."[61] Cranfield adds: "The command to watch is addressed not only to the four, but also to the rest of the Twelve, to Mark's readers in the Church of Rome, and to the whole Church throughout the Last Times."[62]

The first people to receive the command to "watch" are the disciples, and this comes during the final week of Jesus' life when decisive events are unfolding before their very eyes. They need to pay attention so as to understand the mean-

59. Best, *Following Jesus*, p. 136.
60. Lane, p. 456.
61. Lane, p. 484.
62. Cranfield, p. 412.

ing of what is happening. Their eyes have been opened. This gift of grace will enable them to understand. Their task is simply to pay attention.

That Mark intends to connect this call to watchfulness to the events of the final week is made clear in 14:32-42 (the Garden of Gethsemane story). Here Jesus calls the disciples to "watch" *(grēgoreite)* with him while he prays (14:34, 37, 38). Three of the disciples who are with him in the garden were also with him on the Mount of Olives where he first stressed watchfulness (cf. 13:3 and 14:33).[63] This call to watchfulness is made necessary because the disciples are in fact sleeping when they should be involved in the events which are taking place (and which, if understood, would enable them to understand Jesus). But their eyes are "heavy," Mark says (14:40). The word "heavy" suggests difficulty in sight.[64] It seems that the disciples have not yet availed themselves of the gift of full sight.[65] Potentially they can now see and understand; practically this will not happen until the cross.

There is a close connection in both language and theme between 13:33-37 and 14:32-42.

> Both "sleep" and "watchfulness" are set firmly . . . in a passion and not a parousia context; the "hour" is not the "hour" of the return but of the cross. Should we not then interpret the "watchfulness" of 13:33-7 in terms of that of Gethsemane? The failure of the disciples to be watchful is seen directly after Gethsemane in Peter's denial and in the flight of all of them at the time of the arrest. Finally we should note the passion context of the whole of Mk 13, which Lightfoot first indicated so clearly.[66]

Betrayal: Mark 14:1-11, 27-52, 66-72

Since the disciples do not "watch" in Gethsemane, they are unprepared for the arrest of Jesus. Being unprepared, they flee (14:50). Then Peter betrays Jesus. And so Jesus is left alone at the cross. But it is not just the disciples who have forsaken Jesus. All have rejected him. He is rejected by both the religious

---

63. See Charles B. Cousar, "Eschatology and Mark's *Theologia Crucis:* A Critical Analysis of Mark 13," *Interpretation* 24 (1970): 333.

64. Best, *Following Jesus,* p. 151. W. H. Kelber, "The Hour of the Son of Man and the Temptation of the Disciples (Mk 14:32-42)," in *The Passion in Mark: Studies in Mark 14–16,* ed. Werner H. Kelber (Philadelphia: Fortress, 1976), p. 49.

65. Best feels that they have not yet obtained full sight, i.e., they have not received the "second touch." He does not, however, indicate when such an experience takes place. See Best, *Following Jesus,* p. 151.

66. Best, *Following Jesus,* p. 153.

and secular leadership of Israel (14:43–15:20); he is rejected by the crowds who had only the week before acclaimed him (cf. 11:8-10 and 15:6-15);[67] and even God forsakes him (15:34). And probably even Mark, the author, has fled from Jesus — if he is, as many feel, the young man who flees naked into the night when caught by the guards (14:51-52). Of all these betrayals, the one on which Mark focuses the most attention is that of Peter. In Peter's betrayal is seen the betrayal of all the disciples.

The process of defection by the Twelve begins in the opening pericope of unit six at the anointing of Jesus. The disciples' lack of understanding of Jesus is seen in their reactions. They are annoyed at Jesus for allowing this incident to occur, though they express their anger to the woman: "But some were there who said to one another in anger, 'Why was the ointment wasted in this way? For this ointment could have been sold for more than three hundred denarii, and the money given to the poor.' And they scolded her" (14:4-5). This general impatience on the part of the Twelve is set in the context of Judas's betrayal, which is described next (14:1-2, 10-11). The less lethal but none-the-less critical reaction of the other eleven disciples is different only in order of magnitude to what Judas does. Judas may be the first to betray Jesus, but the others will soon do the same.[68]

> Mark's sole purpose seems to have been to place this account of treachery alongside the preceding account of the complete devotion of the unnamed woman (vv. 3-9). In doing so, Mark gives the most striking example of how the gulf between Jesus and members of the Twelve had widened. Earlier, there are examples of the Twelve being insensitive to Jesus' teaching . . . but with Judas' plan to betray Jesus we see the beginnings of their complete collapse described in 14:50, 66-72.[69]

67. While it is true that historically there was probably little or no similarity between the crowds that greeted Jesus and those that rejected him (given the enormous number of people in Jerusalem for Passover and the secrecy of the trial that prevented Jesus' supporters from attending it), Mark does not make this distinction. The crowds are like the seed sown in rocky soil that fades away in the heat of the day (4:5, 16-17). Mark shows this very thing happening.

68. There is a question as to why Mark does not say, as Matthew does (Matt. 26:8), that it is the disciples who are angry. Mark simply says, "some were there who said to one another in anger . . ." (14:4). Perhaps the incident was well enough known in the early church that everyone knew who had protested this act of anointing. Perhaps the incident is meant to illustrate the general reaction to Jesus on the part of those who were close to him (which would have included the Twelve).

69. Larry W. Hurtado, *Mark: A Good News Commentary* (San Francisco: Harper & Row, 1983), p. 217.

The betrayal by the other eleven disciples is made explicit in the third incident in unit six (the Lord's Supper — 14:12-31). Jesus states quite openly that they will deny him (14:27-31). "You will all become deserters," he says (14:27). The Twelve, of course, deny that they will do this (14:31). However, the first step in this predicted falling away takes place almost immediately. In the very next incident, at Gethsemane, Jesus asks Peter, James, and John to "keep watch" with him (14:34 NIV). He repeats this request twice (14:34, 38), yet three times they fail to do so (14:37, 40, 41). These three failures parallel what Jesus had said earlier to Peter: "This very night, before the cock crows twice, you will deny me three times" (14:30). Peter's coming betrayal is part of a general falling away that is taking place.

The falling away of the Twelve culminates in Judas's betrayal (14:43-46) and Peter's denial (14:66-72). These incidents serve to reveal the true state of the Twelve when it comes to discipleship. With Judas the situation is quite straightforward. Not only has he gone over to the enemies of Jesus, he is willing to identify Jesus by means of a kiss. That which is meant to be a mark of relationship and love becomes a mark of betrayal. Peter is no better. He crumples before the accusations, not of a magistrate or other official, but of a servant girl (14:66-67, 69) and some of the spectators (14:70). Not only is he cowardly, he resorts to lies. His denials start with a mild (but untrue) declaration: "I do not know or understand what you are talking about" (14:68), and move to strong declarations that most likely invoke the name of God to guarantee his truthfulness: "He began to curse, and he swore an oath, 'I do not know this man you are talking about'" (14:71).

Judas is revealed to be without inner commitment to Jesus, but so too is Peter. When Peter states: "I do not know this man," what he says is literally true. He does not (yet) know who Jesus is. When he declares that he is not with Jesus (14:67-68), this is also literally true. He has yet to become a disciple in the way Jesus described in unit four. Peter's statements are examples of the irony that pervades chapters 14 and 15. In the same way that the high priest and Pilate both speak what is absolutely true about Jesus without believing it (14:61; 15:2), so too does Peter (though Peter is unaware of what he is really saying). Peter did indeed know Jesus (certainly in the way his questioners meant), but in fact, he did not know him in the way he needed to know him. Jesus had taught that those who would be his disciples must deny themselves, take up their crosses, and follow him. In fact, Peter denies Jesus, not himself! And he turns his back on cross bearing (in the sense of suffering) because an association with Jesus might result in his own arrest. This incident reveals in a clear way the assertion of this book: that Peter and (by association) the other eleven were not Jesus' disciples in the full sense as defined by Jesus.

The story of Judas ends with his betrayal of Jesus. But Peter's story has a different conclusion. In the very act of denying Jesus, Peter comes to see the truth about himself. He remembers the words of Jesus: "Before the cock crows twice, you will deny me three times" (14:72). As a result, Peter breaks down and weeps. These are the tears of insight, the tears of a man who has suddenly seen the betrayal in his heart and is overwhelmed by the vision. Peter has come to the very end of himself. He has confronted his pretension. He has discovered the inadequacy that lies deep within himself.[70] He who vowed never to fall away from Jesus even if all the others did so, has fallen away (14:29). He who vowed never to disown Jesus even to the point of death, has caved in not at the threat of death but because of the question of a servant girl and the challenge of strangers — none of whom had any real power over him. Peter had stated his allegiance to Jesus using the strongest of language: he insisted "vehemently" that he would not fall away (14:31). And yet, this is exactly what he has done. Furthermore, his denial was couched in the same kind of strong language in which he stated his allegiance. When challenged about Jesus, Peter actually lies, and furthermore, he involves God's name in calling down curses on himself. What depths he has sunk to!

However, when he is confronted with himself by remembering the words of Jesus, Peter finally comes to understand the truth about himself. He is not utterly committed to Jesus and his way as he had supposed. He sees the "hardness of heart" that Jesus spoke to the disciples about (6:52 and 8:17-21). And in seeing this he is enabled to choose another way. He can repent. Seeing the false way he has been walking, he can now choose the new way of cross-bearing discipleship.

The parallel between Paul's experience on the Damascus road and Peter's experience here is very strong. For Paul it simply took one question from Jesus to open his eyes to who he really was (Acts 9:4). For Peter it was the remembered words of Jesus that unlocked for him who he was. The response of Paul to this new insight about himself was that of repentance. So too, by implication, was the response of Peter. His tears are the tears of repentance.

Once again Peter functions as a representative of the Twelve. When Peter vowed that he would never deny Jesus, so did the others (Mark 14:31). Mark then goes on to describe Peter's denial. By implication, the others deny Jesus in like manner. But Peter comes to himself and weeps tears of repen-

---

70. This sort of distress prior to conversion is regularly reported in the literature of conversion. See, for example, William James, *The Varieties of Religious Experience: A Study in Human Nature* (New York: Longmans, Green and Co., 1902; reprint, New York: Random House, The Modern Library, n.d.), chap. 8, and Paul E. Johnson, *Psychology of Religion* (New York: Abingdon, 1954), pp. 103-8.

tance. So too will the other disciples (except for Judas, who by his own choice has moved outside the circle of disciples). For all of them, then, their betrayal of Jesus would be the shock that jolts them into awareness and understanding of who they are and that, therefore, makes repentance possible.

The betrayal by Peter is the last direct description of any of the disciples in Mark's Gospel. However, they are mentioned once more in the epilogue by the young man in white. He instructs the women to tell the disciples and Peter that Jesus is risen and is going ahead of them to Galilee. There, by implication, they will start their journey together all over again. This time the Twelve (with Judas replaced by Matthias — Acts 1:23-26) will be true disciples, having left behind their old, self-centered ways and trusting Jesus, whom they now know as the Messiah, the Son of God. This time they will, indeed, walk the way of true disciples.

The Return to Galilee: Mark 14:28; 16:7

Mark does not describe the change that eventually took place in the disciples. In his account the reader does not see the disciples coming to understand fully who Jesus is or becoming the kinds of disciples Jesus desired. Nor does Mark show them coming to understand the meaning of Jesus' death. And he does not relate the story of their encounters with the resurrected Jesus nor their subsequent ministries in the early church. That story is told by others. However, Mark does give abundant hints that all this will take place. And certainly those to whom Mark originally wrote were well aware of what the disciples had become. They know that the disciples did come to understand what Jesus was trying to teach them. They know that the disciples did open themselves to Jesus in repentance and faith as the Messiah who is the Son of God. They know the place of each of the original Twelve in the ministry of the early church. But Mark's Gospel is not a postresurrection account of the disciples.

What Mark does focus on is the step-by-step process by which the disciples came to understand Jesus, themselves, and the Way to which Jesus called them. These Twelve were ordinary people with ordinary ideas and ordinary failings. As such, their turning charts the way for other ordinary people who would turn to Jesus. Their failings and misunderstandings resonate with the failings and misunderstandings that most people experience. So perhaps the lack of closure in the Gospel account is a good thing. It leaves the question still in the air: Will they or won't they grasp who Jesus is? Will they or won't they turn to him in repentance and faith and so enter the Way of cross-bearing discipleship? The reader is faced with these same questions. Will I come to

Jesus? Will I believe that Jesus is the Messiah, the Son of God? Will I turn from my self-oriented way of life and become an other-oriented disciple of Jesus? Will I return to Galilee and join the band of the disciples as together we join in the mission to which Jesus calls us?

The final and strongest hint of what the disciples will become is found in the epilogue (in particular, 16:7). The young man in white instructs the women to "go, tell his disciples and Peter that he is going ahead of you to Galilee; there you will see him, just as he told you." Four observations need to be made about these instructions. First, Peter is singled out for mention. Perhaps this was necessary because he had separated himself from the others since he was so distraught over his act of betrayal. But whatever the situation, just as it was he who actually betrayed Jesus (the others just fled), so too it is he who is invited by name to Galilee. There is a hint of forgiveness in these words. Jesus has now given his life as a ransom for many, as he predicted (10:45). Peter is certainly among those who will experience the fruits of his redemptive activity.

Second, there is the question of what the disciples will find in Galilee. The suggestion is that they will begin their pilgrimage with Jesus all over again, but this time it will be with eyes wide open and full of understanding. This time they will be his true disciples. This is implied by the word used here for "going ahead." It is *proagei,* the same word used in 6:45; 10:32; 11:9; and 14:28. The meaning of the word in 16:7 is probably the same as in 10:32: "They were on the road, going up to Jerusalem, and Jesus was *walking ahead* of them" (italics mine). In the same way that Jesus once led them on the way to Jerusalem, this time he leads the way back to Galilee.

> Galilee is not just a place. We can see this more clearly if we understand that the geographical journey which Mark constructs and on which Jesus reveals to the disciples the meaning of discipleship is a journey to Jerusalem; right from the north they come down through Galilee and Judea to Jerusalem; there the first part of the journey ends; but it recommences and goes back to Galilee, to the place where Jesus had taught and healed and preached. In the gospel there is a sharp division between Galilee and Jerusalem; the former is the place of mission; the latter the place of death. Once they are through death they are sent back on the mission with Jesus at the head.[71]

The nature of this mission is made clear when the words by which Jesus began the first Galilee mission are recalled: "I will make you fish for people" (1:17). Up to this point in the account there has been little evidence that the

---

71. Best, "Discipleship in Mark," p. 336.

disciples have become "fishers of men" (NIV). The implication is that now they will become what Jesus promised to make them.[72] Prior to the crucifixion this was not possible. Now it is.

Third, the close parallel between the words in 16:7 and those in 14:28 is important. The prophecy of Jesus in 14:28, "But after I am raised up, I will go before you to Galilee," is given in the context of his prediction of their coming betrayal. "The initial prophecy of Jesus *that he would go before them to Galilee is proclaimed as a counteraction to the falling away of the whole company of disciples. . . .* Galilee then becomes the place of *restoration* to Jesus and *reformation* of the scattered company of disciples."[73]

Fourth, in Galilee they will meet the risen Lord. This is the final event that will complete their journey to faith. "Only after the final meeting in Galilee do the disciples really understand — and hence become transformed from those taught into proclaimers of the gospel of Jesus Christ, the Son of God (Mark 1:1)."[74] The disciples have come full circle and their transformation is complete.

The Conversion of the Twelve: A Summary

Did the Twelve undergo the process of conversion, and is this what Mark is writing about in his Gospel? This is the question that was asked at the beginning of this study. To answer it, the experience of Paul on the Damascus road was examined in Part I in order to determine the shape of Christian conversion in the New Testament documents, since most people consider Paul's experience to be the quintessential example of Christian conversion. Three categories were derived from Acts 26:18 as the distinguishing marks of Christian conversion: insight, turning, and transformation. Insight or understanding is what launches conversion. Without a sense of need and an understanding of Jesus, there is no motivation for turning. Why change when all is well? It is insight that prepares the ground for repentance. Having seen reality, you make the decision, on a cognitive level, to turn around and go the other direction. But the decision to turn is one thing; the turning itself is another. When repentance is paired with faith, turning takes place. This is conversion proper. Having understood that you are not walking in God's way, you turn around from that old way and reach out to Jesus by faith so as to walk in his new way.

72. Meye, pp. 83-84. Best, "Discipleship in Mark," p. 336.
73. Meye, p. 84.
74. Meye, p. 85.

The result is new life in Christ. The nature and character of the transformation that takes place is shaped by the walk of discipleship.

When we turn to Mark's Gospel, we find ourselves in the same world of concern. The focus is on Jesus and turning to him in repentance and faith. We watch the Twelve take this journey of turning in which they leave behind both their misunderstanding of Jesus and their hardened hearts. Step by step they come to understand who Jesus is and how to respond to him so as to become his disciples. The prologue to the Gospel tips off the reader as to the central themes. The Gospel is all about Jesus the Messiah who is the Son of God (1:1). The desired response to this good news, we are told, is repentance and faith (1:15). These are the themes that are then explored within the body of Mark's Gospel. In unit one Mark examines the question of how to respond to Jesus. He defines three inadequate responses and sets these over against the one fruitful response. In unit two he looks at the vital role of faith as one responds to Jesus. In unit three he explores the need to understand who Jesus is as well as the need by the disciples to understand the hardness of their hearts. In these first three units the reader watches the slow turning of the Twelve. The concepts of insight, repentance, faith, and turning are not merely discussed, they are experienced by the Twelve. True, the turning is slow and incomplete, but in the first three units the Twelve have moved to a significant new level of understanding. They know Jesus to be a great teacher from God, a powerful prophet inspired by God, and the Messiah sent by God.

Part II of the Gospel begins with a nuanced reflection on the nature of discipleship (i.e., the kind of transformation to which Jesus is calling people). Then in units five and six the Gospel moves to the final weeks of Jesus' life. Here the role of the Twelve is largely reduced to that of observers, as Jesus walks the path that leads to his death and resurrection. At the conclusion of Mark's account the Twelve have all the data before them. They have come to understand who Jesus really is. They know how to turn to him. The final challenge to them (and to the reader) is to return to Galilee. There they will meet the resurrected Jesus and begin their lives of true discipleship.

In other words, the same concerns, the same categories, the same turnings pervade the Gospel of Mark that one finds in the literature about Paul's conversation. Mark shows his readers whom to follow (the focus on Christology in all six units); how to begin following Jesus (the nature of response, the need to understand, and the dynamics of faith and repentance are found in units one to three); and how to continue following Jesus (discipleship in unit four). The experience of Paul and the experience of the Twelve are different, to be sure. The turning of Paul is rapid; the turning of the Twelve is slow. But the core characteristics that define each of these turnings are the same. There is insight (into self and into Jesus); there is the turning itself (from sin/hardness-of-heart to Jesus by repentance and faith); and there is transformation (forgiveness, discipleship, new life). In both accounts — the account of Paul and the account of the Twelve — we are in the same world of conversion.

PART III

EVANGELISM

CHAPTER ELEVEN

Encounter Evangelism: A Critique

In the introduction I described this book as an examination of conversion from the vantage point of practical theology. As such, it is not enough simply to explore various ideas about conversion. It is also necessary to take the next step and ask of these ideas, "So what?" and to do so from the vantage point of the church. Practical theology is, if nothing else, analysis in aid of ministry. So in these final three chapters I want to reflect on the question, What are the implications for the work of evangelism that arise from understanding that there are two paradigms in the New Testament for conversion?

My own sense is that were the church to understand on a deep level *how* Mark is preaching the gospel, this would alter how *we* preach the gospel. So, for example, we would develop new ways to aid those who are "on the way" in their understanding of Jesus, rather than focusing exclusively on individuals who are at the point where they are ready and able to give their lives to Jesus. Likewise, we need to go back to the story of Paul's conversion and make sure we have actually understood what happened there on the Damascus road. Otherwise evangelistic efforts that aim at sudden conversion may owe more to culture than Scripture. Do those activities which seek to reproduce the experience of Paul result in genuine encounters with Jesus, or do they inoculate people against the gospel by offering them an inadequate experience of Jesus? Put another way, do our current practices of evangelism actually draw people to Jesus or repel people from a thoughtful consideration of the gospel? These are the kinds of questions we must raise as we seek to assess our efforts at evangelism on the basis of our understanding of Scripture.

My core perspective in all this is quite simple. I have come to believe that *how we conceive of conversion determines how we do evangelism.* The equation is really that straightforward.

If you conceive of conversion as an event like that which happened to St. Paul, then it is appropriate in your evangelism to confront people with the question, "Will you receive Jesus as your Lord and Savior?" You assume that all people at all times are interested in this question and able to make a meaningful response to it. Thus you will arrange evangelistic events that promote such encounters. So mass evangelism becomes a primary tool of outreach, since it is a structure that enables you to declare publicly who Jesus is and then issue an invitation to accept him as Lord and Savior. Visitation evangelism also makes sense. You knock on doors with the intention of engaging in the kind of conversation that allows you to confront individuals with the need to accept Jesus, then and there, lest they miss out on the free gift of salvation. It even makes sense to pick up hitchhikers, talk with strangers in the mall, or buttonhole relatives at family dinners in order to engage them in conversation the point of which is to encourage them to decide for Jesus.

If, however, you understand conversion to be a process that unfolds over time, as it did for the Twelve, then your question to others is apt to be "Where are you in your spiritual pilgrimage and with what issue are you wrestling when it comes to God?" You assume that different people are at different places in their spiritual pilgrimages and that they need to be assisted in conscious reflection on that pilgrimage (even as you too are engaged in a spiritual pilgrimage and need the help of others to walk in the way of Jesus). The events that you arrange to promote such reflection will assume many forms (and not just a few forms), including such things as small-group Bible studies, seminars on troubling life issues, conversations in which faith journeys are shared, and practical workshops on spiritual disciplines. The point of all these activities will be to assist others in determining where they are in their spiritual pilgrimages, to know what question God is asking of them at each point in that pilgrimage, and at that point to take the next step in a Godward direction.

Since the majority of evangelistic activities in the United States for the past fifty years (at least) have focused on sudden conversion (and the methods that arise from this viewpoint), the challenge to the church is to develop more holistic ways of outreach that take into account the fact that the majority of people come to faith slowly, not suddenly. Of course, this is not an either/or question. People do still come to faith suddenly. So we need to continue to urge people to decide here and now to follow Jesus (though we have to learn to do this in a less combative way). However, the most pressing need is to develop ways of outreach that assist people who are at various places in their spiritual pilgrimages and not only at one point (the point of decision).

What follows here in Part III may be thought of as a reflection on conversion (rather than more research into conversion). It is an attempt to take the key ideas of the book and explore ways in which they impact the work of ministry. Here in chapter 11 I want to begin with an analysis of what I call *encounter evangelism*. This is the term I use for those methods of outreach which seek to bring about in the lives of people Pauline-like encounters with Jesus. In large part, these are the evangelistic methodologies that have been used by the church since World War II. The result is that when you use the word "evangelism," what comes to mind for most people are activities of this sort. The question is: Have we got it right? When we examine these ways of outreach on the basis of the two paradigms for conversion in the New Testament, what we do find?

Then in chapter 12 I want to shift focus and look at *process evangelism,* a term I use for outreach that seeks to assist others to continue on in their spiritual pilgrimages so that they eventually become conscious disciples of Jesus. This way of thinking about evangelism is based on the Marcan paradigm for conversion. In chapter 12 I will propose a theoretical basis for this form of outreach by suggesting a way of thinking about spiritual pilgrimage and then using Mark's sixfold path to a full of understanding of Jesus as a template by which to organize evangelistic activities. Finally, in chapter 13 I want to suggest various ways of doing process evangelism. I cannot describe in full detail these various methods of outreach, but I hope to offer sufficient information so that a thoughtful pastor can develop such programs in his or her church.

There are two parts to what follows here in chapter 11. First I want to describe three general ways of engaging in encounter evangelism: mass evangelism, personal evangelism, and media evangelism. It is important to have clearly in mind the actual character of such evangelistic activities before any assessment of them is made. However, this first section is not just descriptive, as I will begin here my interaction with these forms of outreach. Then, second, I want to use the three-part definition of conversion drawn from Acts 26:18 (insight, turning, transformation) as a way to critique encounter evangelism in general.[1] What can we learn from the two paradigms for conversion that will make our outreach efforts more effective?

1. See above, pp. 25-27.

Encounter-Oriented Evangelistic Activities

Evangelistic activities that create the possibility of sudden conversion are well known in our society. They cluster around three types of outreach: mass evangelism, personal evangelism, and media evangelism.

Mass Evangelism

Mass evangelism is, perhaps, the most familiar form of encounter evangelism. The distinguishing characteristics of mass evangelism include the size of the audience (too large to be engaged individually), the central vehicle of communication (an evangelistic sermon), and the call to decide for Jesus (the invitation or altar call). This type of evangelism occurs in a variety of settings: stadiums, large auditoriums, church sanctuaries, outdoors in tents or on beaches, etc. But venue is not the crucial issue. What sets this style of evangelism apart from other styles is the way in which the audience connects to the presentation. The presentation is almost always in the form of a monologue. As such, no real interaction with the content of that message is possible. Even when potential converts go forward and talk to counselors, discussion is generally not possible. Counselors have very narrowly focused training. Their task is simply to explain how to receive Jesus. In my experience, counselors are often disconcerted by questions and are not prepared to engage in dialogue with the new or potential convert.

At first glance, mass evangelism appears to be a highly effective way of drawing outsiders to Jesus and then into the church. However, research indicates that mass evangelism reaches mostly nominal Christians and helps them to become committed Christians. For example, during the 1956 Graham crusade in Glasgow, Scotland, there were 52,253 decisions for Christ, but only 3,802 joined a local church (a little over 7 percent); and in the Toronto crusade, of the 8,161 inquirers, only 902 joined a church or said they intended to do so (11 percent).[2] One reason for this low response is that many of the people coming forward were already members of churches.

That this is the case was demonstrated via the research that surrounded the 1976 Billy Graham campaign in Seattle. Win Arn, one of the leaders of the church growth movement, was the first to analyze the crusade.[3] This particular

---

2. William G. McLoughlin, *Modern Revivalism* (New York: Ronald Press, 1959), pp. 516-18.

3. Win Arn, "Mass Evangelism: The Bottom Line," *Church Growth: America* 4, no. 1 (1978).

crusade was identified by the Graham organization (in their periodical, *Decision* magazine) as the "most exciting and successful U.S. Billy Graham Crusade in years."[4] A total of 434,100 people attended the crusade, and 18,136 went forward (or stood in place) when the evangelistic invitation was given by Billy Graham.[5] Those who responded filled out a card indicating that they had made some sort of decision for Christ. A year later a follow-up study was conducted by Win Arn and reported in *Church Growth: America* magazine. It was discovered that only 1,285 (15 percent) of those who professed conversion had been incorporated into a church.[6] The conclusion that Arn drew from this study is that there are more effective ways of doing evangelism.

Several years later the Graham organization replied to this criticism via a study (which they commissioned) done by Glenn Firebaugh, an assistant professor of sociology at Vanderbilt University. Firebaugh concluded, as a result of his much more carefully conducted survey, that the Seattle crusade received "relatively high marks in most areas."[7] But he agreed with the main charge in the Arn article, namely, that most of the people who responded during the crusade were already members of churches.[8] Apparently, what happens in mass evangelism is that those with a nominal faith in Jesus take the next step to a vital faith in Jesus. This is a valuable outcome and does justify mass evangelism. However, it also points out that this style of evangelism does not seem to reach many of those who are outside the church.

But it is not just a question of who is reached via mass evangelism. A second question has to do with how many are actually reached (be they nominal church members or genuine outsiders). Mass evangelistic crusades are often quite impressive at first glance. One sees crowds of people streaming to the front of the stadium when the invitation to receive Christ is given. The assumption is that all these people are coming to faith for the first time. And clearly, something important is happening in the lives of people. But are great numbers of people actually, then and there, becoming disciples of Jesus? Again, the research seems to indicate a huge falloff in numbers between those who indicate they have "received Jesus for the first time" and those who actually become disciples of Jesus. For example, Jerry Reed reports the results of an evangelistic crusade in Latin America.

4. As quoted in Arn, p. 5.
5. Arn, p. 5.
6. Arn, p. 7. Of the 434,100 who attended the crusade, only 0.29 percent became new members of a church.
7. Glenn Firebaugh, "How Effective Are City-Wide Crusades?" *Christianity Today,* March 27, 1981, p. 417.
8. Firebaugh, p. 413.

During the Evangelism-in-Depth movement in Ecuador I was responsible for organizing the follow-up for the end-of-the-year evangelistic crusade in the country's capital, Quito. By the close of the crusade 1,234 people had responded to the evangelist's invitation to commit their lives to Jesus Christ. We had well-trained counselors and a good follow-up system networking with most of the area churches and leaders. Yet one year later when I went back to study the results of that big evangelistic campaign, only 64 people (5%) could be found in churches and most of those churches were within easy walking distance of the coliseum where the meetings had been held. . . . I might add that the net results for Ecuador of that year-long saturation-evangelism thrust of Evangelism-in-Depth, was a grand total of sixteen more people added to the church than would have been added without the movement!

The same was true for the Luis Palau crusade a couple of years later in Quito.[9]

In addition, there is some indication that Generation X is being reached by mass evangelism — at least in some places by some evangelists. For example, Greg Laurie, a Calvary Chapel pastor with a substantial ministry to people in their teens, twenties, and early thirties, uses this methodology to good effect. His Harvest Crusades are an annual event in southern California. However, even here a gap is evident between those who respond and those who continue to follow Jesus. "Greg Laurie's staff estimates that 16,000 conversions occurred at Harvest Christian Fellowship in the five-year period from 1986 to 1991. Admittedly, perhaps only 10 percent of these decisions result in long-term changes in personal behavior, but even with these attrition rates a substantial number of people have been affected."[10]

Mass evangelism has had a long history in America, extending from the revivalism of the Great Awakenings (in the eighteenth and nineteenth centuries) to the mass rallies of Billy Sunday and Billy Graham (and others) in the twentieth century.[11] Up until the 1960s this form of outreach was the predominant way of doing evangelism in the United States.[12] However, a shift

9. Jerry Reed, "Lasting Fruit in Evangelism," *Journal of the Academy for Evangelism in Theological Education* 11 (1995-96): 48-49.

10. Donald Miller, *Reinventing American Protestantism: Christianity in the New Millennium* (Berkeley: University of California Press, 1997), pp. 171-72. See also Miller's description of Harvest Crusades on pp. 53-54.

11. See John Mark Terry, *Evangelism: A Concise History* (Nashville: Broadman & Holman, 1994), chaps. 9–12.

12. It is true, however, that during this time period many people joined churches as the result of the ministry of local churches. Sometimes this was the result of intentional

took place in the sixties. Visitation evangelism became the new method of choice.

Personal Evangelism

Personal evangelism (of which visitation evangelism is one example) is the second major type of encounter evangelism, and is distinguished from mass evangelism in several ways. First, the audience is an individual, not a group. Second, the presentation is via personal testimony in which there is a description of a "plan of salvation" rather than via a sermon. Third, the call to commitment comes in the context of a conversation and not in an after-meeting.

At the heart of personal evangelism is conversation. This is not random conversation nor general conversation about religion or spirituality. This is carefully crafted conversation in which the Christian "witness" (which is how people generally view themselves in such situations) seeks to guide the dialogue in predetermined ways. Such conversations are initiated by means of provocative questions (e.g., "Suppose you were to die today and stand before God and He were to say to you, 'Why should I let you into My heaven?' what would you say?"),[13] religious surveys (which are often never tallied), or personal testimony (a carefully prepared description of one's conversion). The aim of the conversation is to come to the point at which a gospel outline can be presented via a brief monologue. The same outline is presented to all people. (There are, however, many different outlines, ranging from the Four Spiritual Laws of Campus Crusade to the Bridge Illustration of the Navigators.) The culmination of the presentation is a challenge to accept Jesus now, by praying a prayer of commitment.

The context of such conversations varies. Sometimes they take place with a friend or family member in a casual setting; more often such witness is given to strangers at a shopping mall, to a person you happen to sit next to on an airplane, or to individuals in other chance encounters. The best-organized form of personal witness comes in the form of door-to-door visitation.

Visitation is not a new methodology. In fact, it was used by the Ameri-

---

evangelistic activities on the part of the church, but mostly people came into churches because of the general activities of the church. The major exception to this generalization is the Southern Baptist Convention, which was actively involved in intentional evangelism between 1900 and 1960 via revival meetings, Sunday schools, and simultaneous crusades through local associations. See Terry, pp. 187-88.

13. D. James Kennedy, *Evangelism Explosion* (Wheaton, Ill.: Tyndale House, 1970), p. 22.

can church as early as the 1870s when Dwight L. Moody made it a part of his crusades. From 1913 to 1929 citywide visitation efforts were organized in many places. One evangelist, A. Earl Kernahan, using visitation methodologies he refined, claimed that between 1923 and 1929 some 370,750 people were visited, with 185,867 being converted.[14] But it was not until the Evangelism Explosion program of D. James Kennedy that this methodology came to the attention of the church in general. Kennedy's church, Coral Ridge Presbyterian, grew from an initial membership of 45 in 1959 to become a megachurch with 4,500 members in 1977 — all through the use of visitation evangelism.[15] Kennedy wrote about this form of outreach and organized training programs which were attended by thousands of pastors and laypeople.

In the 1980s a new form of personal evangelism was developed. It came to be known as lifestyle evangelism.[16] Lifestyle evangelism emerged because of the problems inherent in prior forms of personal evangelism. For one thing, while personal evangelism defined itself as a "conversation," in actual fact the potential convert was the passive recipient of a preprepared presentation. Real dialogue, including wrestling with hard questions and confronting genuine doubt, was not encouraged. The point of personal evangelism was to "make the pitch" and "close the deal." It seemed, at times, more like a religious sales presentation than a genuine dialogue between friends. And in fact, some literature consciously describes personal evangelism in business transaction terms.[17] For a second thing, personal evangelism focused on a standard presentation that was seldom, if ever, personalized. The assumption was that everybody was able to understand and connect to the same outline of the gospel.

But can the gospel be reduced to an outline? Does not this sort of outline simplify and codify the message in such a way as to obscure the multifaceted richness of the good news? This is not to say that the "gospel" cannot be

14. Terry, pp. 185-86.

15. See his book *Evangelism Explosion* for a description of this method.

16. For a discussion of lifestyle evangelism, see Rebecca Pippert, *Out of the Salt Shaker and into the World* (Downers Grove, Ill.: InterVarsity Press, 1979); Jim Petersen, *Evangelism as a Lifestyle* (Colorado Springs: NavPress, 1980); Joseph C. Aldrich, *Life-Style Evangelism* (Portland, Oreg.: Multnomah Press, 1981); and Paige Patterson, "Lifestyle Evangelism," in *Evangelism in the Twenty-First Century: The Critical Issues*, ed. Thom S. Rainer (Wheaton, Ill.: Harold Shaw, 1989), pp. 41-49.

17. Jim Petersen talks about his original conception of what a "good witness" was like. ". . . I imagined a good witness was like a good salesman — unabashed, aggressive, fearless of strangers." His book was written in order to suggest a new way of understanding witness. Petersen, p. 27.

defined. The gospel is a limited domain of doctrine.[18] But people connect in different ways to the death and resurrection of Jesus. Would it not be better simply to be in touch with the key aspects of the gospel (such as the nature, work, and call of Jesus and the dynamics of repentance and faith) and let the conversation flow around these issues? Different people will make different (life-changing) connections to this message. But, alas, such a way of talking about the gospel is not easily or quickly taught to impatient American Christians who want quick results and easy systems.

> Evangelicals may be far too eager to erase the unruly elements of the conversion process, while packaging the gospel for easy, rapid, and strain-free consumption. Such cognitive reductionism means that the "spiritual" aspects of evangelical life are increasingly approached by means of and interpreted in terms of principles, rules, steps, laws, codes, guidelines, and so forth.
>
> A uniformity of process quite often aims at a uniformity of product, while ignoring the uniqueness of the individual and the varieties of religious experiences.[19]

Personal evangelism turns out to be impersonal evangelism. There is little space for making links between the needs and aspirations of the seeker and that aspect of the gospel that speaks to these particular needs or aspirations. Furthermore, the language of the gospel outline is often laden with theological terms that are seldom explained, unpacked, or translated. Again, the assumption is that anyone is able to grasp the essential meaning of the gospel even if that person has little or no understanding of the biblical terms being used.

Furthermore, it seems that personal evangelism works best in anonymous situations rather than with friends and family who demand real dialogue, genuine conversation, and honesty. So evangelists knocked on doors in neighborhoods or dormitories, passed out tracts in public buildings or on street corners, and picked up hitchhikers. The name often given to this form of personal outreach was "cold turkey" evangelism.

Lifestyle evangelism sought to address these issues. It did this by focusing on friendship. Christians were urged to build relationships with people outside

18. See the provocative discussion of the kerygma in Harry L. Poe, *The Gospel and Its Meaning: A Theology for Evangelism and Church Growth* (Grand Rapids: Zondervan, 1996).

19. Darius Salter, *American Evangelism: Its Theology and Practice* (Grand Rapids: Baker, 1996), pp. 208-9.

the church. It was in the context of these relationships that the gospel could be discussed. The words one spoke about Christ would make sense since your friend would have seen how you lived out these commitments in your daily life. Furthermore, conversations about Christianity would take place over time in response to the interest and needs of the friend as well as through your own openness about your spiritual pilgrimage. In the course of conversation you could confront and discuss the questions of your friend so that these impediments to faith could be defused. Stories could be shared that communicated the reality of the spiritual. An appeal for decision was still needed, but this would come in the context of ongoing conversation that is the natural activity of real friends. Clearly, lifestyle evangelism had moved away from encounter evangelism in the direction of process-oriented evangelism.

The biggest problem in lifestyle evangelism, however, was developing friendships with non-Christians. Aldrich (and others) points out that many Christians do not have meaningful relationships with anyone but other Christians. This raises the whole question of motives for friendship. Should one cast about for a relationship with a non–church person simply because this will give one the opportunity to witness (albeit in a nonmechanistic way)? Surely this is a flawed motivation that cannot reap true friendship. Rather, the challenge is for a person to be open to friendship with all sorts of people and not just seek relationships with people who might be interested in one's church or in Christianity.

Media Evangelism

Media evangelism is a variation on mass evangelism in that the gospel is presented to a large audience. The key difference between the two is that the media evangelist is separated by space and time from the actual audience. There are various forms of media evangelism. Radio was the first medium used for evangelism.[20] In 1925 approximately 10 percent of the 600 radio stations in the United States were owned by churches and other religious organizations.[21] By the 1940s evangelist Charles E. Fuller had a weekly audience of over twenty million listeners for his *Old Fashioned Revival Hour*.[22] When tele-

20. The first broadcast of a church service took place on January 2, 1921, over KDKA in Pittsburgh, Pennsylvania. Terry, p. 199.

21. Jeffrey K. Hadden and Charles E. Swann, *Prime Time Preachers* (Reading, Mass.: Addison-Wesley, 1981), pp. 73-75.

22. Daniel P. Fuller, *Give the Winds a Mighty Voice: The Story of Charles E. Fuller* (Waco, Tex.: Word, 1972), p. 238.

vision became a national medium in the 1950s, it too was used for evangelism. Figures such as Oral Roberts, Rex Humbard, Pat Robertson, Jim Bakker, Jimmy Swaggart, and Robert Schuller flourished in the 1970s and 1980s. However, due to the scandal connected to some of these televangelists (related to sex and money), their popularity began to decline in the late 1980s.

Film is a third media format that has been used evangelistically. Pioneers in this form of outreach include the Moody Science Films and Billy Graham films. The first film made by the Billy Graham organization was in 1950. Since then, via World Wide Pictures (their film production arm), the Billy Graham organization has produced over one hundred films, including the widely acclaimed story of Corrie ten Boom entitled *The Hiding Place.*[23]

At first glance, media evangelism appears to be the vehicle of choice to deliver the gospel. Vast audiences can be reached simultaneously. People who would not darken the door of a church can watch and listen in the privacy of their own homes. Media presentations can be done professionally so that they are attractive, entertaining, and interesting (in comparison with some church services). But there is a real question as to how many people are actually reached for Christ via this medium.

Media evangelism is a useful test case in assessing the essence of encounter evangelism. According to encounter evangelism, the task is to proclaim the gospel message. The assumption is that once this is done, people can and will "make decisions for Jesus." What is meant by this is, they will come to Jesus in the way St. Paul did, i.e., they will have sudden conversions. Furthermore, it is assumed that these converts can and will continue to follow Jesus as his lifelong disciples. And yet, even though the gospel message has been presented endlessly in America via radio and television and in evangelistic films, the fact is that relatively few people seem to be reached in this way. A key problem is that most viewers and listeners are already Christians. Seekers do not watch much Christian television or film, nor do they pay much attention to Christian radio. Furthermore, those who do respond to the message are not often followed up on (nor can they be incorporated easily into a Christian community, given the distance that separates the audience from the evangelist). There is an intense individualism to media evangelism. Television threatens to become an "electronic church" with a congregation of one, with no personal contact, and where "my minister" is a figure who appears on a screen. But being a disciple of Jesus means joining the community of others who seek to follow him.

The challenges are all here in media evangelism. Is "preaching the gos-

23. McLoughlin, p. 492.

pel" all there is to evangelism — when this is understood to mean a verbal presentation that focuses on a standard outline?[24] Does the call to "accept Jesus now" cover the situation and needs of all the people? Is not follow-up an essential aspect of evangelism? Does encounter evangelism actually bring people to the place where they meet Jesus the way Paul did?

The Problem of Overfamiliarity

The problem with a lot of these evangelistic activities is that they have lost their effectiveness because of their familiarity. Most Americans, for example, have a rough idea of what to expect in an evangelistic rally even though they may have never personally attended such an event. Billy Graham Crusades are often broadcast on television, and enough films portray evangelistic meetings (though often in caricatured form) that the phenomenon is familiar. Likewise, visitation evangelism is well known, so much so that most people have a built-in response when they see two strangers dressed in dark suits and holding Bibles knocking on their doors.[25] The tracts we receive from well-meaning strangers on a street corner contain messages we have heard before.[26]

Of course, it is one thing to read or hear familiar words and quite another for those words to impress themselves deeply upon you in a way that causes you to respond to them. So an argument can be made that we just have to keep repeating the message over and over until it finally sinks in. But it can also be argued (as George Barna does) that America is saturated with the gospel. He points out the following facts:

- More than $200 million is spent every year on television evangelism.
- An additional $100 million is spent on radio evangelism.
- In the decade of the 1990s, the goal is to start forty thousand new

24. See William J. Abraham, *The Logic of Evangelism* (Grand Rapids: Wm. B. Eerdmans Publishing Co., 1989), pp. 40-69, for a penetrating discussion of the problem of defining evangelism as proclamation.

25. Even Gary Larson has cartoons about visitation evangelism. In one, a cow is at the door of another cow's house, saying, "Listen, — just take one of our brochures [entitled *Cowintology*] and see what we're all about. . . . In the meantime, you may wish to ask yourself, 'Am I a happy cow?'" In another cartoon, entitled "The Blob Family at Home," the father "blob" spots two people coming to the door and shouts out, "Jehovah's Witnesses! Jehovah's Witnesses! . . . Everyone act like bean bag chairs!" (The Blob family look like oversized beanbags.)

26. Campus Crusade alone has distributed literally millions of tracts containing "The Four Spiritual Laws."

churches as a means of reaching every person in the nation with the gospel.

- There are more than five thousand nonchurch organizations whose primary purpose is evangelism.
- There are more than two thousand itinerant evangelists.
- The aggregate revenues each year from Christian books and music exceed $1 billion, and as much as 10 percent of this total is associated with products that are evangelistic in nature.[27]

With such an outpouring of evangelistic effort, why have not more people been converted?[28] And why are so few people (including many who claim conversion) able to answer even the most rudimentary questions about the Christian faith?[29] Why is it that even though, according to Barna, roughly nine out of ten Americans (88 percent) label themselves Christians, the lifestyle, social involvement, ethical conduct, and relational life of this nation are in such chaos?[30] Apparently we are preaching the gospel but nobody is listening, or if they are listening they are not responding, or if they are responding it is in a partial way that seems to have little impact on mind, will, or behavior.

With such poor results from traditional evangelism, a good case can be made for reorienting how we do evangelism. This would involve both a rethinking of how we engage in encounter evangelism and the development of new means by which to engage in process evangelism. When we do evangelism, we need to give ourselves over to the task of helping people become disciples of Jesus and not simply be content with making converts. All this is an

27. George Barna, *Evangelism That Works* (Ventura, Calif.: Regal, 1995), pp. 33-35.

28. Part of the issue, of course, has to do with how one determines whether a person is or is not a Christian. While it is doubtful that the 81 percent of the American population who claim to be Christians are, in fact, committed disciples of Jesus (this figure is taken from the Gallup polls; see chap. 12, p. 314; Barna puts this figure at 88 percent), it is probably also true that the pessimistic assessment of Barna (and others) that only 29 percent of our population (75 million people out of 262 million; Barna, p. 22) is actually Christian is also suspect. Where the truth lies is impossible to determine. Such a pessimistic assessment is a product of the encounter paradigm, where all people are either in or out and little notice is taken of the fact that many people are involved in a faith pilgrimage.

29. For example, nine out of ten adult Americans are unable to define the meaning of the Great Commission; seven out of ten do not know what the term "John 3:16" means; and only one-third know the meaning of the expression "the gospel" (Barna, p. 35). Barna goes on to say: "More adults are capable of accurately naming the top-rated prime-time television shows . . . than are able to accurately state the defining theme of the Christian faith" (p. 36).

30. Barna call this a "culture in crisis" (pp. 19-21).

argument for the *unfamiliar* when it comes to evangelism. The familiar, it seems, is being tuned out.

An Assessment of Encounter Evangelism

The challenge is to rework these traditional methods of evangelism so that they regain their effectiveness. Here is where Mark and Luke can help. When encounter evangelism is viewed through the lens of the two New Testament paradigms, what does one see? What are the strengths of such approaches? What are the issues that need attention or correction? What are the challenges to these ways of doing evangelism that come from the New Testament? A helpful way of getting at these issues is by means of the three categories that define conversion: insight, turning, and transformation. By examining the practices of encounter evangelism in light of these three issues, it is possible to hear what Mark and Acts have to say to us.

Insight

Conversion begins with insight. Without insight the whole process is stopped even before it starts. Unless people have a reason to respond to Jesus they will not respond to Jesus. Such insight needs to extend in two directions: insight into who Jesus is and insight into who we are. Sometimes it is the amazing appeal of Jesus and his call to be part of the in-breaking of the kingdom of God that draws us to him. At other times it is the awareness of our lostness, our brokenness, or our neediness that draws us to Jesus as the one who can heal, forgive, and restore us. How well does contemporary evangelism do when it comes to assisting others to "see" who Jesus is and to discern their need for him?

Understanding Jesus

Within American culture the name of Jesus is well known, but the question is whether people have an accurate view of who he really is. Mark reminds us that in order to be disciples of Jesus we must know the real Jesus. So the call to follow Jesus dare not be reduced to a call to follow the Jesus of popular culture. It was the Jesus of popular culture that the Twelve began to follow. In first-century Israel most agreed that Jesus was an effective teacher — both his allies (the crowds) who loved his teaching and his enemies (the religious leaders) who hated his popularity. But if Mark's Gospel says nothing else, it says it is not enough to follow this Jesus. He is so much more than a great teacher. And he requires a different kind of commitment than the one a person gives to a teacher.

Look at what happened to the crowds who flocked to his teaching. In the end they left Jesus. Their commitment was not strong enough to withstand the pressure. It withered because it had no root. Presumably they went on to follow other teachers. Nor was it enough to follow Jesus as if he were just a powerful prophet. In the end, this too is self-serving because it is all about what we can get from Jesus. The Twelve learned that it was not even enough to follow him as the Messiah. They had to understand what kind of Messiah he was before their commitment was complete (which is what the second half of Mark's Gospel is all about). To whom do we call people in our evangelism?

When we engage in encounter evangelism, we must be quite clear about the Jesus we preach. We need to make sure that the Jesus we present is the Jesus of the New Testament and not the Jesus of culture. Mark's sixfold description of Jesus is a useful gauge for us to make sure that our presentation is accurate. Do we present Jesus as one who teaches a particular way which we are called to follow (Teacher)? Do we present Jesus as one empowered by God to do God's works in this world (Prophet)? Do we present Jesus as the one who is chosen of God to fulfill the purposes of God (Messiah)? Do we present Jesus as the one who gave his life for us and all humankind in a redemptive way (Son of Man)? Do we present Jesus as the Lord of the Universe and our rightful King to whom we owe allegiance and obedience (Son of David)? Do we present Jesus as God amongst us (Son of God)?

Of course, no one presentation can hope to capture all this content, much less nuance it as Mark has done. But we can replicate the central vision found in Mark's Gospel. Even when time and circumstance do not allow us to express fully who Jesus is, what we do say must be in accord with the basic blueprint found in Mark (and elsewhere in the New Testament). So many presentations seem to portray a Jesus who is a product of our own making: one who gives gifts we desire, who demands nothing, and who is what we want to make him. I suspect that if we were to make the Jesus of the New Testament the core of the message, fewer might respond but more would stay on with Jesus.

This is not to say that before one can become a follower of Jesus, he or she needs a theologically nuanced understanding of Jesus. Clearly men and women down through the ages have followed Jesus even though their understanding of him was minimal. But what little they knew was accurate: that he was touched by God; that he was a person like us; that he made forgiveness and the way back to God possible; that he called us to follow him, and the way in which he led us was God's way. There are different ways of phrasing this, but each phrase focuses on Jesus as sent by God, Jesus as God, Jesus as one whose death and resurrection is redemptive, and Jesus as one come to lead us in God's way. Each carries the sense that to commit oneself to Jesus is to enter into a Way. As people begin to follow that Way, they grow in their under-standing of Jesus. In fact, this is part of the adventure: to grow in our knowl-edge of Jesus. This is a venture that takes a lifetime. This is what discipleship is all about.

Understanding Ourselves

A second question relates to this whole issue of insight. Why bother with Je-sus at all if all is well in our lives? Part of the evangelistic task is to alert men and women to the reality of their situations from a spiritual point of view. They need to know that though they are created to know God, by nature they are cut off from God. They are called to love God, but by instinct they love lesser gods. They are called to be part of the kingdom of God, but by default they inhabit the kingdom of this world. How can we help others to see clearly who they are and what they are missing by living apart from God?

Traditionally, "sin" has been a major theme in evangelistic presenta-tions. In order to alert people to their spiritual peril, evangelists have painted vivid and graphic pictures of hell (as the outcome of lostness) and described human nature in extreme and unflattering ways (to puncture false under-standings of the self). In recent years human "need" has often been cast into psychological terms. The focus has been on such issues as broken relation-ships and addictive behaviors as signs of lostness. In addition, the appeal has been to the yearning for wholeness or the longing for reconciliation as a rea-son to come back to God. Clearly, both Mark and Luke would recognize the legitimacy of such appeals as ways to bring about the kind of personal insight that sets the stage for conversion. Luke uses terms such as "darkness," "Satan," and "sin" to describe these realities. Mark talks about hardness of heart and hypocrisy. Whatever the language, the aim is personal insight.

However, the problem in some encounter evangelism is that the meth-ods used to bring about such insight have been so confrontational that they have become counterproductive. In fact, to many people the word "evange-list" brings to mind a finger-pointing, in-your-face, angry person who de-mands that you accept Jesus because otherwise you are going to hell since you are such an evil person. While there is caricature in this image, there is also some truth. A lot of evangelism does feel like religious confrontation that arises more out of anger and judgment than out of love and hope. It is almost as if such evangelists feel it their responsibility to set people right and to make it abundantly clear to them that they are in deep trouble when it comes to God. They may say, "God loves you and has a wonderful plan for your life," but what they actually communicate is "God is really mad at you, and unless you get with his plan you are in deep trouble."

Confrontation is often antithetical to both communication and commitment. Confrontation raises defenses — just as Jesus told us would happen ("Do not judge, so that you may not be judged" [Matt. 7:1]). If our true desire is for people to face clearly the reality of God, to understand who Jesus is, and to decide to follow Jesus as his disciples, then this goal is better served via the path of love, not judgment. God judges; we do not. The challenge is to present a clear and accurate picture of the human situation, and to do so in ways that draw people to Jesus as the one who answers our deepest needs and brings out in us our true callings.

Turning

Conversion begins with insight. But insight must result in turning. It is not enough to know; we must also act. To turn requires that we respond to our insight in various ways. First, we must turn around in terms of ourselves. To repent means to decide to stop living the way we once did (in sin, apart from God) and to start living in a new way (as a follower of Jesus walking in the way of God). Second, we must turn around in terms of Jesus. To have faith means to reach out to Jesus and to leave behind the darkness in which we once lived. At the center of this turning is Jesus, nothing else. He is the pivot point of the turning. We turn from not understanding who he is to understanding that he is the Messiah, the Son of God; from not following him to following him; from not being his disciple to being his disciple. So the challenge is to make this call to commitment one that reflects the nature of turning as portrayed in the New Testament.

One Call or Many Calls?

This whole issue of the call to commitment is important in evangelism because it distinguishes evangelism from other activities in the church: urging others to respond to God through Jesus Christ.

This call to respond characterizes both process evangelism and encounter evangelism. However, the way in which a call to commitment is expressed distinguishes the two approaches to evangelism. In encounter-oriented evangelism there are one call, one response, one commitment. Jesus is presented as the person to whom allegiance is due, here and now, in the moment. Either you believe in Jesus or you do not.[31] For those who are at the point in their pilgrimages where they can respond, this is a life-changing call. For all others this single call fails to define how they need to respond to God. In process-oriented evangelism there are many calls to commitment, each of which moves a person closer to Jesus or further along as a disciple of Jesus. Another way of saying this is that there is a single call to become a disciple of Jesus in encounter evangelism. But in process evangelism this call is broken up into a number of smaller calls to respond, each of which moves people step-by-step to Jesus until they become his committed disciples. In both cases the aim is the same: that men and women open themselves to Jesus and by repentance and faith become his disciples.

The challenge for traditional encounter evangelism is to see that while some people are ready and able to respond to Jesus, not all are. Conversion can be sudden, but mostly it is gradual. Furthermore, the validity of conversion is not found in the speed of turning. It is found in the nature of commitment (to Jesus by repentance and faith). This being the case, evangelistic activities need to be more broadly targeted. Rather than always focusing on a single issue ("Accept Jesus now"), a more nuanced presentation of Jesus could be made. For example, a sermon could be preached at a rally in which people are challenged, as a first step in investigating Jesus, to accept Jesus as a great religious teacher and then to study his teachings with an eye to following these teachings in their lives. Concrete help, such as a set of Bible studies, could be provided to facilitate such a process. When people actually study what Jesus taught, they quickly encounter what he taught about himself, which in turn leads to new insight into Jesus and, hopefully, new commitment to Jesus.

But there is another side to this. From Paul we learn that there are people ready and able to commit their lives to Jesus, and we learn that it is possible to decide for Jesus in the moment. The strength of encounter evangelism is found in the clarity of the call to decide for Jesus and in the constant urging

---

31. See the paper by Paul Hiebert ("Conversion, Culture, and Cognitive Categories," *Gospel in Context* 1 [1978]: 24-29) for a useful discussion of different cognitive paradigms and how such paradigms influence our understanding of conversion. For example, when we think in bounded-set terms this "in or out" mentality dominates, whereas when we begin to think in centered-set terms we come to view people in relationship to which direction they are traveling when it comes to God: toward or away from God.

of others to become disciples of Jesus here and now. The challenge for process evangelism is not to lose sight of the fact that the aim in evangelism is full commitment to Jesus and not just progress in the spiritual pilgrimage. The danger in process evangelism is that people are always questing after but never finding God, much less giving their allegiance to Jesus.

Mystical Encounters

The aim of encounter evangelism is sudden conversion, and the model for this is what happened to St. Paul on the Damascus road. Events are organized to replicate this experience in the lives of others. However, it is important to notice that *for Paul to be converted in an instant, it took a mystical encounter with Jesus.* Mystical encounters cannot be orchestrated. They simply happen — to some people (and not all), and then only on certain unpredictable occasions. Yet at the heart of the sudden conversion paradigm is a mystical encounter with Jesus.

So the question must be asked as to whether we are, in fact, bypassing this central feature of Paul's experience in our evangelistic efforts. While it is true that in certain evangelistic contexts (e.g., an evangelistic meeting in a stadium) men and women do sometimes have mystical encounters with Jesus, this is the exception and not the rule. Yet people who "come forward" are treated as though they have just encountered Jesus in this kind of way. Might it not be better to assume that most of the people gathered at the front of the stadium for the after-meeting are simply responding to a new understanding of Jesus? For some, their journey to Jesus culminates in this act of coming forward, but most of those coming forward have more steps to take in order for their commitment to be fully formed. Do we not, at times, short-circuit the work of the Holy Spirit by positing that when someone says yes to Jesus, he or she is fully committed to Jesus? We need to develop ways to help people build upon the genuine response they have to Jesus (no matter its specific content) so as to move them in the direction of fuller commitment to Jesus.

What about this thing of a mystical experience? According to the Greeley and McCready study, fully one-third of adult Americans have had mystical experiences.[32] However, a mystical experience is not the same as a conversion experience. Paul had a mystical experience, but for that event to change his life (conversion) he had to own his past (repentance) and affirm a new future (acceptance of his call to follow Jesus). Thus the question for those

32. See p. 88.

who have had present-day mystical experiences is whether these have led to conversion. My own sense is that the mystical experience of many people has remained merely an experience — an important experience, even an experience that changed their view of God, of death, etc., but still not something that has been integrated into who they are on a daily basis in their lives. This touch by God has not transformed them into disciples.

My suggestion is that we build into our evangelistic efforts the awareness that a lot of people have had mystical experiences but most have not responded to them. In other words, it makes good sense to ask people to recall those moments in their lives in which they were aware of the presence, power, and love of God and then invite them to respond to the God they met in such mystical moments. Our point of contact is with their deepest aspirations, since mystical experiences create a longing for the Divine. For such people Jesus becomes the bridge between an experience of God and a lifestyle rooted in the presence of God.

Transformation

The proof that we have turned is found in the transformation of our lives. Without transformation there is no real conversion. But transformation is expressed in different ways: e.g., via the experience of forgiveness, through the sense of call, or in the activities of discipleship. In each case something discernible takes place in how we live and who we are. Conversion does not stay in the head as mere information. The challenge to the evangelist is to help people move from being converts to becoming disciples. The temptation for the evangelist is to move on too quickly to other people before helping those just reached to be firmly established in the faith.

The Problem of Follow-Up

It is one thing to call men and women to commitment; it is another to see them grounded enough in the faith so that they are functioning as followers of Jesus. In American evangelism we have been quite good at creating *converts* (i.e., those who respond at the conclusion of an evangelistic presentation) but not nearly as good at generating *disciples* (i.e., those who actively pursue a life given over to following Jesus). The statistics cited above in the discussion of mass evangelism indicate the extent of the problem. This problem may be the most severe in mass or media evangelism because of the distance that separates the convert from both the evangelist and the church. But helping converts become disciples is a troubling issue in all forms of evangelism.

The traditional name for this sort of activity is "follow-up." In some mass evangelistic contexts follow-up has been quite sophisticated. For example, when I was working with African Enterprise doing citywide preaching missions in South Africa, we developed a five-tiered form of follow-up. On the first level we sent literature to the new convert. This consisted of a series of letters, each of which touched on a particular issue related to following Jesus; booklets that dealt with specific problems that new converts wonder about; and a Bible study series that focused on what it meant to be a disciple of Jesus.[33] On the second level we arranged a series of small groups to which converts were invited and in which themes in Christian living were explored. On a third level we conducted a series of weekly follow-up lectures in which a skilled teacher covered these same areas. On a fourth level we arranged weekend retreats as a way of helping people connect together as disciples of Jesus seeking to be active members of a church. Finally, on a fifth level we assisted local churches to provide specific activities designed around the needs of new converts. Of course, not all converts availed themselves of each set of activities, and some activities worked better in certain locations than in others. Still, the goal was to help converts become disciples, and our motivation was to deal with the sometimes appalling gap between those who respond positively at evangelistic events and those who actually continue following Jesus.

Whatever means we use, we cannot bypass the problem of follow-up. This is not an optional activity. As seen in both Mark and Acts, transformation is part of the conversion experience.

It might be argued that the failure to do effective follow-up is most noticeable in encounter evangelism. The statistics indicate that on average only 10 percent of those who respond at an evangelistic meeting become active disciples of Jesus. So the question becomes: What about the other 90 percent? Could it be that for these "lost converts" the whole experience might turn out to be counterproductive? In their minds, they "tried Jesus" and it didn't work (for whatever reason), so they are less likely to make such a response in the future. It is almost as if they have been immunized against Christianity by being given a small dose of the gospel.

33. This was the original version of the three-part Learning to Love Bible study series: *Learning to Love God; Learning to Love Ourselves;* and *Learning to Love Others,* published jointly by InterVarsity Press (Downers Grove, Ill., 1968) and Zondervan Publishing House (Grand Rapids, Mich., 1968).

Another related issue is the whole question of "results." In evangelism numbers have come to be very important. Police are asked to estimate the size of crowds at evangelistic rallies. Supporters are encouraged by glowing reports as to how many "responded to Jesus" at the latest crusade. Books are promoted by indicating how many were reached using the method of outreach described by the author. But is it really responsible to count converts? Should we not be counting disciples (if we count at all)? And then, what about all those who do not respond to our evangelistic efforts? Have we helped them or hindered them in their spiritual pilgrimages? Sometimes manipulative methods may yield a lot of converts, but the very methods used repel those who do not respond and make them wary of evangelism (and of Jesus?). Can the positive impact on the few justify the negative impact on the many?

The Clarity of Call

I think there may be another reason why so many converts fail to become disciples. This has to do with the lack of clarity in our call to turn to Jesus. Sometimes in evangelistic events it sounds as if the call is to come to Jesus in order to get what you need in life. "What you need" is framed differently in different events. In some cases the gift is salvation which protects one from eternal damnation. In other cases the gift is a new life in which one's problems are dealt with. In the worst cases the gift that is promised if you come to Jesus is the realization of your fantasies: wealth, health, success, power. This is not to say that Jesus does not bring salvation, new life, healing, aid in troubling situations, or any other gift. It is to say that the end result of commitment is a relationship with Jesus, not a gift of some sort. Such gifts emerge out of the very character of our relationship with Jesus.

For example, the meaning of salvation is that we will continue on in relationship to Jesus after this life ends. Even death cannot sever our relationship to Jesus. The gift of salvation is endemic to our relationship with Jesus. So too are the other gifts. New life emerges as we reorient ourselves around the way of life to which Jesus calls us. The forgiveness we offer to others and which repairs relationships is made possible by the forgiveness we receive from Jesus. The truth we find by listening to Jesus brings clarity and a worldview that enables us to navigate through life. The love we experience in knowing Jesus casts out fear. The community that comes as we connect with others who seek to follow Jesus brings support, care, and burden bearing. The worship we offer God produces joy and gratitude. And so the list goes on. To follow Jesus is good for us, as E. Stanley Jones (amongst others) has pointed out, but the reason we follow Jesus is not to gain a good life.[34] We become disciples of Jesus because of who he is and who we are. Love, longing, need, and aspiration motivate discipleship, not "what's in it for me." When we make the outcome of commitment into something other than discipleship to Jesus, we blur, mute, distort, obscure, or even deny what conversion is all about.

Critiquing Encounter Evangelism

It is important that the comments in this chapter be understood in the way they are intended. My aim has not been to dismiss encounter evangelism as an undesirable activity for the church. Encounter evangelism is not wrong; it is certainly not ineffective; nor is it illegitimate. To suggest this would be to wash away with the stroke of a pen much of the faithful, sacrificial work of evangelism that has gone on in the previous fifty years. It would be to rule out-of-court all the many conversions that have resulted from these activities. On the other hand, we do need to recognize that evangelism has developed a negative reputation in this country amongst many people both inside and outside the church, and that this reaction is in response to what is perceived to be the manipulative character of encounter evangelism. As with any aspect of ministry, we need to critique carefully the evangelism we do and ask whether what we do reflects a biblical perspective.

Part of what we need to do is to set alongside our current encounter-oriented evangelistic activities other forms of outreach that take seriously the fact that for many people conversion is a process. Evangelism is not an either/or activity in which we do encounter evangelism or process evangelism. We need to do both, and we need to learn from each activity. Those doing encounter evangelism need to be sensitive to the fact that not all are able to say yes to Jesus at any given time even with the best will in the world. We need to create space for a variety of decisions, each of which leads a person even closer to Jesus in his or her pilgrimage. Those doing process evangelism need to make sure that they call for commitment. Dialogue, story, exploration, and processing is one thing; decision is another. It is not good enough to leave the process so open-ended that no one ever really gets beyond the questions and actually becomes a disciple of Jesus.

So the aim of this chapter has been to raise questions about how we do evangelism and to suggest some correctives that might enhance the process.

---

34. See chap. 10 (pp. 158-74) in E. Stanley Jones, *A Song of Ascents: A Spiritual Autobiography* (Nashville: Abingdon, 1968).

In fact, what we really need is the development of innovative ways of doing encounter evangelism that will reach the many people who are ready to come to Christ while not alienating those who are still on the way. My hope is that the church will find ways to move beyond the stereotypes and negative reactions to evangelism and embrace both new forms of outreach and reinvigorated older forms. In this way we will have taken seriously the two paradigms in the New Testament for conversion.

CHAPTER TWELVE

Process Evangelism: Theory

The Twelve came to faith over time via a series of incidents and encounters with, and experiences of, Jesus. Each such event assisted them to move from their initial assumptions about Jesus to a radically new understanding of who he actually was. In his Gospel Mark invites his readers to make this same pilgrimage of discovery. He invites them to walk with the Twelve on their journey. When we adopt this point of view, evangelism becomes the process of assisting others to move beyond their assumptions about Jesus to a new and radical understanding of who he actually is.

In this chapter I want to explore ways of thinking about process evangelism. It is one thing to assert that we need to assist others to take the various steps that lead to active discipleship. It is another to know what this means in practice. I want to focus on two issues. First, I will suggest a way by which to conceptualize the process of coming to faith over time. By using the metaphor of spiritual journey, it becomes possible to identify various typical stages of pilgrimage. Each stage requires different input from us. So rather than just saying we must help people grow in their understanding of God and Jesus and leaving it at that, this way of thinking helps us to see and understand exactly where a person is in spiritual pilgrimage. Then second, I want to use Mark's six-step process by which the Twelve came to understand Jesus as a model for how we might go about helping others come to a full realization of who Jesus is. I am suggesting that the pattern in Mark is as relevant today as it was in the first century.

Spiritual Pilgrimage

At the heart of process evangelism is the assumption that all people are involved in a spiritual pilgrimage. They cannot help it. This is simply a fact of creation. Human beings are made in the image of God (Gen. 1:26-27) and were created to know God. This means that there is a divine restlessness in us until we open ourselves to the life of the Spirit and to the presence of God. Process evangelism takes seriously that people need to connect to the spiritual side of life and that this will often be a long process.

But not all people are aware that they are on a spiritual pilgrimage. Nor do they understand their need for God. They may sense an inner restlessness, but they call it by names other than "a desire for God." It may feel like loneliness of a cosmic sort; it may show itself in the search for relationships that they hope will give significance to life; it may express itself in acts of care for others even though they do not quite understand where this urge to love comes from; or it may wake them up in the middle of the night with questions about why they are alive. As they seek to understand this part of themselves, this may or may not lead them in the direction of spiritual inquiry since many people are unclear about the origin of this inner longing.

So our task in the ministry of evangelism is to help others discern their hunger for God, then help them discover where they are in their own spiritual pilgrimages, help them understand how they view God, and help them wrestle with their questions about God and Jesus in such a way that they respond to God and take the next step in their spiritual pilgrimages. The goal of evangelism is to help others discover who Jesus is and that Jesus is the way back to God, and then to see them respond to Jesus in love and commitment.

Put this way, it sounds very logical and very linear. Get in touch with your desire for God. Find out what you think about God. Explore the questions you have about God and God has for you. Respond to God and eventually commit your life to God by repentance and faith in Jesus. While it is true that spiritual pilgrimage is this neatly defined for some people, the search for God is much messier for most. It involves times of intense activity and other times of disinterest. Questions surface and then are forgotten. It involves searching, conversation, Bible study, stories, experiences, reading, worship services, small groups, etc. And often, what impacts people in all of this is not logic as much as it is love. In other words, this whole process of coming to faith in Jesus is more apt to be disjointed than systematic. To be with a person in his or her spiritual pilgrimage is to be a friend who is willing to walk with that person on an uncertain journey that has many curves and byways. What is required of us is love, honesty, the willingness to engage and then disengage, the ability to share what we have learned and know by virtue of having walked this way for a longer time, the ability to challenge our friend gently even as we are being challenged by God. We also need to know that in the end it is God the Holy Spirit who brings conviction, insight, motivation, and the ability to respond to God in repentance and faith. Our role as companion/ guide, though vital, is secondary.

The Geography of Pilgrimage

In order to be involved with others in this way, we need to understand something about the shape of spiritual pilgrimage. In a previous book I proposed a three-part process as one way to describe spiritual pilgrimage.[1] Pilgrimage begins with what I call the Quest phase in which people search for God. It moves to the Commitment phase in which people respond to Jesus. And it concludes with the Formation phase in which people seek to follow God as disciples of Jesus. This three-part paradigm enables us to talk about the various aspects of pilgrimage in ways that are useful to others on the pilgrim way.

Quest

In the Quest phase people search for meaning; they ask questions about God's existence and identity; and they explore the nature of reality. This is a quest to understand how the universe operates and what place one has in the scheme of things. This phase of pilgrimage has both an intellectual and an experiential tone to it.

Intellectual questions are sometimes as basic as whether God exists. At other times these questions have to do with the problems that are presented by the fact of God, such as the old puzzle of how an all-good and all-powerful God can allow suffering. Such questions trouble the mind. A person cannot believe what he or she suspects is untrue. The mind needs to know before the heart can respond in love and trust. The good thing about intellectual questions is that the church has had two thousand years to reflect on them. So people can find ample help as they struggle to know about God, if they know where to look.

If intellectual questions focus on whether Christianity is true, then experiential questions revolve around whether Christianity works or matters.

---

1. See *Pilgrimage: A Handbook on Christian Growth* (Grand Rapids: Baker, 1984), especially Part II.

Experiential questions deal with such issues as whether commitment to Christ will bring purpose to life, if and how God answers prayer, what difference it makes whether or not we are in touch with the spiritual, how to find peace (or joy, love, hope, etc.). With these issues it is not so much answers a person wants as it is experience. Sometimes this may involve seeing these realities in others who have committed their lives to Jesus.

In the Quest phase people need to discover that a Christian worldview gives them a helpful way of looking at these tough issues of living as well as a way of getting through them with grace and love. In fact, people often come to faith when they discover that God is alive, that God is real and with them in the midst of the messiness and meanness of life.

The exploration of the spiritual side of reality during the Quest phase is driven by both *need* and *aspiration*. Sometimes inner need drives the search. People are troubled by issues that arise out of their past: how to deal with guilt over what they have done, how to mend broken relationships, how to go beyond the limitations imposed on them by growing up in a dysfunctional family, how to cope with errant emotions, how to overcome destructive behavioral patterns. Each of these issues (and many others like them) creates anxiety, disturbs harmony, and stresses people deeply. In exploring these problems, people can encounter the power of God to bring healing, forgiveness, insights, and new life. Need can open eyes to the reality of the spiritual. The role of the evangelist is to help people make the link between individual need and gospel solutions.

But it is not only need that opens people to God. Unfulfilled aspirations also drive men and women to explore the spiritual. People long for purpose in life. We all want to be part of something that draws out the best in us, uses our gifts, and makes a difference on this planet. We want a challenge; we crave a calling. These sorts of longings open people to God and to God's purpose for us as individuals in the light of God's purpose for the world. The role of the evangelist is to help people see that God is calling each person to discover his or her God-given role and to find his or her place in the unfolding work of the kingdom of God. By following Jesus we realize our deepest aspirations.[2]

On one level, what I am suggesting is not new. Evangelists have long known that before you can get people even to consider Christ, you have to deal with issues that keep them from faith. Bishop Stephen Neill once commented that much of what he did when he conducted a preaching mission at

---

2. George Hunter has written perceptively about reaching out to people on the basis of aspiration and not just on the basis of need. See his *The Contagious Congregation* (Nashville: Abingdon, 1979), pp. 48-51.

a university was "jungle clearing."[3] By this he meant that he was involved in cutting away objections that were raised to Christianity so that faith can flourish. The popular term for this sort of activity is "pre-evangelism." But on another level, what I am suggesting is new. We sometimes think that if we "answer the question," this will lead to faith. But most of the time this just allows a person to move a bit forward in his or her pursuit of faith. This is a useful step in one's spiritual pilgrimage, but it is not the only step or the final step. We need to remember that it was a long process for the Twelve in their coming to faith, and so it will be for most people as well.

The evangelistic challenge in the Quest phase is to discern the issues that trouble people and the challenges that motivate people and then to address these in ways that promote movement in a Godward direction.

Commitment

The second part of the process is what I call the Commitment phase. The Quest phase ends when people are convinced that God exists and have decided that they want to know this God. Now the issue becomes one of response. How can we know God? What is involved in following God? Here is where Jesus becomes the central focus, because the biblical answer to the question of how to know God involves faith in Jesus.

Commitment is not easy, however. People are open to commitment on some levels but not on all levels. For example, some people are willing to be committed to the church (as a community) but are dubious about the doctrines of Christianity (the issue of truth). Others try to live by the ethics of Jesus (moral behavior) but are hesitant to get involved in the activities of the Christian community (ministry). Still others get involved in justice issues as a Christian response to evil (social action) but stop short of commitment to Christ as his follower (discipleship). All commitments are good, of course, and should be encouraged, but in the end the core Christian commitment is to the person of Jesus.

A lot of people in the United States are, apparently, in the Commitment phase of their pilgrimages. As George Gallup, Jr., has shown, America is a very religious nation. It seems that 95 percent of Americans believe in God;[4] nine

---

3. This remark was made to the author in a private conversion that took place in Johannesburg, South Africa, during a university mission in the late 1960s.

4. George Gallup, "Religion in America: Fifty Years: 1935-1985," *Gallup Report* 286 (May 1985): 50.

out of ten Americans say they pray;[5] seven in ten are members of a church or synagogue;[6] four out of ten adults attended church or synagogue during a typical week in 1984;[7] 86 percent feel that religion is "important," with 56 percent saying it is "very important";[8] and 61 percent say religion can answer all or most of today's problems.[9] Eighty-one percent of American adults consider themselves to be Christians,[10] and three out of four believe Jesus is God.[11] Forty percent claim to have had a "born-again" experience.[12]

But Gallup has also shown that the level of commitment is quite shallow, at least when measured by people's depth of understanding of Christianity.[13] In the 1978 Gallup survey, only 42 percent could name five of the Ten Commandments (which almost everyone claims to believe in). Fewer than three in ten correctly identified "Ye must be born again" as Jesus' words to Nicodemus, and only two in five knew that Jesus delivered the Sermon on the Mount. Only 46 percent could name the first four books of the New Testament, and only 70 percent knew Jesus was born in Bethlehem (despite years of Christmas pageants).[14] In other words, while it is easy to claim (at least to a pollster) that you believe in God and are born again, it is much harder to translate these "commitments" into discernible characteristics. To be committed to Christ as his disciple should show itself in how a person thinks, feels, and acts. Thus the challenge for the evangelist is to help those committed to Christianity on some level to continue their faith pilgrimage so that they become genuine disciples of Jesus. This too is part of the evangelistic task.[15]

Clearly, there are different levels of commitment within the wider Christian community. This issue has engaged the attention of numerous people down through the ages, beginning with Jesus himself, who spoke out against the institutionalized religion of his day. His comments to the scribes

5. Gallup, p. 45.
6. Gallup, p. 40.
7. Gallup, p. 42.
8. Gallup, p. 22.
9. Gallup, p. 18.
10. George Gallup, Jr., and George O'Connel, *Who Do Americans Say That I Am?* (Philadelphia: Westminster, 1986), p. 18.
11. Gallup, p. 51.
12. Gallup, p. 38.
13. See also p. 297 n. 29.
14. Gallup and O'Connel, p. 62.
15. For a helpful discussion of the evangelization of nominal Christians, see the thoughtful book by Eddie Gibbs: *In Name Only: Tackling the Problem of Nominal Christianity* (Wheaton, Ill.: Victor Books/BridgePoint, 1994).

and Pharisees were scathing, to say the least. He called them hypocrites and compared them to whitewashed tombs that look beautiful on the outside but are full of the bones of the dead.[16] The scribes and the Pharisees to whom Jesus spoke were considered by their contemporaries to be the most committed of all religious people, and yet they had missed the point. Nearer our own day, Søren Kierkegaard spoke out against "official Christianity," which was to be distinguished from the "radical Christianity" he espoused.

But how does one distinguish between true and false commitment, much less between partial commitment and full commitment? Or perhaps a better way to put this question is the way Mark expresses it in the parable of the sower (Mark 4:1-20): What type of commitment does a person have when it comes to Jesus? Mark identifies four options. The crowds receive the word of God with joy but their commitment is not deep, so when trouble comes they fall away. The religious leaders harden their hearts against the word, so it never takes root in them at all. The family of Jesus is tentative, receiving the word but letting other issues choke its power. But the Twelve accept the word and it produces a miraculous crop in them. Clearly there are different levels of commitment to Jesus, as Mark indicates. However, Mark is quite clear. There is only one true commitment: the commitment that produces fruit. This is the evangelistic mandate: to aid people to move beyond their limited commitments to full commitment to Jesus.

Gordon Allport, the Harvard psychologist, has a useful way of expressing the difference between partial and full commitment. He uses the terms "intrinsic faith" and "extrinsic faith" to distinguish between different ways of being religious. An extrinsic religious orientation is one in which religion is "strictly utilitarian: useful for the self in granting safety, social standing, solace, and endorsement for one's chosen way of life. . . . By contrast, the intrinsic form of the religious sentiment regards faith as a supreme value in its own right. . . . A religious sentiment of this sort floods the whole life with motivation and meaning. Religion is no longer limited to single segments of self-interest."[17] Allport and Ross developed a questionnaire called the Religious Orientation Scale to distinguish between these two ways of connecting to religious faith. Other researchers have proposed different scales that seek to get at the various levels of commitment that characterize the religious community. The most interesting of these was developed originally by C. Daniel

16. See Matt. 23:2-28 and Mark 7:1-23.
17. G. W. Allport, "The Religious Context of Prejudice," *Journal for the Scientific Study of Religion* 5 (1966): 455. See also the description of these concepts in the paper co-written with J. M. Ross, "Personal Religious Orientation and Prejudice," *Journal of Personality and Social Psychology* 5 (1967): 432-43.

Batson and then revised and extended with the aid of his colleagues Patricia Schoenrade and W. Larry Ventis. This is a six-scale measure that looks at the extrinsic, intrinsic, external, internal, quest, and orthodoxy aspects of religious commitment.[18] Each of these scales makes the same point: commitment is not a single response. Instead, commitment is multidimensional and can grow (or shrink) over time.

This being the case, the evangelistic challenge, when it comes to people in the Commitment phase of pilgrimage, is to help them build on what commitments they have until they become true disciples of Jesus. It is possible to be committed to the church, to Christian doctrine, to Christian ethics, or even on some level to the idea of Jesus without being fully committed to Jesus as a living person with whom one can have a relationship. And clearly, Christian conversion is all about a commitment to Jesus. It is in this aspect of pilgrimage that Mark's six-step paradigm is most helpful (see below).

Formation

But the spiritual pilgrimage does not stop with an initial commitment to Jesus, no matter how deep, serious, or dramatic such a commitment might be. One's spiritual pilgrimage simply moves to a new stage. This third stage might be called the Formation phase. The Formation process never ends, since no one is ever fully conformed to the image of Christ (which is the goal of Formation). For those newly committed to Jesus, it is important that they be helped to take the first formational steps in following after Jesus. Such initial formational activities are part of the evangelistic responsibility. Mark describes the nature and process of discipleship in unit four of his evangelistic book. For him it is not just a matter of believing in Jesus (which is crucial but insufficient); it is a matter of following Jesus. If formational assistance is not given to new believers, what evangelism produces is converts (who may or may not last) and not disciples (which is what Jesus desires, according to Matt. 28:19).

William Abraham argues persuasively that evangelism can be conceived of as the process of initiation into the kingdom of God.[19] As such, evangelism has various aspects. Abraham names six: conversion (which has to do with

18. A description of this scale can be found in their book entitled *Religion and the Individual* (New York and Oxford: Oxford University Press, 1982, 1993), pp. 168-90.

19. William J. Abraham, *The Logic of Evangelism* (Grand Rapids: Wm. B. Eerdmans Publishing Co., 1989), especially chap. 5 (pp. 92-116). Abraham's book is a groundbreaking theological reflection on the work of evangelism.

conscious awareness that one is committed to God and God's way), baptism (which is about public affirmation that one is a follower of Jesus), morality (which focuses on the demands of the Great Commandment), creed (which has to do with understanding basic Christian doctrine and with developing a Christian worldview), spiritual gifts (which involve openness to, awareness of, and participation in the life of the Spirit), and spiritual disciplines (which have to do with the ongoing formation process in the life of the convert). Clearly, each of these six aspects touches upon different aspects of Formation. In other words, the aim of evangelism is not just to bring people to Jesus; it is to help them become established in a lifestyle of active discipleship. Not a few of the problems that have plagued American evangelism can be traced back to a view of evangelism that stops short of including formational activities into the process of evangelism.

Implications

There is another way of thinking about this whole process of pilgrimage. During the Quest phase the focus is on God the Father. The issues with which people wrestle have to do with such things as the existence of God, the nature of God, the way to know God, and other problems related to coming to grips with the reality of the spiritual side of life. During the Commitment phase the focus is on God the Son. The movement that takes place is all about responding to Jesus and becoming his disciple. During the Formation phase the focus is on God the Holy Spirit. Now it is a matter of sanctification: openness to the Spirit of God that brings about spiritual growth. This is a useful perspective in that it enables the evangelist to concentrate on the appropriate set of theological issues for each person.

By conceiving of the process of conversion in terms of three stages, Quest, Commitment, and Formation, it is possible to target evangelistic activities more carefully. If your audience is in the Quest phase, it does no good urging them to accept Jesus, whom they do not understand much less believe in. It is better to raise and respond to the intellectual and/or experiential questions that trouble them. In so doing you will be able to reveal what Christianity has to say by way of perspective on such issues and how being a Christian enables one to cope with these problems. This, then, would open the way to serious consideration of Jesus. However, if your audience is already aware of Jesus and prone to believe in him, then the challenge is to broaden their understanding of and commitment to Jesus. A lot of people are quite comfortable thinking of Jesus as a wonderful religious teacher. They are not so sure, however, what his death and resurrection are all about or how these events can have any meaning for them. In still other circumstances, the issue is not helping people believe in Jesus (they already do that); it is getting them to follow Jesus in ways that change how they live, feel, and think. While on one level this is all about Christian growth and nurture and, as such, is the responsibility of the teaching arm of the church, on another level this too is part of our evangelistic responsibility. It is often the evangelist who can help people move beyond their first step in following Jesus and begin to develop a Christian lifestyle.

Of course, it almost goes without saying that the three-part process for spiritual pilgrimage that I have proposed here does not describe accurately the experience of every person. Some people never go through a Quest phase, for example. They grow up in Christian homes and cannot remember not believing in Jesus. It is not uncommon for such people to wrestle with Quest issues within the context of faith (Formation). Others seem to jump from the point of no commitment to full commitment to Jesus, grasping the whole in an instant and giving themselves fully to Jesus. Still others stay suspended at the edges of Formation: forever the new convert, never the conscious disciple. For still others, this particular way of describing pilgrimage simply does not represent how their lives have unfolded. Other schemes must be adduced to capture what they have experienced. All this points to the fact that what I have proposed is a generalization about pilgrimage and not an irreducible pattern through which all must go. It does give us, however, a starting point in listening to the story of others. It is useful in identifying typical stopping points in spiritual exploration. But it must be abandoned when it ceases to describe accurately the reality of another life in pursuit of God.

In using this three-part schema, it becomes clear that the focus of Mark's Gospel is on the Commitment phase of pilgrimage, since Mark deals primarily with how a person comes to know and respond to Jesus. Mark has little to say about the issues in the Quest phase (except when these deal with certain lifestyle matters). He does not wrestle with issues such as the existence of God or the reality of the spiritual. Nor does Mark ever really deal with the nature of the Christian life and community (Formation) beyond outlining in broad terms a kingdom lifestyle. But when it comes to the Commitment phase, Mark provides us with a useful way for helping people go through the process of committing their lives to Jesus.

A Model for Process Evangelism

In his Gospel Mark describes how the Twelve came both to know who Jesus was and to understand how to be committed to him. I would argue that this six-step process is not just the description of what happened to a few Jewish men in the first century. It is also a powerful model for how to reach out to people in any century, including the twenty-first. Mark's schema of conversion is a fine outline to follow as we seek to make Jesus known in this culture. While not every person will go through each of these six steps of understanding, by using these six titles as a way of talking about Jesus we make connections to people who are at various places in their understanding of Jesus. In what follows, each of the six Marcan titles for Jesus will be considered in terms of how it can be a focal point for evangelism, particularly in contemporary American culture.[20] Taken together, this discussion offers a model for how one does process evangelism.

Jesus as a Great Teacher

Jesus is highly regarded today in American culture if the polls can be believed. There seems to be a cultural consensus that Jesus is a great spiritual teacher. For the most part people feel positive about him. However, this interest in Jesus is not accompanied by much insight into Jesus. In fact, people do not seem to know a lot about what Jesus actually taught. So this is a good point to begin one's evangelistic work. We start with our shared assumption that Jesus is a great teacher and then explore together what Jesus actually taught. This kind of point of contact is what we are looking for in evangelism: a way to begin the conversation that links together evangelist and seeker.

What, then, do we actually talk about (in a personal conversation) or what kind of presentation should we make (in a meeting)? I suggest that it is best to begin with those teachings by Jesus that are the most readily understood and accepted. For example, the Great Commandment about loving God and loving others generates good conversation. That we should love others is a widely accepted axiom. Likewise, the call to love God resonates with people. But when we get into the specifics of this all-embracing call to love, it becomes apparent that this is not so easy to do. Loving others in a sustained way, over time, in the midst of struggle and pain is difficult. Loving the unlov-

---

20. Other cultures will relate in other ways to these titles. The task of the evangelist is to make the appropriate cultural connections in whatever setting he or she is working.

able outcasts of our society (whom Jesus seemed to favor) is even harder. Even loving God is not easy once we get beyond the kind of pious sentimentality we feel at Christmas. Thus as the Great Commandment is discussed, it becomes apparent that we need help if, in fact, we are to live by this central teaching of Jesus. We need to be loved to have any hope of loving others. In fact, we need to be loved by God so as to be free to love others. But for the love of God to be a sustaining reality for us, we need to be in relationship to God. To be committed to the axiom that God loves us is one thing; to be in a loving relationship with God is quite another. In other words, by exploring this central teaching of Jesus about love, we come quickly to the heart of the gospel and to Jesus himself, the one who brings us back to God, and to his love that sustains our lives.

Many other aspects of Jesus' teaching lead easily to this sort of fruitful conversation: conversation that begins with shared assumptions and moves to new insight into the gospel and to the challenge to respond to it. For example, it is stimulating to discuss the appealing but baffling teaching of Jesus in the Sermon on the Mount. People like the Lord's Prayer in Matthew 6:9-13 but are confused to read, in the same sermon, the call to gouge out a lusting eye (Matt. 5:29). So it becomes natural to talk about the kingdom of God and what it means to live out a kingdom ethic. In doing this we come quickly to Jesus' call to become part of the kingdom by repentance and faith (Mark 1:15). Exploring the parables of Jesus is also fruitful. As we wrestle with them so as to hear them in the same way that Jesus' first-century audience heard them, we are as baffled, as delighted, and as challenged by the parables as they were. One of the most powerful aspects of this sort of conversation is that the gap between evangelist and seeker disappears. There is no "us and them" any longer. Both those who are committed to Christ and those who are coming to Christ are challenged by the words of Jesus. Both are called to respond to Jesus in terms of where they are in their own spiritual pilgrimages.

Implied in Mark's six-step process for discovering Jesus is a pattern for evangelism. For those who are in the Commitment phase of pilgrimage, begin with that aspect of Jesus which resonates most deeply with them. Explore it together. Let the conversation move in a natural way to gospel realities and to the challenge which a particular aspect of Jesus has for us. In terms of Jesus as a great teacher, the question is: If we say that we consider Jesus to be a great spiritual teacher, are we actually living by his teachings? If not, how can we do so? This is a challenging evangelistic question.

Jesus as Powerful Prophet

But Jesus is not just a wise teacher; he is also a powerful prophet. The question of power engages the attention of many people today in the light of our relative powerlessness before the forces that afflict us. In the first-century world there was a similar feeling of helplessness in the face of the four foes: the *elements* that can so easily destroy and kill, *evil* that is able to possess us, *illness* that wastes us, and *death* that takes us. In the twenty-first century we still face these same enemies. We have learned to protect ourselves against many of the rages of nature, but hurricanes, floods, fire, and earthquakes still burst easily through our barriers. When it comes to evil, we have defined it away and sanitized its force, but still we have to confront the randomness of gang violence, the fact of serial killers, the impersonality of bureaucracies that bind us, the horrors of genocide, as well as the senselessness of war. On a personal level we know the power of evil when we confront life-destroying demons of addiction. We still get ill in the twenty-first century, and even with antibiotics and laparoscopic surgery we continue to face plagues like cancer and AIDS. As for death, we may have prolonged our life span but we still must die. In other words, we have as much a need for a powerful prophet as did the people of the first century. In our spiritual pilgrimages we need to confront our own powerlessness and be in touch with one who has power over all these issues.

It is at the point of need as symbolized by our powerlessness in the face of various forces that evangelistic conversation can focus in helpful ways. For example, one of the reasons the church in Africa has been growing steadily in numbers since the turn to the twentieth century is that Jesus is perceived as the Lord over all the powers. In a cultural context in which the powers are known to exist, to meddle in harmful ways with human affairs, and to be difficult to avoid, much less control, this is good news indeed. To name Jesus as Lord is to experience his power over these supernatural forces. Likewise in America, to address issues of suffering, pain, evil, and helplessness is to touch the heart of many people's concern. To discover Jesus as the powerful one is as good news to us as it is to Africans.

However, in our conversation with others about these matters, we need to be very careful not to trivialize evil or to overpromise power. Yes, Jesus still heals, but not magically, not always, and not everyone — as was also true in the first century. Yes, Jesus is the Lord of nature and can and does protect us, but not always in the ways we want. Yes, Jesus is more powerful than any evil we can imagine, but his followers can still be captive to evil. And yes, Jesus is the Lord of Life who has gone through death, but we still die, and dying is often hard even when we know the hope of resurrection.

321

We also need to be careful not to underpromise. God is alive and active in this world as surely as God was active in the first-century world. Miracles still happen, power is unleashed, prayer is potent, resurrection is promised, and faith is rewarded. To be committed to Jesus, who is the Lord over all powers, is to make a powerful commitment which makes a discernible difference in our lives at the level of affliction.

In fact, it is at this point that the reality of commitment to Jesus is sometimes put to the test. Donald Jacobs expresses this well in his discussion of culture and conversion in reference to East Africa.

> When a person is converted to Jesus Christ, what happens at the level of these powers? I am convinced that for a sustained conversion experience, a person must elevate Jesus Christ to a position of Lordship in his or her power constellation and keep him there through Christ-honoring living. Unless this happens little else really matters. . . .
>
> . . . [O]ne might well scrutinize a so-called conversion experience in which Jesus Christ is not exalted above all powers. It is not easy to ascertain the place of Jesus Christ in another person's world, and sometimes not even in one's own. Most of the world's Christians would no doubt score high on a doctrinal questionnaire as to the person of Christ. The test comes, however, in times of crises when we require power or knowledge which we feel Jesus withholds. Such crises bring out one's true cosmology.[21]

Once again it becomes evident that conversion is not a one-way street. The evangelist is as challenged as the seeker to respond to Jesus in terms of his role as powerful prophet. The difference is that for the evangelist this is an aspect of his or her formational process and not the first such response to Jesus. For the seeker this may well be the next step of turning, with more turnings ahead before commitment is complete.

Jesus as the Messiah

When we come to the issue of the messiahship of Jesus, we begin to confront a certain amount of cultural resistance. It is widely accepted that Jesus is a great teacher. Likewise, the idea of Jesus as a prophet with power does not move beyond our cultural comfort zones (even though we are not quite sure what Jesus as a powerful prophet means to us personally). But when we come

---

21. Donald Jacobs, "Culture and the Phenomena of Conversion: Reflections in an East African Setting," *Gospel in Context* 1, no. 3 (July 1978): 8.

to the whole idea of *chosenness,* hesitation emerges. And surely the idea of chosenness is what messiahship means — on one level at least. Jesus the Messiah was the Chosen One of God who was the focus of God's word to the world. In the first century the coming of the Messiah was widely expected. Such a one had been foretold. It was understood that the Messiah would represent God's presence in this world. The people knew that the Messiah would come from God to do God's work.

But in our culture today this view becomes offensive when it is asserted that Jesus was not just *a* messiah but *the* Messiah. It is this assertion of uniqueness that clashes with modern sensibilities. But surely this is the teaching of the New Testament. Nowhere is Jesus portrayed as simply the latest incarnation of a messiah. And it is this very offense that moves the evangelistic conversation to a whole new level, because now a choice is involved. Will I break with my cultural assumptions about how God is supposed to work in the world (by creating many diverse paths to spiritual reality) and instead come to view Jesus as the unique Messiah (the way, the truth, and the life [John 14:6])? This is not to say that truth is found only in Christianity. Truth is truth and all truth is of God. But it is to say that in Jesus, God had a unique purpose.

But the assertion that in Jesus the Messiah, God accomplished a unique work that forever altered the character of this planet is also very appealing. Yes, there is resistance to the audacity of this claim, but there is also resonance. For those with growing openness to the spiritual, the good news that God intervened in the course of human affairs in a redemptive way is persuasive. Such a proclamation needs to be part of our evangelistic appeal. For those who wish to explore this topic (in the course of evangelistic dialogue), the history of redemption as recorded in the Bible can be fascinating.

The challenge is to be able to say, as Peter did: "You are the Messiah" (Mark 8:29). One is able to say this in the same way that Peter was: via the healing touch of God that opens eyes. At this point in the spiritual pilgrimage it becomes clear that conversion is a process which involves the work of God. While it is true that the ability to commit oneself to Jesus as teacher or prophet also requires the inner work of the Spirit, this is not always as evident. It seems "natural" to want to follow a wise teacher or to have faith in a powerful prophet. But to say "Yes, I believe Jesus is the Messiah" requires a qualitatively new level of insight and new depth of faith. The ability to make such a commitment is evidence of the work of the Spirit in a person's life.

However, it is one thing to assert that Jesus is the Messiah. It is another to understand what it means for Jesus to be Messiah. Peter still had a

long way to go in his commitment even after he made his astonishing assertion. So, too, people in the twenty-first century must take the next steps in
commitment by probing the meaning of Jesus' messiahship. The three titles
in the second half of the Gospel of Mark give content to the concept of
messiahship.

Jesus as the Son of Man

To confront the fact that Jesus is the Son of Man is to confront the fact of his
atoning death. It is easy to be committed to a person like Jesus when we come
to believe that in him the intentions of God reside. In fact, a certain glamour
is attached to association with a figure so wise, so powerful, and so important
as Jesus. That kind of Jesus is almost a cult figure — one who knows what is
true and has the power and the connections to work his will in this world.
This is Jesus Christ Superstar. But when we move beyond this image into the
reality of his messiahship, we find lurking there the scepter of death. To be the
Messiah is to die for others. That Jesus "died for our sins" has always been understood to be an essential part of the gospel.[22] In coming to this point in a
pilgrimage of commitment, people shed some of the glamour of Christian
commitment and enter the realm of serious discipleship. They have to ask:
Do we really want to be associated with this kind of Messiah? It is not by accident that in unit four where Mark focuses on Jesus as Son of Man, he also introduces Jesus' teaching about discipleship and its cost. Unit four ends with a
powerful assertion about what it means to be the Son of Man and what it
means to follow such a one as this: "Whoever wishes to become great among
you must be your servant, and whoever wishes to be first among you must be
slave of all. For the Son of Man came not to be served but to serve, and to give
his life a ransom for many" (Mark 10:43-45).

On one level, commitment to this kind of Messiah is to the benefit of
people. Jesus has become their ransom. He has died for them — and not just
for the world in general. They appropriate all the benefits of his atoning
death. They experience what it means to be forgiven, rescued, and redeemed.
But on another level this calls them to a new seriousness in following Jesus.
They now enter into the way of servant discipleship. And this is not a step that
can be missed. Incomplete commitment to Jesus which stops short of the

---

22. See Harry L. Poe, *The Gospel and Its Meaning: A Theology for Evangelism and
Church Growth* (Grand Rapids: Zondervan, 1996), especially chap. 5: "Death for Sins," pp.
134-62.

cross and cross-bearing discipleship results in nominal faith and partial discipleship.

By following Mark's schema for conversion, we assist others to move beyond a mere cultural view of Jesus (which may be accurate but is incomplete) to the kind of view that gets inside them and starts to transform them. As the disciples learned, it is not enough simply to know that Jesus is the Messiah. It is necessary to grasp on a deep, inner level what kind of Messiah he is and what this means if people are to follow after him. The kind of evangelistic discussion one will find when it comes to the title Son of Man is deep and rich. It wrestles with the scandal of the cross. As such it is a vital part of the pilgrimage of faith.

Jesus as the Son of David

On the other side of the cross is glory. This is implied in the title Son of David. The Son of David is the rightful king in the kingdom of God. Here also is the proactive Jesus who takes on the structures and the powers. He is the Lord of Lords and the King of Kings (to use language from other parts of Scripture).

The evangelistic conversation at this point gets into issues of justice. The model in unit five of Mark's Gospel is that of Jesus taking on the corrupt practices of the money changers and animal merchants at the temple. Righteous anger is displayed for all to copy. So we learn yet another lesson if we are to be fully committed to Jesus. We too are called to confront the structures that make a mockery of the kingdom of God. Here also in this unit we hear the Great Commandment to love God and to love others with the whole of our being. The kingdom of God is the kingdom of love.[23] The way of Jesus is the way of love but also the way of conflict. It is illustrative that the Great Commandment about love is given in the context of the fierce debate which has just taken place between Jesus and the religious leaders. Apparently the kind of love of which Jesus spoke can be directed even to one's enemies.

By dealing with these issues we have left behind the kind of simplistic and undemanding call that characterizes some versions of evangelism. The call to come to Jesus who is the Son of David is not a call to feel good about

---

23. See the unusual and highly provocative book by Edward John Carnell, *The Kingdom of Love and the Pride of Life* (Grand Rapids: Wm. B. Eerdmans Publishing Co., 1960). This is an apologetic effort on Carnell's part in which he tries to show how the gospel connects to our search for meaning and purpose in life.

yourself in the midst of a life of leisure, happiness, and the American way. This is a call to a demanding love in the midst of a complex and flawed world.

However, this kind of call does not necessarily put off people, as we sometimes imagine. Implicit in much evangelism is the sense that we need to sugarcoat what it means to be a disciple of Jesus. We emphasize the wonderful plan which God has for our lives. We point out the unconditional love that God has for all human beings. We tell people about the free gift of salvation which is theirs for the asking. "Just accept Jesus. It's good for you. You can't lose." While this has a superficial appeal, for many people it is just too easy, too undemanding, too simple. Jesus does have a plan for our lives (and a purpose for us in his kingdom that is far beyond what we can imagine). Jesus does love us and we do find salvation in him. But all this comes in the context of his call to be his disciple. To be a disciple is, at the root, to fall in step behind Jesus and follow him where he is going, and this is never simple and never predictable. Ernest Best expresses this well.

> "Come after me" is a general command which specifically links discipleship to Jesus; discipleship is not just the readiness to suffer, howbeit in ever so good a cause; it is a step to fall in behind Jesus, and no other, in the way in which he is going. The call is not one to accept a certain system of teaching, live by it, continue faithfully to interpret it and pass it on, which was in essence the call of a rabbi to his disciples; nor is it a call to accept a philosophical position which will express itself in a certain type of behaviour, as in Stoicism; nor is it the call to devote life to the alleviation of suffering for others; nor is it the call to pass through certain rites as in the Mysteries so as to become an initiate of the God, his companion — the carrying of the cross is no rite! It is a call to fall in behind Jesus and go with him.[24]

Such a call to discipleship is a call to expand oneself, to move beyond oneself, to be involved in matters of great importance. This is a call worthy of all of us. This is a call which puts Jesus at the center of who we are, not at the polite periphery where nice people live. As such, there is great appeal to this sort of call. When we come to Jesus out of a deep sense of need, we discover the Son of Man who died for our sins. When we come to Jesus out of a strong desire to have purpose and meaning in life, we discover the Son of David who will not tolerate injustice. George Hunter argues that the appeal in much of American evangelism is to come to Jesus since you are a lost, needy sinner, and while this connects with many people, it turns off those who are getting

24. Ernest Best, "Discipleship in Mark: Mark 8.22–10.52," *Scottish Journal of Theology* 23 (August 1970): 329.

on well in this life. For those who have learned to cope with life, the more powerful appeal is to follow after the magnificent Son of David, who will lead them in a way that brings genuine meaning and purpose to their lives and who will involve them in kingdom matters which have eternal significance.[25]

Jesus as the Son of God

There is one more level of commitment to be given. Jesus is the Son of God. He is God incarnate. It is at this point that Christian commitment moves into an entirely new realm. It is not just that God has worked out his purposes via the life, ministry, death, and resurrection of this man Jesus. It is that God himself has done all this. When the high priest asked Jesus, "Are you the Messiah, the Son of the Blessed One?" Jesus said, "I am" (Mark 14:61-62). Jesus does not dodge the question. Neither can we. The time for the "messianic secret" is passed. Now everything needs to be out in the open. He is the Messiah, and the Messiah is the Son of God. Mark has already shown his readers what this means. At both the baptism and the transfiguration of Jesus, the God of Elijah and Moses declares, "This is my Son, the Beloved; listen to him!" (Mark 9:7; see also 1:11).

With the title Son of God the evangelistic conversation comes to the whole question of incarnation: the Divine Word who is God, God come in human flesh (to use categories from elsewhere in the Gospels). Again this is a challenge to our modern mind-set, though not such a formidable challenge as it once was. As recently as twenty-five years ago, to point to Jesus as divine was to court incredulity. But during that era we were captivated by a deterministic worldview which had no space for the supernatural. Today, whatever else one might say about postmodernism, we live in a much more open universe. It is not "beyond belief" that God might have taken on human flesh and dwelt on this planet. It may not necessarily be easy to believe this, but such an event is not automatically ruled out of the realm of possibility.

What does it mean to say that you believe that Jesus is the Son of God? It means that in Jesus you have found the human face of God. Jesus is what God looks like in flesh. It means that God is not a disinterested force or spirit that wafts mindlessly through the universe. God is personal. God can be known. We can have a relationship with God. It means that while the five other titles

---

25. See Hunter, pp. 48-51. Hunter calls this the Inductive-Mission model, in which one appeals to those on the higher levels of Maslow's hierarchy of need by inviting them to join Christ in one of his causes.

accurately describe who Jesus is, this one sums it all up. No wonder he is a wise teacher, a powerful prophet, the chosen Messiah, the Son of Man who is able to be a ransom for our sin, and the Son of David who is Lord of all powers, be they on earth or in heaven. He is God. To follow such a one is the goal of the Commitment phase.

Turning to Jesus

Mark helps us understand that the evangelistic mandate is wider and deeper than we often make it out to be. To change our minds about Jesus; to move from our cultural assumptions about who he is; to move beyond what is easy and comfortable to believe about him — all this is a challenge. For some, such a change of heart is quick; for most it is a process. To do the work of evangelism is to urge others to follow this way of conversion so that they discover the true Jesus (as against the cultural Jesus) — be it a long or short journey. Paul understood who Jesus was in a flash; others take a lifetime to move as far. But then again, how much did Paul really understand about Jesus there on the Damascus road? He experienced the resurrected Jesus, and this was enough to bring him to commitment. It also jolted him into learning all he could about this mysterious presence who knew his name and his story. For Paul, it seems, commitment led to reflection. For others, reflection leads to commitment as they explore the various facets of Jesus until they finally understand and believe. Mark's schema offers a way of conceptualizing how to go about the work of evangelism. It defines the path that people need to follow (slowly or rapidly) as they move to full commitment to Jesus.

Mark also tells us how to turn to Jesus once a person has discovered who he is. With the language of repentance, faith, and discipleship, we understand how we are to respond to Jesus.

We are tempted to say that this paradigm describes how outsiders are converted to Jesus, but I would assert that this is the same path that many who are already in the church need to walk. It is quite possible to be a faithful church member of long standing and know Jesus only as teacher or prophet (or even Messiah) and never take all the steps necessary for full understanding. As Witherup has shown, in the Old Testament the "message of conversion is addressed *internally* to the people of God and not *externally* to others."[26] As was true in Old Testament times, so too today insiders in the church

---

26. Ronald D. Witherup, *Conversion in the New Testament* (Collegeville, Minn.: Liturgical Press, 1994), p. 18, italics in original.

are also called to conversion. I would go one step further. Not just nominal Christians need to walk the path to full commitment, but all Christians at all times need to walk the path to fuller commitment to Jesus. Again, as Witherup has demonstrated, "Conversion is depicted [in the Old Testament] not as a singular event but an *ongoing process* of realignment to God. God continually reaches out to human beings in relationship, yet we continue to stray from that relationship. Through conversion we make frequent course correction in order to embrace the relationship to God anew."[27] Part of the stigma of evangelism has to do with the supposed dichotomy between insiders and outsiders: those who have "got it" and those who have not. With this more holistic view of evangelism everyone is challenged always to respond to God: insider-outsider; nominal-committed; seeker-evangelist. Those who evangelize may have made progress in their pilgrimages, but no one has yet arrived at a full knowledge of or commitment to Jesus. Church member, skeptic, believer, clergy, seeker, agnostic — all are called to respond to Jesus, and Mark identifies issues that each needs to face.

27. Witherup, p. 18, italics in original.

CHAPTER THIRTEEN

Process Evangelism: Practice

I t is one thing to assert that evangelism needs to take into account the long process by which many people come to faith. It is another actually to do evangelism in this way. We know what evangelism looks like when it is organized around events that seek to produce immediate decisions for Christ. But what does evangelism look like when it is process oriented?

In this final chapter I want to suggest four ways to do process evangelism: small-group evangelism, growth-oriented evangelism, evangelism via the spiritual disciplines, and worship evangelism. This is not meant to be an exhaustive list, but rather an illustrative list of a few of the many ways to do process evangelism. These four methods of outreach are known and used to varying degrees. Certainly worship evangelism is widely used in seeker-sensitive churches. And small-group evangelism is growing in popularity. But in many cases there is not a clear sense of how people come to faith in these contexts. My hope is that the theoretical framework developed in chapter 12 will enrich and enliven these methodologies. Before I describe these four ways of outreach, it is necessary to make a series of general comments that apply to all forms of process evangelism.

An Overview of Process-Evangelism Activities

First, process evangelism will entail great variety simply because people face a host of issues in their spiritual pilgrimages. Event-oriented evangelism can be narrowed down to a rather limited number of activities. But not so with process evangelism, where one must constantly ask: Am I connecting with the real issues of these particular people at this point in time in their pilgrimages? Each issue and each question has the potential for creating new ways of expressing the gospel.

Second, what we do by way of evangelism emerges out of our understanding of whom we seek to reach. Outreach is tailored to a particular group of people. It is this targeting that makes process evangelism so powerful. This means, of course, that activities which connect with one group may miss (or even turn off) a second group of people. For example, while it might be helpful on a university campus to present a lecture that deals with reasons for our faith (because intellectual inquiry is at the heart of a university), this would not necessarily connect with a group of young parents who are struggling daily with the issue of raising small children and keeping marriages and careers going simultaneously. The young parents are more likely to respond to a Bible study focused on these struggles (with child care provided) than to abstract argument about "truth." In fact, even for college students today in this postmodern environment, a debate about "truth" will be of less interest than conversation concerning a Christian view of saving our planet.

Third, since process evangelism is targeted to specific issues and specific audiences, the activities will tend to be smaller and more focused rather than larger and more general (i.e., "mass" events). One of the great appeals of mass evangelism is that so many people can be reached simultaneously. The reality is that while this is true in certain cultural contexts (e.g., mass evangelism is quite effective in many African settings), in other cultural settings there is great wariness about mass evangelism (e.g., in America where mass appeals, in general, fall on deaf ears). And in fact, smaller, more focused activities can generate greater response since the outreach is so personal and specific.

Fourth, process evangelism flows out of a particular attitude toward people. When people are viewed as engaged in spiritual pilgrimage (whether they know it or not), they are treated as pre-Christian[1] and not as anti-Christian. The one attitude assumes that people are not in the kingdom of God, are not interested in the kingdom, and are probably hostile to God (and to us as Christians, by extension). This sets up an "us/them" confrontation which tends to create walls between people. Whereas with a pilgrimage perspective we assume that the people we meet are made to know God, want to know God, and are open to God (even when they are closed to religion, church,

---

1. George Hunter draws attention to the word "pre-Christian" in his book *Church for the Unchurched* (Nashville: Abingdon, 1996), p. 15, attributing it to the leaders of New Song Church in West Covina, California, a church founded in 1986 by Dieter Zander and others to reach Generation X.

doctrine, etc.). Furthermore, we know that we too as evangelists are engaged in the same pilgrimage to which we call others and that the only difference between us is that we have different issues to face. This creates a climate of warmth and openness. The succinct way of stating these differing attitudes is to say that the one perspective assumes people are hostile to God, the other assumes people are open to God. The one perspective assumes that we as evangelists have to overcome this hostility and work at generating interest in the spiritual world. The other assumes that all people would really like to believe in God if only they knew that God was actually alive, real, and knowable. These two attitudes result in different approaches to evangelism.

Fifth, in process evangelism the assumption is that most activities in a church have evangelistic potential and that the challenge is to create the kind of mind-set that sees that potential. For example, take the church choir. In most churches the choir exists simply to provide music for the worship service. This is its task and its ministry. But if a choir understands that one aspect of its existence involves helping people in their pilgrimages of faith, then ample opportunity presents itself for this to happen. The very music that is sung raises all the life and faith issues one can hope for. Furthermore, many choirs develop a strong sense of community. The same group of people meet weekly, work hard together, and minister together on Sundays so that over time deep bonds develop between people. The very existence of this sort of community provides the perfect context in which to assist one another to move toward full commitment to Jesus. A choir may even decide to recruit members outside the ranks of the church and thereby draw in folk who are not yet consciously aware of their spiritual pilgrimages.

This contrasts with the assumption that evangelism is a special activity that requires new structures and particular methodologies. I need to be clear at this point, however. It is true that certain activities are organized solely for the sake of doing outreach. This is their purpose and reason for existence. I am not advocating that such activities cease. Clearly they are vital. What I am saying is that we need to go beyond such directly evangelistic activities and work evangelistically in as many structures as possible. When evangelism is seen as "something special," it is done only occasionally and only in specific ways that will reach some people but miss most. Furthermore, experience demonstrates that entropy takes hold of evangelism. We have to keep at it or it dies away (even in churches that owe their existence to vigorous evangelistic programs). So if evangelism is seen as that which requires special structures, then, over time, it will become marginalized. Whereas if you have the attitude that most all church activities have evangelistic potential and that it is merely a matter of realizing it, continuous involvement in outreach by a church is more likely.

Another distinction needs to be made as well. In the sixties and seventies, when mainline churches started to decline and rediscovered evangelism, it was sometimes asserted that "everything we do is evangelism." However, experience showed that when evangelism was made this amorphous, it ceased to exist as a specific activity and, in fact, no evangelism actually took place. When everything we do is evangelism, then nothing we do is evangelism. In contrast, what I am saying is that each activity in a church needs to be assessed as to its potential for evangelism. This is not the same as saying that such activities are automatically evangelistic. People need to be helped to see the evangelistic potential in what they do and then act upon it. If one is alert to the fact of spiritual pilgrimage, then it becomes possible to respond to pilgrimage issues in the context of those activities in which one is already engaged. However, most of the time we are not aware of such matters, so we fail to take advantage of the natural opportunities we have to help people move toward God. Attitude is key. We need an evangelistic mind-set in all our activities. In this way all events in the church, from worship to adult education to pastoral counseling, can have an evangelistic function.

One of the great benefits of viewing outreach in this way is that these "normal activities of a church" are not understood by outsiders to the church to be "evangelistic" and so do not carry the stigma that evangelism has developed in our society today. As a result, people can respond comfortably rather than warily to the activities. They are open, not defensive, and so are able to hear the gospel and not just resist an evangelist.

Finally, since so many different kinds of activities can be used to do process evangelism, the danger is that the evangelistic aspect of the activity will soon be forgotten. For example, to invite people to a seminar in which they will learn how to do spiritual journaling is attractive in this era when spirituality is of great interest to so many people. But it is possible to do such a seminar and never get to the evangelistic challenge — which is to use one's journal as a way to identify where one is in one's spiritual journey and to discern how to respond to God. We can teach journaling, provide people with a useful tool of growth, but never raise the evangelistic issue. So we must constantly be aware of the evangelistic purpose of the activity, lest it be muted, downplayed, or lost altogether. For an activity to be evangelistic it must challenge people to be open to where they are in terms of God, to consider Jesus, and to respond in repentance and faith and so take that next step in a Godward direction.

Rather than talk further in generalities about process evangelism, I want to suggest four styles of outreach that connect with people in their various pilgrimages to faith. The intention is not to give detailed instructions in how to go about such evangelistic activities. Rather, it is to raise possibilities and to describe in general terms the core of such process-oriented activities.

Small-Group Evangelism

Small-group evangelism meets all the criteria for process evangelism. It focuses on the needs and issues of individuals. It allows for ample reflection and discussion of these issues. It creates space for all sorts of input from the Bible about Jesus. It makes it possible for people to process this material in the context of their own lives. It provides the opportunity for those who are further along in their pilgrimages to assist those who are just beginning. It enables the group itself to walk with each person through each new decision and each new step of faith. And a small group meets together for long enough periods of time to make growth over time possible. Finally, a small group is conducive to growth since at its center are care and community.

This sort of outreach typically begins when a group of committed Christians decides that it would be a good idea to invite nonchurch friends, relatives, co-workers, and neighbors to a small group in order to explore spiritual issues. A topic or theme is chosen that connects directly to the needs and interests of these friends. Invitations are issued and hopefully a group forms — made up of equal numbers of people from the church and from outside the church (but no more than a total of thirteen people). Community is built as people share their stories with one another. Study and discussion ensue. Trust grows in an atmosphere of confidentiality and vulnerability. Prayer becomes a central part of the group experience. People move consciously into new commitments, especially as Jesus becomes more and more central to the conversation.[2]

A small-group Bible study on the Gospel of Mark is the perfect example of process evangelism. There are various reasons for saying this. First, people are interested in the Bible today. Unlike earlier decades when a friend would be puzzled and even put off by an invitation to join a Bible study ("Why would I be interested in something like that?"), today a lot of people are curious about the Bible. They would welcome an invitation to join such a group. Second, to study Mark is to engage in exactly the sort of pilgrimage of discovery about Jesus that Mark has as his primary intention. Third, it would be possible to explore together each of the six titles for Jesus in Mark and to re-

2. See my book *Small Group Evangelism* (Downers Grove, Ill.: InterVarsity Press, 1985) for a description of how a group of Christians can plan small-group outreach.

flect on how each person in the small group relates to Jesus in each of his roles. By the way, this is as challenging to those who are already disciples of Jesus as it is to those just discovering Jesus. Many Christians have not reflected deeply on what it means in our lives to assert that we believe Jesus to be, for example, a prophet. Do we, in fact, trust his power and open ourselves to it? Each title has its own challenge which needs to be faced by all people in the group and not just the "pre-Christians." Fourth, the small group is a natural bridge into the church and its many ways of helping people move forward in pilgrimage.

There is great power and value in small-group evangelism. For one thing, small groups are quite popular today. Robert Wuthnow and George Gallup, Jr., discovered that 40 percent of the adult American population is in "a small group that meets regularly and provides caring and support for those who participate in it."[3] This means that some 75 million adult Americans are involved in a small group. (In comparison, each week some 80 million adults attend church.)[4] This figure does not take into account all the children and teenagers in small groups. Furthermore, these small groups are highly valued. Nearly three-quarters say their group is very important to them, with 30 percent saying it is extremely important.[5] Sixty-three percent of these small groups focus on religious or spiritual matter.[6] All these statistics point in the same direction: small groups are an ideal vehicle for outreach. They have great appeal to people; they are seen as valid ways to explore spiritual issues; and they are a comfortable habitat for people (as opposed to a worship service, for example, which feels alien to many newcomers).

For another thing, small groups offer an ideal learning environment. Small groups not only expose people to new data and information, they also make it possible to discuss this information with others so as to move the data from the mind to the heart. Furthermore, all this learning takes place in the context of community. Learning is enhanced when it occurs in the context of the love, care, support, trust, and mutuality of those whom one has come to know and trust. Finally, the small group is the best climate in which to make decisions. When people are involved with others who are also seeking to

---

3. Robert Wuthnow, *Sharing the Journey: Support Groups and America's New Quest for Community* (New York: Free Press, 1994), p. 45. There are at least 3 million small groups in America, or one group for every eighty people. So in a small city of fifty thousand people, at least six hundred small groups would be operating at any given time (p. 46).

4. Wuthnow, p. 52.

5. Wuthnow, p. 51.

6. Wuthnow, p. 55.

grow, they are especially open to new options, new choices, and new commitments. Small groups are the ideal environment for process evangelism.

Growth-Oriented Evangelism

Sometimes the outreach method of choice will involve tackling head-on the issues that trouble people. For each of us as we go through life, problems emerge that cause great distress. Oftentimes hidden in these problems are keys to our spiritual progress. For example, adolescence is a troubling time for everyone: parents, child, society in general. However, adolescence is a necessary developmental stage through which each child must progress so as to emerge as an independent adult. But the passage itself is, in varying degrees, stormy. In the midst of this turmoil both parent and child can discover the reality of God. Many teenagers discover God. In fact, more conversions take place in adolescence than in any other period of life.[7] Groups like Young Life that work with teens know that it is by developing relationships and patiently sharing the gospel over time in the context of these life issues that kids will grow in their spiritual pilgrimages. For parents, too, this can be a time of spiritual discovery. If they were to avail themselves of a church-sponsored support group or seminar on parenting teenagers, they could easily discover their need to be loved by God so as to be able to love better their teens.[8] They might also discover more about themselves as they ponder their own reactions during this time of stress, out of which their need for God might emerge.

This is what growth-oriented evangelism is all about: focusing on life issues, helping people through them in concrete ways, and doing so in ways that reveal the spiritual dimension of the problem.

Another example of growth-oriented evangelism is outreach to newly married couples. The aim of such a seminar (or small-group series) would be to help couples develop a healthy marriage.[9] Healthy marriages are a problem

7. Robert W. Crapps, *An Introduction to Psychology of Religion* (Macon, Ga.: Mercer University Press, 1986), p. 107.

8. For example, there are the small-group guidebook entitled *Parenting Adolescents: Easing the Way to Adulthood,* by William Cutler and Richard Peace, in the Serendipity Support Group Series (Littleton, Colo.: Serendipity House, 1990), and the small-group video series also entitled *Parenting Adolescents,* featuring Kevin Huggins, which includes two videocassettes, a small-group discussion guide, and a book (Colorado Springs: NavPress, 1989).

9. For an example of a small-group series that addresses this issue, see David Brown, assisted by Richard Peace and Dietrich Gruen, *Newly Married: How to Have a Great First*

these days, especially for Generation X couples who have not had adequate models for long-term marriages. Between 1960 and 1979 — the era in which Generation X was born — the American divorce rate tripled. And by 1986 the United States had the highest divorce rate in the Western world.[10] Not surprisingly, X-ers are marrying later. The number of "never marrieds" twenty-five to twenty-nine years old was 19 percent of the men and 10 percent of the women in 1970 (baby boomers), whereas by 1988 (Generation X) these figures had risen to 43 percent and 29 percent, respectively.[11]

Various themes could be addressed in such a seminar that would provide authentic help to a new couple. These include such things as discerning the expectations we bring to marriage, how to fight fairly, the nature of gender-based communication, developing intimacy, learning to enjoy life together, and dealing with tough issues in marriage (like money). It becomes quickly evident that there is a spiritual dimension to forming a strong marriage: unless we feel loved and valued, we find it difficult to love and value another person, even our spouse. But the sort of unconditional love we crave is in short supply in the world today. In fact, the only real source of this sort of love is God. So we need to be open to God and God's love in order to love better our spouse. Discussing the issue of God's love in this context would not feel contrived or inappropriate since it strikes right at the heart of the question of forging a solid marriage. In discussing such a concept we get into the question of spiritual pilgrimage in a natural, nonpressured, and helpful way.

Many types of issues can be addressed in this way. There are other *relational issues* that could form the basis for outreach groups, such as marriage enrichment or renewal, divorce recovery, parenting preschoolers, single parenting, blended family issues, coping with aging parents, and dealing with out-of-control children. *Developmental issues* are of concern to people and can be addressed helpfully in a spiritual context. These include such topics as dealing with midlife, coping with an empty nest, parenting adolescents, and facing retirement. Coping with *life problems* is yet another fruitful area of inquiry. The sorts of life problems that can be addressed include such things as

---

Year, Serendipity Support Group Series (Littleton, Colo.: Serendipity House, 1990). This book consists of fourteen small-group sessions which alternate between sessions that focus on an issue in developing a marriage (e.g., Session One deals with the dynamics of moving from single life into married life) and sessions that focus on the study of a Bible passage related to this issue (e.g., Session Two deals with Gen. 2 and the meaning of marriage).

10. Jimmy Long, *Generating Hope: A Strategy for Reaching the Postmodern Generation* (Downers Grove, Ill.: InterVarsity Press, 1997), p. 43.

11. Long, pp. 43-44.

unemployment or underemployment, raising learning-disabled children, recovery from failure, dealing with infertility, living with depression, coping with illness, dealing with grief and loss, and cancer recovery. *Developing a healthy lifestyle* can be addressed. This includes such issues as forming healthy eating patterns, engaging in a weight-loss or exercise program, and learning about stress management. *Addictive behavior* of all sorts is fair game for church-based programs, given the fact that the twelve-step program is a thinly restated version of the dynamics of transformation found in the New Testament.[12]

But it is not just *problems* that need to be addressed in growth-oriented evangelism. It is also important to explore the deep *longings* that people have: longings for purpose, longings for a place to serve, longings for "more" in life. Activities of this sort could focus on such things as finding one's calling in life, discerning gifts and skills, locating a place of service, and training in ways to help others. This also could involve a search for the meaning of life, exploration of the question of God, or involvement in various spiritual disciplines or practices (as will be discussed below). Each of these topics provides an opportunity for growth. Each can be used as a window into the state of one's spiritual pilgrimage.

The actual form of the activity will vary according to topic. Some issues can best be dealt with in a seminar format in which information is presented, case studies examined, and personal stories shared. Other issues can best be addressed in a small group in which data is presented (usually in written form, to be studied individually prior to each session) and then discussed thoroughly and applied individually with the help of the whole group. Certain topics such as the need for physical exercise require a practice format along with the opportunity to be part of a support group that will keep one involved in the exercise program.[13] Some issues might require a weekend retreat in which a variety of learning activities are utilized. Still other topics may best be dealt with via personal exercises that then lead to group activities.

---

12. See Richard Peace, *Twelve Steps: The Path to Wholeness,* Serendipity Support Group Series (Littleton, Colo.: Serendipity House, 1990), for a discussion of this assertion and as an example of a small-group approach to recovery.

13. It might well be asked how evangelism can take place in such a setting. The answer is that exercise is never an end in itself; it is a means to an end, which in this case is a healthy life. But many people need to come to grips with the whole Christian meaning of the body (as a gift from God to be used for God). They need to understand the interrelationship between body, mind, and soul and the importance of leading a balanced life. A spiritual understanding of the body provides the rationale for such an activity as exercise, and it gives the needed motivation to keep on exercising.

For example, stress management is best approached by means of a combination of events. First, information is needed: What is stress, how does it develop, and how can it be controlled?[14] But it is not enough to know about stress; it is also important to pinpoint the sources of stress in each individual's life. This is why the second form of activity would be small-group based, in which participants use a discussion protocol to examine their lives and discuss together the sources of their own stress. Third, stress management is not just a concept but a practice. So it is vital to involve the group in the experience of stress-reduction activities. This would include teaching and practicing the process of meditation and prayer. An experience of meditation and prayer would lead naturally into conversation about spiritual reality. A workshop on stress management would appeal to a wide range of people both with and without church connection. Furthermore, the discussion of spirituality is essential to a responsible presentation of the topic of stress management.

To do evangelism in this way it is necessary to have the right perspective. First, it is important that when offered, such seminars provide authentic help with no strings attached. There must be integrity, expertise, and skillful teaching so that anyone attending the event is helped in concrete ways. Such events must never be mere excuses to preach. Second, what is communicated about spiritual truth must emerge from the consideration of the topic itself and be directly related to the issue at hand. There must be a seamless whole to the event. The spiritual aspect can never just be tacked on. This is generally not a problem since many life issues do have a spiritual dimension to them so that in approaching the topic, it is not just desirable but necessary to raise these issues in order to deal responsibly with the topic. For example, any addiction group must deal with the question of God because the path to health in the twelve-step scheme rests on submission of oneself to God.[15] In this context it would be irresponsible not to raise spiritual issues. Third, these activities need to be situated right in the midst of the activities of the church community. Sometimes growth-events seem merely an adjunct to the real work of the church. In the worst case, they simply take place in a church building with no organic connection to the worshiping community. However, when such activities are part of the life of the Christian community, new possibility is opened up for participants. Then the event is not an end in itself.

14. The sort of information needed is discussed in a book like Arch Hart's *Adrenaline and Stress* (Waco, Tex.: Word, 1986).

15. While it is true that the Twelve Steps speak of "a Power greater than ourselves" (step 2), more frequently the reference is to God (steps 3, 5, 6, 11), although on two occasions this is qualified as "God as we understood Him" (steps 3 and 11).

People have the option of getting connected with other aspects of the community life as part of their ongoing growth.

The Spiritual Disciplines

People are fascinated by spirituality these days. As Jack Miles asks in a *New York Times Magazine* article entitled "Religion Makes a Comeback. (Belief to Follow)":

> Is America in the grip of a religious revival? Hundreds of thousands of Christian Promise Keepers rally in Washington, and hundreds of thousands of black men gather, at a Muslim's call, to make "atonement." Religion comes to life on television in series like "Seventh Heaven," "Touched by an Angel" and "Nothing Sacred." Religious books, once ghettoized by the publishing trade, are promoted heavily by the biggest chains, reviewed in major newspapers and monitored closely by Publishers Weekly. The Pope, of all people, writes a runaway best seller. Time and Newsweek seem virtually obsessed with religion: everything from the Infant Jesus to the Baby Dalai Lama.[16]

One of the substantial streams in this renewed interest in spirituality is the exploration of ancient forms of spirituality. New editions of spiritual classics are being issued (e.g., The Classics of Western Spirituality series by Paulist Press). And people are reading these spiritual classics (e.g., *The Interior Castle,* by Teresa of Avila) as well as books about saints like Teresa (e.g., *Holy Daring: An Outrageous Gift to Modern Spirituality from Saint Teresa the Grand Wild Woman of Avila,* by Mother Tessa Bielecki).[17] Kathleen Norris's two books on spirituality have become best-sellers *(Dakota: A Spiritual Geography* and *The Cloister Walk).*[18] It is not just active Christians who are reading such books. A wide range of people have joined in this exploration of the spiritual.

So it makes sense for the church to institute programs that enable people to get in touch with spirituality, both its concepts and its practices. And these programs need to be made accessible and attractive to people outside the church. This is a direct form of process evangelism. Such programs need

16. This was published in a special edition of the *New York Times Magazine* (December 7, 1997, p. 56) on the subject of the proliferation of new religious expressions in America. Miles is the author of *God: A Biography,* which won a Pulitzer Prize.

17. Rockport, Mass.: Element, 1994.

18. *Dakota: A Spiritual Geography* (Boston: Houghton Mifflin, 1994); *The Cloister Walk* (New York: Riverhead Books, 1996).

to be characterized by exploration of various approaches to spirituality, by immersion in the actual practices themselves, and by focused discussion concerning the God one seeks to connect with by means of such practices.

For example, I have written a series of four books on the spiritual disciplines.[19] Each book explores a different topic (spiritual journaling, spiritual autobiography, *lectio divina,* and meditative prayer). Each book is designed to be used by a small group that meets for between six and fourteen sessions. My assumption is that a small group is the ideal environment in which to learn spiritual disciplines, given the fact that few people are able to spend long periods of time in a monastic setting. People are able, however, to schedule weekly meetings during which they can explore spiritual disciplines with like-minded others. The books are written without a heavy use of theological language with the hope that they will be accessible to people with a limited background in the church. The anticipation is that these small groups will consist of people from both within and without the church. The aim of each book is to guide the group into an encounter with the living God.

How this process works is illustrated by the first book in the Spiritual Disciplines series, which explores the process of journaling. There is great interest in journaling these days, as is evident from the large number of blank journals one can purchase from any Barnes & Noble or Borders bookstore. However, most journaling consists of diary entries which are often little more than musings on the day. The aim of this small-group program is to help people discover a variety of new ways to use a journal that will help them get in touch with their spiritual journey. Each small-group session consists of information about a new aspect of journaling, instructions in that particular process of journaling, time for individual journaling, and group discussion following the journaling exercise. In addition, there are homework assignments, excerpts from journals, and Bible studies that examine the lives of individuals from a journal point of view. It is almost impossible to be part of such a group and not gain new insight into your spiritual pilgrimage.

A variety of themes can be explored in a spiritual disciplines program. *Prayer* is a topic of great interest to all sorts of people these days. There is a deep desire to learn ways of prayer that go beyond merely asking God for in-

---

19. The Spiritual Disciplines series of books consists of four titles: *Spiritual Journaling: Recording Your Journey toward God* (Colorado Springs: NavPress/Pilgrimage Publications, 1995, 1998); *Spiritual Autobiography: Discovering and Sharing Your Spiritual Story* (Colorado Springs: NavPress/Pilgrimage Publications, 1996, 1998); *Contemplative Bible Reading: Experiencing God through Scripture* (Colorado Springs: NavPress/Pilgrimage Publications, 1996, 1998); and *Meditative Prayer: Entering God's Presence* (Colorado Springs: NavPress, 1998).

tervention when problems arise. There is also a renewed interest in *Bible study,* especially by the baby boom generation, which grew up biblically illiterate but now is fascinated by the Bible. Their interest, however, is not just in learning facts from the Bible. They want Bible study that makes a difference in their lives. As a result, *lectio divina* (which is the earliest form of monastic Bible study) is a type of Bible study that connects with people. It is also possible to put together reading groups that examine and discuss *devotional classics* — ranging from Augustine's *Confessions* to Evelyn Underhill's *Mysticism* and Julian of Norwich's *Revelations of Divine Love.* Modern spiritual writers are also of great interest, so a group might meet to study one of the books by Thomas Merton, Henri Nouwen, or C. S. Lewis. The book *Devotional Classics,* edited by Richard J. Foster and James Bryan Smith, is a fine resource for small groups to use.[20] It consists of brief readings from over fifty authors, Bible passages related to each reading, reflection questions, and suggested exercises.

Another way to reach out to people evangelistically is via spiritual direction, which is experiencing a revival of interest, mainly due to its discovery by Protestants. All sorts of people are now seeking out spiritual directors as a way of exploring this side of life. Ben Campbell Johnson argues that it is via spiritual direction that clergy can make contact with seekers.[21] He talks about how ministers have become marginalized from the mainstream of society. They work with members of their church but have little natural contact with culture in general. But this renewal of interest in spirituality opens a new role to them. They are the ones recognized by society as the "experts" about God, so it is conceivable that people would seek out pastors who make known their availability to give spiritual direction. Spiritual direction, by definition, focuses on discerning the nature of one's spiritual pilgrimage and the challenges that God is giving to him or her. It is the ideal evangelistic environment.[22]

Given their new popularity, *retreat centers* can also become a place in which process evangelism takes place. People are open to weekend retreats which deal with a host of subjects. Attendees anticipate (and desire) that these issues be dealt with from a spiritual point of view. In this context a person is wide open to developing a relationship with God.

20. San Francisco: Harper San Francisco, 1991, 1992, 1993.

21. Ben Campbell Johnson, *Speaking of God: Evangelism as Initial Spiritual Guidance* (Louisville: Westminster/John Knox, 1991), p. 10.

22. However, it is important to resist the pressure to "tell" the directee what he or she should do. Spiritual direction is all about assisting a directee to discern on his or her own what God is saying. Of course, this is exactly what one desires when doing evangelism.

Worship Evangelism

The megachurches have discovered how powerful worship itself can be for evangelism. In the so-called seeker-sensitive and seeker-driven churches, the needs, interests, and questions of "pre-Christians" are factored into the whole worship experience. Music is based on the tastes of outsiders. Sermons are preached with little overt theological vocabulary. Offerings are not taken during the service (since research indicates that one of the major complaints by outsiders is that churches always seem to be asking for money). Drama and media are used during the service. Multiple programs are available during the week that deal with issues that trouble people and open them up to the spiritual side of life. In fact, many seeker churches go so far as to have an architectural design that helps outsiders feel comfortable in the church building. Such spaces include few liturgical symbols, and the meeting place feels more like an auditorium than a sanctuary. People can slip in and out anonymously if they choose. Church looks different when it is designed for seekers.[23]

Seeker churches understand intuitively what I am calling process evangelism. They do not expect immediate "decisions for Christ." They urge people to explore, to question, and to get involved as a way of coming to faith.

Most churches are not (nor ever will be) seeker oriented, but all churches can develop a seeker sensitivity. Even as simple a process as walking through the entire worship experience from the vantage point of a first-time visitor can result in significant changes that aid outreach. Imagine that you are new to the church. What is your experience as you try to park, are greeted at the door, find a seat, look at the bulletin, participate in the service, listen to the sermon, visit the coffee hour? Is the experience easy? Is it positive? Does the service respond to spiritual hunger? Does it promote links to the Christian community? Will it assist people in their spiritual pilgrimages?

Once a church is made seeker friendly, it can evaluate how to use its liturgical activities as a way to reach out to new people. One good point of contact is via ritual events such as marriages, baptisms, confirmations, and funerals. In such services the presence of Christ and the power of the gospel will be evident. Needless to say, these services cannot be transformed into something other than what they are meant to be. For example, too many funeral

---

23. There is no one model for seeker churches. What I have described is typical of some but not all seeker churches. For further information see such books as Ed Dobson, *Starting a Seeker Sensitive Service: How Traditional Churches Can Reach the Unchurched* (Grand Rapids: Zondervan, 1993); Lynne Hybels and Bill Hybels, *Rediscovering Church: The Story and Vision of Willow Creek Community Church* (Grand Rapids: Zondervan, 1995); and Rick Warren, *The Purpose Driven Church* (Grand Rapids: Zondervan, 1995).

services consist mostly of a gospel sermon directed at the "unsaved" who have come to mourn the loss of a friend. Such sermons are seldom effective and mostly serve to confirm the negative stereotypes people have about Christianity. On the other hand, a funeral service that rings with the hope of the resurrection, even as it celebrates the life of the one who has died, is a powerful witness to the reality of God.

A second natural point of contact with the community is via holiday worship services. People who might not otherwise come to church are there on Easter and Christmas. Such services are wonderful opportunities to reflect basic Christian realities so as to spark interest in spiritual pilgrimage. And they can be used to make connections with those who attend so as to foster further contact. Special worship events can also be planned, such as concerts (churches have kept alive both classical and folk music), celebrations (of community events), and presentations (like the Black Nativity at Christmas). The aim in all these events is to give people the opportunity to participate in powerful worship experiences which awaken or encourage spiritual inquiry and forge personal links with those in the church and with the truth of the gospel.

Conclusions

The fact that there are two patterns for conversion in the New Testament opens up rich new possibilities for evangelism. And certainly evangelism in the United States is badly in need of renewal. The very term "evangelism" has come to have negative connotations to many people in this culture. Evangelism is often seen as coercive, manipulative, and dishonest. Its practitioners are portrayed as hostile, falsely superior, and often just plain rude. More recently, evangelism has become suspect because some of the televangelists have been associated with deceptive financial practices and dishonest morality. In some denominations pastors joke about the "E word," by which they mean that evangelism is not something to be discussed in polite theological company.

The problem is, these negative stereotypes contain some truth. Not all of our evangelistic activities have been worthy of the name of Jesus (though it needs to be stated that only a minority practice evangelism in such less-than-loving ways). Where do these coercive behaviors come from? My own feeling is that in America, since the turn to the twentieth century, our thinking about evangelism has all too often been shaped more by cultural paradigms than by biblical ones. For example, I think many current evangelistic methodologies owe more to business than to the Bible. We have come to understand evangelism in terms of buying and selling. To evangelize is to seek out potential customers. Once they are located, then you manipulate the situation by means of clever questions or strong emotions so that you get to deliver your sales pitch on behalf of Jesus. The aim in all of this is to close the deal by getting the customer to sign on the dotted line by praying a brief prayer of commitment. Then it is off to the next customer. I overstate the case, of course, by putting it in such raw terms. But it makes the point: to preach the gospel is not the same as selling Jesus to a needy customer.

There is a second cultural metaphor that shapes our practice of evangelism. We sometimes think of evangelism in terms of a military enterprise. We talk about evangelistic crusades. We think of beachheads and strategies. We are concerned about enemies. I do not think all this is just an innocent or naive use of language. We justify questionable actions because, after all, it is a battle of good with evil. Furthermore, the whole enterprise is strongly male in tone and character, as befits the American view of war.

By recovering biblical paradigms by which to think about evangelism, we can redeem our methodologies so that we are proud of what we are doing, not embarrassed, and can be confident that evangelism is a worthy enterprise. Over time it might even be possible to erase the negative cultural stereotypes about evangelism. Even more importantly, with reinvigorated methodologies fueled by a genuine enthusiasm based on a deep relationship to Jesus, people in this culture can be reached with the good news about Jesus. And it will sound like the good news it is.

I began Part III by asserting in chapter 11 that how we think about conversion determines how we do evangelism. With a clear and nuanced understanding of how Paul and the Twelve were converted, we are able to forge ways of evangelism that will draw people to Jesus.

APPENDIX

A Lexical Summary of Conversion

In the New Testament, the word *epistrophē* is translated "conversion." But in fact, there are three related word groups that express the concept of conversion: *epistrephō, metanoeō,* and *metamelomai.* The first two word groups are similar in that they convey the idea of turning around, of reversing direction and going the opposite way. The idea of turning around is the core meaning of the concept of conversion. There are, however, important distinctions between these two word groups. *Epistrephō* is the broader term. It defines the actual turning itself. *Epistrephō* involves both repentance *(metanoeō)* and faith *(pistis)*. *Metanoeō*, on the other hand, is a more focused word. It describes the *decision* to turn; it emphasizes the inner, cognitive (mental) decision to make a break with the past. *Metanoeō* must be combined with *pistis* in order to bring about *epistrophē.* The third word group, *metamelomai*, carries the idea of feeling sorry for failure. It focuses on past sin, error, debt, or failure and is connected with the concept of repentance. In the Bible it has less to do with conversion proper than do the other two words.

Epistrophē

The idea of conversion *(epistrophē)* is found in the writings of secular Greek authors. "In the classical philosophical literature *epistrephō* and its sub. *epistrophē* mean *inter alia* the turning of the soul to piety or the divine. This concept passed from secular Gk. via the LXX into the vocabulary of the NT."[1]

---

1. F. Laubach, *"Epistrephō,"* in *The New International Dictionary of New Testament Theology,* ed. Colin Brown (Grand Rapids: Zondervan, 1975), vol. 1, p. 354.

The Hebrew word which underlies the concept of *epistrophē* in the LXX is *shubh*. *Shubh* occurs over a thousand times in the Old Testament. It is, in fact, the twelfth most frequent verb in the Old Testament.[2] It means "turn around, return (qal), bring back, restore (hiph.)."[3] Most often it is used in the normal sense of physical motion, as in Ruth 1:16: "Don't urge me to leave you or to *turn back* [*lashuv*] from you" (NIV).[4] "It appears with its specifically theological meaning c. 120 times: turn around, return, be converted, bring back, in the sense of a change in behaviour and of a return to the living God."[5] An example of this use is Isaiah 55:7:

> Let the wicked forsake his way
> and the evil man his thoughts.
> Let him *turn to* the LORD, and he will have mercy on him. (NIV)

When used in this theological sense, *shubh* has rich connotations. The nature of the turning is described as being *from* evil (Jer. 18:8) *to* God (Mal. 3:7); the impulse for turning originates with God (Jer. 31:18; Lam. 5:21), though it can be resisted by human beings (Hos. 5:4); the result of turning is forgiveness (Isa. 55:7), remission of punishment (Jon. 3:9ff.), prosperity and fertility (Hos. 14:5ff.), and life (Ezek. 33:14ff.); the result of not turning is disaster (Amos 4:6-8; Hos. 11:5; 1 Kings 9:6-9) and death (Ezek. 33:9, 11); the call to turn comes both to the nation (Jon. 3:10; Deut. 4:30-31; Hos. 3:5; Mal. 4:5f.; Ezek. 11:19, 36:26f.; 37:14) and to individuals (2 Kings 23:25; Jer. 32:31ff.; Ezek. 18:30-31). When *shubh* was used in both rabbinic and Hellenistic Judaism, it retained the Old Testament sense. There is an interesting variation at one point, however. In the Qumran community, in order to be admitted one had to be "converted." The "turning" in this case was defined as turning from evil (as in the OT) to the Law of Moses (and not to God, as in the OT). The members of the community called themselves "those who had turned from transgression."[6]

In the New Testament, *epistrephō* is used some thirty-six times. In each case it has one of two possible meanings. It means either "turn around" in the sense of physical motion (e.g., Matt. 9:22: "Jesus *turned* and saw her" [NIV]) or "turn around and follow after God" in the theological sense (e.g., Acts 3:19: "Repent, then, and *turn* to God" [NIV]).

2. Jacob W. Heikkinen, "'Conversion': A Biblical Study," National Faith and Order Colloquium, World Council of Churches, June 12-17, 1966, p. 3.

3. Laubach, "*Epistrephō*," p. 354.

4. All italics in Scripture quotations in the appendix are mine.

5. Laubach, "*Epistrephō*," p. 354.

6. Laubach, "*Epistrephō*," pp. 354-55.

18 times it has its secular meaning of turning, returning, turning away, etc. (cf. Matt. 10:13; 2 Pet. 2:22), and 18 times with its theological meaning of conversion especially in Acts and the Epistles (cf. Mk. 4:12 par.; Lk. 1:16f.; 22:32; Acts 15:19; 2 Cor. 3:16; Jas. 5:19f.). Here, unlike the LXX, it is often synonymous with *metanoeō*. Only in Matt. 18:3 and Jn. 12:40 is *strephō* used with the meaning of turning oneself (be converted); likewise *apostrephō* only in Acts 3:26. The noun *epistrophē* is found only once in the NT in Acts 15:3.[7]

The use of *epistrephō* in the New Testament bears a lot of similarity to the way *shubh* is used in the Old Testament. The turning is from wicked ways (Acts 3:26), from the error of one's ways (James 5:20), from darkness to light and from the power of Satan to God (Acts 26:18), from worthless things to the living God (Acts 14:15), from idols to serve the living and true God (1 Thess. 1:9), from going astray to the Shepherd and Overseer of one's soul (1 Pet. 2:25); the turning is to the Lord (Acts 9:35; 11:21; 15:19; 26:20; 2 Cor. 3:16); the result of turning is forgiveness of sin and times of refreshment (Acts 3:19; 26:18), it is finding a place in the community of faith (Act 26:18), and it is finding (or in this case, not finding) healing (Matt. 13:15; see also Mark 4:12; John 12:40; Acts 28:27). In contrast, *epistrephō* in the negative sense is turning back to weak and miserable principles (Gal. 4:9) or turning one's back on the sacred command (2 Pet. 2:21).

Although, as these verses show, what one turns from is sometimes in view when *epistrephō* is used, the emphasis is on what one turns to (or more properly, to whom one turns). The focus is on God or the Lord. It is *metanoeō* that looks at the past, at that from which the person (or nation) has turned. *Metamelomai*, then, is related to *metanoeō* in that it captures the sense of regret over the life that was once led but from which there has been turning.

The distinction between *metanoeō* and *epistrephō* is seen most clearly in the instances in which both words are found: Acts 3:19-20, "Repent, then, and turn to God, so that your sins may be wiped out, that times of refreshing may come from the Lord, and that he may send the Christ, who has been appointed for you — even Jesus" (NIV), and Acts 26:20, "I preached that they should repent and turn to God and prove their repentance by their deeds" (NIV). Were there not a difference in focus between *metanoeō* and *epistrephō*, it would not be necessary to use both in verses like these. But as it is, *metanoeō* looks backs to past sins while *epistrephō* looks ahead to the one who is now and will be the Lord.

---

7. Laubach, *"Epistrephō,"* p. 355.

There is yet another key word paired with *epistrephō*. It is *pisteuō*. The connection between belief and conversion is seen in Acts 11:21: "A great number of people believed and turned to the Lord" (NIV). The believing (faith) looks to the future, to the one in whom the faith is placed, namely, the Lord. Thus the New Testament equation seems to be repentance plus faith equals conversion. "*Epistrephō* has a wider meaning than *metanoeō*, for it always includes faith, while *metanoeō* and *pisteuō* can stand together and complement each other. . . ."[8]

However, lest too fine a distinction be made between these words, the comment of J. Schniewind must be kept in mind:

> The word "repent" really means "be converted." We sometimes translate it by "change your mind." Certainly this translation is founded on a literal interpretation of the Greek word, but it is questionable if in New Testament times the meaning of the word was understood so literally. At any rate, John the Baptist and Jesus Himself spoke Aramaic. In that language the word which we translate with "repent" must have been the same which in the Old Testament Luther always translated "convert." Much more is at stake than just a change of mind. Certainly to get a new heart is implied too, but our actions also are involved even to the smallest and the least; and above all our relationship to God is at stake and not merely a change of our Self. It is very important to remember that repentance is the same as conversion, and nothing less than that. It was a fundamental discovery for Luther that "repent ye" really means "be converted."[9]

Metanoeō

The *metanoia* word group is seldom found in classical literature. When it was used, however, "the verb *metanoein* means to take subsequent note of something, to adopt another view, and therefore to regret the prior viewpoint."[10] In classical literature "the noun *metanoia* signified a change of mind."[11] "In the non-canonical Jewish literature, two meanings attach to it, namely that of

8. Laubach, "*Epistrephō*," p. 355.
9. Julius Schniewind, "The Biblical Doctrine of Conversion," *Scottish Journal of Theology* 5 (September 1952): 270.
10. Richard J. Sklba, "The Call to New Beginnings: A Biblical Theology of Conversion," *Biblical Theology Bulletin* 11 (July 1981): 67.
11. Heikkinen, p. 4. He offers an example by citing a passage from Xenophon: "But when we reflected that Cyrus . . . had brought very many men under his sway . . . we were forced to change our mind *metanoein* . . ." (*Cyropaedia* 1.1.3), p. 13.

change of mind and of regret."[12] Likewise, there are few uses of this word group in the LXX. Only the verb is used, and then to render the Hebrew *niham* (niph.), which means "to be sorry about something,"[13] although it would appear that *metamelomai* better captured the sense of *niham*.[14] The whole concept of turning around and coming back to God which is expressed by the Hebrew verb *shubh* is unfailingly translated by *epistrephō*. Summing up the sense of the word prior to the New Testament:

> If the change of mind involves the recognition that the previous opinion was false or bad, we get the meaning of feel remorse or regret for the vb. and that of a change of mind, remorse, regret for the noun. In pre-Biblical Gk. the word-group does not develop the precision which characterizes its use in the NT. Gk. society never thought of a radical change in a man's life as a whole, of conversion or turning around, even though we may find some of the factors which belong to conversion. This shows that the concept of conversion is not derived from Gk. thought, and its origin must be sought elsewhere.[15]

The distinctive New Testament meaning of *metanoia* is discerned first and foremost in the preaching of John the Baptist in the light of the Qumran movement. The Qumran community called itself the "covenant of repentance," *berith teshuba*. "John the Baptist appeared in the wilderness preaching the baptism of *metanoia*, that is, we may safely assume, the baptism of *teshuba*. *Metanoia*, therefore, is to be understood as the equivalent for the Hebrew *shuv* [*shubh*], as expressed by the great prophets, who appealed to Israel 'to turn,' or 'to return,' to true obedience to the covenant."[16] In other words, whereas the Septuagint translators failed to translate *shubh* by *metanoeō*, the writers of the New Testament felt that it correctly captured the prophetic sense of the word.

---

12. Heikkinen, p. 13. He illustrates: "So it appears in Philo's writings. 'Shall anyone endure to come near to God, the most pure, when he himself is impure in soul and without the intention to *change his purpose, metanoein* in regard to these impurities?' (I, 274). The book of Sirach (48:15) contains this passage: 'During all these events, the people did not change their purpose, *metanoese* and did not withdraw from their sins.' . . . The Palestinian use of *metanoein* followed not the classical sense but indicated regret and change of purpose" (p. 13).

13. J. Goetzmann, *"Metanoia,"* in *The New International Dictionary of New Testament Theology*, ed. Colin Brown (Grand Rapids: Zondervan, 1975), vol. 1, p. 357.

14. Heikkinen, p. 4.

15. Goetzmann, p. 357.

16. Heikkinen, p. 4.

Interestingly, both John the Baptist and Jesus preached the identical message: "Repent, for the kingdom of heaven is near" (NIV).[17] The baptism of John was anticipatory in nature; he was challenging Israel to prepare for the coming of the kingdom. The coming of Jesus inaugurated that kingdom. "Hence, repentance is now no longer obedience to a law but to a person. The call to repentance becomes a call to discipleship. So repentance, faith and discipleship are different aspects of the same thing (Mk. 1:15, 'Repent and believe')."[18]

> *Metanoia*, then, is the key word symbolizing the character of the response on the part of men to the preaching of the judgment and the rule of God. It marks a total turning on God's terms, a movement from the direction in which they are going to its opposite in order to be re-established in a relationship of faithfulness to their covenant-God. It draws its force, in part from the past, that is, from the prophets, and this serves as the bearer of the verb *shuv* [*shubh*] in its highest potency. But, it also draws its force, in part, from the present events marking the end-time. The new motif which gives a unique energy to the *metanoia* of the New Testament is the eschatological reality in face of the imminent rule of God.[19]

Metamelomai

The third word group, *metamelomai*, is related to *metanoeō* in that it involves regret over past actions — a change of mind about them. However, it differs from *metanoeō* in that *metamelomai* is more a feeling than a decision, much less an action. The sense of *metamelomai* is that one regrets a past deed but does not decide necessarily never to do it again, much less to express this new view in concrete action (e.g., restitution). *Metanoeō* is the stronger word and the one that bears upon the process of conversion.

In both the classical and Old Testament contexts, *metamelomai* is not, however, distinguished from *metanoeō*. But by the New Testament the two words cease to have identical meanings. Two examples illustrate the differentiation between the two words:

> Judas recognized that Jesus had been wrongly condemned. He regretted his betrayal (Matt. 27:3), but he did not find the way to genuine repentance.

17. Matt. 3:2 records these words for John while Matt. 4:17 records them for Jesus.
18. Goetzmann, p. 358.
19. Heikkinen, p. 5.

We find the same differentiation in 2 Cor. 7:8-10. Paul did not regret that he had written a sharp letter to the Corinthians, for the sorrow caused to its recipients had led them to true repentance *(metanoia)*, to an inner turning to God. There is no need to regret such a repentance, for it always serves only our salvation.[20]

Conversion in the Bible

Various conclusions can be drawn from the lexical meaning of the words translated "conversion" and "repentance." First, the theological sense of these words derives its meaning from the secular use made of them. At the heart of both *epistrophē* and *metanoia* is the idea of "turning." Whatever else conversion is, it is a turning. Second, when these words are used in the Bible in a theological sense, the turning always has to do with God. It is a turning away from that which is against God and God's ways (sin, idols, darkness, Satan), and it is a turning to God (the Lord, the living God). Conversion is always seen in relationship to God. Third, in the Old Testament it is often the nation as a whole that is called upon to turn or return to God, whereas in the New Testament it is more often individuals who turn to God (though even here this turning takes place in the context of the kingdom of God with all that implies about becoming part of a kingdom). Fourth, the more comprehensive of the two words is *epistrephō,* which describes the act of turning. While *metanoeō* is used at times as almost an equivalent of *epistrephō,* when the two words are used together it becomes clear that *metanoeō* is a word that looks backwards — back to sin or wrongdoing or error from which one decides to turn. Fifth, the root meaning of *metanoeō* focuses on a decision of the mind (a cognitive choice), and this sense is never completely lost. Repentance *(metanoia)* begins with the cognitive decision to turn. A choice is made. A decision is reached. Sixth, the decision to turn, however, is not the turning itself. That which activates repentance and moves it from a mental decision to a behavioral activity is faith *(pistis).* When a person looks back and decides to leave behind (turn away from) certain errant ways or false gods, that is repentance. When that same person looks ahead in trust and confidence to Jesus as the one who can and will forgive, that is faith. Repentance and faith taken together result in conversion in the New Testament sense.

There is a picture implicit in this schema (harking back to the root no-

20. F. Laubach, "Metamelomai," in *The New International Dictionary of New Testament Theology,* ed. Colin Brown (Grand Rapids: Zondervan, 1975), vol. 1, p. 356.

tion of physical movement). A person is walking along a path in pursuit of certain goals (or gods). Something causes that person to recognize the error of his ways, the futile nature of his life, the destructive quality of that around which he has oriented his life. He decides that he no longer wants to follow this old path. That is repentance. The decision is made to go in the opposite way. But can he go in a new direction? Is there a new way? Will he be forgiven the past and welcomed into the new way? In confident trust and with joy he realizes and accepts the gospel message that Jesus is the Way. That is faith. Thus he stops, turns around, and goes in the opposite direction (toward Jesus Christ and away from sin). The experience of this turning is conversion.

Thus far the focus has been on the person: the person who repents, reaches out in faith, and experiences conversion. Yet, it is quite clear from the New Testament that God the Holy Spirit is an active agent in this whole process. "But to all who received him, who believed in his name, he gave power to become children of God, who were born, not of blood or of the will of the flesh or of the will of man, but of God" (John 1:12-13). The theological term for this work of God in the hearts and lives of those who turn to God is regeneration. Without regeneration conversion is mere human effort at self-improvement; without the work of the Holy Spirit evangelism becomes manipulation. But having said this, I must note that regeneration will not be considered in this book. It is a vast subject in its own right.[21] The focus here is on the human side of the equation, on the experience of conversion. The inner work of God both in leading people to the point of conversion and in bringing about this conversion is assumed though not dealt with, except at a few points where it is necessary to focus on God's work in order to understand the event in view.

---

21. See Peter Toon, *Born Again: A Biblical and Theological Study of Regeneration* (Grand Rapids: Baker, 1987), and Bernhard Citron, *New Birth: A Study of the Evangelical Doctrine of Conversion in the Protestant Fathers* (Edinburgh: University Press, 1951), for informative discussions of regeneration.

Selected Bibliography

Biblical and Theological Studies

Abraham, William J. *The Logic of Evangelism.* Grand Rapids: William B. Eerdmans Publishing Co., 1989.

Achtemeier, Paul J. *Mark.* Proclamation Commentaries. Philadelphia: Fortress, 1975.

————. "An Exposition of Mark 9:30-37." *Interpretation* 30 (1976): 178-83.

————. "Mark as Interpreter of the Jesus Traditions." *Interpretation* 32 (October 1978): 339-52.

————. "'And He Followed Him': Miracles and Discipleship in Mark 10:46-52." *Semeia* 11 (1978): 116-45.

————. "'He Taught Them Many Things': Reflections on Marcan Christology." *Catholic Biblical Quarterly* 42 (1980): 465-81.

Aingers, Geoffrey. "Conversion and Church Practice." *Study Encounter* 1 (1965): 102-5.

Aldrich, Joseph C. *Life-Style Evangelism.* Portland, Oreg.: Multnomah Press, 1981.

Arias, Mortimer. *Announcing the Reign of God: Evangelism and the Subversive Memory of Jesus.* Philadelphia: Fortress, 1984.

Arn, Win. "Mass Evangelism: The Bottom Line." *Church Growth: America* 4, no. 1 (1978): 4-7, 16-19.

"At Cross Purposes: Jesus and the Disciples in Mark." *Furrow* 33 (June 1982): 331-39.

Augustine, A. *The Confessions.* Garden City, N.Y.: Doubleday, 1960.

Aune, David E. "Magic in Early Christianity." In *Aufstieg und Niedergang der römischen Welt* II.23.2 (1980), pp. 1507-57.

Bacon, Benjamin W. "The Purpose of Mark's Gospel." *Journal of Biblical Literature* 29 (1910): 41-60.

Baillie, John. *Baptism and Conversion.* New York: Scribner, 1963.

Baird, William. "Mark 1:14-15." *Interpretation* 33 (October 1979): 394-98.

Barclay, William. *Turning to God: A Study of Conversion in the Book of Acts and Today.* Grand Rapids: Baker, 1973.

————. *The Gospel of Mark.* Rev. ed. Philadelphia: Westminster, 1975.

Barna, George. *Evangelism That Works.* Ventura, Calif.: Regal, 1995.

Barrett, C. K. *New Testament Essays.* London: SPCK, 1972.

————. "The House of Prayer and the Den of Thieves." In *Jesus und Paulus,* edited by E. Earle Ellis and Erich Grässer, pp. 13-20. Göttingen: Vandenhoeck & Ruprecht, 1975.

Bauer, Walter. *A Greek-English Lexicon of the New Testament and Other Early Christian Literature.* Translated and adapted by William F. Arndt and F. Wilbur Gingrich from the 4th Ger. ed., 1952. Chicago: University of Chicago Press, 1957.

Beavis, Mary Ann. "Mark's Teaching on Faith." *Biblical Theology Bulletin* 16 (October 1986): 139-42.

Beker, J. Christiaan. *Paul the Apostle: The Triumph of God in Life and Thought.* Philadelphia: Fortress, 1980.

Bernard, J. H. "A Study of St. Mark 10:38, 39." *Journal of Theological Studies* 28 (1927): 262-70.

Bertram, Georg. "Strephō." In *Theological Dictionary of the New Testament,* edited by Gerhard Friedrich, translated and edited by Geoffrey W. Bromiley, vol. 7, pp. 714-29. Grand Rapids: William B. Eerdmans Publishing Co., 1971.

Best, Ernest. *The Temptation and the Passion: The Markan Soteriology.* Cambridge: University Press, 1965.

————. "Discipleship in Mark: Mark 8.22–10.52." *Scottish Journal of Theology* 23 (August 1970): 323-37.

————. "The Camel and the Needle's Eye (Mark 10:25)." *Expository Times* 82 (1970-71): 83-89.

————. "Mark 10:13-16: The Child as Model Recipient." In *Biblical Studies: Essays in Honour of William Barclay,* edited by Johnston R. McKay and James F. Miller, pp. 119-34, 209-14. London: Collins, 1976.

————. "The Role of the Disciples in Mark." *New Testament Studies* 23 (July 1977): 377-401.

————. *Following Jesus: Discipleship in the Gospel of Mark.* Sheffield: JSOT Press, 1981.

————. *Mark: The Gospel as Story.* Edinburgh: T. & T. Clark, 1983.

————. *Disciples and Discipleship: Studies in the Gospel according to Mark.* Edinburgh: T. & T. Clark, 1986.

Betz, Hans Dieter, ed. *Christology and a Modern Pilgrimage: A Discussion with Norman Perrin.* N.p.: Society of Biblical Literature, 1971.

Birdsall, J. Neville. "The Withering of the Fig-Tree (Mark 11:12-14, 20-22)." *Expository Times* 73 (1961-62): 191.

Blatherwick, David. "The Markan Silhouette?" *New Testament Studies* 17 (January 1971): 184-92.

Bligh, Philip H. "A Note on *Huios Theou* in Mark 15:39." *Expository Times* 80 (November 1968): 51-53.

Boozer, Jack. "A Biblical Understanding of Religious Experience." *Journal of Bible and Religion* 26, no. 4 (October 1958): 291-97.

Bornkamm, Günther. *Paul.* Translated by D. M. G. Stalker. New York: Harper & Row, 1971.

Borsch, F. H. "Mark 14:62 and I Enoch 62:5." *New Testament Studies* 14 (1967-68): 565-67.

Bowker, J. W. "'Merkabah' Visions and the Visions of Paul." *Journal of Semitic Studies* 16 (1971): 157-73.

Bratcher, Robert G. "A Note on *Huios Theou* (Mark 15:39)." *Expository Times* 68 (October 1956): 27-28.

————. "Mark 15:39: The Son of God." *Expository Times* 80 (June 1969): 286.

Bratcher, Robert G., and Eugene A. Nida. *A Translator's Handbook on the Gospel of Mark*. London: United Bible Societies, 1961.

Brauer, Jerald C. "Conversion: From Puritanism to Revivalism." *Journal of Religion* 58 (1978): 227-43.

Brett, Laurence F. X. "Suggestions for an Analysis of Mark's Arrangement." In *Mark: A New Translation with Introduction and Commentary*, by C. S. Mann, pp. 174-90. Garden City, N.Y.: Doubleday, 1986.

Brown, Colin, ed. *The New International Dictionary of New Testament Theology*. 3 vols. Exeter: Paternoster, 1976.

Brown, David, with Richard Peace and Dietrich Gruen. *Newly Married: How to Have a Great First Year*. Serendipity Support Group Series. Littleton, Colo.: Serendipity House, 1990.

Bruce, F. F. *Paul: Apostle of the Heart Set Free*. Grand Rapids: Wm. B. Eerdmans Publishing Co., 1977.

————. *The Epistle to the Galatians: A Commentary on the Greek Text*. The New International Greek Testament Commentary. Grand Rapids: Wm. B. Eerdmans Publishing Co., 1982.

Brueggemann, Walter. *Biblical Perspectives on Evangelism: Living in a Three-Storied Universe*. Nashville: Abingdon, 1993.

Buchanan, George Wesley. "Mark 14:54." *Expository Times* 68 (October 1956): 27.

Buck, Charles, and Greer Taylor. *Saint Paul: A Study of the Development of His Thought*. New York: Scribner, 1969.

Bultmann, Rudolf. *Theology of the New Testament*. Translated by Kendrick Brobel. New York: Scribner, 1965.

Burkill, T. A. "Strain on the Secret: An Examination of Mark 11:1–13:37." *Zeitschrift für die neutestamentliche Wissenschaft* (1960): 31-46.

————. *Mysterious Revelation: An Examination of the Philosophy of St. Mark's Gospel*. Ithaca, N.Y.: Cornell University Press, 1963.

————. *New Light on the Earliest Gospel: Seven Markan Studies*. Ithaca, N.Y.: Cornell University Press, 1972.

Burkitt, F. C. "On Romans 9:5 and Mark 14:61." *Journal of Theological Studies* 5 (1904): 451-55.

Burrell, David B., C.S.C., and Franzita Kane, C.S.C., eds. *Evangelization in the American Context*. Notre Dame, Ind.: University of Notre Dame Press, 1976.

Burt, Robert L. *Good News in Growing Churches*. New York: Pilgrim, 1990.

————, ed. *Affirming Evangelism: A Call to Renewed Commitment in the United Church of Christ*. Cleveland: United Church Board Homeland Ministries, 1993.

Callahan, Kennon L. *Twelve Keys to an Effective Church*. San Francisco: Harper & Row, 1983.

Calloud, Jean. "Toward a Structural Analysis of the Gospel of Mark." *Semeia* 16 (1980): 133-65.

Carl, William J., III. "Mark 10:17-27 (28-31)." *Interpretation* 33 (1979): 283-88.

Carnell, Edward John. *The Kingdom of Love and the Pride of Life.* Grand Rapids: Wm. B. Eerdmans Publishing Co., 1960.

Carroll, Jackson, Carl Dudley, and William McKinney. *Handbook for Congregational Studies.* Nashville: Abingdon, 1986.

Charlesworth, James H., ed. *The Old Testament Pseudepigrapha.* 2 vols. Garden City, N.Y.: Doubleday, 1983.

Citron, Bernhard. *New Birth: A Study of the Evangelical Doctrine of Conversion in the Protestant Fathers.* Edinburgh: University Press, 1951.

"Common Witness and Proselytism: A Study Document." *Ecumenical Review* 23 (January 1971): 1-12.

Conn, Walter E., ed. *Conversion: Perspectives on Personal and Social Transformation.* New York: Alba House, 1978.

Costas, Orlando. "Conversion as a Complex Experience." *Gospel in Context* 1 (1978): 14-24, 40.

Cousar, Charles B. "Eschatology and Mark's *Theologia Crucis:* A Critical Analysis of Mark 13." *Interpretation* 24 (1970): 321-35.

Cranfield, C. E. B. *The Gospel according to Saint Mark.* Cambridge: University Press, 1959.

————. *A Critical and Exegetical Commentary on the Epistle to the Romans.* Edinburgh: T. & T. Clark, 1975.

Crosby, Michael H. "The Biblical Vision of Conversion." In *The Human Experience of Conversion: Persons and Structures in Transformation,* edited by Francis A. Eigo, pp. 31-74. Villanova, Pa.: Villanova University Press, 1987.

Cross, Whitney R. *The Burned Over District. The Social and Intellectual History of Enthusiastic Religion in Western New York, 1800-1850.* New York: Harper & Row, 1950.

Culpepper, R. Alan. "Mark 11:15-19." *Interpretation* 34 (1980): 176-81.

Daube, David. *The New Testament and Rabbinic Judaism.* London: University of London, The Athlone Press, 1956.

————. "Responsibilities of Master and Disciples in the Gospels." *New Testament Studies* 19 (October 1972): 1-15.

Davies, W. D. *The Setting of the Sermon on the Mount.* Cambridge: Cambridge University Press, 1964.

DeGidio, Sandra, O.S.M. *RCIA: The Rites Revisited.* Minneapolis: Winston, 1984.

De Jonge, M. "The Use of the Word 'Anointed' in the Time of Jesus." *Novum Testamentum* 8 (1966): 132-48.

Derrett, J. Duncan M. "Law in the New Testament: The Palm Sunday Colt." *Novum Testamentum* 13 (1971): 241-58.

————. *The Making of Mark: The Scriptural Bases of the Earliest Gospel.* 2 vols. Shipston-on-Stour: P. Drinkwater, 1985.

Dewey, Joanna. *Markan Public Debate: Literary Technique, Concentric Structure, and Theology in Mark 2:1–3:6.* SBL Dissertation Series 48. Chico, Calif.: Scholars Press, 1980.

————. "Point of View and the Disciples in Mark." In *Society of Biblical Literature*

1982 Seminar Papers, edited by Kent Harold Richards, pp. 97-106. Chico, Calif.: Scholars Press, 1982.

———. "The Literary Structure of the Controversy Stories in Mark 2:1–3:6." In *The Interpretation of Mark,* edited by William Telford, pp. 109-18. Philadelphia: Fortress, 1985.

Dewey, Kim E. "Peter's Curse and Cursed Peter." In *The Passion in Mark: Studies in Mark 14–16,* edited by Werner H. Kelber, pp. 96-114. Philadelphia: Fortress, 1976.

———. "Peter's Denial Reexamined: John's Knowledge of Mark's Gospel." In *SBL Seminar Papers 16,* edited by Paul J. Achtemeier, pp. 109-12. Missoula, Mont.: Scholars Press, 1979.

Dixon, Bernard. *Journeys in Belief.* London: George Allen & Unwin, 1968.

Dobson, Ed. *Starting a Seeker Sensitive Service: How Traditional Churches Can Reach the Unchurched.* Grand Rapids: Zondervan, 1993.

Dodd, C. H. *The Epistle of Paul to the Romans.* The Moffatt New Testament Commentary. London: Collins, Fontana Books, 1959.

Donahue, John R. *Are You the Christ? The Trial Narrative in the Gospel of Mark.* SBL Dissertation Series 10. Missoula, Mont.: Scholars Press, 1973.

———. "Jesus as the Parable of God in the Gospel of Mark." *Interpretation* 32 (October 1978): 369-86.

Donaldson, James. "'Called to Follow': A Twofold Experience of Discipleship in Mark." *Biblical Theology Bulletin* 5 (February 1975): 67-77.

Drane, John. *Evangelism for a New Age: Creating Churches for the Next Century.* London: Marshall Pickering, 1994.

Dupont, Jacques. "The Conversion of Paul, and Its Influence on His Understanding of Salvation by Faith." In *Apostolic History and the Gospel,* edited by W. Ward Gasque and Ralph P. Martin, pp. 176-94. Grand Rapids: Wm. B. Eerdmans Publishing Co., 1970.

Dyrness, William A. *How Does America Hear the Gospel?* Grand Rapids: Wm. B. Eerdmans Publishing Co., 1989.

Engel, James F. "The Road to Conversion: The Latest Research Insights." *Evangelical Missions Quarterly* 26 (1990): 84-95.

Englishman's Greek Concordance of the New Testament. London: Samuel Bagster and Sons, 1903.

Fackre, Gabriel. *Do and Tell: Engagement Evangelism in the '70s.* Grand Rapids: Wm. B. Eerdmans Publishing Co., 1973.

———. "Conversion." *Andover Newton Quarterly* 14 (1974): 171-89.

———. *Word in Deed: Theological Themes in Evangelism.* Grand Rapids: Wm. B. Eerdmans Publishing Co., 1975.

Farmer, William R. *The Last Twelve Verses of Mark.* Cambridge: Cambridge University Press, 1974.

Faw, Chalmer E. "The Outline of Mark." *Journal of Bible and Religion* 25 (1957): 19-23.

Fee, Gordon D. *The First Epistle to the Corinthians.* Grand Rapids: Wm. B. Eerdmans Publishing Co., 1987.

Ferch, Arthur J. *The Son of Man in Daniel 7.* Andrews University Seminary Doctoral

Dissertation Series, vol. 6. Berrien Springs, Mich.: Andrews University Press, 1979.

Firebaugh, Glenn. "How Effective Are City-Wide Crusades?" *Christianity Today,* March 27, 1981, pp. 412-17.

Fisher, Loren R. "'Can This Be the Son of David?'" In *Jesus and the Historian: Written in Honor of Ernest Cadman Colwell,* edited by F. Thomas Trotter, pp. 82-97. Philadelphia: Westminster, 1968.

Fletcher, Donald R. "Condemned to Die: The Logion on Cross-Bearing: What Does It Mean?" *Interpretation* 18 (1964): 156-64.

Fowler, Robert M. *Loaves and Fishes: The Function of the Feeding Stories in the Gospel of Mark.* SBL Dissertation Series 54. Chico, Calif.: Scholars Press, 1981.

———. "Who Is 'the Reader' of Mark's Gospel?" In *Society of Biblical Literature 1983 Seminar Papers,* edited by Kent Harold Richards, pp. 31-53. Chico, Calif.: Scholars Press, 1983.

France, R. T. "Mark and the Teaching of Jesus." In *Gospel Perspectives: Studies of History and Tradition in the Four Gospels,* edited by R. T. France and David Wenham. Vol. 1. Sheffield: University of Sheffield, 1980.

Freyne, S. *The Twelve: Disciples and Apostles, a Study in the Theology of the First Three Gospels.* London: Sheed & Ward, 1969.

Fuller, Daniel P. *Easter Faith and History.* Grand Rapids: Wm. B. Eerdmans Publishing Co., 1965.

———. *Give the Winds a Mighty Voice: The Story of Charles E. Fuller.* Waco, Tex.: Word, 1972.

Galilea, Segundo. *The Beatitudes: To Evangelize as Jesus Did.* Translated by Robert R. Barr. New York: Orbis, 1984.

Gallup, George. "Religion in America: Fifty Years: 1935-1985." *Gallup Report* 286 (May 1985).

Gallup, George, Jr., and George O'Connel. *Who Do Americans Say That I Am?* Philadelphia: Westminster, 1986.

Gardner, Helen. "The Poetry of St. Mark." In *The Business of Criticism.* Oxford: Clarendon Press, 1959.

Gasque, W. Ward. "Apocalyptic Literature." In *Zondervan Pictorial Encyclopedia of the Bible,* pp. 200-204. 1975.

Gaventa, Beverly Roberts. *From Darkness to Light: Aspects of Conversion in the New Testament.* Overtures to Biblical Theology. Philadelphia: Fortress, 1986.

Geddert, Timothy J. "Mark 13 in Its Markan Interpretative Context." Ph.D. diss., University of Aberdeen, 1986.

Gelpi, Donald. *Charisma and Sacrament: A Theology of Christian Conversion.* New York: Paulist, 1976.

———. "Conversion: The Challenge of Contemporary Charismatic Piety." *Theological Studies* (1982): 43:606-28.

———. "The Converting Jesuit." *Studies in the Spirituality of Jesuits* 18 (1986): 1-38.

———. "The Converting Catechumen." *Lumen Vitae* 42 (1987): 401-15.

———. "Religious Conversion: A New Way of Being." In *The Human Experience of Conversion: Persons and Structures in Transformation,* edited by Francis A. Eigo. Villanova, Pa.: Villanova University Press, 1987.

———. "Conversion: Beyond the Impasses of Individualism." In *Beyond Individual-*

ism, edited by Donald J. Gelpi. South Bend, Ind.: University of Notre Dame Press, 1989.

Gerberding, G. *New Testament Conversion.* Philadelphia: Lutheran Press, 1889.

Gerhardsson, Birger. *Memory and Manuscript: Oral Tradition and Written Transmission in Rabbinic Judaism and Early Christianity.* Translated by E. J. Sharpe. Acta Seminarii Neotestamentici Upsaliensis 22. Uppsala: C. W. K. Gleerup, 1961.

Gibbs, Eddie. *In Name Only: Tackling the Problem of Nominal Christianity.* Wheaton, Ill.: Victor Books/BridgePoint, 1994.

Gillespie, V. Bailey. *Religious Conversion and Personal Identity.* Birmingham, Ala.: Religious Education Press, 1979.

———. *The Dynamics of Religious Conversion: Identity and Transformation.* Birmingham, Ala.: Religious Education Press, 1991.

Glasson, T. F. "The Reply to Caiaphas." *New Testament Studies* 7 (1960-61): 88-93.

———. *The Second Advent.* 3rd rev. ed. London: Epworth Press, 1963.

———. "Mark 15:39: The Son of God." *Expository Times* 80 (June 1969): 286.

Goetzmann, J. "Metanoia." In *The New International Dictionary of New Testament Theology,* edited by Colin Brown, vol. 1, pp. 357-59. Grand Rapids: Zondervan, 1975.

Gowan, Donald E. *Bridge between the Testaments: A Reappraisal of Judaism from the Exile to the Birth of Christianity.* Pittsburgh: Pickwick Press, 1976.

Graham, Helen R. "A Passion Prediction for Mark's Community: Mark 13:9-13." *Biblical Theology Bulletin* 16 (January 1986): 18-22.

Green, Michael. *Evangelism in the Early Church.* London: Hodder & Stoughton, 1970.

Green, Michael P. "The Meaning of Cross-Bearing." *Bibliotheca Sacra* 140 (1983): 117-33.

Griffin, Emilie. *Turning: Reflections on the Experience of Conversion.* Garden City, N.Y.: Doubleday, 1980.

Griffiths, J. Gwyn. "The Disciple's Cross." *New Testament Studies* 16 (1969-70): 358-64.

Guder, Darrell L. *Be My Witnesses: The Church's Mission, Message, and Messengers.* Grand Rapids: Wm. B. Eerdmans Publishing Co., 1985.

———, ed. *Missional Church: A Vision for the Sending of the Church in North America.* Grand Rapids: Wm. B. Eerdmans Publishing Co., 1998.

Guelich, Robert A. "'The Beginning of the Gospel': Mark 1:1-15." *Biblical Research* 27 (1982): 5-15.

———. *Mark 1–8:26.* Word Biblical Commentary, vol. 34a. Dallas: Word, 1989.

Gundry, Robert H. *Mark: A Commentary on His Apology for the Cross.* Grand Rapids: Wm. B. Eerdmans Publishing Co., 1993.

Guy, Harold A. "Son of God in Mark 15:39." *Expository Times* 81 (February 1970): 151.

Hadden, Jeffrey K., and Charles E. Swann. *Prime Time Preachers.* Reading, Mass.: Addison-Wesley, 1981.

Hahn, Ferdinand. *The Titles of Jesus in Christology.* London: Lutterworth Press, 1969.

Happel, Stephen, and James J. Walter. *Conversion and Discipleship.* Philadelphia: Fortress, 1986.

Harrington, Daniel J. "A Map of Books on Mark (1975-1984)." *Biblical Theology Bulletin* 15 (January 1985): 12-16.

Hawkins, David J. "The Incomprehension of the Disciples in the Marcan Redaction." *Journal of Biblical Literature* 91 (1972): 491-500.

————. "The Symbolism and Structure of the Marcan Redaction." *Evangelical Quarterly* 49 (1977): 98-110.

Heikkinen, Jacob W. "'Conversion': A Biblical Study." National Faith and Order Colloquium, World Council of Churches, June 12-17, 1966.

————. "Conversion to God and Service to Man." Central Committee Minutes, Heraklion, Greece, World Council of Churches, Geneva, 1967, pp. 155-66.

————. "Notes on 'Epistrepho' and 'Metanoeo.'" *Ecumenical Review* 19 (July 1967): 313-16.

Hengel, Martin. *The Charismatic Leader and His Followers.* Translated by James C. G. Grieg. Edited by John Riches. Edinburgh: T. & T. Clark, 1981.

Hiebert, Paul G. "Conversion, Culture, and Cognitive Categories." *Gospel in Context* 1 (1978): 24-29.

Hiers, Richard H. "Purification of the Temple: Preparation for the Kingdom of God." *Journal of Biblical Literature* 90 (1971): 82-90.

Higgins, A. J. B. "St. Mark 10:36." *Expository Times* 52 (1940-41): 317-18.

————. *The Son of Man in the Teaching of Jesus.* Cambridge: Cambridge University Press, 1980.

Hofinger, Joannes, S.J. *Evangelization and Catechesis.* New York: Paulist, 1976.

Holladay, William L. *The Root Subh in the Old Testament with Particular Reference to Its Usage in Covenantal Contexts.* Leiden: E. J. Brill, 1958.

Holmes, Urban T. *Turning to Christ: A Theology of Renewal and Evangelization.* New York: Seabury Press, 1981.

Hong Kong Call to Conversion, The. "Initial Report about the 'Consultation on Conversion.'" Hong Kong, January 4-8, 1988.

Hooker, Morna D. *The Son of Man in Mark.* London: SPCK, 1967.

————. "Trial and Tribulation in Mark 13." *Bulletin of the John Rylands University Library of Manchester* 65 (1982): 78-99.

Howard, Virgil. "Did Jesus Speak about His Own Death?" *Catholic Biblical Quarterly* 39 (1977): 515-27.

Huggins, Kevin. *Parenting Adolescents.* Colorado Springs: NavPress, 1989.

Hulsbosch, A. *The Bible on Conversion.* De Pere, Wis.: St. Norbert Abbey, 1966.

Humphrey, Hugh M. *A Bibliography for the Gospel of Mark: 1954-1980.* New York and Toronto: Edwin Mellen Press, 1981.

Hunter, George. *The Contagious Congregation.* Nashville: Abingdon, 1979.

————. *How to Reach Secular People.* Nashville: Abingdon, 1992.

————. *Church for the Unchurched.* Nashville: Abingdon, 1996.

Hurtado, Larry W. *Mark: A Good News Commentary.* San Francisco: Harper & Row, 1983.

Hybels, Lynne, and Bill Hybels. *Rediscovering Church: The Story and Vision of Willow Creek Community Church.* Grand Rapids: Zondervan, 1995.

Inglis, G. J. "The Problem of St. Paul's Conversion." *Expository Times* 40 (1929): 227-31.

Jackson, Blomfield. "Note on Matt. 20:23 and Mark 10:40." *Journal of Theological Studies* 6 (1905): 237-40.

Jacobs, Donald R. "Culture and the Phenomena of Conversion: Reflection in an East African Setting." *Gospel in Context* 1, no. 3 (1978).

Jeremias, Joachim. *New Testament Theology.* Pt. 1, *The Proclamation of Jesus.* London: SCM Press, 1971.

Johnson, Ben Campbell. *Speaking of God: Evangelism as Initial Spiritual Guidance.* Louisville: Westminster/John Knox, 1991.

Johnson, E. S. "Mark 10:46-52: Blind Bartimaeus." *Catholic Biblical Quarterly* 40 (1978): 191-204.

―――. "Mark 8:22-26: The Blind Man from Bethsaida." *New Testament Studies* 25 (1979): 370-83.

Jones, E. Stanley. *Conversion.* New York: Abingdon, 1959.

―――. *A Song of Ascents: A Spiritual Autobiography.* Nashville: Abingdon, 1968.

Juel, Donald. *Messiah and Temple: The Trial of Jesus in the Gospel of Mark.* SBL Dissertation Series 31. Missoula, Mont.: Scholars Press, 1977.

Kähler, Martin. *The So-Called Historical Jesus and the Historic, Biblical Christ.* Translated by Carl E. Braaten. Philadelphia: Fortress, 1964.

Kasdorf, Hans. *Christian Conversion in Context.* Scottdale, Pa.: Herald, 1980.

Keck, Leander E. "The Introduction to Mark's Gospel." *New Testament Studies* 12 (1966): 352-70.

―――. "Mark 3:7-12 and Mark's Christology." *Journal of Biblical Literature* 84 (1966): 341-58.

Kee, Howard Clark. "The Function of Scriptural Quotations and Allusions in Mark 11–16." In *Jesus und Paulus,* edited by E. Earle Ellis and Erich Grässer, pp. 165-88. Göttingen: Vandenhoeck & Ruprecht, 1975.

―――. *Community of the New Age: Studies in Mark's Gospel.* London: SCM Press, 1977.

―――. "Mark's Gospel in Recent Research." *Interpretation* 32 (October 1978): 353-68.

Kelber, Werner H. "Mark 14:32-42: Gethsemane. Passion, Christology, and Discipleship Failure." *Zeitschrift für die neutestamentliche Wissenschaft* 63 (1972): 166-87.

―――. *The Kingdom in Mark: A New Place and a New Time.* Philadelphia: Fortress, 1974.

―――. "The Hour of the Son of Man and the Temptation of the Disciples (Mk 14:32-42)." In *The Passion in Mark: Studies in Mark 14–16,* edited by Werner H. Kelber, pp. 41-60. Philadelphia: Fortress, 1976.

―――. *Mark's Story of Jesus.* Philadelphia: Fortress, 1979.

―――. "Mark and Oral Tradition." *Semeia* 16 (1980): 7-55.

―――, ed. *The Passion in Mark: Studies on Mark 14–16.* Philadelphia: Fortress, 1976.

Kempthorne, Renatus. "The Marcan Text of Jesus' Answer to the High Priest (Mark 14:62)." *Novum Testamentum* 19 (1977): 197-208.

Kennedy, D. James. *Evangelism Explosion.* Wheaton, Ill.: Tyndale House, 1970.

Kerr, Hugh T., and John M. Mulder, eds. *Conversions: The Christian Experience.* Grand Rapids: Wm. B. Eerdmans Publishing Co., 1983.

Kertelge, Karl. "The Epiphany of Jesus in the Gospel (Mark)." In *The Interpretation of Mark,* ed. William Telford, pp. 78-94. Philadelphia: Fortress, 1985.

Kim, Seyoon. *The Origin of Paul's Gospel.* Grand Rapids: Wm. B. Eerdmans Publishing Co., 1981.

Kingsbury, Jack Dean. "The Gospel of Mark in Current Research." *Religious Studies Review* 5 (April 1979): 101-7.

————. *The Christology of Mark's Gospel.* Philadelphia: Fortress, 1983.

Kittel, Gerhard, and Gerhard Friedrich, eds. *Theological Dictionary of the New Testament.* Translated and edited by Geoffrey W. Bromiley. 10 vols. Grand Rapids: Wm. B. Eerdmans Publishing Co., 1964-76.

Klaiber, Walter. *Call and Response: Biblical Foundations of a Theology of Evangelism.* Translated by Howard Perry-Trauthig and James A. Dwyer. Nashville: Abingdon, 1997.

Klausner, Joseph. *The Messianic Idea in Israel from Its Beginning to the Completion of the Mishnah.* London: George Allen & Unwin, 1956.

Knibb, M. A. "The Date of the Parables of Enoch: A Critical Review." *New Testament Studies* 25 (1979): 345-59.

Kolb, Robert. *Speaking the Gospel Today: A Theology for Evangelism.* St. Louis: Concordia, 1984.

Kolenkow, Anita Bingham. "Relationships between Miracle and Prophecy in the Greco-Roman World and Early Christianity." In *Aufstieg und Niedergang der römischen Welt* II.23.2 (1980), pp. 1470-1506.

Kraft, Charles H. *Communication Theory for Christian Witness.* Rev. ed. Maryknoll, N.Y.: Orbis, 1983, 1991.

Krailsheimer, A. J. *Conversion.* London: SCM Press, 1980.

Krass, Alfred C. *Five Lanterns at Sundown: Evangelism in a Chastened Mood.* Grand Rapids: Wm. B. Eerdmans Publishing Co., 1978.

————. "Conversion in the United States Today." *International Review of Missions* 68 (1979): 161-66.

————. *Evangelizing Neopagan North America: The Word That Frees.* Institute of Mennonite Studies, Missionary Studies, no. 9. Scottdale, Pa.: Herald, 1982.

Kümmel, W. G. *Introduction to the New Testament.* Translated by Howard C. Kee. Nashville: Abingdon, 1975.

Lambrecht, J. "Q-Influence on Mark 8,34–9,1." In *Logia: The Sayings of Jesus,* edited by Joël Delobel. Leuven: Leuven University Press, 1982.

Lane, William L. *The Gospel according to Mark.* Grand Rapids: Wm. B. Eerdmans Publishing Co., 1974.

————. "The Present State of Markan Studies." 1988. Typewritten.

Laubach, F. "*Epistrephō.*" In *The New International Dictionary of New Testament Theology,* edited by Colin Brown, vol. 1, pp. 354-55. Grand Rapids: Zondervan, 1975.

————. "*Metamelomai.*" In *The New International Dictionary of New Testament Theology,* edited by Colin Brown, vol. 1, pp. 356-57. Grand Rapids: Zondervan, 1975.

Laurence, David. "Jonathan Edwards, Solomon Stoddard, and the Preparationist Model of Conversion." *Harvard Theological Review* 72 (1979): 267-83.

Laws, Sophie. *A Commentary on the Epistle of James.* London: Adam & Charles Black, 1980.

Liefeld, Walter L. "The Wandering Preacher as a Social Figure in the Roman Empire." Ph.D. diss., Columbia University, 1967.

Lightfoot, R. H. *The Gospel Message of St. Mark.* London: Oxford University Press, 1950.

Lilly, Joseph L. "The Conversion of Saint Paul: The Validity of His Testimony to the Resurrection of Jesus Christ." *Catholic Biblical Quarterly* 6 (1944): 180-204.

Lincoln, A. T. "'Paul the Visionary': The Setting and Significance of the Rapture to Paradise in II Corinthians XII.1-10." *New Testament Studies* 25 (January 1979): 204-20.

Lindars, Barnabas. "Salvation Proclaimed VII. Mark 10:45: A Ransom for Many." *Expository Times* 93 (1981-82): 292-95.

Loffler, Paul. "The Biblical Concept of Conversion." *Study Encounter* 1 (1965): 93-101.

———. "Conversion — an Introduction." *Ecumenical Review* 19 (July 1967): 249-51.

———. "Conversion in an Ecumenical Context." *Ecumenical Review* 19 (July 1967): 252-60.

Lohfink, Gerhard. *The Conversion of St. Paul: Narrative and History in Acts.* Translated and edited by Bruce J. Malina. Chicago: Franciscan Herald Press, 1976.

Lohse, Eduard. "Rabbi." In *Theological Dictionary of the New Testament,* vol. 6, pp. 961-65. 1968.

Long, Jimmy. *Generating Hope: A Strategy for Reaching the Postmodern Generation.* Downers Grove, Ill.: InterVarsity Press, 1997.

Lyons, George. *Pauline Autobiography: Toward a New Understanding.* SBL Dissertation Series, no. 73. Atlanta: Scholars Press, 1985.

Malbon, Elizabeth Struthers. "Mythic Structure and Meaning in Mark: Elements of a Lévi-Straussian Analysis." *Semeia* 16 (1980): 97-132.

———. "Fallible Followers: Women and Men in Mark's Gospel." *Semeia* 28 (1983): 29-48.

———. "Mark: Myth and Parable." *Biblical Theology Bulletin* 16 (October 1986): 8-17.

Malone, Daniel. "Riches and Discipleship: Mark 10:27-31." *Biblical Theology Bulletin* 9 (April 1979): 78-88.

Mann, C. S. *Mark: A New Translation with Introduction and Commentary.* Garden City, N.Y.: Doubleday, 1986.

Manson, T. W. "The Cleansing of the Temple." *Bulletin of the John Rylands Library* 33 (1951): 271-82.

———. *The Teaching of Jesus: Studies of Its Form and Content.* Cambridge: Cambridge University Press, 1951.

Marcus, Joel. *The Mystery of the Kingdom of God.* SBL Dissertation Series 90. Atlanta: Scholars Press, 1986.

Marsh, J. "Conversion." In *The Interpreter's Dictionary of the Bible,* edited by George A. Buttrick. Vol. 1. New York: Abingdon, 1962.

Marshall, I. Howard. *The Gospel of Luke.* The New International Greek Testament Commentary. Grand Rapids: Wm. B. Eerdmans Publishing Co., 1978.

Martin, Ralph. *Mark: Evangelist and Theologian.* Grand Rapids: Zondervan, 1973.

Marxsen, W. *Introduction to the New Testament: An Approach to Its Problems.* Translated by G. Buswell. Oxford: Basil Blackwell, 1968.

————. *Mark the Evangelist: Studies on the Redaction History of the Gospel.* Nashville: Abingdon, 1969.

Masuda, Sanae. "The Good News of the Miracle of the Bread: The Tradition and Its Markan Redaction." *New Testament Studies* 28 (1982): 191-219.

Matera, Frank J. *The Kingship of Jesus: Composition and Theology in Mark 15.* SBL Dissertation Series 66. Chico, Calif.: Scholars Press, 1982.

Mays, James L. "Jesus Came Preaching: A Study and Sermon on Mark 1:14-15." *Interpretation* 27 (January 1972): 30-41.

————. "An Exposition of Mark 8:27–9:1." *Interpretation* 30 (1976): 174-78.

McArthur, H. K. "Mark 14:62." *New Testament Studies* 4 (1958): 156-58.

McGavran, Donald A. *Effective Evangelism: A Theological Mandate.* Phillipsburg, N.J.: Presbyterian and Reformed Publishing Co., 1988.

McGavran, D. A., et al. *Church Growth and Group Conversion.* Lucknow, U.P., India: Lucknow Publishing House, 1936.

McGlashan, Robin. "Conversion — a Comparative Study." Department of the Laity, World Council of Churches. Document no. VIII. July 1960.

McLoughlin, William G. *Modern Revivalism.* New York: Ronald Press, 1959.

Mead, Loren B. *Transforming Congregations for the Future.* Bethesda, Md.: Alban Institute, 1994.

Meagher, John C. *Clumsy Construction in Mark's Gospel: A Critique of Form- and Redaktionsgeschichte.* New York: Edwin Mellen Press, 1979.

Mearns, Christopher L. "Dating the Similitudes of Enoch." *New Testament Studies* 25 (1979): 360-69.

Menoud, Philippe H. "Revelation and Tradition: The Influence of Paul's Conversion on His Theology." *Catholic Biblical Quarterly* 6 (1953): 131-41.

Meye, Robert P. *Jesus and the Twelve: Discipleship and Revelation in Mark's Gospel.* Grand Rapids: Wm. B. Eerdmans Publishing Co., 1968.

Miller, Donald. *Reinventing American Protestantism: Christianity in the New Millennium.* Berkeley: University of California Press, 1997.

Minear, Paul S. "The Needle's Eye." *Journal of Biblical Literature* 61 (1942): 157-69.

Moloney, Francis J. "The Vocation of the Disciples in the Gospel of Mark." *Salesianum* 43 (1981): 487-516.

Moo, Douglas J. *The Old Testament in the Gospel Passion Narratives.* Sheffield: Almond Press, 1983.

Moore, Robert L. "Pauline Theology and the Return of the Repressed: Depth Psychology and Early Christian Thought." *Zygon* 13 (June 1978): 158-68.

Morris, George E. *The Mystery and Meaning of Christian Conversion.* Nashville: Discipleship Resources, 1981.

Mott, Stephen Charles. "Greek Ethics and Christian Conversion: The Philonic Background of Titus II 10-14 and III 3-7." *Novum Testamentum* 20 (January 1978): 22-48.

Moule, C. F. D. *The Gospel according to Mark.* Cambridge: University Press, 1965.

Mowinckel, Sigmund. *He That Cometh: The Messianic Concept in the Old Testament and Later Judaism.* Translated by G. W. Anderson. Oxford: Basil Blackwell, 1956.

Navone, John. "The Story Told by Mark: God's Word of Love." *Clergy Review* 67 (June 1982): 199-203.

Neill, Stephen C. "Conversion." *Scottish Journal of Theology* 3 (December 1950): 352-62.

Neirynck, Frans. *Duality in Mark: Contributions to the Study of the Markan Redaction.* Bibliotheca Ephemeridum theologicarum Louvaniensium 31. Leuven: Leuven University Press, 1972.

Newbigin, Lesslie. "Context and Conversion." *International Review of Mission* 68 (1979): 301-12.

————. *Sign of the Kingdom.* Grand Rapids: Wm. B. Eerdmans Publishing Co., 1980.

————. *Foolishness to the Greeks: The Gospel and Western Culture.* Grand Rapids: Wm. B. Eerdmans Publishing Co., 1986.

————. *The Gospel in a Pluralistic Society.* Grand Rapids: Wm. B. Eerdmans Publishing Co., 1989.

————. *Truth and Authority in Modernity: Christian Mission and Modern Culture.* Valley Forge, Pa.: Trinity Press International, 1996.

Nineham, D. E. *The Gospel of St. Mark.* London: Adam & Charles Black, 1968.

Nissiotis, Nikos A. "Conversion and the Church." *Ecumenical Review* 19 (July 1967): 261-70.

Nock, A. D. *Conversion: The Old and the New in Religion from Alexander the Great to Augustine of Hippo.* London: Oxford University Press, 1933.

————. *St. Paul.* New York: Harper & Brothers, 1938.

Norborg, S. V. *Varieties of Christian Experience.* Minneapolis: Augsburg, 1937.

Norris, Kathleen. *Dakota: A Spiritual Geography.* Boston: Houghton Mifflin, 1994.

————. *The Cloister Walk.* New York: Riverhead Books, 1996.

Obersteiner, Jakob. "Messianism." In *Sacramentum Verbi: An Encyclopedia of Biblical Theology,* edited by Johannes B. Bauer, vol. 2, pp. 575-82. New York: Herder & Herder, 1970.

O'Brien, John A., ed. *Road to Damascus.* Garden City, N.Y.: Doubleday, 1955.

O'Grady, John F. "The Passion in Mark." *Biblical Theology Bulletin* 10 (April 1980): 83-87.

Otto, Rudolf. *The Idea of the Holy.* Translated by John W. Harvey. Harmondsworth, Middlesex, England: Penguin Books, 1917.

Pannell, William. *Evangelism from the Bottom Up: What Is the Meaning of Salvation in a World Gone Urban?* Grand Rapids: Zondervan, 1992.

Parrinder, E. G. "The Feeding of the Four Thousand: Mark 8:1-10." *Expository Times* 51 (May 1940): 397-98.

Parrott, H. W. "Blind Bartimaeus Cries Out Again." *Evangelical Quarterly* 32 (1960): 25-29.

Patte, Daniel. "Jesus' Pronouncement about Entering the Kingdom like a Child: A Structural Exegesis." *Semeia* 29 (1983): 3-42.

Peace, Richard. *Pilgrimage: A Workbook on Christian Growth.* Los Angeles: Acton House, 1976.

————. *Small Group Evangelism.* Downers Grove, Ill.: InterVarsity Press, 1985.

————. *Twelve Steps: The Path to Wholeness.* Serendipity Support Group Series. Littleton, Colo.: Serendipity House, 1990.

————. *Learning to Love God.* Colorado Springs: NavPress/Pilgrimage Publishing, 1994.

————. *Learning to Love Others*. Colorado Springs: NavPress/Pilgrimage Publishing, 1994.

————. *Learning to Love Ourselves*. Colorado Springs: NavPress/Pilgrimage Publishing, 1994.

————. *Spiritual Journaling: Recording Your Journey toward God*. Colorado Springs: NavPress/Pilgrimage Publications, 1995, 1998.

————. *Contemplative Bible Reading: Experiencing God through Scripture*. Colorado Springs: NavPress/Pilgrimage Publications, 1996, 1998.

————. *Spiritual Autobiography: Discovering and Sharing Your Spiritual Story*. Colorado Springs: NavPress/Pilgrimage Publications, 1996, 1998.

————. *Meditative Prayer: Entering God's Presence*. Colorado Springs: NavPress, 1998.

Peace, Richard, and William Cutler. *Parenting Adolescents: Easing the Way to Adulthood*. Serendipity Support Group Series. Littleton, Colo.: Serendipity House, 1990.

Peisker, C. H. "Prophet." In *The New International Dictionary of New Testament Theology*, vol. 3, pp. 74-84. 1978.

Perrin, Norman. *Christology and a Modern Pilgrimage: A Discussion with Norman Perrin*. Edited by Hans Dieter Betz. N.p.: Society of Biblical Literature, 1971.

————. "The Interpretation of the Gospel of Mark." *Interpretation* 30 (April 1976): 115-24.

Petersen, Jim. *Evangelism as a Lifestyle*. Colorado Springs: NavPress, 1980.

Petersen, Norman R. "'Point of View' in Mark's Narrative." *Semeia* 12 (1978): 97-121.

————. "The Composition of Mark 4:1–8:26." *Harvard Theological Review* 73 (1980): 185-217.

Pettit, Norman. *The Heart Prepared: Grace and Conversion in Puritan Spiritual Life*. 2nd ed. Middletown, Conn.: Wesleyan University Press, 1989.

Pippert, Rebecca. *Out of the Salt Shaker and into the World*. Downers Grove, Ill.: InterVarsity Press, 1979.

Poe, Harry L. *The Gospel and Its Meaning: A Theology for Evangelism and Church Growth*. Grand Rapids: Zondervan, 1996.

Posterski, Donald. *Reinventing Evangelism: New Strategies for Presenting Christ in Today's World*. Downers Grove, Ill.: InterVarsity Press, 1989.

Quesnell, Quentin. *The Mind of Mark: Interpretation and Method through the Exegesis of Mark 6:52*. Analecta Biblica 38. Rome: Pontifical Biblical Institute, 1969.

Rahner, Karl. "Conversion." *Sacramentum Mundi* 2 (1968): 6.

Rainer, Thom S., ed. *Evangelism in the Twenty-First Century: The Critical Issues*. Wheaton, Ill.: Harold Shaw, 1989.

Reed, Jerry. "Lasting Fruit in Evangelism." *Journal of the Academy for Evangelism in Theological Education* 11 (1995-96): 46-56.

Rengstorf, Karl H. "*Apostellō*." In *Theological Dictionary of the New Testament*, edited by Gerhard Kittel, translated and edited by Geoffrey W. Bromiley, vol. 1, pp. 398-447. Grand Rapids: Wm. B. Eerdmans Publishing Co., 1964.

————. "*Didaskō*." In *Theological Dictionary of the New Testament*, edited by Gerhard Kittel, translated and edited by Geoffrey W. Bromiley, vol. 2, pp. 135-65. Grand Rapids: Wm. B. Eerdmans Publishing Co., 1964.

————. "*Dōdeka*." In *Theological Dictionary of the New Testament*, edited by Gerhard

Kittel, translated and edited by Geoffrey W. Bromiley, vol. 2, pp. 321-28. Grand Rapids: Wm. B. Eerdmans Publishing Co., 1964.

———. "Manthanō." In *Theological Dictionary of the New Testament,* edited by Gerhard Kittel, translated and edited by Geoffrey W. Bromiley, vol. 4, pp. 390-461. Grand Rapids: Wm. B. Eerdmans Publishing Co., 1967.

Rhoads, David, and Donald Michie. *Mark as Story: An Introduction to the Narrative of a Gospel.* Philadelphia: Fortress, 1982.

Richardson, Alan. "The Feeding of the Five Thousand." *Interpretation* 9 (1955): 144-49.

Rite of Christian Initiation of Adults: Provisional Text. Washington, D.C.: United States Catholic Conference, 1974.

Robbins, Vernon K. "The Healing of Blind Bartimaeus (10:46-52) in the Marcan Theology." *Journal of Biblical Literature* 92 (1973): 224-43.

———. "Summons and Outline in Mark: The Three-Step Progression." *Novum Testamentum* 23 (April 1981): 97-114.

———. "Mark 1:14-20: An Interpretation at the Intersection of Jewish and Graeco-Roman Traditions." *New Testament Studies* 28 (1982): 220-36.

———. "Pronouncement Stories and Jesus' Blessing of the Children: A Rhetorical Analysis." *Semeia* 29 (1983): 43-74.

———. *Jesus the Teacher: A Socio-Rhetorical Interpretation of Mark.* Philadelphia: Fortress, 1984.

Robin, A. De Q. "The Cursing of the Fig Tree in Mark 11: A Hypothesis." *New Testament Studies* 8 (April 1962): 276-81.

Robinson, J. A. *St. Paul's Epistle to the Ephesians.* 2nd ed. London: Macmillan, 1904.

Robinson, J. A. T. "The Second Coming — Mark 14:62." *Expository Times* 67 (1956): 336-40.

———. *Jesus and His Coming.* London: SCM Press, 1957.

Robinson, James M. *The Problem of History in Mark and Other Markan Studies.* Philadelphia: Fortress, 1982.

Roof, Wade Clark. *A Generation of Seekers: The Spiritual Journeys of the Baby Boom Generation.* San Francisco: Harper San Francisco, 1993.

Roth, Cecil. "The Cleansing of the Temple and Zechariah 14:21." *Novum Testamentum* 4 (1960): 174-281.

Roth, Wolfgang. *Hebrew Gospel: Cracking the Code of Mark.* Oak Park, Ill.: Meyer-Stone Books, 1988.

Roxburgh, Alan J. *Reaching a New Generation.* Downers Grove, Ill.: InterVarsity Press, 1993.

Salter, Darius. *American Evangelism: Its Theology and Practice.* Grand Rapids: Baker, 1996.

Sample, Tex. *U.S. Lifestyle and Mainline Churches.* Philadelphia: Westminster, 1990.

Sanders, E. P. "Mark 10:17-31 and Parallels." In *Society of Biblical Literature 1971 Seminar Papers I,* pp. 257-70. Atlanta: Society of Biblical Literature, 1971.

———. *Jesus and Judaism.* London: SCM Press, 1985.

Sandmel, Samuel. "Prolegomena to a Commentary on Mark." *Journal of Bible and Religion* 31 (October 1963): 294-300.

Schilling, Frederick A. "What Means the Saying about Receiving the Kingdom of God as a Little Child *(Tēn Basileian Tou Theou Hōs Paidioi)?* Mark 10:15; Luke 18:17." *Expository Times* 77 (November 1965): 56-58.

Schmidt, Henry J., ed. *Conversion: Doorway to Discipleship.* Hillsboro, Kans.: Board of Christian Literature of the General Conference of Mennonite Brethren Churches, 1980.

Schniewind, Julius. "The Biblical Doctrine of Conversion." *Scottish Journal of Theology* 5 (September 1952): 267-81.

Scholem, Gershom. *The Messianic Idea in Judaism.* New York: Schocken Books, 1971.

Schürer, Emil. *The History of the Jewish People in the Age of Jesus Christ (175 B.C.–A.D. 135).* Edited by Geza Vermes and Fergus Millar. Rev. ed. 3 vols. Edinburgh: T. & T. Clark, 1975.

Schweizer, Eduard. "The Son of Man Again." *New Testament Studies* 10 (1963): 256-61.

—————. *The Good News according to Mark.* Translated by Donald H. Madvig. London: SPCK, 1971.

—————. "The Portrayal of the Life of Faith in the Gospel of Mark." *Interpretation* 32 (October 1978): 387-99.

Scott, M. Philip. "Chiastic Structure: A Key to the Interpretation of Mark's Gospel." *Biblical Theology Bulletin* 15 (January 1985): 17-26.

Segal, Alan F. *Paul the Convert.* New Haven: Yale University Press, 1990.

Sena, Patrick J. "The Nature and Function of the Catholic Parish Mission." *Journal of the Academy for Evangelism in Theological Education* 4 (1988-89): 33-38.

Sheridan, Mark. "Disciples and Discipleship in Matthew and Luke." *Biblical Theology Bulletin* 3 (October 1973): 235-55.

Sklba, Richard J. "The Call to New Beginnings: A Biblical Theology of Conversion." *Biblical Theology Bulletin* 11 (July 1981): 67-73.

Smalley, Stephen. "Conversion in the New Testament." *Churchman* 78 (September 1964): 193-210.

Smart, James D. "Mark 10:35-45." *Interpretation* 33 (1979): 288-93.

Smith, Charles W. F. "No Time for Figs." *Journal of Biblical Literature* 79 (1960): 315-27.

Smith, John E. "The Concept of Conversion." World Council of Churches, Faith and Order Colloquium, June 1966.

Smith, Marion. "The Problem of Christ." *Month* 17 (March 1984): 93-96.

Smith, Morton. *Clement of Alexandria and a Secret Gospel of Mark.* Cambridge: Harvard University Press, 1973.

—————. *Jesus the Magician.* San Francisco: Harper & Row, 1978.

Smith, Stephen Harry. "Structure, Redaction and Community in the Markan Controversy-Conflict Stories." Ph.D. diss., University of Sheffield, 1985.

Sparrow, G. Scott. *I Am with You Always: True Stories of Encounters with Jesus.* New York: Bantam Books, 1995.

Stallings, James O. *Telling the Story: Evangelism in Black Churches.* Valley Forge, Pa.: Judson Press, 1988.

Stanley, David M. "Paul's Conversion in Acts: Why the Three Accounts?" *Catholic Biblical Quarterly* 15 (1953): 315-38.

Steinhauser, Michael G. "Part of a 'Call Story'?" *Expository Times* 94 (1982-83): 204-6.

————. "The Form of the Bartimaeus Narrative (Mark 10:46-52)." *New Testament Studies* 32 (1986): 583-95.

Stendahl, Krister. *Paul among Jews and Gentiles.* Philadelphia: Fortress, 1976.

Stock, Augustine. *Call to Discipleship: A Literary Study of Mark's Gospel.* Dublin: Veritas Publications, 1982.

————. "Hinge Transitions in Mark's Gospel." *Biblical Theology Bulletin* 15 (January 1985): 27-31.

Stoffel, Ernest Lee. "An Exposition of Mark 10:46-52." *Interpretation* 30 (1976): 288-92.

Stonehouse, Ned B. *The Witness of Matthew and Mark to Christ.* Philadelphia: Presbyterian Guardian, 1944.

Stott, John R. W. *Christian Mission in the Modern World.* Downers Grove, Ill.: InterVarsity Press, 1975.

Strachan, James. "Conversion." In *Encyclopedia of Religion and Ethics,* ed. James Hastings, vol. 4, pp. 104-10. New York: Scribner, 1914.

Strecker, Georg. "The Passion and Resurrection Predictions in Mark's Gospel." *Interpretation* 22 (1968): 421-42.

Swartley, Willard M. *Mark: The Way for All Nations.* Scottdale, Pa.: Herald, 1979.

————. "The Structural Function of the Term 'Way' *(Hodos)* in Mark's Gospel." In *The New Way of Jesus: Essays Presented to Howard Charles,* edited by William Klassen, pp. 73-86. Newton, Kans.: Faith and Life Press, 1980.

Sweet, William Warren. *Revivalism in America: Its Origin, Growth, and Influence.* New York: Abingdon, 1944.

Synge, F. C. "Common Bread: The Craftsmanship of a Theologian." *Theology* 75 (1972): 131-35.

Tannehill, Robert C. *The Sword of His Mouth.* Semeia Supplements 1. Philadelphia: Fortress; Missoula, Mont.: Scholars Press, 1975.

————. "The Disciples in Mark: The Function of a Narrative Role." *Journal of Religion* 57 (1977): 386-405.

————. "The Gospel of Mark as Narrative Christology." *Semeia* 16 (1980): 57-95.

Taylor, Vincent. "The Apocalyptic Discourse of Mark 13." *Expository Times* 60 (1948): 94-98.

————. *The Gospel according to St. Mark.* New York: St. Martin's Press, 1966.

Telford, William R. *The Barren Temple and the Withered Tree.* Journal for the Study of the New Testament Supplement Series 1. Sheffield: JSOT Press, 1980.

————, ed. *The Interpretation of Mark.* Philadelphia: Fortress, 1985.

Terry, John Mark. *Evangelism: A Concise History.* Nashville: Broadman & Holman, 1994.

Thiede, Carsten Peter, and Matthew D'Ancona. *Eyewitness to Jesus.* New York: Doubleday, 1996.

Thompson, E. F. *Metanoeo and Metamelei in Greek Literature until 100 A.D.* Chicago: University of Chicago Press, 1908.

Tiede, David Lenz. *The Charismatic Figure as Miracle Worker.* Dissertation Series, no. 1. Missoula, Mont.: Society of Biblical Literature, 1972.

Tödt, H. E. *The Son of Man in the Synoptic Tradition.* Translated by Dorothea M. Barton. London: SCM Press, 1965.

Toon, Peter. *Born Again: A Biblical and Theological Study of Regeneration.* Grand Rapids: Baker, 1987.

Towner, W. Sibley. "An Exposition of Mark 13:24-32." *Interpretation* 30 (1976): 292-96.

Traina, Robert A. *Methodical Bible Study: A New Approach to Hermeneutics.* Wilmore, Ky.: By the Author, Asbury Theological Seminary, 1952.

Trocmé, Étienne. *The Formation of the Gospel according to Mark.* Translated by Pamela Gaughan. London: SPCK, 1975.

Turner, C. H. "Marcan Usage: V. The Movements of Jesus and His Disciples and the Crowd." *Journal of Theological Studies* 26 (1925): 225-40.

Tyson, Joseph. "The Blindness of the Disciples in Mark." *Journal of Biblical Literature* 80 (1961): 261-68.

Vermes, Geza. *Jesus the Jew: A Historian's Reading of the Gospels.* London: Collins, 1973.

Via, Dan O. "Mark 10:32-52 — a Structural, Literary and Theological Interpretation." In *Society of Biblical Literature 1979 Seminar Papers Vol. II,* edited by Paul J. Achtemeier, pp. 187-203. Missoula, Mont.: Scholars Press, 1979.

Vincent, John J. "The Evangelism of Jesus." *Journal of Bible and Religion* 23 (1955): 266-71.

Wallis, Jim. *The Call to Conversion: Recovering the Gospel for These Times.* San Francisco: Harper & Row, 1981.

Warren, Rick. *The Purpose Driven Church.* Grand Rapids: Zondervan, 1995.

Watson, David. *I Believe in Evangelism.* Grand Rapids: Wm. B. Eerdmans Publishing Co., 1976.

Webber, Robert E. *Celebrating Our Faith: Evangelism through Worship.* San Francisco: Harper & Row, 1986.

Weeden, Theodore J. *Mark — Traditions in Conflict.* Philadelphia: Fortress, 1971.

Weisberger, Bernard A. *They Gathered at the River: The Story of the Great Revivalists and Their Impact upon Religion in America.* Chicago: Quadrangle Books, 1958.

Wells, David F. *God the Evangelist: How the Holy Spirit Works to Bring Men and Women to Faith.* Grand Rapids: Wm. B. Eerdmans Publishing Co., 1987.

————. *Turning to God: Biblical Conversion in the Modern World.* Grand Rapids: Baker, 1989.

————. "Conversion." *Evangelism* 5 (August 1991): 172-77.

Wickham, E. R. "Conversion in a Secular Age." *Ecumenical Review* 19 (July 1967): 291-96.

Wiebe, Phillip H. *Visions of Jesus: Direct Encounters from the New Testament to Today.* New York and Oxford: Oxford University Press, 1997.

Williams, James G. *Gospel against Parable: Mark's Language of Mystery.* Bible and Literature Series 12. Sheffield: Almond (JSOT Press), 1985.

Williamson, Lamar. "An Exposition of Mark 6:30-44." *Interpretation* 30 (1976): 169-73.

Winter, Paul. "The Marcan Account of Jesus' Trial by the Sanhedrin." *Journal of Theological Studies* 14 (1963): 94-102.

Witherup, Ronald D. *Conversion in the New Testament.* Collegeville, Minn.: Liturgical Press, 1994.

Wood, H. G. "The Conversion of St. Paul: Its Nature, Antecedents and Consequences." *New Testament Studies* 1 (1955): 276-82.

Wrede, W. *The Messianic Secret.* Translated by J. C. G. Greig. Greenwood, S.C.: Attic Press, 1971.

Wuthnow, Robert. *Sharing the Journey: Support Groups and America's New Quest for Community.* New York: Free Press, 1994.

Psychology

Alland, Alexander. "Possession in a Revivalistic Negro Church." *Journal for the Scientific Study of Religion* 1 (spring 1962): 204-13.

Allison, Gerold E. "Psychiatric Implications of Religious Conversion." *Canadian Psychiatric Association Journal* 12 (1967): 55-61.

Allison, Joel. "Recent Empirical Studies of Religious Conversion Experiences." *Pastoral Psychology* 17 (September 1966): 21-23.

———. "Adaptive Regression and Intensive Religious Experience." *Journal of Nervous Mental Diseases* 145 (1967): 452-63.

Allport, Gordon W. "The Roots of Religion." *Pastoral Psychology* 5 (April 1954): 13-24.

———. "Religion and Prejudice." *Crane Review* 2 (1959): 1-10.

———. *The Individual and His Religion: A Psychological Interpretation.* 2nd ed. New York: Macmillan, 1962.

———. "The Religious Context of Prejudice." *Journal for the Scientific Study of Religion* 5 (1966): 447-57.

Allport, Gordon W., and J. M. Ross. "Personal Religious Orientation and Prejudice." *Journal of Personality and Social Psychology* 5 (1967): 432-43.

Ames, Edward S. *The Psychology of Religious Experience.* Boston: Houghton and Mifflin, 1910.

Argyle, Michael. *Religious Behaviour.* London: Routledge & Kegan Paul, 1958.

Austin, R. L. "Empirical Adequacy of Lofland's Conversion Model." *Review of Religious Research* 18 (1977): 282-87.

Bartman, Paul. "The Relationship of Personality Modes to Religious Experience and Behavior." *Journal of the American Scientific Affiliation* 20 (1968): 27-30.

Batson, C. Daniel, Patricia Schoenrade, and W. Larry Ventis. *Religion and the Individual.* New York and Oxford: Oxford University Press, 1982, 1993.

Bauer, Raymond A. "Brainwashing: Psychology or Demonology." *Journal of Social Issues* 13 (1957): 41-47.

Beardsworth, Timothy. *A Sense of Presence.* Oxford: Religious Experience Research Unit, Manchester College, 1977.

Beck, Robert N. "Hall's Genetic Psychology and Religion Conversion." *Pastoral Psychology* 15 (September 1965): 45-51.

Bergman, Paul. "A Religious Conversion in the Course of Psychotherapy." *American Journal of Psychotherapy* 7 (January 1953): 41-58.

Boisen, Anton T. *The Exploration of the Inner World: A Study of Mental Disorders and Religious Experience.* New York: Harper & Row, 1936.

Bourguignon, Erika, ed. *Religion, Altered States of Consciousness, and Social Change.* Columbus: Ohio State University Press, 1973.

Bowker, John. *The Sense of God: Sociological, Anthropological, and Psychological Approaches to the Origin of the Sense of God.* Oxford: Clarendon Press, 1973.

Brandon, Owen. "Religious Conversion in the Context of Pastoral Work." *Church Quarterly Review* 159 (1958): 396-407.

————. *The Battle for the Soul: Aspects of Religious Conversion.* London: Hodder & Stoughton, 1960.

Brantl, George. *The Religious Experience.* 2 vols. New York: Braziller, 1964.

Broch, Timothy C. "Implications of Conversion and Magnitude of Cognitive Dissonance." *Journal for the Scientific Study of Religion* 1 (spring 1962): 198-203.

Brown, J. A. C. *Techniques of Persuasion.* Harmondsworth, Middlesex, England: Penguin Books, 1963.

Brown, L. C., ed. *Psychology and Religion: Selected Readings.* Harmondsworth, Middlesex, England: Penguin Books, 1973.

Browning, Don S. *Atonement and Psychotherapy.* Philadelphia: Westminster, 1966.

Cesarman, F. C. "Religious Conversion of Sex Offenders during Psychotherapy: Two Cases." *Journal of Pastoral Care* 11 (1957): 25-35.

Christensen, Carl W. "Religious Conversion." *Archives of General Psychiatry* 9 (1963): 207-16.

————. "Religious Conversion in Adolescence." *Pastoral Psychology* 16 (September 1965): 17-23.

Clark, E. T. *The Psychology of Religious Awakening.* New York: Macmillan, 1929.

Clark, W. H. *The Psychology of Religion.* New York: Macmillan, 1958.

————. "William James: Contributions to the Psychology of Religious Conversion." *Pastoral Psychology* 16 (September 1965): 29-36.

————. *Chemical Ecstasy: Psychedelic Drugs and Religion.* New York: Sheed & Ward, 1969.

Clark, W. H., H. Newton Malony, James Daane, and Alan R. Tippett. *Religious Experience: Its Nature and Function in the Human Psyche.* The First John G. Finch Symposium on Psychology and Religion. Springfield, Ill.: Charles C. Thomas, 1973.

Coe, George A. *The Spiritual Life: Studies in the Science of Religion.* New York: Eaton and Mains, 1900. Reprint, Philadelphia: Westminster, 1903.

————. *The Religion of a Mature Mind.* Chicago: Revell, 1902.

————. *The Psychology of Religion.* Chicago: University of Chicago Press, 1916.

Coles, Robert. *The Spiritual Life of Children.* Boston: Houghton Mifflin, 1990.

Conklin, Edmund S. *The Psychology of Religious Adjustment.* New York: Macmillan, 1929.

Conn, Walter, ed. *Conversion: Perspectives on Personal and Social Transformation.* New York: Alba House, 1978.

————. "Adult Conversions." *Pastoral Psychology* 34 (1986): 225-36.

————. *Christian Conversion: A Developmental Interpretation of Autonomy and Surrender.* New York: Paulist, 1986.

————. "Pastoral Counseling for Self-Transcendence: The Integration of Psychology and Theology." *Pastoral Psychology* 36 (1987): 29-48.

Conway, Flo, and Jim Siegelman. *Snapping: America's Epidemic of Sudden Personality Change.* Philadelphia: Lippincott, 1978.

Crapps, Robert W. *An Introduction to Psychology of Religion.* Macon, Ga.: Mercer University Press, 1986.

Cutten, George B. *The Psychological Phenomena of Christianity.* London: McGraw-Hill, 1946.

D'Arcy, M. *The Nature of Belief.* London: Sheed, 1931.

Davenport, F. M. *Primitive Traits in Religious Revivals: A Study on Mental and Social Evolution.* New York: Macmillan, 1906.

De Sanctis, Sante. *Religious Conversion.* New York: Harcourt, Brace & Co., 1927.

Dean, Stanley R., ed. *Psychiatry and Mysticism.* Chicago: Nelson-Hall, 1975.

Deutsch, Felix, ed. *On the Mysterious Leap from the Mind to the Body: A Workshop Study on the Theory of Conversion.* New York: International Universities Press, 1959.

Dimond, Sydney G. *The Psychology of the Methodist Revival.* London: Oxford University Press, 1926.

Douglas, William, and James Scroggs. "Issues in the Psychology of Religious Conversion." *Journal of Religion and Health* 6 (July 1967): 204-16.

Drakeford, John W. *Psychology in Search of a Soul.* Nashville: Broadman, 1964.

Elkind, David, and Sally Elkind. "Varieties of Religious Experiences in Young Adolescents." *Journal for the Scientific Study of Religion* 2 (fall 1962): 102-12.

Ellis, Charles Calvert. *The Religion of Religious Psychology.* Los Angeles: Biola Book Room, 1928.

Ferm, Robert O. *The Psychology of Christian Conversion.* Westgate, N.J.: Revell, 1959.

Flower, J. C. *An Approach to the Psychology of Religion.* New York: Harcourt, Brace & Co., 1927.

Frank, Jerome D. *Persuasion and Healing.* Baltimore: Johns Hopkins University Press, 1961.

Frankl, Viktor. *The Will to Meaning.* New York: New American Library, 1969.

―――. *The Unconscious God.* New York: Simon & Schuster, 1975.

Freud, Sigmund. "A Religious Experience." *Collected Papers* 5 (1950): 244-45.

Fromm, Erich. *Psychoanalysis and Religion.* New York: Grosset and Dunlap, Bantam Books, 1967.

Furgeson, Earl H. "The Definition of Religious Conversion." *Pastoral Psychology* 16 (September 1965): 8-16.

―――. "The Renewal of Interest in Religious Conversion." *Pastoral Psychology* 16 (September 1965): 5-7.

Gillespie, V. Bailey. *Religious Conversion and Personal Identity.* Birmingham, Ala.: Religious Education Press, 1979.

―――. *The Dynamics of Religious Conversion: Identity and Transformation.* Birmingham, Ala.: Religious Education Press, 1991.

Gilliland, A. R. "Changes in Religious Beliefs of College Students." *Journal of Social Psychology* 37 (February 1953): 113-16.

Glock, C. Y., and P. E. Hammond, eds. *Beyond the Classics in the Scientific Study of Religion.* New York: Harper & Row, 1973.

Godin, André. *The Psychological Dynamics of Religious Experience.* Birmingham, Ala.: Religious Education Press, 1985.

Goodenough, Erwin R. *The Psychology of Religious Experiences.* New York: Basic Books, 1965.

Gordon, Albert J. *The Nature of Conversion: A Study of Forty-Five Men and Women Who Changed Their Religion.* Boston: Beacon Press, 1967.

Granberg, Lars I. "Some Issues in the Psychology of Christian Conversion." Paper delivered to the Eighth Annual Convention of the Christian Association for Psychological Studies, April 4, 1961.

Greeley, Andrew M. *Ecstasy: A Way of Knowing.* Englewood Cliffs, N.J.: Prentice-Hall, 1974.

———. *The Sociology of the Paranormal: A Reconnaissance.* Beverly Hills, Calif.: Sage, 1975.

Greeley, Andrew M., and William C. McCready. "Are We a Nation of Mystics?" *New York Times Magazine,* January 25, 1975, pp. 12-25.

———. *The Ultimate Values of the American Population.* Sage Library of Social Research, vol. 23. Beverly Hills, Calif.: Sage, 1976.

Grensted, L. W. *Psychology and God: A Study of the Applications of Recent Psychology for Religious Belief and Practice.* The Bampton Lectures for 1930. London: Green and Co., 1930.

———. *The Psychology of Religion.* New York: Oxford University Press, 1952.

Hardy, Alister. "A Scientist Looks at Religion." *Proceedings of the Royal Institution of Great Britain* 43 (August 1970): 205-23.

———. *The Spiritual Nature of Man: A Study of Contemporary Religious Experience.* Oxford: Clarendon Press, 1979.

Hart, Arch. *Adrenaline and Stress.* Waco, Tex.: Word, 1986.

Hay, David. "Religious Experience amongst a Group of Post-Graduate Students — A Qualitative Study." *Journal for the Scientific Study of Religion* 18 (1979): 164-82.

Hay, David, and Ann Morisy. "Reports of Ecstatic, Paranormal or Religious Experience in Great Britain and the United States — a Comparison of Trends." *Journal for the Scientific Study of Religion* 17 (1978): 255-68.

Heirich, Max. "Change of Heart: A Test of Some Widely Held Theories about Religious Conversion." *American Journal of Sociology* 83 (1977): 653-80.

Helming, O. C. "Modern Evangelism in the Light of Modern Psychology." *Biblical World* 36 (November 1910): 296-306.

Hickman, Frank S. *Introduction to the Psychology of Conversion.* New York: Abingdon, 1926.

Hill, William S. "The Psychology of Conversion." *Pastoral Psychology* 6 (November 1955): 43-46.

Hiltner, Seward. "Toward a Theology of Conversion in the Light of Psychology." *Pastoral Psychology* 17 (September 1966): 35-42.

Hood, Ralph W., Jr. "Forms of Religious Commitment: An Intense Religious Experience." *Review of Religious Research* 15 (1963): 29-36.

Horton, Robin. "African Conversion." *Africa* 41 (1971): 85-108.

———. "On the Rationality of Conversion, Part I." *Africa* 45 (1975): 219-35.

———. "On the Rationality of Conversion, Part II." *Africa* 45 (1975): 373-99.

Hyde, Douglas. *Dedication and Leadership: Learning from the Communists.* London: Sands & Co., 1966.

Jackson, George. *The Fact of Conversion.* The Cole Lectures for 1908 at Vanderbilt University. New York: Revell, 1908.

Jacobs, Donald. "Culture and the Phenomena of Conversion: Reflections in an East African Setting." *Gospel in Context* 1, no. 3 (July 1978): 4-14, 40.

James, William. *The Varieties of Religious Experience: A Study in Human Nature.* New York: Longmans, Green and Co., 1902. Reprint, New York: Random House, The Modern Library, n.d.

Janis, Irving L. "Personality Correlates of Susceptibility to Persuasion." *Journal of Personality* 22 (June 1954): 504-18.

Jeeves, Malcolm A. *Contemporary Psychology and Christian Belief and Experience.* London: Tyndale Press, 1960.

Johnson, Paul E. *Psychology of Religion.* New York: Abingdon, 1954.

————. *Personality and Religion.* Nashville: Abingdon-Cokesbury, 1957.

————. "Conversion." *Pastoral Psychology* 10 (1959): 51-56.

Jones, Barbara E. "Conversion: An Examination of the Myth of Human Change." Ph.D. diss., Columbia University, 1969.

Jones, W. L. *A Psychological Study of Religious Conversion.* London: Epworth Press, 1937.

Jordan, G. J. *A Short Psychology of Religion.* New York: Harper, 1927.

Jules-Rosette, Benneta. "The Conversion Experience: The Apostles of John Maranke." *Journal of Religion in Africa* 7 (1976): 132-64.

Jung, Carl G. *Modern Man in Search of a Soul.* Translated by W. S. Dell and Cary F. Baynes. New York: Harcourt, Brace & World, 1933.

————. *Psychology and Religion: West and East.* Vol. 2 of *The Collected Works.* Bollingen Series 20. 2nd ed. Princeton, N.J.: Princeton University Press, 1969.

Kasdorf, Hans. *Christian Conversion in Context.* Scottdale, Pa.: Herald, 1980.

Kildahl, J. P. "Personality Correlates of Sudden Religious Converts Contrasted with Persons of Gradual Religious Development." Ph.D. diss., New York University, 1957.

————. "The Personalities of Sudden Religious Converts." *Pastoral Psychology* 16 (September 1965): 37-44.

Klausner, Samuel Z. *Psychiatry and Religion.* Glencoe, Ill.: Free Press, 1964.

Knudson, A. C. *The Validity of Religious Experience.* New York: Abingdon, 1937.

Kotsuji, Abraham. *From Tokyo to Jerusalem.* New York: Geis, 1946.

Lang, L. Wyatt. *A Study of Conversion.* London: George Allen & Unwin, 1931.

Laski, Marghanita. *Ecstasy: A Study of Some Secular and Religious Experiences.* New York: Greenwood, 1968.

Leuba, James H. "A Study in the Psychology of Religious Phenomena." *American Journal of Psychology* 7 (April 1896): 309-85.

————. "Introduction to a Psychological Study of Religion." *Monist* 2 (January 1901): 195-225.

————. *The Psychological Origin and the Nature of Religion.* London: A. Constable & Co., 1909.

————. *The Psychological Study of Religion.* New York: Macmillan, 1912.

————. *The Belief in God and Immortality: A Psychological, Anthropological, and Statistical Study.* Boston: Sherman, French & Co., 1916.

————. *The Psychology of Religious Mysticism.* London: Kegan Paul, Trench, Trubner & Co., 1925.

Levinson, Henry S. *Science, Metaphysics, and the Chance of Salvation: An Interpretation of the Thought of William James.* Missoula, Mont.: Scholars Press, 1978.

Leys, Wayne A. R. "Soul-Saving in the Light of Modern Psychology." *Religious Education* 25 (April 1930): 340-45.

Liebman, Joshua L., ed. *Psychiatry and Religion.* Boston: Beacon Press, 1948.

Lifton, Robert J. "Thought Reform of Chinese Intellectuals: A Psychiatric Evaluation." *Journal of Social Issues* 13 (1957): 5-20.

————. *Thought Reform and the Psychology of Totalism: A Study of "Brainwashing" in China.* New York: Norton, 1961.

————. *Boundaries: Psychological Man in Revolution.* New York: Random House, 1967.

Linn, L., and L. W. Schwary. *Psychiatry and Religious Experience.* New York: Random House, 1958.

Lloyd-Jones, M. *Conversion: Spiritual and Psychological.* London: InterVarsity Press, 1959.

Loder, James E. *The Transforming Moment: Understanding Convictional Experiences.* San Francisco: Harper & Row, 1981.

Loftland, John. "'Becoming a World-Saver' Revisited." *American Behavioral Scientist* 20 (1977): 805-18.

————. *Doomsday Cult: A Study of Conversion, Proselytization, and Maintenance of Faith.* New York: Wiley, 1977.

Loftland, John, and Norman Skonovd. "Conversion Motifs." *Journal for the Scientific Study of Religion* 20 (1981): 373-85.

Loftland, John, and Rodney Stark. "Becoming a World-Saver: A Theory of Conversion to a Deviant Perspective." *American Sociological Review* 30 (1965): 862-75.

MacDonald, D. J. "Psychological Factors in Conversion." *American Ecclesiastical Review* 88 (April 1933): 337-51.

MacIntosh, Douglas Clyde. *Personal Religion.* New York: Scribner, 1942.

MacMurray, John. *The Structure of Religious Experience.* 2nd ed. New York: Hillary House, 1956.

Malony, H. Newton, and Samuel Southard, eds. *Handbook on Conversion.* Birmingham, Ala.: Religious Education Press, 1992.

Maslow, Abraham H. *Religions, Values, and Peak-Experiences.* New York: Viking Press, 1964.

Mavis, W. Curry. *The Psychology of Christian Experience.* Grand Rapids: Zondervan, 1963.

————. *Personal Renewal through Christian Conversion.* Kansas City, Mo.: Beacon Hill, 1969.

McKenzie, J. G., Jr. *Psychology, Psychotherapy, and Evangelicalism.* New York: Macmillan, 1941.

Meehl, Paul, Richard Klann, Alfred Schmieding, Kenneth Breimeier, and Sophie Schroeder-Slomann. *What, Then, Is Man?* A Symposium of Theology, Psychology and Psychiatry. St. Louis: Concordia, 1958.

Moore, John M. *Theories of Religious Experience: With Special Reference to James, Otto, and Bergson.* New York: Round Table Press, 1938.

Mudge, E. Leigh. *The God-Experience: A Study in the Psychology of Religion.* Cincinnati: Caxton Press, 1923.

Myers, David G. *The Human Puzzle: Psychological Research and Christian Belief.* New York: Harper & Row, 1978.

Neill, Stephen. *A Genuinely Human Existence.* Garden City, N.Y.: Doubleday, 1959.

Nicholi, Armand M. "A New Dimension of the Youth Culture." *American Journal of Psychiatry* 131 (April 1974): 396-401.

Norberg, S. V. *Varieties of Christian Experience.* Minneapolis: Augsburg, 1937.

Oates, Wayne. *What Psychology Says about Religion.* New York: Association Press, 1958.

————. *The Psychology of Religion.* Waco, Tex.: Word, 1973.

Olt, R. *An Approach to the Psychology of Religion.* Boston: Christopher Press, 1956.

Pahnke, Walter N., and William A. Richards. "Implications of LSD and Experimental Mysticism." *Journal of Religion and Health* 5 (1966): 175-208.

Paterson, W. P. *Conversion.* New York: Scribner, 1940.

Pettersson, Thorleif. *The Retention of Religious Experiences.* Acta Universitatis Upsaliensis, Psychologia Religionum, 3. Uppsala: n.p., 1975.

Pratt, James Bissett. *The Psychology of Religious Belief.* New York: Macmillan, 1921.

————. *The Religious Consciousness.* New York: Macmillan, 1921.

Prince, Morton. "The Psychology of Sudden Religious Conversion." *Journal of Abnormal Psychology* 1 (1906): 42-54.

Pruyser, Paul W. *A Dynamic Psychology of Religion.* New York: Harper & Row, 1968. Reprint, 1976.

————. *Between Belief and Unbelief.* New York: Harper & Row, 1974.

Ramage, Ian. *Battle for the Free Mind.* London: George Allen & Unwin, 1967.

Rambo, Lewis R. "Current Research on Religious Conversion." *Religious Studies Review* 8 (April 1982): 146-59.

————. *Understanding Religious Conversion.* New Haven: Yale University Press, 1993.

Roberts, D. E. *Psychotherapy and the Christian View of Man.* New York: Scribner, 1950.

Roberts, F. J. "Some Psychological Factors in Religious Conversion." *British Journal of Social Clinical Psychology* 4 (1965): 185-87.

————. "Psychopathology and the Religious Belief of Families." *British Journal of Social Psychiatry* 1 (1967): 147-50.

Robinson, Edward. *The Original Vision: A Study of the Religious Experience of Childhood.* Oxford: Religious Experience Research Unit, 1977.

————. *Living the Questions.* Oxford: Religious Experience Research Unit, 1978.

————, ed. *The Time-Bound Ladder.* Oxford: Religious Experience Research Unit, 1978.

Routley, Erik. *Conversion.* Philadelphia: Muhlenberg Press, 1960.

————. *What Is Conversion?* Derby, Pa.: Peter Smith, 1965.

Rudin, Josef. *Psychotherapy and Religion.* Translated by Elisabeth Reinecke and Paul C. Bailey, C.S.C. London: University of Notre Dame Press, n.d.

Salzman, Leon. "The Psychology of Religious and Ideological Conversion." *Psychiatry* 16 (1953): 177-87.

————. "The Psychology of Regressive Conversion." *Journal of Pastoral Care* 8 (1954): 61-75.

————. "Spiritual and Faith Healing." *Journal of Pastoral Care* 11 (1957): 146-55.

————. "Types of Religious Conversion." *Pastoral Psychology* 17 (September 1966): 8-20.

Sargant, William. *Battle for the Mind.* Baltimore: Pelican Books, 1961.

————. *The Mind Possessed: A Physiology of Possession, Mysticism, and Faith Healing.* New York: Lippincott, 1974.

Schaer, Hans. *Religion and the Care of Souls in Jung's Psychology.* London: Routledge & Kegan Paul, 1951.

Schaub, Edward L. "The Psychology of Religion in America during the Past Quarter-Century." *Journal of Religion* 6 (March 1926): 113-34.

Schein, E. H. "The Chinese Indoctrination Program for Prisoners of War." *Psychiatry* 19 (1956): 149.

————. "Reaction Patterns to Severe, Chronic Stress in American Army Prisoners of War of the Chinese." *Journal of Social Issues* 13 (1957): 21-30.

Scobie, Geoffrey E. W. *Psychology of Religion.* New York: Wiley, 1975.

Segal, Julius. "Correlates of Collaboration and Resistance Behavior among U.S. Army P.O.W.'s in Korea." *Journal of Social Issues* 13 (1957): 31-40.

Selbie, W. B. *The Psychology of Religion.* Oxford: Clarendon Press, 1924.

Silverstein, Steven M. "A Study of Religious Conversion in North America." *Genetic, Social, and General Psychology Monographs* 114 (1988): 261-305.

Snow, David A., and Richard Machalek. "The Convert as a Social Type." In *Sociological Theory 1983,* edited by Randall Collins. San Francisco: Jossey-Bass, 1983.

————. "The Sociology of Conversion." *Annual Review of Sociology* 10 (1984): 167-90.

Snow, David A., Richard Machalek, and Cynthia L. Phillips. "The Lofland-Stark Conversion Model: A Critical Reassessment." *Social Problems* 27 (1980): 340-47.

Spellman, Charles M., Glen D. Baskett, and Don Byrne. "Manifest Anxiety as a Contributory Factor in Religious Conversion." *Journal of Consulting Clinical Psychology* 36 (April 1971): 245-47.

Spinks, C. Stephen. *Psychology and Religion: An Introduction to Contemporary Views.* Boston: Beacon Press, 1967.

Starbuck, Edwin Diller. "A Study of Conversion." *American Journal of Psychology* 8 (January 1897): 268-308.

————. *The Psychology of Religion.* New York: Scribner, 1899.

————. "The Psychology of Conversion." *Expository Times* 25 (1914): 219-23.

Stewart, Charles W. "The Religious Experience of Two Adolescent Girls." *Pastoral Psychology* 17 (September 1966): 49-55.

Stratton, George Malcolm. *Psychology of the Religious Life.* London: George Allen & Co., 1911.

Strickland, Francis L. *Psychology of Religious Experiences: Studies in the Psychological Interpretation of Religious Faith.* New York: Abingdon-Cokesbury, 1924.

Strunk, Orlo, Jr., ed. *Readings in the Psychology of Religion.* Nashville: Abingdon, 1959.

————. *Religion: A Psychological Interpretation.* New York: Abingdon, 1962.

Tawney, G. A. "The Period of Conversions." *Psychological Review* 2 (1904): 210-16.

Thomas, W. B. *The Psychology of Conversion.* London: Allenson, 1935.

Thouless, Robert H. *An Introduction to the Psychology of Religion.* New York: Macmillan, 1923.

Tiebout, Harry M. "Conversion as a Psychological Phenomenon in the Treatment of the Alcoholic." *Pastoral Psychology* 2 (April 1951): 28-34.

Tippett, A. R. "Religious, Group Conversion in the Non-Western Society." Research-in-Progress. Pamphlet Series No. 11. Fuller Theological Seminary School of World Missions, Pasadena, Calif., 1967.

Turner, Victor W. *The Ritual Process: Structure and Anti-Structure*. Chicago: Aldine, 1969.

Underhill, Evelyn. *Mysticism*. New York: Dutton, 1961.

Underwood, A. C. *Conversion: Christian and Non-Christian*. New York: Macmillan, 1925.

Unger, Johan. *On Religious Experience: A Psychological Study*. Translated by David C. Minagh. Acta Universitatis Upsaliensis, Psychologia Religionum, 6. Uppsala: n.p., 1976.

Uren, A. Rudolph. *Recent Religious Psychology*. Edinburgh: T. & T. Clark, 1924.

Valentine, Cyril H. *Modern Psychology and the Validity of Christian Experience*. London: SPCK, 1926.

Wach, Joachim. *Types of Religious Experiences: Christian and Non-Christian*. London: Routledge & Kegan Paul, 1951.

Wallace, A. F. C. "Revitalization Movements." *American Anthropologist* 58 (1956): 264-81.

Weininger, Benjamin. "The Interpersonal Factor in the Religious Experiences." *Psychoanalysis* 3 (1955): 27-44.

White, Ernest. *Christian Life and the Unconscious*. New York: Harper & Brothers, 1955.

White, Victor, O.P. *God and the Unconscious*. London: Fontana Books, 1960. Original ed., London: Harvill Press, 1952.

Whitney, Harold J. "The Place of Emotion in Evangelism with Specific Reference to the Studies of William Sargant." M.Th. diss., Melbourne College of Divinity, Australia, 1964.

Windemiller, Duane Arlo. "The Psychodynamics of Change in Religious Conversion and Communist Brainwashing: With Particular Reference to the Eighteenth Century Evangelical Revival and the Chinese Thought Control Movement." Ph.D. diss., Boston University, 1960.

Winter, Terry W. R. "Effective Mass Evangelism: A Study of Jonathan Edwards, George Whitefield, Charles Finney, Dwight L. Moody and Billy Graham." Doctor of Pastoral Theology diss., Fuller Theological Seminary, Pasadena, Calif., 1968.

Wise, Carroll A. "Conversion." *Journal of Pastoral Care* 2 (1957): 40-42.

Witherington, Henry C. *Psychology of Religion*. Grand Rapids: Wm. B. Eerdmans Publishing Co., 1955.

Woodburne, A. S. "The Psychological Study of Conversion in India." *Journal of Religion* 1 (1921): 641-45.

Zaehner, R. C. *Mysticism: Sacred and Profane*. London: Oxford University Press, 1957.
———. *Zen, Drugs, and Mysticism*. New York: Pantheon Books, 1972.

Zangwill, D. L. Review of *Battle for the Mind*, by William Sargant. *British Journal of Medical Psychology* (1958): 60-62.

Zetterberg, H. L. "The Religious Conversion as a Change of Social Roles." *Sociology and Social Research* 36 (1952): 159-66.

Zilboorg, Gregory. *Psychoanalysis and Religion*. Edited by Margaret Stone Zilboorg. New York: Farrar, Straus & Cudahy, 1962.

Author Index

AUTHOR INDEX

Subject Index

Scripture Index